Poland on its Way to a Federal State?

T0316501

Schriften zur Internationalen Entwicklungs- und Umweltforschung

Herausgegeben vom

Zentrum für internationale
Entwicklungs- und
Umweltforschung

der Justus-Liebig-Universität Gießen

Band 22

PETER LANG

Frankfurt am Main · Berlin · Bern · Bruxelles · New York · Oxford · Wien

Armin Bohnet (ed.)

Poland on its Way
to a Federal State?

PETER LANG
Internationaler Verlag der Wissenschaften

Bibliographic Information published by the Deutsche Nationalbibliothek
The Deutsche Nationalbibliothek lists this publication in the Deutsche Nationalbibliografie; detailed bibliographic data is available in the internet at <http://www.d-nb.de>.

ISSN 1615-312X
ISBN 978-3-631-57148-4

© Peter Lang GmbH
Internationaler Verlag der Wissenschaften
Frankfurt am Main 2008
All rights reserved.

Printed in Germany 1 2 3 4 5 7

www.peterlang.de

FOREWORD OF THE EDITOR

The Center for International Development and Environmental Research (Zentrum für internationale Entwicklungs- und Umweltforschung, ZEU) was founded in 1998 as an interdisciplinary and interdepartmental research institute of the Justus-Liebig-University, Giessen. Presently, faculty members from the following disciplines are associated with ZEU: Agricultural and Nutritional Sciences, Economics, Environmental Safety, Geography, Law, Statistics and Econometrics as well as Social and Cultural Sciences. Upon ZEU's foundation, the following five sections were established:

- The use of natural resources and environmental preservation,

- Nutrition security,

- Human capacity in socio-economic systems,

- Institutional foundation of regional development processes,

- Transformation of economy and society.

These sections also indicate the issues which research is currently focused on. A restriction of ZEU's activities to specific geographic regions is not considered.

The series 'Schriften zur Internationalen Entwicklungs- und Umweltforschung' (Publications on International Development and Environmental Research) aims to present the results of ZEU's research activities and the state of discussions in the fields of our research to a broader public. The authors appreciate suggestions and critical remarks, in order to reconsider their own positions.

The volumes of the series will appear intermittently and may be purchased in bookstores or directly from the publisher.

Giessen, January 2008
　　　　　　　　　　　　　　　　Professor Dr. Ingrid-Ute Leonhäuser
　　　　　　　　　　　　　　　　Chairwoman of the Board

V

PREFACE

The submitted volume is the outcome of a common research project of Polish and German scientists on Polands fiscal equalization system. In order to find a common basis for the description and the evaluation of this system the volume starts with a chapter on theoretical foundations of fiscal equalization and on special requirements which should be taken into account for countries in transition.

Chapter II concentrates on the legal framework of the assignment of expenditures, on own revenues and on intergovernmental transfer payments. In addition it includes the financial data of expenditures, revenues and intergovernmental transfers thus enabling the authors to describe the financial situation of all self-government units – gminas, poviats, and voivodships – and to give a basis for analyzing the Polish fiscal equalization system from the point of view of the theory if fiscal equalization and of the Polish constitution.

Chapter III gives an overview of the "Laender"-fiscal equalization system and the municipal fiscal equalization system in Germany. It is regarded as a basis for comparing Polands fiscal equalization system with that of Germany and to find out weaknesses and strengths of the Polish system. A special part of this chapter describes the outcome of an empirical study on the allocation of unemployment policy between the central and the local level of governments.

The final chapter IV is devoted to reform proposals for the Polish fiscal equalization system. As there was no common consent between the project partners on the question which changes should be recommended and realized, chapter IV includes three different catalogues of recommendations, giving the reader an apportunity to set up his own opinion.

The project partners are:

1. Professor Dr. Krystyna Piotrowska-Marczak (group-leader), Dr. Magda Godek, Dr. Radek Witczak and Magister Tomasz Uryszek from the University of Lódz;

2. Dr. Wojcziech Misiag (group leader), Dr. Marta Mackiewicz, Elżbieta Malinowska-Misiąg, and Magister Marcin Tomalak from the Gdańsk Institute for Market Economics;

3. Dr. Margit Schratzenstaller from the Austrian Institute of Economic Research;

4. Professor Dr. Armin Bohnet (project-coordinator and group leader), PD Dr. Ivo Bischoff, and Diplomvolkswirt Lars Ponterlitschek from the University of Giessen.

I am very greatful for the financial support which was given by the Volkswagen-Foundation. Dr. Wolfgang Levermann and also Dr. Alfred Schmidt were especially helpful in the application phase. Dr. Matthias Höher from the Center for International Development and Environmental Research solved all administrative problems for us and was also responsible for the printing of this volume.

Giessen, May 2008   Professor Dr. Dr. h.c. Armin Bohnet

CONTENT

I. THEORETICAL FOUNDATIONS

THE THEORY OF FISCAL FEDERALISM
LARS PONTERLITSCHEK

FISCAL DECENTRALIZATION - PROBLEMS AND SPECIAL REQUIREMENTS FOR TRANSITION ECONOMIES
LARS PONTERLITSCHEK

II. POLAND'S SYSTEM OF INTERGOVERNMENTAL
FISCAL RELATIONS

DECONCENTRATION, DECENTRALIZATION, FEDERALISM: TERMS
AND DEFINITIONS IN THE POLISH LITERATURE

Magdalena Godek, Radosław Witczak,Tomasz Uryszek

**INTERGOVERNMENTAL TRANSFERS IN POLAND – LEGAL
FRAMEWORK**

TOMASZ URYSZEK AND LARS PONTERLITSCHEK

THE SELF-GOVERNMENT UNITS IN POLAND FINANCIAL DATA

MARTA MACKIEWICZ, ELŻBIETA MALINOWSKA-MISIĄG, MARCIN TOMALAK

LIMITATIONS ON THE FISCAL POLICY OF A LOCAL GOVERNMENT

PIOTR BURY

III. SELECTED TOPICS OF GERMANY'S SYSTEM OF INTERGOVERNMENTAL FISCAL RELATIONS

THE FEDERAL FINANCIAL EQUALISATION SYSTEM IN GERMANY

ANDREAS KIENEMUND

THE LOCAL FISCAL CONSTITUTION IN GERMANY – AN OVERVIEW

Wolfgang Scherf und Kai Hofmann

UNEMPLOYMENT INSURANCE AND MICRO-LEVEL LABOR MARKET POLICY IN A FEDERAL STATE – THEORETICAL CONSIDERATIONS AND THE GERMAN EXPERIENCE

STEFAN SCHÄFER AND IVO BISCHOFF

IV. REFORM PROPOSALS FOR THE POLISH
FISCAL SYSTEM

REFORM PROPOSALS FOR THE POLISH FISCAL EQUALIZATION SYSTEM DERIVED FROM THE THEORY OF FISCAL FEDERALISM

LARS PONTERLITSCHEK

PROPOSALS FOR THE IMPROVEMENT OF THE POLISH LOCAL FINANCE SYSTEM **311**

TOMASZ URYSZEK RADOSŁAW WITCZAK

SELF-GOVERNMENT FINANCE RECOMMENDATIONS FOR POLAND

WOJCIECH MISIĄG, MARCIN TOMALAK

FIGURES

TABLES

I. THEORETICAL FOUNDATIONS

THE THEORY OF FISCAL FEDERALISM

LARS PONTERLITSCHEK

1   Introduction

Throughout Eastern and Central Europe new systems of local and intergovernmental relations are being established as part of the transformation away from the old central planning system to a market economy. China is another example where (fiscal) decentralization is regarded as an important change of the institutional framework, having allowed high growth-rates in the last two decades.[1] The theory of fiscal federalism analyzes the specific fiscal problems that arise in federal countries, but can also be applied for unitary countries and is therefore an appropriate theoretical framework to describe and evaluate these transformation processes. The theory of fiscal federalism is based on the theories of public goods, taxation and public debt, on public choice theories of political processes, and on various aspects of locational theory.[2] The analyses conducted from a fiscal federalism perspective include both normative and positive issues, whereas our focus for the present will concentrate on the normative aspects. Traditionally, public finance theory and welfare economics, respectively, approach such issues based on the assumption that government is motivated by pursuit of the 'public interest' and of general welfare.[3]

This introductory chapter deals with several basic concepts related to the design of fiscal relations within a state to provide a theoretical foundation for the issues the project focuses on. The first task is to find a definition of the term "fiscal federalism". This will be done in section 2. The second task is to find out which level of government is best able to provide public goods and services to the individuals in the private sector.

---

[1]   See Bardhan, P. (2002), p. 185.

[2]   See Groenewegen, P. (1988), p. 366.

[3]   See Cullis, J. and Jones, P. (1998), p. 293.

This will be analyzed in section 3 along with Musgrave's distinction of the three "branches" of government – the allocation, the distribution, and the stabilization branch. In the ensuing section we will concentrate on the question of how subnational governments should finance the expenditures needed to fulfill the assigned tasks: Should they raise their own funds, should they participate in common financial sources (cooperative federalism), or should they – at least partly – be financed by transfer payments from the central government? Furthermore, we have to treat the tax assignment problem (section 4), i.e. to answer the normative question of an appropriate assignment of the different types of taxes to the different levels of government.[4] Finally we have to discuss if and how revenues raised by individual levels of government should be redistributed to ensure fiscal equity, to internalize fiscal externalities and to equip the subnational governments with sufficient resources to fulfill their tasks. The theory of intergovernmental grants in section 5 will help to find solutions to these problems. In sections 4 and 5 the current debate about a "competitive federalism" versus a "cooperative federalism" will also receive some attention.

2 What Does "Fiscal Federalism" Mean?

In this section we will give a very general review of what the term "fiscal federalism" means and how it is used in the public finance literature. This literature presents different views and definitions of the term "fiscal federalism", and the reality is characterized by different ways of organizing federal systems (e.g. the German versus the US federal system). We therefore need to find a minimum consensus on what fiscal federalism means.

Following Oates (1994) the term "fiscal federalism" applies to a public sector with two or more levels of decision-making. Tresch (2002) refers to federalism as "a hierarchical structure of governments in which each person is, simultaneously, a citizen of more than one government." Both definitions do not exclude unitary countries (like Poland) from the analysis.

The theory of fiscal federalism deals with the vertical structure of the public sector, analyzing the roles of the different levels of government and their interactions. The term "fiscal federalism" is closely connected to that of (fiscal) decentralization, which represents a genuine possession of independent decision-making power by

---

[4] See Oates, W. E. (1999), p. 1125.

decentralized units (i.e. [fiscal] autonomy). In this context, the term decentralization describes the *status* or *structure* of the allocation of tasks, expenditures, and revenues among the different levels of government. From this static perspective fiscal decentralization is equal to fiscal federalism.

From another, dynamic angle decentralization can be understood as a political *process* entailing a transfer of competencies or decision-making authority from the central level to subnational levels of government. This process can take place either within a given organizational structure or by creating new dependent or independent lower levels. Then, fiscal federalism could be characterized as the result of the process of decentralization.

For a detailed analysis it is necessary to separate the political and administrative aspects of decentralization from those of fiscal decentralization.[5] According to Bird and Vaillancourt (1998) we may distinguish between three varieties of fiscal decentralization, corresponding to the degree of independent decision-making exercised at the local level. First, *deconcentration* as one type of decentralization describes the distribution of responsibilities within a central government to regional branch offices or local administrative units. Second, *delegation* refers to a situation in which local governments act as agents for the central government, executing certain functions on their own behalf. Third, *devolution* characterizes a situation in which not only implementation but also the authority to decide what is done is in the hands of local governments.[6]

Oates (1972) suggests integrating the term "decentralization" into the definition of federalism as follows: A federal government is a "public sector with both centralized and decentralized levels of decision-making in which choices made at each level concerning the provision of public services are determined largely by the demands for these services of the residents of (and perhaps others who carry on activities in) the respective jurisdiction."[7]

This definition is more inclusive than a narrow political definition that would include only systems with formal federal constitutions.[8] It implies that in *economic terms* most if not all systems are federal so that the real issue is the determination of the appropriate

---

[5] See Bardhan, P. (2002), p. 186.

[6] See Bird, R. M. and Vaillancourt, F. (1998), p. 3.

[7] Oates, W. E. (1972), p. 17.

[8] See Oates, W. E. (1994), p. 127.

degree of (de)centralization within the public sector.[9] Instead of being either federal or non-federal, governments vary along some multidimensional spectrum in the degree to which fiscal decision-making is decentralized.[10] A federal system is more centralized than another if more of its decision-making power is in the hands of authorities with a larger jurisdiction.[11] The central issue of federalism then, to put it simply, is to decide whether public goods and services should be defined, provided, and financed at the federal (central), state, or local level of government.[12]

In Germany and the European Union (EU) proponents of fiscal decentralization refer to the principle of subsidiarity, which requires that a public task should be carried out on the lowest level of government with the capacity to achieve the objectives aimed at. This principle has been accepted as part of the Maastricht Treaty for the EU.

3   The Division of Tasks among Different Levels of Government

One important question that needs to be addressed is: What is the economic rationale for having a federal division of public sector functions? One argument and at the same time justification for a federal system is the existence of different preferences for local public goods whose benefits are restricted to a particular geographical area. In a federal system of government, each local government decides independently how much of each type of local public good to provide, and what types of taxes as well as which tax rates to use in financing these public goods.[13] In most cases, issues of provision and financing are considered together.[14] As it is unlikely that the residents of different localities want to consume the same amounts of local public goods, there will be a different supply structure of these goods. This would be different if a single higher level of government were responsible for choosing them.[15] Thus the primary rationale

---

9   See Oates, W. E. (1972), pp. 18-19.

10   See Oates, W. E. (1977), p. 4.

11   See Rosen, H. S. (2002), p. 472.

12   See Rubinfeld, D. L. (1987), p. 626.

13   See Gordon, R. H. (1983), p. 567.

14   See Gillette, C. P. (2001), p. 123.

15   See Boadway, R. W. and Wildasin, D. E. (1984), p. 498.

for a federal system of government lies in the better knowledge of local preferences for local public goods.

In analyzing the division of fiscal rights and responsibilities among the different levels of government we will revert to Richard Musgrave's view[16] that the purposes of government budgets are the allocation of fiscal resources, the redistribution of income, and the stabilization of growth. The question to be answered in this section is which level of government is best able to fulfill these functions, taking into account the benefits of decentralization as well as the fact that decentralization can cause inefficiencies and inequities as well as instabilities in the national economy.

3.1   THE ALLOCATION FUNCTION – EFFICIENCY ASPECTS

This section addresses the question which level of government is best able to provide public goods according to the preferences of the people, or, to use the words of Musgrave (1971) "... what goods should be provided where and by whom".[17] For a certain class of goods and services there is a clear case for centralized provision: these are pure public goods and services (characterized by non-rivalry in use and non-excludability of potential users) which imply benefits for everyone in the nation.[18] Thus central authorities should be responsible for national defense, national roads and highways, as these services provide benefits beyond a single jurisdiction, i.e. are connected with regional spillovers. Also judicial functions, national law enforcement, and foreign affairs are usually seen as examples for centralized provision. Another argument for centralization is that it can better exploit economies of scale in the provision of public goods than local suppliers. This is the case for goods with high fix costs and low marginal costs of use. Central provision of these goods can secure cost efficiency.

But centralized provision is not the most efficient solution for all public goods. Hayek (1945) suggests that local governments and consumers will make better decisions than the national government because they have better information about local conditions and preferences.[19] This view is also supported by Oates (1972).

---

[16]   See Musgrave, R. A. (1959), p. 6 et sqq.

[17]   Musgrave, R. A. (1971), p. 4.

[18]   See Oates, W. E. (1972), pp. 8-9.

[19]   See Hayek, F. A. (1945), pp. 524-526.

As already indicated, centralized provision may not be the most efficient solution for all public goods, because uniform levels of provision do not take into consideration different tastes (i.e. heterogeneous preferences) of residents of differing communities. Local governments possess knowledge of both local preferences and cost conditions that a central agency will probably not have.[20] Different demands for types and levels of public goods and services may be due to geographical, demographic or economic differences.[21] Economic (structural) efficiency is achieved by providing the mix of public goods and services that best matches individual preferences. This can be achieved by a multilevel government which offers a bundle of public goods that corresponds to the differing tastes of groups of consumers.[22] The optimal allocation of local public goods can be determined by the Samuelson condition according to which the sum of the marginal benefits generated should equal marginal costs. In the case of local public goods, which are not characterized by regional spillovers, marginal benefits only accrue to residents of the appropriate geographical area.[23]

The welfare gains of decentralization can be explained by using Figure I - 1. We assume that the population can be divided into two regionally separated groups. Each group is presumed to have homogeneous preferences for the local public good G. D_A represents the aggregate demand of individuals in group A, D_B the aggregate demand of individuals in group B. The marginal costs of providing G are constant, the price each individual has to pay is P=MC.

The optimal amount of G is Q^a for members of group A, and Q^b for members of group B. The basic assumption we make now is that "the spirit of the centralized solution to the provision of the public service is a standardized level of the service to everyone."[24] Thus, if the central government decides to provide a uniform amount of the public good to both groups, it might choose the quantity Q as a compromise between the demands of the individuals in groups A and B.[25] This uniform quantity is lower than the amount demanded by group A, but more than the amount demanded by group B. The resulting

---

[20] See Oates, W. E. (1999), p. 1123.

[21] See Boadway, R. (2001), p. 99.

[22] See Oates, W. E. (1972), p. 12.

[23] See Boadway, R. W. and Wildasin, D. E. (1984), p. 498.

[24] Oates, W. E. (1977), p. 10.

[25] This is valid for those public goods or services for which we can assume that a compromise between the groups is possible. If, for example, group B preferred one school per 5,000 inhabitants and group A preferred three schools per 5,000 inhabitants, the central government would provide two schools per 5,000 inhabitants as a compromise.

welfare loss of the central provision of G is the sum of the deadweight loss for group A (triangle 123), plus the deadweight loss for group B (triangle 145). Decentral provision of G would avoid these deadweight losses because the central state could be divided into two regions which would be permitted to provide themselves with the quantity of the public good they prefer. The welfare gains from decentralization become more important the more heterogeneous the preferences for the public good are across different regions. The welfare loss increases with the price inelasticity of demand. As the demand for local public goods is regarded as highly price inelastic, the welfare gains from decentralized financing are assumed to be quite large.[26]

Figure I - 1: The welfare gains of decentralization

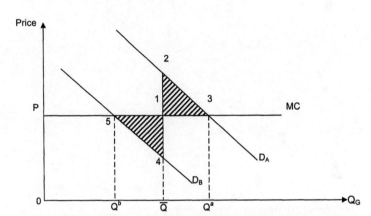

Source: See CULLIS and JONES (1998), p.193; OATES (1977), p. 10.

This situation illustrates the well-known decentralization theorem described by Oates (1972): "For a public good – the consumption of which is defined over geographical subsets of the total population, and for which the costs of providing each level of output of the good in each jurisdiction are the same for the central or the respective local government – it will always be more efficient (or at least as efficient) for local governments to provide the Pareto-efficient levels of output for their respective

---

[26]   See Oates, W. E. (1999), p. 1123.

jurisdictions than for the central government to provide *any* specified and uniform level of output across all jurisdictions."[27]

Figure I - 2 illustrates the derivation of the optimal degree of centralization for a special public good which results from the minimization of welfare losses due to centralization (arising from heterogeneous preferences) and welfare losses due to decentralization (arising from foregone economies of scale).

Figure I - 2:   The optimal degree of centralization for a public good

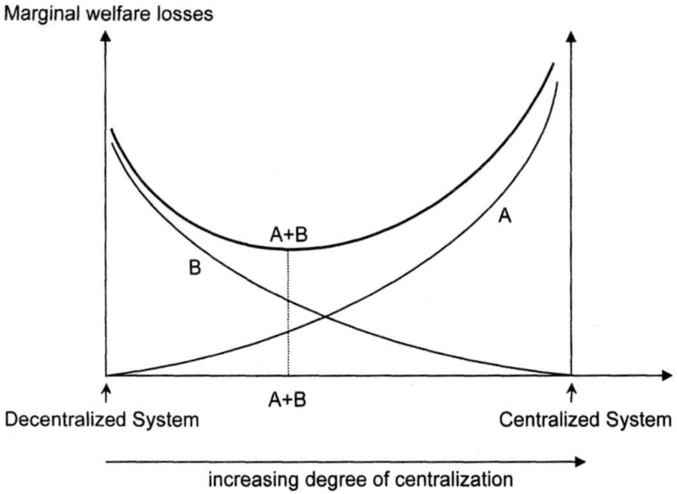

Marginal welfare losses

increasing degree of centralization

Source: Author's illustration following FREY and KIRCHGAESSNER (2002), p. 63.

Curve A represents the marginal welfare losses increasing with a rising degree of centralization, e.g. increasing deadweight losses and congestion costs. Congestion costs occur when the consumption of a public good is not independent of the number of persons who consume the good[28], i.e. the criterion of "nonrival" consumption is no longer satisfied.[29] This may lead to a reduction in benefits to those already consuming

---

[27]   Oates, W. E. (1972), p. 35.

[28]   See Oates, W. E. (1972), p. 50.

[29]   See Musgrave, R. A. and Musgrave, P. B. (1989), p. 452.

the congested public good. Thus curve A represents the marginal benefits of decentralization. Curve B represents the decreasing welfare losses with a rising degree of centralization, e.g. through economies of scale. Thus B represents the marginal benefits of centralization. The steeper the slope of curve A and the flatter the slope of curve B, the more decentralized the government structure should be with respect to the public good regarded.[30] The optimal degree of (de-)centralization will of course be different for different public goods and services.

However, the existence of interregional externalities, i.e. regional benefit spillovers for such public goods as local transportation facilities, education or health services, can lead to an underprovision of the public good in question. To illustrate this problem, suppose that a public good G is provided by jurisdiction A. In Figure I - 3 D_A represents the aggregate demand by residents of A for the public good G. Benefits spill over into neighboring jurisdictions and D_N is the demand for G of non-residents. Adding up D_A and D_N vertically yields the total demand curve D_T. S is the supply curve for G.

Figure I - 3: Benefit spillover

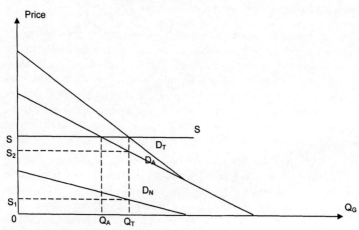

Source: See DAVIS, J./MEYER, C. (1983), p. 325.

---

[30]   See Frey, B. S. and Kirchgaessner, G. (2002), p. 64.

The quantity provided by locality A is Q_A, while the optimum quantity taking into account the aggregate demand of all beneficiaries would be Q_T. This underprovision of the public good is likely because taxpayers and politicians in A have no incentive to finance a quantity of G which also satisfies the demand of non-residents who do not contribute to the financing of G. Nevertheless, it is still reasonable to decentralize the provision of these public goods, especially when preferences in the various regions are heterogeneous. In this case it is necessary to introduce intergovernmental grants in order to correct regional spillovers. This will be elaborated in more detail in section 5, in which the use of intergovernmental grants will be discussed.

Another argument in favor of centralized provision of public goods is the existence of economies of scale: For certain publicly provided goods, the cost per user decreases with the number of users.[31] If the central government can achieve cost savings by providing a uniform level of a public good, these savings must be weighed against the potential welfare loss if individual preferences are not met optimally.[32]

3.2 THE DISTRIBUTION FUNCTION

If redistribution of income is regarded as one of the central aims of governments, the question arises which level of government should take over responsibility for the redistribution function. An important point in this discussion emphasizes the principle of horizontal equity which suggests that individuals in equal circumstances should be treated equally no matter where they reside. In a decentralized nation with an unequal distribution of income and property and different redistribution programs on the subnational level this principle cannot be realized.[33] Hence, some authors have argued that the central government should carry out the redistribution function.[34]

One of the main reasons for this assertion is the mobility of individuals among jurisdictions. If one jurisdiction decides to pursue stronger redistributive policies than others, there will be an incentive for the poor to migrate into this jurisdiction due to the higher level of redistribution, while the rich will migrate out due to the higher level of taxation necessary to finance generous redistributive policies. This argument relies on the notion that people's decisions to locate in a given community are influenced by the

---

[31] See Rosen, H. S. (2002), p. 479.

[32] See Oates, W. E. (1977), p. 6.

[33] See Boadway, R. (2001), p. 109.

[34] See Musgrave, R. A. (1959), p. 181 and Oates, W. E. (1972), pp. 6-8.

provided "tax-welfare package".[35] In anticipation of such behavior from their citizens, fear of unintended results might even induce the local government to supply less redistribution than it thinks appropriate for its citizens.[36]

Boadway and Wildasin (1984) use a very simple numerical example to demonstrate that even if all jurisdictions undertake the same redistributive policy, the presence of local government redistribution would itself induce migration if incomes are distributed unevenly among inhabitants[37]: Consider two states A and B that differ in their mix of high- and low-income inhabitants. In the wealthier state A, there are two persons with incomes of $30,000 p.a. for every one person with an income of $10,000. The poorer state B has one person with an income of $30,000 for every two persons with incomes of $10,000. Both states levy a proportional income tax of 20 percent, and both use the revenues to provide public services in equal amounts to all citizens. The effect of this budget package will be redistributive because all persons receive the identical benefits from public expenditures, whereas tax payments rise with income. Thus the impact of the public budget on real income will differ across the rich and the poor in each state and across states.

Table I - 1 illustrates the impact of the state budgets on the real income of the two types of persons. Persons of the same income pay the same amount of taxes in each state, but they receive different net benefits (per capita expenditures minus tax payments) because of the population mix.

Table I - 1: The impact of state budgets on real income

	State A		State B	
	Person with $30,000 income	Person with $10,000 income	Person with $30,000 income	Person with $10,000 income
Tax Payment	6,000	2,000	6,000	2,000
Per capita public expenditures	4,667	4,667	3,333	3,333
Net fiscal benefit/loss	-1,333	2,667	-2,667	1,333

Source: See BOADWAY and WILDASIN (1984), p. 506.

---

[35] See Rosen, H. S. (2002), p. 481.

[36] See Aronson, J. R. (1985), p.149.

[37] See Boadway, R. W. and Wildasin, D. E. (1984), pp. 505-507. These considerations are based on Buchanan, J. M. (1950).

We can see that the net fiscal benefit[38] (NFB) is $1,333 higher for the persons living in state A than for those in state B. Those in the richer state receive more than those in the poorer state. At the same time rich people in A face a lower net fiscal loss than those in B. Net fiscal benefit differentials lead to fiscal inequity and obviously occur simply as a result of decentralization.[39] As a consequence there is an incentive for the inhabitants of B to migrate to state A. Buchanan (1950) suggests to apply intergovernmental grants to ensure "equal fiscal treatment for equals".[40] Only distributionally neutral budgets do not cause incentives to migrate. This neutrality can only be realized by centralizing the redistributive function.

The question arises whether redistribution should only deal with distribution among individuals or whether intercommunity distribution should be included. Musgrave (1971) answers this question as follows: "Fiscal Federalism cannot function properly without either a central policy of interindividual or (second best) intercommunity equalization."[41] Intercommunity redistribution would not be necessary if the interindividual income distribution (as the first-best solution) was adjusted properly, but it seems unrealistic to assume that the desirable state of interindividual distribution can be established by national policy alone. This leaves the local fiscal authorities responsible for such redistributional functions as welfare, health care, and other public services. On the other side, this can lead to imbalances between fiscal capacities and needs in the jurisdictions, so that policies of interjurisdictional fiscal equalization are needed in order to avoid the migration tendencies mentioned above.

Altogether, arguments in favor of assigning the distribution function – or at least a large part of it – to the central government seem to dominate the theoretical discussion.

3.3 ASSIGNMENT OF THE STABILIZATION FUNCTION

With regard to the stabilization branch there seems to exist a broad consensus in economic literature that this function should be taken over by the central government. The first reason for this position is that monetary policy should not and cannot be controlled by subnational agencies. In the European Community we even observe a development towards an economic and monetary union. With the common currency

---

[38] Buchanan called this "fiscal residuum". See Buchanan, J. M. (1950), p. 588.

[39] See Boadway, R. (2001), p. 109.

[40] Buchanan, J. M. (1950), p. 591.

[41] Musgrave, R. A. (1971), p. 9.

and thus a common monetary policy by the European Central Bank, member states are no longer able to influence their local economies through exchange rate or monetary policies when state-specific economic shocks appear.[42]

In the European Union, the instrument left to ease the burdens of macroeconomic shocks at the level of the member states is fiscal policy. Thus the remaining question is whether it is reasonable to decentralize fiscal policies. The newer view on fiscal policy and its stabilization potential is that in really open economies with flexible exchange rates and free mobility of capital, fiscal policy has only weak stabilization effects and that stabilization should primarily be the task of monetary policy.[43]

The traditional view on the assignment of fiscal policy within multilevel governments is that it must be largely centralized because "any attempts to influence the level of local economic activity by deliberate fiscal measures will be dissipated by the deflection of most of the new demand to goods and services produced elsewhere; typically the local economy is highly open, i.e., it has a large average and marginal propensity to import, so the local authority is unable to contain the new spending within its borders."[44] Inman and Rubinfeld (1991) point out that even if state deficit policies are economically feasible, their management may be non-optimal because the benefits from local demand creation through deficit financing may spill over to other states, while the interest costs of deficits remain with the borrowing state. As a result there will be an under-provision of expansionary fiscal policies by the state level.[45]

Gramlich (1987) on the other side argues that subnational governments can play some role in countercyclical policy. He contends that macroeconomic shocks can have different impacts on the various regions of a country and shows that states should try to offset spending shocks by at least a small degree.[46] Nevertheless, the scope for decentralized stabilization policy is quite narrow, so that the primary responsibility for this function should be at the central level.

---

[42]   See Inman, R. P. and Rubinfeld, D. L. (1991), pp. 1-2.

[43]   See Gramlich, E. M. (1993), p. 234.

[44]   Oates, W. E. (1977), p. 5.

[45]   See Inman, R. P. and Rubinfeld, D. L. (1991), p. 3.

[46]   For details see Gramlich, E. M. (1987), pp. 310-311.

4 Revenue Assignment in a Federal System

4.1 BASIC PRINCIPLES OF REVENUE RAISING IN A FEDERAL SYSTEM

One key issue in fiscal federalism literature is the question of funding principles of subnational governments. Rationally designed financing patterns should meet several, sometimes conflicting, objectives.[47] There is no easy solution to this complex issue, neither in theory nor in practice. We are confronted with a variety of systems in different countries. The main sources of income for subnational governments are fees and user charges, taxes, grants-in-aid, and local public debt. In this section, we will concentrate on the two former revenue sources (fees/user charges and taxes), with taxes being the most important source of revenue for subnational governments. Local borrowing will be neglected in the following;[48] the use of intergovernmental grants will be described in section 5. Questions of revenue assignment are always related to the problem of expenditure assignments across different levels of government.[49]

The following section discusses the question, which source of finance is preferable for a local authority and whether control over tax instruments can and should be decentralized. This complex of questions is called "the tax assignment problem". We will include the appropriate use of fees and user charges into the discussion of the tax assignment problem. The basic issue here is the normative question which fees/user charges and taxes should be used at what level of government.

4.2 THE ALLOCATION OF TAXING POWERS AMONG DIFFERENT LEVELS OF GOVERNMENT – THE TAX ASSIGNMENT PROBLEM

In a decentralized state, we assume in general that state and local governments should be allowed to set their own tax rates, constrained by the requirement to balance their budgets so that borrowing is unnecessary.[50] If subnational governments do not have independent sources of revenue they will not truly enjoy fiscal autonomy, but will be

---

[47] See Joumard, I. and Kongsrud, P. M. (2003), p. 182.

[48] Borrowing is necessary when total public expenditures exceed revenues. The access of local governments to capital markets is rather restricted in most developed countries. See Bird, R. M. and Wallich, C. I. (1993), p. 60.

[49] See Norregaard, J. (1997), p. 49.

[50] See Inman, R. P. and Rubinfeld, D. L. (1996), p. 313.

under the "financial thumb" of the central government.[51] Gordon (1983) assumes that the states are short-sighted when setting their tax rates: Any effects on other units of government are ignored and the actions of other local governments are taken as given.[52] To find a solution to the tax assignment problem the following questions have to be answered:[53]

- Which level of government chooses the taxes that a given level imposes?
- Which level of government defines the tax base?
- Which level of government sets the tax rates?
- Which level of government administers the diverse taxes?

In his classic article on the tax assignment problem, Musgrave (1983) establishes the following six tax assignment rules:[54]

1. middle and especially lower-level jurisdictions should tax those bases which have low inter-jurisdictional mobility;

2. personal taxes with progressive rates should be used by those jurisdictions within which a global base can be implemented most efficiently;

3. progressive taxation, designed to secure redistributional objectives, should be primarily central;

4. taxes suitable for purposes of stabilization policy should be central, while lower-level taxes should be cyclically stable;

5. tax bases which are distributed highly unequally among sub-jurisdictions should be used centrally; and

6. benefit taxes and user charges are appropriate at all levels.

Combining these principles, Musgrave suggests the following assignment of taxes to the three levels of government:

In accordance with Musgrave's three-branch system of government, progressive individual income taxes and corporate income taxes can be used for purposes of redistribution and, through their countercyclical effects on revenues and disposable

---

[51]   See McLure Jr., C. E. (1999)

[52]   See Gordon, R. H. (1983), p. 577.

[53]   See McLure Jr., C. E. (2001), p. 341.

[54]   See Musgrave, R. A. (1983), p. 11.

income, macroeconomic stabilization.[55] Therefore, these two taxes should be assigned to the central government.[56]

Central Level	Regional Level	Local Level
Integrated Income Tax	Resident Income Tax	Property Tax
Expenditure Tax	Non-resident Income Tax	Payroll Tax
Natural Resource Tax	Destination-Type Product Tax	Charges
Charges	Natural Resource Tax	
	Charges	

Source: See MUSGRAVE (1983), p. 13.

Taxes pursuing allocation goals should closely reflect benefits of public services. The different levels of government should be assigned taxes that are related to benefits generated by their expenditures. As the theoretical considerations in section 3 suggest, subnational governments should be responsible for expenditures which are characterized by limited economies of scale and limited spillovers of benefits to neighboring jurisdictions.[57] They should also have enough 'own' revenues to finance their provision of goods and services. In this regard, shared taxes[58] and tax surcharges collected and then remitted by the central government can also be seen as own revenues.[59] Furthermore, "subnational governments must be assigned sources of marginal own revenues – own revenues whose level they can control – if they are to be truly autonomous."[60] Shared taxes are not marginal revenues in this sense because subnational governments cannot affect the amount of revenue they receive as they cannot influence the tax parameters, whereas they have that possibility if they are

---

[55] See McLure Jr., C. E. (2001), pp. 342-343.

[56] This does not mean that subnational governments should not levy taxes on the income of individuals.

[57] See McLure Jr., C. E. (1999), section I.C.

[58] In tax sharing systems one level of government (usually the central level) collects the revenue from a tax and shares it with other levels of government (usually subnational levels). In most of the cases this is done on the basis of a formula which includes factors like population, tax capacity, and tax effort of the subnational governments. See Bird, R. M., et al. (1995a), p. 46; Boadway, R. W. and Wildasin, D. E. (1984), p. 539.

[59] See McLure Jr., C. E. (1999), section II.A.

[60] McLure Jr., C. E. (1999), section II.A. See also Bird, R. M. (2003a), section 1.

allowed to impose surcharges on taxes levied by the national government. In sum, efficiency requires that subnational jurisdictions refrain from nonbenefit taxation of mobile economic units, and that they use benefit taxes when public services are provided. If nonbenefit taxes are considered necessary and desirable – for example, a progressive income tax for redistribution and stabilization purposes – they are generally best employed by the central level.[61]

According to Bird (1993), a proper local tax can be defined as one that is assessed by a local government, at rates decided by that government, collected by that government, and whose profits accrue to that government.[62] In addition, he lists the following characteristics of an ideal local tax:[63]

1. The tax base should be immobile to give local authorities some scope in varying rates without driving away the tax base.

2. The tax revenues should be adequate to meet local needs and sufficiently buoyant (i.e. expand at least as fast as expenditures) over time.

3. The tax revenues should be stable and predictable over time.

4. The tax should be perceived to be reasonably fair by taxpayers.

5. The tax should be easy to administer efficiently and effectively.

6. It should not be possible to export much, if any, of the tax burden to non-residents.

7. The tax base should be visible to ensure accountability of the tax-collecting local government.

In the subsequent sections, fees and user charges as well as the different taxes usually suggested for local and regional use will be reviewed in order to find out whether they are appropriate for use at subnational levels of government.

4.2.1 Fees and User Charges

As a general guideline, fees and user charges should be used at any level of government as they realize the benefit principle for public services.[64] To the extent possible, local public services should be financed by user charges and fees. Thus a

---

[61] See Oates, W. E. (1999), pp. 1125-1126.

[62] See Bird, R. M. (1993), p. 213.

[63] See Bird, R. M. (1993), p. 214.

[64] See Cullis, J. and Jones, P. (1998), p. 313.

first rule for subnational finance is: "Wherever possible, charge!"[65] User charges and fees are not burdened with the spillover problem because outsiders automatically pay the marginal share of benefits received.[66] Bird (2003a) distinguishes three types of user charges – service fees, public prices, and specific benefit charges.[67] The correct prices of those user charges are marginal cost prices, which make sure that the right public services are provided to those who are willing to pay for them. In reality, however, user charges often are not employed to a desirable extent so that by far they do not provide sufficient revenue for subnational activities.[68]

Where it is not possible to impose fees or user charges, another possible source of revenue should be taxes levied on local residents to the extent they benefit from public services.[69]

4.2.2 Property Taxes

For decades, the property tax has been regarded as the most important general tax source for local governments, at least in the Anglo-Saxon countries.[70] Property taxes are widely accepted for local taxation because they largely assess land or immobile homeowners.[71] Property tax revenues are also regarded as relatively predictable and stable over time.[72] Besides, property taxes are among the few taxes that can be implemented by the local levels with relatively little assistance from higher levels of government. The taxation of intangible and nonresidential property should be avoided at the local level as it is often very difficult to identify the owners of intangible assets and taxing nonresidential property may result in inefficient tax exporting.[73]

---

[65] Bird, R. M. (2003a), section 2.

[66] See Gramlich, E. M. (1993), p. 230.

[67] Service fees are license fees, e.g. marriage, business, or vehicle. Public prices are revenues received by local governments from selling goods and services, e.g. admission charges to recreation areas. Specific benefit charges are imposed on the assessed value of real property, changes in that value, or some characteristic of that property. See Bird, R. M. (1993), pp. 212-213.

[68] See Bird, R. M. (2003a), section 2.

[69] See Bird, R. M., et al. (1995a), p. 40.

[70] See Prud'homme, R. (1987), p. 1189.

[71] See Gramlich, E. M. (1993), p. 231.

[72] See Joumard, I. and Kongsrud, P. M. (2003), p. 186.

[73] See McLure Jr., C. E. (1999), section VI.E., and Bird, R. M. (1993), p. 216.

The main problem of the property tax is that it is difficult to administer in a horizontally equitable fashion. For example, it is often difficult and consequently costly to identify the market value of a property.[74] A second problem is the inelasticity of the property tax. As its base does not automatically increase over time, increased nominal tax rates are required to maintain real revenues when price levels rise.[75] Furthermore, the property tax is a very visible tax and therefore nominal increases in taxes may cause resistance from the taxpayers.

Despite these problems, the property tax still seems to be a good option for raising revenue at the local level. It is the predominant local tax in most developing and transitional countries, although the resulting revenues will not be sufficient to finance local governments' expenditures.[76]

4.2.3 Personal Income Taxes

In principle, personal income taxes are suitable for use by different levels of government. As mentioned above, the central government can use a progressive income tax for purposes of redistribution and stabilization. Personal income tax revenues are an important component of subnational government financial resources in a large number of countries.[77] But in countries like Austria, Germany, or Poland the lower levels of government have no autonomy to set the personal income tax base and rates. Such a system can be characterized as a tax-sharing arrangement rather than a truly local tax.[78]

A progressive local or regional income tax seems inappropriate because the benefits of public spending are not likely to rise more rapidly than income, as income rises.[79] Alm (1996), in terms of the optimal taxation theory, contends that optimal income taxes in general should be raised "at constant marginal tax rates on broadly defined tax bases above some level of income determined by generously defined exemptions and (standard) deductions with minimal use of special tax incentives."[80]

---

[74] See Bird, R. M. (2003a), section 3.

[75] See Bird, R. M. (1993), p. 215.

[76] See Bird, R. M. (2003a), section 3.

[77] See Joumard, I. and Kongsrud, P. M. (2003), pp. 187-188.

[78] See Prud'homme, R. (1987), p. 1194.

[79] See McLure Jr., C. E. (2001), p. 345.

[80] Alm, J. (1996), p. 129.

Bird (1993) in contrast suggests levying a local income tax as a surcharge on national income taxes, which means that the tax would remain a progressive one. This is desirable on equity grounds, but he concedes that in the local context this is not the center of discussion.[81] The main argument in favor of local surcharges on national income taxes as a source of local finance is that it can provide high amounts of revenue, which would guarantee subnational governments' fiscal autonomy. Besides, income taxes are visible taxes and thus satisfy the criteria of political responsibility and accountability.[82]

One of the questions that need to be answered is whether income taxes should be residence-based or source-based, a problem which occurs when people do not work in the jurisdiction they live in.[83] Source-based taxes are often used at lower levels of government because they are easier to administer. The problem with source-based taxes is that public services are mostly consumed where people live, not where they work. This means that the distribution of revenues from source-based income taxes among jurisdictions would not match the costs of providing public services.[84] Consequently, subnational governments should levy residence-based taxes on income, even though these are more difficult to administer.

4.2.4 Payroll Taxes

Payroll taxes can be used if governments want beneficiaries to pay for costs of public services related to the place of employment instead of residence, as would be the case with the personal income tax. Payroll taxes have the advantage that they are easy to administer — if levied as a tax on payrolls at the enterprise level — and relatively productive at relatively low rates. But there are two important demerits: First, they act as a tax barrier to employment as they favor the use of capital over the use of labor,

---

[81] See Bird, R. M. (1993), pp. 216-217.

[82] See Bird, R. M. (2003a), section 5.

[83] Broadly speaking, residence-based taxes (also referred to as destination-based taxes in reference to consumption taxes) tax factors based on the owner's residence and tax goods and services by the consumer's residence, while source-based taxes (also referred to as origin-based taxes with respect to consumption taxes) tax factors where they are employed and tax goods and services where they are purchased. See Inman, R. P. and Rubinfeld, D. L. (1996), p. 309.

[84] McLure Jr., C. E. (1999), section VI.A.

and second, in most countries the basis for payroll taxes is already heavily exploited to finance social security systems.[85]

4.2.5 Excise Taxes

Excise taxes are commonly charged on special consumer goods like, for example, alcohol and tobacco. There are also strong arguments to impose vehicle-related taxes, like the fuel tax and the motor-vehicle tax. The level of government which should impose excise taxes depends strongly on the mobility of the tax base. Taxes with a mobile base are less appropriate for regional and local governments (e.g. the fuel tax). Regionally differential tax rates would have distortionary effects since tax competition would prevent the maintenance of an efficient level of the tax. If the tax base is immobile, as is the case for the motor-vehicle tax, such a tax will be appropriate for use at the regional or local level.

Especially the latter tax can satisfy the benefit principle if the revenues of this tax are used to finance construction and maintenance of roads and highways.[86] Excise taxes can be easily administered by subnational governments. Moreover, in terms of efficiency, such taxes, levied as destination-based taxes, should have little distortionary effect.[87]

4.2.6 General Sales Taxes

The most common forms of general sales taxes are value added taxes (VATs) and retail sales taxes. Today, the VAT is the most important form of general sales tax in use (all EU member states are obliged to apply VATs). Some 20 years ago, Musgrave (1983) favored the retail sales tax (RST) as a regional tax, but this tax is now rarely used in comparison to the VAT.[88] In theory, both taxes are adequate for financing benefits provided by both central and subnational governments. In general, these types of taxes should be assigned to the jurisdiction in which consumption occurs (i.e. destination-based taxation), rather than to the producing jurisdiction (origin-based

---

[85]   See Bird, R. M. (2003a), section 6.

[86]   See McLure Jr., C. E. (1999), section IV.

[87]   See Bird, R. M. (2003a), section 4.

[88]   See Bird, R. M. and Gendron, P.-P. (2001), p. 2.

taxation) because it is assumed that consumption is more closely related to the benefits of public expenditures than is production.[89]

The question remains whether subnational governments should be allowed to levy a VAT, either with or without a VAT at the federal level. The traditional view on this question was that standalone VATs, since they entail severe administrative problems as, for example, experienced in Brazil[90], should not be imposed by subnational governments. The main reasons for this view are excessive compliance and administrative costs incorporated in standalone VATs. To avoid such difficulties, most federal countries solved the problem by maintaining all VAT at the central level and then sharing the revenues with subnational governments. This was either done by using a formula (as in Germany) or by using consumption statistics, as has recently been recommended for the European Union.[91]

4.2.7 Business Taxes

Regional and local business taxes – levied for instance as corporate income taxes or capital taxes – are found in most countries. They are quite popular because they offer substantial revenue and are more elastic than, for example, the property tax.[92] Nonetheless, there are some important caveats concerning subnational business taxes from the theoretical point of view. First of all, such taxes fail to satisfy the principle of benefit taxation because the benefits a corporation receives do not vary with a corporation's profits.[93] Second, subnational taxes on business capital seem likely to be economically costly. "The international and intra-national mobility of the tax base, the ease with which businesses can shift income across boundaries, and the difficulty that small governments may have in enforcing taxes in such circumstances all point in the same direction."[94] Third, it is often difficult to determine the geographic source of income if a corporation is doing business in more than one jurisdiction. Therefore, it is common to divide a corporation's income among different jurisdictions with the aid of a

---

[89] See McLure Jr., C. E. (1999), section IV and section II C.

[90] See Bird, R. M. (2003a), section 7, and Bird, R. M. and Gendron, P.-P. (2001), pp. 18-20 for details on the problems of the Brazilian VAT.

[91] See Bird, R. M. and Gendron, P.-P. (2001), p. 4.

[92] See Bird, R. M. (2003a), section 8.

[93] See McLure Jr., C. E. (1999), section IV.

[94] Bird, R. M. (2003b), section 2.

formula.[95] To perform such a formula apportionment, subnational governments need to have large administrative resources.

5 Theory and Use of Intergovernmental Grants

In the following section we will first give justifications for the implementation of a system of intergovernmental grants. After that we will introduce the different types of grants used in intergovernmental transfer systems before we will finally describe the effects associated with the different types of grants.

5.1 JUSTIFICATIONS FOR INTERGOVERNMENTAL TRANSFERS

Intergovernmental grants can be justified with several arguments. First of all, intergovernmental grants are needed to achieve what is called "vertical fiscal balance". That means, revenues and expenditures of each level of government are supposed to be approximately equal. Reality, however, is characterized by vertical fiscal imbalances[96] (VFI) because the central government has more revenue-raising capacity than the lower levels. It may be efficient that the central government raises more revenues than it needs for its expenditures and transfers the excess to lower levels of government which collect fewer revenues than they need for their expenditures. Transfers from higher to lower levels of government are then used to fill the existing vertical fiscal gap (VFG). But transfers from the central to the regional governments do not only close the VFG, they also have "important objectives in their own right."[97] They may be given either for efficiency or equity reasons.

Second, as shown in the preceding sections, there are a number of problems associated with the decentralization of (fiscal) decision-making. It is often suggested to correct such negative results of decentralization by introducing intergovernmental

---

[95]   See McLure Jr., C. E. (1999), section VI.D.

[96]   Also known as vertical fiscal gap. That is the difference between expenditures and own-source revenues at different levels of government. In most nations, the central government raises more revenue than it needs and transfers the excess to subnational levels. See Bird, R. M. and Smart, M. (2002), p. 909 and Boadway, R. (2001), p. 111. The extent of the vertical fiscal imbalance varies across countries. Germany, for instance, has a much larger VFI than the USA or Canada. See Boadway, R. (2001), p. 111.

[97]   Boadway, R. (2001), p. 112.

grants[98]. The most common justification for the introduction of intergovernmental grants put forward in the relevant economic literature is the existence of benefit spillovers. Additionally, grants can be used to remedy vertical and horizontal fiscal externalities.

Other possible objectives of an intergovernmental transfer system could be the reduction of horizontal imbalances between poor and wealthy regions to achieve fiscal equalization, the stimulation of subnational tax efforts by encouraging localities to raise more own-source-revenue, and to influence subnational spending decisions.[99] A well designed system of intergovernmental transfers is thus essential to any decentralization strategy.

5.2 TYPES OF GRANTS

Intergovernmental grants can take two basic forms: they may be conditional or unconditional (see Figure I - 4).

Figure I - 4:   Types of Intergovernmental Grants

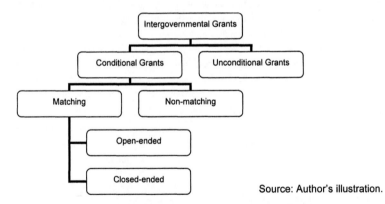

Source: Author's illustration.

Conditional grants – also called categorical or earmarked grants – are to be used for specified purposes by the recipient. They can be grouped into matching grants, which

---

[98]   Also referred to as grants-in-aid.

[99]   See Bird, R. M., et al. (1995a), p. 51.

again can be open-ended or closed-ended, and non-matching grants. The different types of grants will now be discussed in more detail.

5.2.1 Conditional Matching Grants

Matching grants are used when the donor wants to influence the behavior of the recipient government. For every Euro a community spends on a certain activity it will receive – according to a specified formula – a certain amount by the donor to support this activity. Figure I - 5 shows the effects of an open-ended matching grant.[100] The horizontal axis measures the quantity of a public good G provided by a local government. The vertical axis measures the jurisdiction inhabitants' total consumption c. It is assumed that the price for one unit of G and c is €1 each. As we assume no savings, c is equal to after-tax income.

Figure I - 5:   An open-ended matching grant

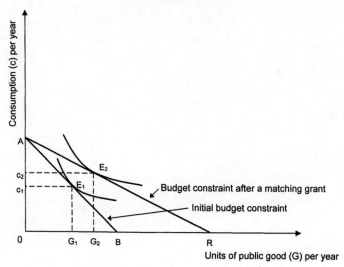

Source: Rosen (2002), p. 498

---

[100]   See Rosen, H. S. (2002), pp. 498-499 for this section.

With these assumptions, the initial budget constraint (AB) between G and c is a straight line with a slope in absolute value of one. This means that for each Euro the jurisdiction spends, it can get one unit of public good. The jurisdiction's preferences for G and c are represented by the indifference curves. Initially the jurisdiction will choose point E_1, which maximizes the collective preferences of the community. Here public good consumption is G_1 and after-tax income is c_1.

Now, a matching grant at a rate BR/0R is introduced whereby the jurisdiction will get two units of G for each Euro it spends. The slope of the new budget constraint line (AR) becomes one-half (in absolute value). In other words, the matching grant halves the price of G for the jurisdiction. A higher indifference curve is reached and the consumption of the public good rises to G_2. The jurisdiction's after-tax income increases to c_2.

Figure I - 6: A closed-ended matching grant

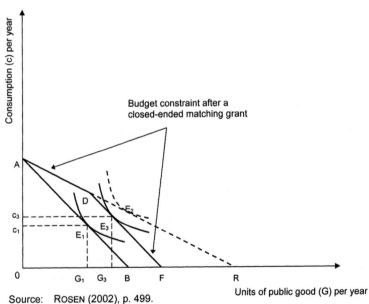

Source: ROSEN (2002), p. 499.

When the indifference curves are drawn as they are in Figure I - 6, the grant leads to a situation in which the jurisdiction uses part of the grant to consume more of the public good and the rest to reduce its tax burden so that the after-tax income can rise from c_1 to c_2. Thus the effectiveness of a matching grant depends on the preferences for the public good in question. Obviously the costs of a matching grant can be substantial – depending on the recipient's behavior or preferences. The donor, however, has the opportunity to put a ceiling on the cost by specifying a maximum amount that will be spent.

This is called a closed-ended matching grant. The effect of a closed-ended matching grant is illustrated in Figure I - 6. In the absence of the transfer, the equilibrium is represented by point E_1. After the introduction of the closed-ended grant, the new budget constraint is described by a kinked line (ADF), as we find in . Segment AD of this line again has a slope of minus one-half, describing the one-for-one matching grant as discussed above. But now, after some point D, the donor does not match Euro for Euro any more and the slope of the segment DF gets steeper again (in minus one). In contrast to the open-ended matching grant a supply of the public good beyond (0F-0B) is not subsidized any longer. The new equilibrium E_3 leads to a consumption level of the public good of G_3 and an after-tax income of c_3, which are both less than under the open-ended matching grant.Matching grants increase the central government's influence and control over the receiving governments. But "they also have the important political advantage of introducing an element of local involvement, commitment, accountability, and responsibility for the aided activities."[101]

5.2.2 Conditional Non-matching Grants

With this type of conditional grant, the donor gives a fixed amount of transfer to the recipient on condition that the money is spent on a certain public good like education or health care. What distinguishes these non-matching grants from the matching grants discussed above is the fact that the fostered jurisdiction does not have to match every Euro it receives by a certain amount. It will receive the grants independent of its own expenditures, it simply has to use the grant on the public good. Figure I - 7 illustrates a non-matching grant to buy AH units of the public good G. At each level of after-tax income AH more units of G can be bought than before the grant. The resulting budget constraint is the kinked line AHM. The new equilibrium is depicted by E_4 where we have a consumption of the public good of G_4 and an after-tax income of c_4. As we can see in Figure I - 7, the difference between G1 and G4 is less than AH. This means that the transfer-receiving community spends the full grant on G, but it also reduces its own expenditures for the public good and is thus able to lower its taxes.[102]

---

[101] Bird, R. M. and Smart, M. (2002), p. 905.

[102] See Rosen, H. S. (2002), pp. 500-501.

Figure I - 7: A non-matching grant

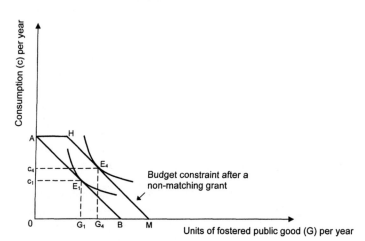

Source: ROSEN (2002), p. 500.

5.2.3 Unconditional Grants

An unconditional grant means that the donor gives an unrestricted lump sum grant to a jurisdiction, which can be spent according to the jurisdiction's own decisions. In contrast to the matching grants discussed in section 5.2.1, an unconditional grant does not change relative prices, but is simply an income-changing phenomenon.[103] Purchasing power is transferred from one level of government to another.

As figure I - 7 shows, the unconditional grant leads to an upward shift of the budget constraint line JM, resulting in a new equilibrium in E4. The grant adds to income and allows the community to expand both its post-tax income and public good consumption. The result here is the same as for the non-matching conditional grant, as long as the community wants to consume an amount of the public good that is at least equal to the grant (AH). The results would only differ if the receiving jurisdiction wanted to consume less than AH. The difference between these two types of grants is that now the receiving jurisdiction is free to decide about how to use the transferred money. Thus the grant is not bound to a specific public good any longer. The magnitude of

---

[103]   See Boadway, R. W. and Wildasin, D. E. (1984), p. 521.

lump sum transfers to lower levels of government often depends on the fiscal capacity and the needs of these lower levels.

Figure I - 8 shows, the unconditional grant leads to an upward shift of the budget constraint line JM, resulting in a new equilibrium in E_4. The grant adds to income and allows the community to expand both its post-tax income and public good consumption. The result here is the same as for the non-matching conditional grant, as long as the community wants to consume an amount of the public good that is at least equal to the grant (AH).

Figure I - 8:   An unconditional grant

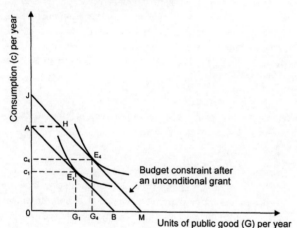

Source: ROSEN (2002), p. 500.

The results would only differ if the receiving jurisdiction wanted to consume less than AH. The difference between these two types of grants is that now the receiving jurisdiction is free to decide about how to use the transferred money. Thus the grant is not bound to a specific public good any longer. The magnitude of lump sum transfers to lower levels of government often depends on the fiscal capacity[104] and the needs[105] of these lower levels.[106]

---

[104]   Often measured by per capita income.

[105]   A measure of need might be the per capita cost of providing a certain level of a public service in the jurisdiction.

5.3 THE IMPACT OF INTERGOVERNMENTAL TRANSFERS

In this section we want to give answers to the following questions: How can the different types of grants be used to internalize spillovers and the various fiscal externalities caused by taxation? And: Which type of transfer is appropriate to achieve equalization?

5.3.1 Internalization of Benefit Spillovers

As described in section 1.4, the benefits of a public good or service provided in one jurisdiction may spill over to non-residents. The government which undertakes an activity does not take into account these spillovers when it decides how much of the public good to provide. If jurisdiction A incurs expenditures which produce benefits in jurisdiction B, the efficient level of output of this expenditure will be that, at which the marginal benefits to residents of A plus the marginal benefits to residents of B equal the marginal cost of the activity:[107]

$MB_A + MB_B = MC$.

But, as government A does not consider the positive externalities of its expenditure decision, it will only select a level of expenditures at which

$MB_A = MC$.

If the central government wants to induce regional government A to spend the 'correct' amount on the public good, a matching grant could be given at the rate of $MB_B/(MB_A + MB_B)$. Not only could the matching grant be given to A in order to obtain the efficient level of expenditure, but an unconditional grant might also be used.

With the help of Figure I - 9 we can show that the matching grant is better able to achieve the goal. Initially we are faced with the budget constraint line AB and the residents of A will choose point E_1, which maximizes their preferences. As discussed above, a matching grant at rate BD/0D will lead to a new budget constraint line of AD and point E_2 will be chosen. Thereby, in principle, the appropriate matching rate should be determined by the size of the spillover.[108] The demand for the public good will rise from G_1 to G_2. In point E_2 the total grant amounts to E_2F. In order to induce the same expenditures on the public good, an unconditional grant of E_3F would have to be given

---

[106] See Boadway, R. W. and Wildasin, D. E. (1984), p. 519.

[107] See Boadway, R. W. and Wildasin, D. E. (1984), p. 519.

[108] See Bird, R. M. and Smart, M. (2002), p. 905.

to jurisdiction A. Such a transfer would shift the budget line to CR. Thus the unconditional grant is more costly than the matching grant; the higher costs are represented by E_3E_2.

Figure I - 9:   Matching vs. unconditional grant

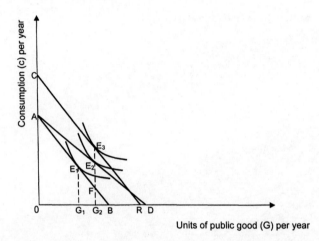

Source: Author's diagram following BOADWAY and WILDASIN (1984), p. 520.

It is evident that in general a matching grant does better in stimulating a jurisdiction's expenditures on a particular good or service than an unconditional lump-sum grant.[109] One substantial problem in the design of matching grants is that they are very demanding in terms of the information needed to set the correct matching rate. For example, the external benefits of a government's activity are difficult to measure.[110]

5.3.2 Establishing Vertical Fiscal Balance

As described in section 4.2 it may be efficient for the central government to collect more tax revenues than it needs and then transfer money to lower levels of government. We referred to this procedure, which results in a vertical fiscal imbalance,

---

[109]   See Cullis, J. and Jones, P. (1998), p. 319.
[110]   See Boadway, R. (2001), p. 115.

as tax sharing. Now, the question is which form of grant is appropriate to be used in such revenue sharing arrangements. Figure I - 10 shows that the highest indifference curve can be reached by using an unconditional grant. Here, we construct a situation in which the total amount transferred, and with it the costs, are identical for both the matching and the unconditional grant.[111]

Figure I - 10: The appropriate grant for closing the VFG

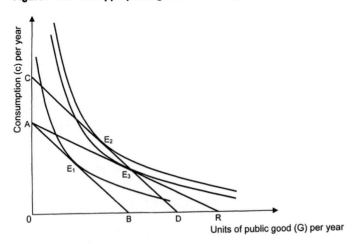

Source: BOADWAY and WILDASIN (1984), p. 522.

Again, AR represents the budget constraint after a matching grant, while CD represents the budget constraint after an unconditional grant. CA is equal to E_3B. If the purpose of such a transfer is to close the vertical fiscal gap by simply transferring purchasing power from the central government to lower levels of government, unconditional grants seem to be the appropriate form because they leave the recipient best off.[112] Such VFGs could also be closed by giving subnational governments more access to own tax revenues, by centralizing expenditure responsibilities, or by reducing

---

[111]   See Boadway, R. W. and Wildasin, D. E. (1984), pp. 521-522.

[112]   See Boadway, R. W. and Wildasin, D. E. (1984), p. 527.

subnational expenditures and service standards, whereby vertical transfers seem preferable to such approaches.[113]

5.3.3 Equalization Grants

The equalization of inter-regional differences in financial capacities requires intergovernmental transfers. Horizontal fiscal imbalances can be corrected by equalization grants in vertical direction from the center, horizontally between regions, or simultaneously in both dimensions.[114] The goal of equalization is accepted in many federations, in some countries it is even written into the constitution.[115] An important and often controversial issue is to what extent equalization is desired. There may be different views in different countries. If horizontal fiscal imbalances are equalized to a large extent, such a grant system can depress incentives for subnational governments to raise their own revenues.[116] Thus fiscal equalization is a disputable issue from an efficiency point of view.[117]

However, the primary justification for fiscal equalization must rest upon equity reasons.[118] One obvious problem here is that intergovernmental grants for redistributive purposes are transfers from one group of people to another. In contrast, the just distribution of income should deal with the distribution among individuals. Persons who are equally well-off before government policy should be equally well-off after government policy.[119] In this case, "fiscal equity" is interpreted in such a way that all equals receive the same net fiscal benefit.[120] Against this background it may be impossible to achieve the desired interindividual income distribution by using intergovernmental grants.

If the goal of the transfers is fiscal equity among regions – as an extension of the principle of interindividual horizontal equity, i.e. the equal treatment of equals – the

---

[113] See Bird, R. M., et al. (1995a), p. 51.

[114] See Ahmad, E. and Craig, J. (1997), p. 76; Musgrave, R. A. (1983), p. 16.

[115] E.g. in the German constitution we find the principle of „Einheitlichkeit der Lebensverhält- nisse".

[116] This effect can be observed, for example, in Germany's Finanzausgleich system.

[117] See Oates, W. E. (1999), p. 1127.

[118] See Oates, W. E. (1999), p. 1128.

[119] See Boadway, R. (2004), p. 213.

[120] See Mieszkowski, P. and Musgrave, R. A. (1999), p. 244. See section 3.1 for the discussion of NFBs.

central government can attempt to equalize the fiscal capacities of all jurisdictions by providing transfer payments to poorer regions.[121] Interjurisdictional equalization has been accepted as a second-best solution when interindividual equalization seems impractical in a federal context.[122] In most countries equalization transfers are given in form of unconditional lump-sum grants.[123] As the receiving jurisdictions are free to decide about the use of the money, they have the possibility to maximize their own welfare.[124] According to different authors, the optimal equalization grants are lump-sum intergovernmental grants which can take the form of inter-state transfers or federal-state transfers.[125] A system of grants should distribute funds on the basis of a formula while discretionary transfers are not desirable. Such grants, mostly based on measures of fiscal need, fiscal capacity, and fiscal effort are designed to reduce differences among localities in their ability to provide the appropriate levels of public goods and services.[126]

---

[121] See Oates, W. E. (1972), pp. 79-84.

[122] See Mieszkowski, P. and Musgrave, R. A. (1999), pp. 245-248 and Musgrave, R. A. (1971), p. 10.

[123] See Ahmad, E. and Craig, J. (1997), p. 90.

[124] See Rubinfeld, D. L. (1987), p. 635.

[125] See, e.g. Dahlby, B. (1996), p. 408, Mieszkowski, P. and Musgrave, R. A. (1999), pp. 241 and 244, or Oates, W. E. (1977), p. 12.

[126] See Oates, W. E. (1999), p. 1127.

6 Bibliography

Ahmad, Ehtisham and Craig, Jon (1997): "Intergovernmental Transfers", in: Ter-Minassian, Teresa: Fiscal Federalism in Theory and Practice. Washington, D.C., International Monetary Fund. pp. 73-107.

Alm, James (1996): "What Is an "Optimal" Tax System?" in: National Tax Journal. March 49(1), pp. 117-133.

Aronson, J. Richard (1985): "Public Finance", New York et al.

Bardhan, Pranab (2002): "Decentralization of Governance and Development", in: Journal of Economic Perspectives. Fall 16(4), pp. 185-205.

Bird, Richard M. (1993): "Threading the Fiscal Labyrinth: Some Issues in Fiscal Decentralization", in: National Tax Journal. June 46(2), pp. 207-227.

Bird, Richard M. (2003a): "Local and Regional Revenues: Realities and Prospects", World Bank, Internet: http://www1.worldbank.org/publicsector/Decentralization SubNational Economics/ June2003Seminar/bird2003.pdf, found 23 Mar 2004.

Bird, Richard M. (2003b): "Local Business Taxes", World Bank, Internet: http://www.worldbank.org/wbi/publicfinance/documents/fiscalfederalism_Russia/B ird_tax.pdf, found 02 Apr 2004.

Bird, Richard M., Ebel, Robert D. and Wallich, Christine I. (1995a): "Fiscal Decentralization: From Command to Market", in: Bird, Richard M., Ebel, Robert D. and Wallich, Christine I.: Decentralization of the Socialist State: Intergovernmental Finance in Transition Economies. Washington, DC. pp. 1-67.

Bird, Richard M. and Gendron, Pierre-Pascal (2001): "VATs in Federal States: International Experience and Emerging Possibilities", World Bank, Internet: http://www.worldbank.org/wbi/publicfinance/documents/ Subnational%20Consumption%20VATs.pdf, found 31 Mar 2004.

Bird, Richard M. and Smart, Michael (2002): "Intergovernmental Fiscal Transfers: International Lessons for Developing Countries", in: World Development. June 30(6), pp. 899-912.

Bird, Richard M. and Vaillancourt, Francois (1998): "Fiscal Decentralization in Developing Countries: An Overview", in: Bird, Richard M. and Vaillancourt, Francois: Fiscal Decentralization in Developing Countries. Cambridge. pp. 1-48.

Bird, Richard M. and Wallich, Christine I. (1993): "Fiscal Decentralization and Intergovernmental Relations in Transition Economies: Toward a Systemic Framework of Analysis", Policy Research Working Paper Series, The World Bank, WPS 1122.

Boadway, Robin (2001): "Intergovernmental Fiscal Relations: The Facilitator of Fiscal Decentralization", in: Constitutional Political Economy. June 12(2), pp. 93-121.

Boadway, Robin (2004): "The Theory and Practice of Equalization", in: CESifo Economic Studies 50(1), pp. 211-254.

Boadway, Robin W. and Wildasin, David E. (1984): "Public Sector Economics", 2nd ed., Boston.

Buchanan, James M. (1950): "Federalism and Fiscal Equity", in: American Economic Review. September 40(4), pp. 583-599.

Cullis, John and Jones, Philip (1998): "Public finance and public choice".

Dahlby, Bev (1996): "Fiscal Externalities and the Design of Intergovernmental Grants", in: International Tax and Public Finance. July 3(3), pp. 397-412.

Frey, Bruno S. and Kirchgaessner, Gebhard (2002): "Demokratische Wirtschaftspolitik", 3rd ed., Muenchen.

Gillette, Clayton P. (2001): "Funding versus Control in Intergovernmental Relations", in: Constitutional Political Economy. June 12(2), pp. 123-140.

Gordon, Roger H. (1983): "An Optimal Taxation Approach to Fiscal Federalism", in: Quarterly Journal of Economics. November 98(4), pp. 567-586.

Gramlich, Edward M. (1987): "Federalism and Federal Deficit Reduction", in: National Tax Journal. September 40(3), pp. 299-313.

Gramlich, Edward M. (1993): "A Policymaker's Guide to Fiscal Decentralization", in: National Tax Journal. June 46(2), pp. 229-235.

Groenewegen, Peter (1988): "Fiscal Federalism", in: Eatwell, John: The new Palgrave: a dictionary of economics. London. pp. 366.

Hayek, Friedrich A. (1945): "The Use of Knowledge in Society", in: American Economic Review. September 35(4), pp. 519-530.

Inman, Robert P. and Rubinfeld, Daniel L. (1991): "Fiscal Federalism in Europe: Lessons From the United States Experience". Cambridge, NBER Working Paper No. 3941.

Inman, Robert P. and Rubinfeld, Daniel L. (1996): "Designing Tax Policy in Federalist Economies: An Overview", in: Journal of Public Economics. June 60(3), pp. 307-334.

Joumard, Isabelle and Kongsrud, Per Mathis (2003): "Fiscal Relations across Government Levels", in: OECD Economic Studies 1(36), pp. 155-229.

McLure Jr., Charles E. (1999): "The Tax Assignment Problem: Conceptual and Administrative Considerations in Achieving Subnational Fiscal Autonomy", World Bank, Internet: http://www1.worldbank.org/wbiep/decentralization/Courses/

Thailand%202.24.99/section5.htm, found 26 Mar 2004, Presented to Seminar on Intergovernmental Fiscal Relations and Local Financial Management organized by National Economic and Social Development Board of the Royal Thai Government and the World Bank, Chiang Mai, Thailand, February 24-March 5.

McLure Jr., Charles E. (2001): "The Tax Assignment Problem: Ruminations on How Theory and Practice Depend on History", in: National Tax Journal. June 54(2), pp. 339-363.

Mieszkowski, Peter and Musgrave, Richard A. (1999): "Federalism, Grants, and Fiscal Equalization", in: National Tax Journal. June 52(2), pp. 239-260.

Musgrave, Richard A. (1959): "The Theory of Public Finance: A Study in Public Economy", Tokyo.

Musgrave, Richard A. (1971): "Economics of Fiscal Federalism", in: Nebraska Journal of Economics & Business 10(4), pp. 3-13.

Musgrave, Richard A. (1983): "Who Should Tax, Where, and What?" in: McLure Jr., Charles E.: Tax Assignment in Federal Countries. Canberra. pp. 2-19.

Musgrave, Richard A. and Musgrave, Peggy B. (1989): "Public Finance in Theory and Practice", 5th ed., New York.

Norregaard, John (1997): "Tax Assignment", in: Ter-Minassian, Teresa: Fiscal Federalism in Theory and Practice. Washington, International Monetary Fund. pp. 49-72.

Oates, W. E. (1999): "An Essay on Fiscal Federalism", in: Journal of Economic Literature. September 37(3), pp. 1120-1149.

Oates, Wallace E. (1972): "Fiscal Federalism", New York.

Oates, Wallace E. (1977): "An Economist's Perspective on Fiscal Federalism", in: Oates, Wallace E.: The Political Economy of Fiscal Federalism. pp. 3-20.

Oates, Wallace E. (1994): "Federalism and Government Finance", in: Quigley, John M. and Smolensky, Eugene: Modern Public Finance. Cambridge. pp. 126-151.

Prud'homme, Remy (1987): "Financing Urban Public Services", in: Mills, Edwin S.: Handbook of Regional and Urban Economics. Amsterdam, Elsevier. pp. 1179-1206.

Rosen, Harvey S. (2002): "Public Finance", 6th ed., Boston.

Rubinfeld, Daniel L. (1987): "The Economics of the Local Public Sector", in: Auerbach, Alan J. and Feldstein, Martin: Handbook of Public Economics. Amsterdam. pp. 571-645.

Tresch, Richard W. (2002): "Public finance: A normative theory", 2nd ed., Amsterdam.

FISCAL DECENTRALIZATION - PROBLEMS AND SPECIAL REQUIREMENTS FOR TRANSITION ECONOMIES

LARS PONTERLITSCHEK

1   Introduction

The process of fiscal decentralization is an important element of the transition from a command to a market economy and it requires many, often difficult, reforms. Important steps of fiscal decentralization are to create – if necessary – new levels of government, to realign expenditure responsibilities among different levels of government, to rethink the structure of tax and intergovernmental transfer systems, and to change views as to what governments can and should do. The level of public sector activity should be reduced significantly. The newly created subnational governments in countries in transition from socialist planned to market economies must be permitted to build up staff and institutional capacities in a way that makes them accountable for their fiscal decisions.[1] Accountability and fiscal transparency are regarded as the vital factors for good governance.[2] "Elected representatives, public officials, government departments, public enterprises, quasi-government bodies and private sector institutions must be held accountable for their actions and be fully transparent in their decision-making, performance and use of public funds."[3]

Over the past fifteen years, a trend towards the devolution of spending and, to a lesser extent, revenue-raising responsibilities to subnational levels of government could be observed in Central and Eastern European transition economies. In 1990, the process of fiscal decentralization in formerly centrally planned economies started in Poland and Hungary. One year later, Romania, Bulgaria and the Russian Federation started comprehensive reforms. Now, about fourty countries are undergoing a transition from central planning to a decentralized government system and a market economy. This

---

[1]   See Bird, R. M., et al. (1995a), p. 2.

[2]   See IMF (1998), p. 122.

[3]   http://www.undp.org.fj/gold/accountability.htm

trend is particularly evident in former unitary countries with a long tradition of centralist governments, but also in some federal systems. It reflects the political evolution towards more democratic and participatory forms of government to ensure a closer correspondence of the quantity, quality and composition of publicly provided goods and services to the preferences of the citizens.[4]

In the pre-transition period, government finances were closely interconnected with the administration of a heavily state-controlled economy with distorted prices, extensive regulation, ill-defined property rights, and incomplete markets. The central elements of economic reform in countries in transition – privatization, liberalization of prices, establishment of legal protection of property rights and contracts, and deregulation – must inevitably have major fiscal consequences.[5] Thus, setting up well-designed intergovernmental fiscal relations is a key factor for a successful economic transition process.[6]

There will be little difference between the desirable outcomes of decentralization in transition economies, developing countries, and the industrialized world. Nevertheless it is likely that countries in transition face specific problems while implementing new systems of intergovernmental finance after the collapse of the socialist system. The aim of this chapter is to identify these problems and to make suggestions to solve them.

The paper is structured as follows. Section 2 gives a short overview of the different forms of government. Sections 3 through 5 review the special problems and considerations concerning the three key components of intergovernmental fiscal relations in transition countries – expenditures, taxes, and inter governmental transfers.

2 Forms of Government

As this study aims at evaluating the Polish financial constitution with Germany as a benchmark, we will, in a first step, discuss the fundamental differences between the different forms of government. Basically, there are three types of the constitutional

---

4   See Ter-Minassian, T. (1997), p. 3.

5   See Wildasin, D. E. (1998), p. 13.

6   See Bird, R. M., et al. (2003), p. 72.

division of powers among various levels of government: unitary, federal and confederal states.[7]

A unitary state is governed constitutionally as one single unit, with one constitutionally created parliament. Governmental power may well be transferred to lower levels, to regionally or locally elected assemblies, governors and mayors, but in a unitary state the central government has the right to recall such delegated power. Under a unitary system, local governments exercise only those powers granted to them by the central government. Local governments are mostly thought of as administrative units of the central government. These administrative units usually have limited decision-making authority. Most of the OECD countries and all East and Southeast European transition countries except Russia, Bosnia & Herzegovina, and Yugoslavia are formally unitary states[8] with a single or multi-tiered government in which effective control of government functions rests with the central government. In most Eastern European transition countries a two-tier structure has been introduced, with a central government and a large number of relatively small local governments. Poland, however, introduced a reform in 1999 that established three levels of local self-government.[9] Today, Poland has sixteen regions (*voivodships*), 314 local districts or counties (*poviats*), and 2478 municipalities (*gminas*) as well as 65 cities with poviat status[10].[11]

A federal system, which can be found in a minority of the OECD countries,[12] divides sovereignty between national and regional governments. It could be characterized as a compromise between a unitary state, where local governments are created by the center and may be dissolved or overruled by it, and a confederation, where the central government is the creation of a group of independent states. Federal arrangements are usually set up by a constitution that divides powers, jurisdictions, and sources of revenue between at least two levels of government. Thus, federal nations have constitutionally protected subnational governments which presumably have stronger

---

[7]   See Shah, A. (1996), p. 614.

[8]   The OECD groups countries depending on whether the political constitution is federalist or unitary. For example, according to article 20 of the German constitution (*Grundgesetz*), Germany is a federal nation, which is divided into states (*Länder*). When talking about federalist and/or unitary countries in our research project, we follow the classification of the OECD.

[9]   See OECD (2001a), p. 8.

[10]   These are gminas with extended tasks.

[11]   See http://www.stat.gov.pl/serwis/polska/2004/dzial2/obrazy2/rys15.htm

[12]   Australia, Austria, Belgium, Canada, Germany, Mexico, Switzerland, and the United States are the federal OECD countries.

possibilities for independent decision-making than subnational governments in a unitary state.[13]

Despite these differences between unitary and federal states, no broad-based generalization can be made about the correlation of federal/unitary states and the degree of fiscal decentralization. Some federal states are highly centralized, while some unitary states have a high degree of decentralization.[14]

In a confederal system (the EU is an important example of such a system), central authority merely coordinates the decisions of sovereign members.[15] The central government serves as the agent of the member states, usually without independent taxing or spending powers.[16]

3 Problems and Requirements Concerning the Expenditure Assignment in Transition Economies

In general, the theoretically advisable assignment of tasks in transition countries (see "The Theory of Fiscal Federalism" starting at page 1) does not differ from that in established market economies. The main reason for decentralizing expenditures is that subnational governments are suspected to be more efficient at delivering public services because they are closer to the preferences of their inhabitants. It is important to note that there is no unique optimum degree of fiscal decentralization that applies to all (transition) countries. In fact, there are country specific factors, such as the level of economic and institutional development, political factors, the size of the country and its population, et al, which have decisive influence on the appropriate degree of decentralization for a country. In either case, the aim of a decentralization of tasks must be to ensure efficiency, accountability, and transparency at all levels of government.[17] Therefore, a clear and well defined institutional framework in the assignment of expenditure responsibilities among the different levels of government should be established by law.[18] However, one has to bear in mind that even in countries where

---

[13]   See http://www1.worldbank.org/publicsector/decentralization/fiscal.htm

[14]   See Cerniglia, F. (2003), p. 751.

[15]   See Shah, A. (1996), p. 614.

[16]   See Shah, A. (2004), p. 4.

[17]   See Dabla-Norris, E. and Wade, P. (2002), p. 14.

[18]   See Martinez-Vazquez, J. (2001), pp. 2 et sqq.

the de jure assignment of expenditure responsibilities is in line with the theoretical principles, practices can and obviously will differ.[19] Some of the reasons why the theoretically recommended assignment of expenditures might not be put into practice in transition countries will be outlined in this section.

3.1 GENERAL BACKGROUND

Expenditure assignments in transition economies have undergone significant changes in the past two decades. Those transition countries that seek accession to the European Union have to follow the EU's guiding principle, the principle of subsidiarity[20], in the assignment of expenditure responsibilities among the different levels of government. Before the transition process began, subnational governments in socialist economies had no spending responsibilities of their own.[21] During the transition and decentralization process, many spending responsibilities were shifted from the direct provision of most goods and services by the central government, which was characteristic of state ownership and central planning, to subnational governments. This does not mean that the level of government that provides a certain good or service must be the one that produces it. Government provision is not necessarily the same as government production.[22] The organization of production of public goods can be realized either by higher-level governments or by the private sector, according to the applicable economies of scale.

To get an impression of how many tasks have been decentralized to subnational governments during the last decade, Figure I - 11 shows the subnational expenditures in countries in transition as a share of total expenditures and as a share of GDP in the year 2004. In this connection Germany – regarded as a country with a medium degree of (de-)centralization[23] – is taken as a benchmark. The figures show that today there are substantial spending responsibilities on the local level of government in the selected transition economies. In five countries, however, subnational expenditures are still less than 20% of total expenditures. Only the most advanced reformers – Poland

---

[19]   See Shah, A. (2004), p. 15.

[20]   This principle suggests that the provision of public goods and services should be assigned to the lowest level of government that is capable of the execution of given tasks.

[21]   See Bird, R. M., et al. (1994), p. 150.

[22]   See Bird, R. M., et al. (1995a), p. 32.

[23]   See Thießen, U. (2003), p. 375.

and Hungary – have a share of subnational expenditures in relation to GDP that is above 10% (Figure I - 12).

Figure I - 11: Subnational expenditures (% of total expenditures) in the year 2004

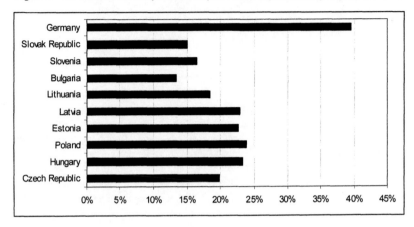

Source: IMF (2006).

Figure I - 12: Subnational expenditures (% of GDP) in the year 2004

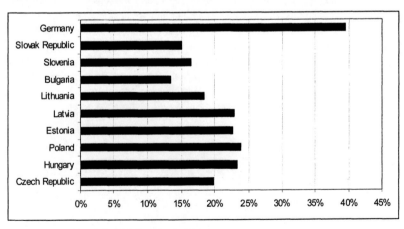

Source: IMF (2006); World Bank (2007).

3.2 PROBLEMS OF EXPENDITURE ASSIGNMENT IN COUNTRIES IN TRANSITION

Thus, subnational governments in transition economies have been assigned many tasks, but their effective expenditure autonomy is still rather limited. Although they are granted some autonomy in the national constitutions and in the acts on local governments, the assignment of tasks mostly follows the enumeration principle. This means that subnational governments may not fulfill any other tasks than those explicitly mentioned in the law.[24] Furthermore, there are still many norms and regulations concerning quality and scope of public service provision set by the central government. These norms and regulations – although they may be reasonable and necessary – constrain the authority of subnational governments to adjust current expenditures according to their preferences. In some transition countries, up to 90 per cent of actual local expenditures in 1999 were not under control of the local authorities.[25] On the other hand, in the more advanced transition countries like Poland, Hungary, or the Czech Republic, the subnational governments have a higher degree of expenditure autonomy. However, with respect to expenditures associated with employment and wages/salaries, central governments interfere with local decisions and thus constrain budgetary autonomy of local governments even among these more advanced reformers. Overall, there seems to be considerable expenditure autonomy in the mentioned advanced transition economies and the Baltic States, whereas in other countries in transition like Ukraine, Bulgaria, or Romania, local spending levels are largely or wholly determined by central authorities.

In several countries in transition, so-called delegated or mandatory tasks absorb the largest part of the budget of decentralized tiers of government. In many cases, these delegated tasks are not even financed by appropriate transfers.[26] Moreover, expenditures formerly borne by state enterprises became the responsibility of local governments (e.g. maintenance of schools, roads, or infrastructure) and this led to new – often unfunded – expenditure burdens for the communes.[27] This process created serious problems for the local governments as they were often not given sufficient revenues to finance these additional expenditures, causing so-called 'unfunded

---

24 See Dafflon, B. (2002), p. 4.

25 For the following see Dabla-Norris, E. and Wade, P. (2002), pp. 24-27.

26 See Dafflon, B. (2002), p. 16.

27 See Bird, R. M., et al. (1995b), pp. 7-8.

mandates', which are still a major problem in Eastern and Central European transition economies.[28]

Another problem (not only in countries in transition) is that it is difficult to assign and design precise expenditure responsibilities. Like contracts, these assignments are never precise and final.[29] This is particularly the case with regard to tasks that require shared responsibilities between different levels of government. Imprecise expenditure assignments often exist in the fields of education, housing, or health care, where different levels of government have responsibilities. In practice, overlapping responsibilities often carry the problem that it is unclear which level of government is responsible for the maintenance of public assets.[30] The laws often do not spell out explicitly, for example, whether local governments' responsibility for primary education implies responsibility for capital spending and maintenance of school buildings or just for current spending.[31]

If responsibilities are imprecise and subnational governments do not have sufficient funds to execute their tasks, subnational government officials might prefer to invest in projects which have benefits in the short run rather than in projects with long term impact on the region's economy, such as education or infrastructure investments. Consequently, local expenditures on maintenance and also on capital infrastructure have declined dramatically in most transition countries.[32] Many investment projects were postponed in order to protect current expenditures, particularly wages and salaries of government employees. This led to a sharply deteriorating infrastructure. Investment needs with regard to infrastructure and maintenance in countries in transition are very high, while capital investment levels on average are below those in OECD countries.[33]

As indicated above, expenditure assignment in transition economies is further complicated by the fact that under central planning, state enterprises usually fulfilled a number of tasks like the provision of social benefits, education, health, or investments in infrastructure. Such services were either privatized or became the responsibility of

---

[28]   See Courchene, T., et al. (2000), p. 93; Shah, A. (2004), p. 16.
[29]   See Tanzi, V. (2000), p. 7.
[30]   See Dafflon, B. (2002), p. 13.
[31]   See Bird, R. M., et al. (1995a), p. 35.
[32]   See Dabla-Norris, E., et al. (2000), p. 8.
[33]   See Alam, A. and Sundberg, M. (2002), p. 15.

subnational governments.[34] However, the decentralization of such services to subnational governments often implicated that local governments became responsible for public services which entail major benefit spillovers. This is contradictory to the theoretically advisable expenditure assignment and is likely to result in the underprovision of these services.[35]

3.3 REQUIREMENTS FOR EXPENDITURE ASSIGNMENT IN COUNTRIES IN TRANSITION

What needs to be done to resolve the problems discussed above? *First* of all institution building is necessary in transition countries for the adjustment of expenditures to the priorities of a market economy. It is a prerequisite for a successful decentralization of tasks that local governments possess the administrative infrastructure which is required to execute the assigned tasks. Important factors are the number and quality of local staff and their equipment. It is also important that subnational levels of government ensure their cooperation and coordination to facilitate efficient service delivery.[36] The more advanced reformers already have such coordinating institutions in place.[37]

Second, as a shortage of skilled administrators on the local level can often be observed, capacity building for subnational governments is needed. Inexperienced, small local governments in transition economies may not have the technical capacity to implement and maintain projects and their staff may not have the required training to effectively manage larger budgets. Therefore, countries that want to further decentralize by transferring more responsibilities and larger budgets to subnational governments will have to build such capacities through measures like training and technical assistance.[38] Herein, higher-level governments can play an important role by "identifying training needs, offering training programs, facilitating staff transfers, providing guidance on organizational structure and management issues, and providing technical assistance."[39]

---

[34]   See Alam, A. and Sundberg, M. (2002), p. 1.

[35]   See Martinez-Vazquez, J. (2001), p. 6.

[36]   See Dabla-Norris, E., et al. (2000), p. 4.

[37]   See Dabla-Norris, E. and Wade, P. (2002), p. 37.

[38]   See Wetzel, D. and Dunn, J. (2001), p. 47.

[39]   Shah, A. (1994), p. 46.

Third, monitoring of expenditures must be ensured. Expenditure control at the subnational level would be enhanced by setting up or improving institutions for budgetary management, including the adoption of a treasury function at the subnational level.[40] Moreover, after budget execution, an external audit or evaluation of the subnational governments is advisable. In all countries in transition overall expenditure control is critical to economic stabilization and was, particularly in the first years of transition, of prime policy concern. Here, building monitoring capacity is important for all levels of government. Organizationally, such monitoring functions could be entrusted to the budget department of the ministry of finance if the required capacities are available.

Fourth, subnational governments need to eliminate unfunded mandates. New unfunded mandates could be prohibited by law[41] in order to avoid the transfer of higher-level governments' responsibilities to lower-level governments without adequate funding. Existing unfunded mandates should be identified and reformed, e.g. through a clarification of spending responsibilities in the respective laws.[42]

Fifth, although some degree of overlap or concurrence of responsibilities between different levels of government seems unavoidable in any decentralized system of government, the role of each level of government in areas of shared responsibilities (e.g. education) should be clarified.

Sixth, following Tanzi (2000), more services can and should be privatized. Examples range from collecting garbage to providing electricity, transportation, water, etc. "Thus, privatization should be considered as an alternative to decentralization for many public activities."[43]

Finally, the system of expenditure assignments in many countries in transition should also allow for a greater subnational autonomy in setting service levels in accordance with local needs. Thus, a central government's influence through norms and regulations should be reduced.

---

[40] See Dabla-Norris, E., et al. (2000), p. 20.

[41] As in Germany, where the "principle of connectivity" (Konnexitätsprinzip) is in force. It says that if a higher-level government decentralizes a task to a local government, it must guarantee that sufficient funds for the execution of this task are provided. In other words: "Who orders must pay the bill".

[42] See Martinez-Vazquez, J. and Boex, L. F. J. (1999), pp. 31-32.

[43] Tanzi, V. (2000), p. 3.

4 Problems and Requirements Concerning the Revenue Assignment in Transition Economies

This section will identify the problems countries in transition encounter in assigning revenues to the subnational governments. Revenues of subnational governments consist of taxes, revenues from tax sharing arrangements, and non-tax revenues like fees and user charges. Intergovernmental grants, which are another important source of subnational revenue, will be discussed in section 5.

Figure I - 13: Revenue structure at subnational levels of government in the year 2004

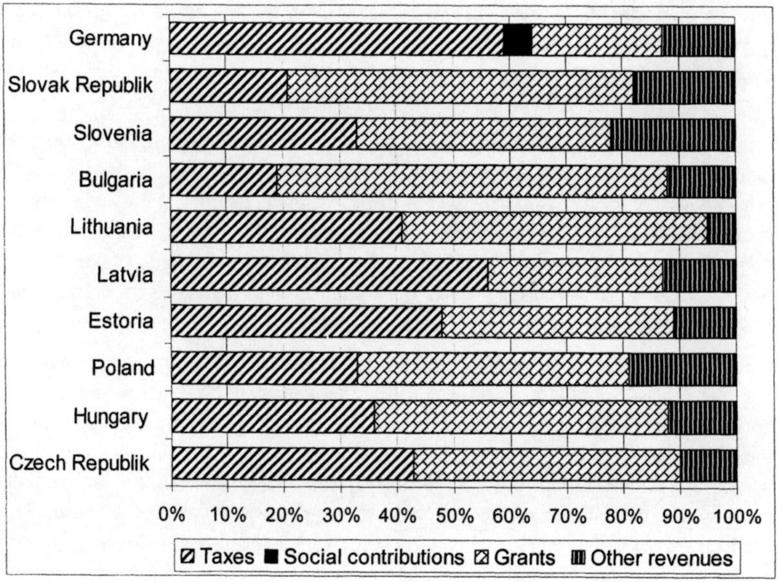

Source: IMF (2006).

Figure I - 13 shows the composition of subnational revenues in selected transition countries and Germany for the year 2004. In this figure, according to the IMF's Government Finance Statistics, subnational taxes include revenues from shared taxes as well as own taxes. Obviously, taxes and grants form the main sources of revenue for subnational governments. In this section, we will concentrate on the former.

4.1 GENERAL BACKGROUND

Under central planning, the finances of the government sector were closely linked with those of the enterprise sector. In particular, state-owned enterprises were the main revenue source for the government. The tax systems and administrations in the former centrally planned economies were directed at the levy of taxes, or rather profit remittances, from public enterprises, often using the banking system as tax collector.[44] Broadly-based privatization programs, which were completed or are nearing completion in most transition countries, have transferred the ownership of enterprise assets to the private sector and have transformed enterprises into separate taxable entities. A new tax system, taking into account these changes, had to be introduced. Recent tax reforms in countries in transition have been driven by the desire to design fiscal regimes according to those of the member countries of the European Union.[45] The evolving obstacles in designing tax systems which are appropriate for a market economy in countries in transition will be outlined below.

Before the reforms of tax systems in the transition economies began, these countries typically had three main sources of tax revenue: taxes on enterprises or profit remittances, turnover taxes, and payroll taxes.[46] During reforms of the tax systems, profit remittances that were lost due to the privatization of public enterprises were compensated for by introducing corporate income taxes. Value-added taxes (VATs) have replaced turnover taxes, which were common in countries in transition, and systems of personal income taxes have been established.

Figure I - 14 shows the structure of the taxes received by subnational governments in the year 2004. Property taxes as well as income and profit taxes are in use in most countries under observation. Bulgaria is the only country to use only property taxes at the local level. In most countries, income and profit taxes are the most important source of subnational tax revenue. In these cases, the income tax is often centrally collected and then shared with the subnational governments. Poland is the only country in which social security contributions account for a substantial share of local revenue.

---

[44]   See Holzmann, R. (1992), p. 236.

[45]   See Bird, R. M., et al. (1994), p. 152.

[46]   See Tanzi, V. and Tsibouris, G. (2000), p. 13.

Figure I - 14: Structure of subnational tax revenues in the year 2004

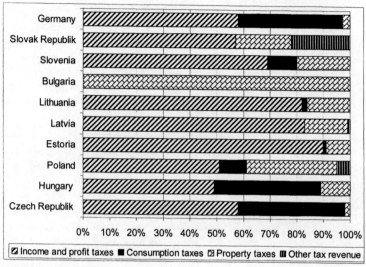

Source: IMF (2006)

4.2 TAX SHARING

Tax sharing between central and subnational governments is – as in most market economies – very common in transition countries. Typically, the central tax administration first collects revenues from a tax and then allocates them on a so-called derivation basis, i.e. a specified share of the revenues flows back to the locality where they were originally collected.[47] Thus, derivation-based tax sharing is counter-equalizing because it channels revenues to high income areas where the tax base and, therefore, revenue collections are largest.[48] Existing interregional disparities are increased. Another shortcoming of shared taxes is that their bases and rates in all countries under observation are determined by the central government, and thus local revenue autonomy is very limited.[49] at the end of this section shows that all revenues

---

[47]   See Bird, R. M., et al. (1995a), p. 6.

[48]   See Bird, R. M., et al. (1994), p. 157.

[49]   See Wetzel, D. and Dunn, J. (2001), p. 27.

from tax sharing in the transition economies under observation are found in groups (d3) and (d4)[50] in which the autonomy of subnational governments is very limited.

In many transition countries subnational governments have been assigned significant shares of income tax revenues. "In Russia a few years ago such governments received all of personal income tax revenues, in Bulgaria, 50 percent, in Poland, 30 percent, and in Hungary, 25 percent."[51] However, the subnational governments in these countries had virtually no autonomy in setting the tax rates. Also, in federal countries like Austria or Germany the lower levels of government have only very limited influence on the tax base and/or rates of shared taxes as the personal income tax.

The discussion above shows that tax sharing arrangements tend to limit local fiscal autonomy. Local tax autonomy requires at least some degree of control over tax base, tax rates, and collection authority. As local governments, especially in countries in transition, may be unable to levy local taxes efficiently due to the initial weakness of localities in all administrative matters, it is often suggested in the literature[52] that higher level governments should instead allow subnational governments to impose a supplementary rate on the same base.[53] This *tax base sharing* is regarded as reasonable especially in countries in transition, where resources for tax administration on the local level are typically scarce, as it minimizes collection and compliance costs.[54] Under such an arrangement, tax base determination usually rests with the higher-level government, but the subnational governments have the possibility to set the tax rates. However, despite the theoretical advantages of imposing such surcharges on central taxes, only a few transition economies have adopted tax base sharing.[55]

4.3 PROBLEMS OF THE PROPERTY TAX AS THE TYPICAL LOCAL TAX

The property tax is the predominant local tax in most developing and transitional countries, although the resulting revenues are usually not sufficient to finance local

---

[50]   For the explanation of the groups, see pages 17-18.

[51]   Bird, R. M. (2003a), p. 14.

[52]   See, e.g., McLure Jr., C. E. (1999), section V; Bird, R. M. (2003a), section 5.

[53]   See Shah, A. (2004), p. 21.

[54]   See McLure Jr., C. E. (1999), section V.

[55]   See Shah, A. (2004), p. 21.

governments' expenditures.[56] Most of the Central and Eastern European transition economies have introduced a property tax at the local level, albeit revenues are not very large (see Figure I - 14). The OECD recommends that subnational governments in a number of countries (e.g. Poland, Czech Republic) should increase their revenues from property taxes "by lowering the administrative barriers to their wider use, by giving subnational governments greater autonomy in setting property tax rates or by updating the land and housing register."[57] The taxation of property is especially difficult where reliable and up-to-date cadastral values or current market values for the taxed properties are missing, as is likely in countries in transition. It may be difficult and consequently costly to identify the market value of a property. Moreover, high inflation rates in many countries in transition cause distorted prices of property. Another major problem concerning the levy of property taxes is the fact that much of the housing stock is still owned by public enterprises or local governments themselves and that housing markets are not well developed in transition economies.[58] Consequently, property tax revenues are relatively low in many transition economies and do not represent a sufficient revenue source.[59]

4.4 FEES AND USER CHARGES

Public sector pricing was one of the areas that had to be reformed in most transition countries. Under the old regime, prices were administratively fixed and rarely changed. Relative prices were heavily distorted; natural resources were seriously under-priced.[60] Both central and subnational governments faced problems in adjusting prices for public services to their production costs because doing so would have implied significant changes in the cost of living and welfare for the private households. Adjusting prices for public services would, for some countries, mean a doubling of the accustomed prices. Therefore, in many cases, governments continue to subsidize prices for water, sewerage, or energy consumption. The price of energy in many countries in transition, for example, is therefore much lower than in market economies.[61] Among the Central

---

[56] See Bird, R. M. (2003a), section 3.

[57] Joumard, I. and Kongsrud, P. M. (2003), p. 186.

[58] See McLure Jr., C. E. (1999), section I.B.

[59] See Bird, R. M. (2003a), section 3.

[60] See de Melo, M. and Gelb, A. (1997), p. 61.

[61] See Tanzi, V. and Tsibouris, G. (2000), p. 21.

and Eastern European transition economies, only Albania and Croatia, in 1994, had household electricity tariffs set at levels that corresponded to the appropriate economic level of long-run marginal cost. As a result of such problems, most subnational governments in transition economies make less use of user charges than seems desirable and economically efficient, and many of the charges that are levied are poorly designed. Moreover, it can be observed that user charges are often still centrally controlled in countries in transition.[62]

4.5 REVENUE AUTONOMY

In most transition economies, truly own revenues cannot be observed, i.e. these countries have no or only little control over tax bases and rates. According to a recent OECD study, among the Eastern European transition countries, only Hungary, Poland and the Slovak Republic allow their local governments some significant degree of tax autonomy.[63] In all other transition countries the central government decides on the definition of the tax bases and sets the rates for subnational taxes. This means that subnational governments will be unable to alter their spending levels as they cannot adjust some of their tax rates or tax bases. They need to be granted a higher degree of taxing autonomy so that they are able to finance their assigned tasks and to reduce their fiscal dependency from the central governments.

The OECD has developed a framework[64] that is able to show the degree of subnational taxing autonomy. In Table I - 2 each country's subnational tax revenues are divided into five main groups (a) to (e), of which group (d), which is concerned with revenue sharing arrangements, is divided into four subgroups. The degree of tax autonomy of the subnational governments is highest in group (a) where subnational governments have control over the tax base and rate. In groups (b) and (c) the subnational government also has significant control over its taxes. In group (d) tax autonomy is limited, and in group (e) there is virtually no autonomy for subnational governments, as the central level sets both tax base and rate.

---

[62] See Bird, R. M., et al. (1995a), pp. 38-39.

[63] See OECD (2002), p. 40.

[64] See OECD (2002), p. 39.

Table I - 2: Autonomy over subnational revenues in transition economies

Country (year)	Subnational government taxes as % of total tax revenue	SNG sets tax rate and base	SNG sets tax rate only	SNG sets tax base
		(a)	(b)	c)
Czech Republic (1999)	11,1	2,7	5,6	
Hungary (1999)	10,4	-	49,2	-
Poland (1999)	8,3	-	41,9	0,6
Estonia (1999)	16,2	-	9,2	-
Latvia (1999)	17,1	-	-	-
Lithuania (1999)	22,0	-	-	-
Bulgaria (2000)	10,0	-	-	-
Romania (2000)	10,5	-	6,0	0,6
Slovak Republic (2000)	4,0	7,0	28,2	-
Slovenia (2000)	7,9	16,7	0,6	0,4
Mean (by country)	**11,8**	**2,6**	14,1	0,2

continued

Country (year)	Revenue sharing where the CG: SNG revenue split...				CG sets both tax rate and base of SNG tax	Total
	... is set by SNG	... can be changed only if SNG agree	... is set in legislation and may be changed uni-laterally by CG	... is set annually by CG as part of the budget		
	(d1)	(d2)	(d3)	(d4)	(e)	a - e
Czech Republic (1999)	-	-	91,7	-	-	100,0
Hungary (1999)	-	-	-	50,8	-	100,0
Poland (1999)	-	-	57,6	-	-	100,0
Estonia (1999)	-	-	90,8	-	-	100,0
Latvia (1999)	-	-	-	-	100,0	100,0
Lithuania (1999)	-	-	-	-	100,0	100,0
Bulgaria (2000)	-	-	39,0	61,0	-	100,0
Romania (2000)	-	-	-	75,0	18,4	100,0
Slovak Republic (2000)	-	-	-	64,8	-	100,0
Slovenia (2000)	-	-	82,3	-	-	100,0
Mean (by country)	**0,0**	**0,0**	**36,1**	**25,2**	**21,8**	**100,0**

Source : OECD (2002), pp. 61-62

Columns (a) – (c) of the table I – 2 show that only 17% of tax revenues in transition economies are totally or substantially under control of the subnational governments. For 83% of the tax revenues – columns (d1) - (e) – the lower level governments have very little or no autonomy. Only in Hungary, Poland and the Slovak Republic, local governments have substantial 'own' tax revenues. In Latvia and Lithuania, the subnational governments have no autonomy at all over local revenues.

5 Problems and Requirements Concerning the Transfer System in Transition Economies

5.1 GENERAL BACKGROUND

As mentioned above, subnational governments in transition economies often have significant spending responsibilities[65], but at the same time do not have sufficient revenues to finance their expenditures. This gives rise to vertical fiscal imbalance (VFI) within a nation's intergovernmental finances. In Poland, for example, gminas were handed over the responsibilities for local education at the kindergarten, elementary school, and high school level, but were not given additional 'own' revenues, i.e. mainly taxes whose bases and/or rates they control, to finance these tasks.[66] As local borrowing tends to be restricted[67] due to the soft budget constraint problem [see first text, "The theory of fiscal federalism", p. 21], subnational governments in transition economies usually have to rely heavily on intergovernmental transfers. Thus the design of the intergovernmental transfer system is an important issue within the decentralization process. It is important that transfers are based on stable principles and specified by formulas that support hard budget constraints.[68]

However, persistent macroeconomic instability in many countries in transition has entailed special challenges which complicate the design of an effective, sound system

---

[65] Major areas of responsibility assigned to local government levels are social welfare, school education, cultural affairs, housing and construction, water and energy supply, waste disposal services as well as the provision of transport systems. See Nam, C. W. and Parsche, R. (2001), p. 2.

[66] See Friedrich, P., et al. (2003), p. 3.

[67] In Poland, for example, a gmina's annual debt service could not exceed 15% of planned revenues, minus the debt service on loans secured by real property. See Wetzel, D. and Dunn, J. (2001), p. 43.

[68] See Dabla-Norris, E. and Wade, P. (2002), p. 14.

of intergovernmental transfers.[69] In most transition economies, intergovernmental transfers remain discretionary and are determined ad hoc by the central government, or the amount of the transfers is subject to negotiations between the central government and local levels of government.[70] Poland is among the exceptions, having a more transparent formula-based system. Generally, the formulas used for determining intergovernmental transfers should include indicators of expenditure needs and tax capacity[71]. More precisely, the amount of transfers should vary with the local expenditure needs and inversely with local fiscal capacity.[72] It is difficult in any case to measure needs (which can be roughly proxied by measures like population or number of pupils) and fiscal capacity, particularly so in the changing circumstances of the transition economies.[73] Moreover, in transition economies, data limitations often make it difficult to acquire appropriate measures of fiscal capacity such as tax base information.[74] Furthermore, to perform such a formula apportionment, subnational governments need to have large administrative resources, which are probably not available.[75]

Intergovernmental transfer mechanisms can be broadly grouped into two main categories, namely revenue-sharing arrangements, which were discussed in section 4, and grants[76], which we will focus on below.

5.2 THE RELEVANCE OF GRANTS IN TRANSITION ECONOMIES

The IMF and the OECD distinguish three groups of subnational revenues[77]: taxes[78], non-tax revenues[79], and grants[80]. If we regard the eight Eastern European states that

---

[69]   See Dabla-Norris, E. and Wade, P. (2002), p. 3.

[70]   See Dabla-Norris, E. and Wade, P. (2002), p. 21.

[71]   The ability of governmental units to raise revenues from their own sources.

[72]   See Nam, C. W. and Parsche, R. (2001), p. 3.

[73]   See Bird, R. M., et al. (1995a), p. 53.

[74]   See Wetzel, D. and Dunn, J. (2001), p. 34.

[75]   See McLure Jr., C. E. (1999), section VI.D.

[76]   See Ter-Minassian, T. (1997), p. 11.

[77]   See OECD (2002), pp. 28-29.

[78]   Including revenue from social security contributions as well as all types of 'own' and shared taxes.

[79]   Including surpluses of trading enterprises, property income, fees and user charges, et al.

joined the EU on May 1, 2004 in Figure I - 15 for instance, we see that grants form the second largest source of subnational revenues in these countries.

Figure I - 15: Percentage shares of the three main sources of revenue for subnational governments in the new EU member countries

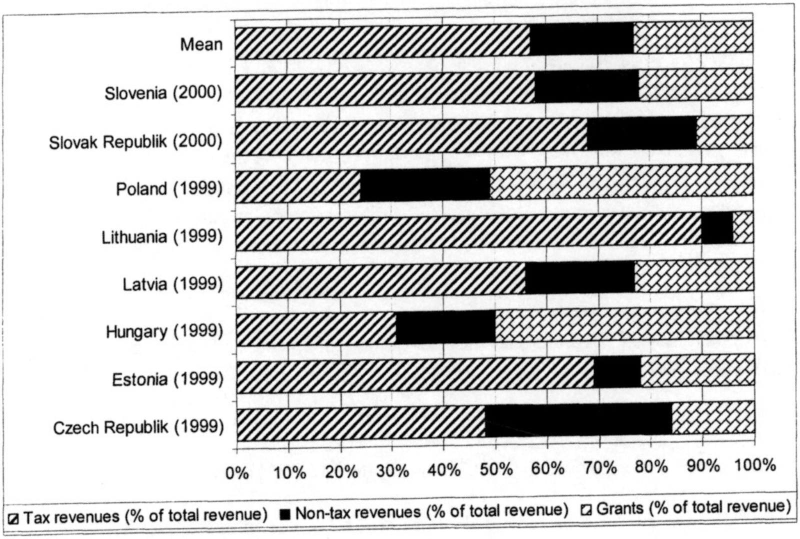

Source: OECD (2002), p. 30.

The large shares of tax revenues in Figure I - 15 include shared taxes over which, as discussed above, subnational governments have virtually no control. On average, subnational governments' 'own' taxes[81] accounted for only about 7% of their revenues in 1999.[82]

Interestingly, in Hungary and Poland, the two countries which are regarded as the leaders in the transition process[83], grants represented the largest share of subnational revenues in 1999. In both countries, where grants accounted for approximately half of

---

[80]   Including any payments received from other levels of government.

[81]   That is taxes whose bases and/or rates they control; groups (a) – (c) in section 4.

[82]   See OECD (2002), p. 5.

[83]   See Tanzi, V. and Tsibouris, G. (2000), p. 15.

the local revenues, the overwhelming reliance on grants is viewed as limiting local autonomy.[84] On average, unconditional grants account for about one-third and conditional grants for about two-thirds of their grants in the new EU member states.[85]

There are, however, some important arguments why subnational governments should not rely chiefly on grants:[86]

- If subnational governments rely chiefly on grants, they will rely on revenues from the central government. The central government raises the sums required from central taxes, and it is responsible to its taxpayers for how these funds are spent. So the central government will probably feel the need and the right to decide how the recipients are to spend their grants. This will make it more difficult for subnational authorities to spend the granted revenues in accordance with local preferences, as they do not have sufficient 'own' revenues and thus no or only limited discretionary spending power.

- If subnational governments rely chiefly on grants, their taxes will give their inhabitants a misleading perception of the tax cost of their services. In other words, if high subnational spending is accompanied by low subnational taxation, then voters may regard subnational services as "cheap", and so they may vote for excessive service levels on the local level.

- If subnational governments rely chiefly on grants, they may become less careful in attempting to meet the preferences of their voters, because they can try to contend that any shortcomings in their services are the result of inadequate or insufficient grants. The desirable link between benefits and costs of public services at the local level is broken and thus accountability is reduced because local governments can attempt to make the central government accountable for their own poor performance.

Taken together, these points seem to suggest a case for reducing grants to a minimum and for allowing subnational authorities to rely on (self-determined) taxation as far as possible. However, there are also serious arguments against such an approach:[87]

- The central government uses grants to support poor and needy subnational governments. The more economic disparities among the lower levels of government exist, the more unconditional grants from the central level will be

---

[84]   See Dabla-Norris, E. and Wade, P. (2002), p. 31.
[85]   See OECD (2002), p. 5.
[86]   See OECD (2002), pp. 31-32.
[87]   See OECD (2002), p. 32.

needed for regional equalization. As an increase in income inequality during transition can be observed empirically[88], the reduction of grants to a minimum would aggravate this process and thus seems inappropriate.

- The central government has the task of managing the country's macroeconomic performance. If a too large portion of a country's taxes is decentralized, the central government's ability to use fiscal policy might be weakened. Moreover, administrative simplicity and economies of scale in tax collection are arguments in favor of centralized taxes with a certain amount of tax revenues being allocated in the form of grants to subnational levels of government.[89]

All these arguments may suggest that *conditional* grants should be reduced to a minimum as they limit the subnational governments' autonomy, whereas *unconditional* grants, which can be used by subnational governments according to their preferences and spending needs, can and should be used for equalization purposes as well as to remedy vertical fiscal imbalances.

5.3 MANAGING FISCAL IMBALANCES AND SPILLOVERS IN TRANSITION ECONOMIES

As mentioned above, the fact that in both unitary and federal countries subnational governments' own revenues are less than their expenditures[90] gives rise to vertical fiscal imbalances (VFIs). Additionally, horizontal fiscal imbalances (HFIs), i.e. differences in net fiscal benefits (NFBs)[91], can occur for the following reasons: Either the capacities of the subnational governments of the same level to raise their 'own' revenues differ, or the subnational governments have different costs in meeting their assigned expenditure responsibilities.[92] It is often stated in literature that fiscal decentralization may aggravate both kinds of fiscal imbalances.[93] The available evidence is that there exist significant VFIs in many transition economies because of the limited revenue autonomy in most of these countries.[94] Also HFIs can be found in

---

[88] See World Bank (2000), pp. 13-14.

[89] See Norregaard, J. (1997), p. 53.

[90] See Ebel, R. D. and Yilmaz, S. (2002), pp. 7-8.

[91] For the concept of NFBs, see first text, *The Theory of Fiscal Federalism*, p. 17.

[92] See Ahmad, E. and Craig, J. (1997), p. 73; Ter-Minassian, T. (1997), p. 11.

[93] See Dabla-Norris, E. and Wade, P. (2002), p. 3.

[94] See McLure Jr., C. E. (2001), p. 347.

many transition countries as these are characterized by wide fiscal disparities among regions and local governments respectively.[95]

Figure I - 16: Vertical Imbalance (grants received from other general government units in % of total expenditures) in the year 2001

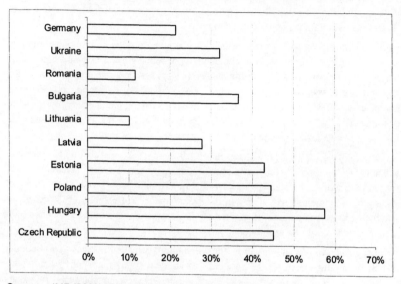

Source: IMF (2003), Government Finance Statistics Yearbook.

As for VFIs, the existing fiscal gap can be closed in different ways: by giving subnational governments more revenue raising power, by transferring responsibilities for expenditures (back) to the central government, by reducing local expenditures, by allowing subnational governments more freedom to borrow on the capital market, by increasing the local share of shared taxes, or by giving vertical grants from the central level. As has been discussed above, there is only limited delegation of taxing autonomy to subnational governments in transition countries.[96] Cutting expenditures is difficult for the subnational governments as their most important tasks, like education or health care, are – to a large extent – defined by the central government (so-called delegated

---

[95]   See Martinez-Vazquez, J. (2001), p. 16.

[96]   See Bahl, R. (2000), pp. 1-2.

tasks). As local borrowing is very restricted[97] in countries in transition due to macroeconomic stability concerns, the arising fiscal gaps are mostly closed by unconditional grants or shared tax transfers from the central level.[98]

A major problem in countries in transition is that they often lack objective criteria[99], such as fiscal capacity and expenditure needs, for the determination of transfers. These 'gap-filling' transfers, however, may provide negative incentives for the lower levels of government to raise own revenues.[100]

HFIs can be alleviated either with equalization grants from the central government to subnational governments, as in most countries, or with transfers between regions, as done partly in Germany. Again, for the design of such grants, measuring the size of the horizontal fiscal imbalances as well as the fiscal capacities of subnational governments is a difficult task which is only carried out in a systematic manner in Australia, Canada, and Germany[101], i.e. only in highly developed federal states. In countries in transition the required data for the design of such grants may be unavailable.

In general, there are three options for dealing with vertical and horizontal imbalances:[102] Either, each imbalance must be corrected by separate policy measures[103], or an integrated system of grants which deals with both kinds of imbalances at the same time needs to be implemented[104], or only the VFI is corrected and the horizontal disparities are ignored[105]. The choice of these options depends on a country's preference with regard to equalization policy.

Another justification for the use of intergovernmental grants is the existence of benefit spillovers. In this case, theory tells us that a conditional matching grant is the appropriate form of intergovernmental transfer to internalize such spillovers. However, it has proved to be extremely difficult to measure the size of spillovers, not only in countries in transition. The information needed to design the required matching grants is difficult to obtain, probably even more so in transition economies. A general problem

---

[97]   Mostly, borrowing is only allowed to finance capital investment projects.

[98]   See Bird, R. M. and Vaillancourt, F. (1998), p. 29.

[99]   Again, Poland is among the exceptions.

[100]   See Ahmad, E. and Craig, J. (1997), p. 74.

[101]   See Ebel, R. D. and Yilmaz, S. (2002), p. 36; Ahmad, E. and Craig, J. (1997), p. 76.

[102]   See Ahmad, E. and Craig, J. (1997), pp. 76-77.

[103]   This is roughly the approach used in Germany.

[104]   This is the Australian and Canadian approach.

[105]   This is broadly the approach in the United States.

with the use of conditional matching grants is that poorer subnational governments may not be able to finance the required matching amount. Thus conditional matching grants tend to benefit wealthier jurisdictions and enhance the problem of interregional inequalities.[106]

In countries in transition, additional efforts are needed to improve the quality of data underlying the transfer mechanism, the ability to monitor and the transparency of the transfer system as a whole.

6 Bibliography

Ahmad, Ehtisham and Craig, Jon (1997): "Intergovernmental Transfers", in: Ter-Minassian, Teresa: Fiscal Federalism in Theory and Practice. Washington, D.C., International Monetary Fund. pp. 73-107.

Alam, Asad and Sundberg, Mark (2002): "A Decade of Fiscal Transition", in: World Bank Working Paper 2835. Washington, D.C.

Bahl, Roy (2000): "Intergovernmental Transfers in Developing and Tansition Countries: Principles and Practice", in: World Bank Working Paper 21097. Washington, D.C.

Bird, Richard M. (2003a): "Local and Regional Revenues: Realities and Prospects", World Bank, Internet: http://www1.worldbank.org/publicsector/DecentralizationSubNationalEconomics/June2003Seminar/bird2003.pdf, found 23 Mar 2004.

Bird, Richard M., Dafflon, Bernard, Jeanrenaud, Claude and Kirchgaessner, Gebhard (2003): "Assignment of Responsibilities and Fiscal Federalism", in: Politorbis 32(1), pp. 58-78.

Bird, Richard M., Ebel, Robert D. and Wallich, Christine I. (1995a): "Fiscal Decentralization: From Command to Market", in: Bird, Richard M., Ebel, Robert D. and Wallich, Christine I.: Decentralization of the Socialist State: Intergovernmental Finance in Transition Economies. Washington, DC. pp. 1-67.

Bird, Richard M., Ebel, Robert D. and Wallich, Christine I. (1995b): "Fiscal Decentralization in Transition Economies: A Long Way to Go", in: Transition: The Newsletter About Reforming Economies 6(3), pp. 7-10.

---

[106] See Joumard, I. and Kongsrud, P. M. (2003), p. 194.

I. Theoretical Foundations

Bird, Richard M., Freund, Caroline and Wallich, Christine I. (1994): "Decentralization of Intergovernmental Finance in Transition Economies", in: Comparative Economic Studies 36(4), pp. 149-160.

Bird, Richard M. and Vaillancourt, Francois (1998): "Fiscal Decentralization in Developing Countries: An Overview", in: Bird, Richard M. and Vaillancourt, Francois: Fiscal Decentralization in Developing Countries. Cambridge. pp. 1-48.

Cerniglia, Floriana (2003): "Decentralization in the Public Sector: Quantitative Aspects in Federal and Unitary Countries", in: Journal of Policy Modeling. November 25(8), pp. 749-776.

Courchene, Thomas, Martinez-Vazquez, Jorge, McLure Jr., Charles E. and Webb, Steven B. (2000): "Principles of Decentralization", in: Giugale, Marcelo M. and Webb, Steven B.: Achievments and Callenges of Fiscal Decentralization: Lessons from Mexico. Washington, D.C., The World Bank. pp. 85-122.

Dabla-Norris, Era, Martinez-Vazquez, Jorge and Norregaard, John (2000): "Making Decentralization Work: The Case of Russia, Ukraine, and Kazakhstan", International Studies Program, Andrew Young School of Policy Studies, Georgia State University.

Dabla-Norris, Era and Wade, Paul (2002): "The Challenge of Fiscal Decentralization in Transition Countries", in: IMF Working Paper 02/103. Washington, D.C., International Monetary Fund.

Dafflon, Bernard (2002): "Fiscal Federalism in Switzerland: Relevant Issues for Transition Economies in Central and Eastern Europe", Department of Political Economy, University of Fribourg, Switzerland.

de Melo, Martha and Gelb, Alan (1997): "Transition to date: a comparative overview", in: Zecchini, Salvatore: Lessons from the Economic Transition. Central and Eastern Europe in the 1990s. Dordrecht. pp. 59-78.

Ebel, Robert D. and Yilmaz, Serdar (2002): "Concept of Fiscal Decentralization and Worldwide Overview", World Bank Institute, Internet: http://www1. worldbank.org/ wbiep/decentralization/library3/Ebel&Yilmaz.pdf, found 10 Sep 2004.

Friedrich, Peter, Gwiazda, Joanna and Nam, Chang Woon (2003): "Development of Local Public Finance in Europe", in: CESifo Working Paper No. 1107. München.

Holzmann, Robert (1992): "Tax Reform in Countries in Transition: Central Policy Issues", in: Pestieau, Pierre: Public Finance in a World of Transition. The Hague. pp. 233-255.

IMF (1998): "Code of Good Practices on Fiscal Transpareny: Declaration on Principles", in: IMF Survey 27, pp. 122-124.

IMF (2006): "Government Finance Statistics Yearbook 2006", Washington, D.C., International Monetary Fund, XXX.

Joumard, Isabelle and Kongsrud, Per Mathis (2003): "Fiscal Relations across Government Levels", in: OECD Economic Studies 1(36), pp. 155-229.

Martinez-Vazquez, Jorge (2001). "The Assignment of Expenditure Responsibilities". Proceedings of the Fiscal Policy Training Program 2001, Atlanta, Georgia.

Martinez-Vazquez, Jorge and Boex, L.F. Jameson (1999): "Fiscal Decentralization in the Russian Federation during the Transition", International Studies Program, Andrew Young School of Policy Studies, Georgia State University.

McLure Jr., Charles E. (1999): "The Tax Assignment Problem: Conceptual and Administrative Considerations in Achieving Subnational Fiscal Autonomy", World Bank, Internet: http://www1.worldbank.org/wbiep/decentralization/ Courses/ Thailand%202.24.99/section5.htm, found 26 Mar 2004, Presented to Seminar on Intergovernmental Fiscal Relations and Local Financial Management organized by National Economic and Social Development Board of the Royal Thai Government and the World Bank, Chiang Mai, Thailand, February 24-March 5.

McLure Jr., Charles E. (2001): "The Tax Assignment Problem: Ruminations on How Theory and Practice Depend on History", in: National Tax Journal. June 54(2), pp. 339-363.

Nam, Chang Woon and Parsche, Rüdiger (2001): "Looking for Appropriate Forms of Intergovernmental Transfers for Municipalities in Transition Economies", in: CESifo Working Paper No. 614. München.

Norregaard, John (1997): "Tax Assignment", in: Ter-Minassian, Teresa: Fiscal Federalism in Theory and Practice. Washington, International Monetary Fund. pp. 49-72.

OECD (2001a): "Fiscal Design Across Levels of Government - Year 2000 Surveys. Country Report: Poland". Paris.

OECD (2002): "Fiscal Decentralisation in EU Applicant States and Selected EU Member States". Paris, OECD.

Shah, Anwar (1994): " The Reform of Intergovernmental Fiscal Relations in Developing and Emerging Market Economies". Washington, D.C., The World Bank Policy and Research Series No. 23.

Shah, Anwar (1996): "On the Design of Economic Constitutions", in: Canadian Journal of Economics 29(2), pp. 614-618.

Shah, Anwar (2004): "Fiscal Decentralization in Developing and Transition Economies: Progress, Problems, and the Promise", in: World Bank Policy Research Working Paper 3282. Washington, D.C., World Bank.

Tanzi, Vito (2000): "On Fiscal Federalism: Issues to Worry About", IMF Conference on Fiscal Decentralization, Washington, D.C.

Tanzi, Vito and Tsibouris, George (2000): "Fiscal Reform Over Ten Years of Transition", in: IMF Working Paper 00/113. Washington, D.C., International Monetary Fund.

Ter-Minassian, Teresa (1997): "Intergovernmental Fiscal Relations in a Macroeconomic Perspective: An Overview", in: Ter-Minassian, Teresa: Fiscal Federalism in Theory and Practice. Washington, International Monetary Fund. pp. 3-24.

Thießen, Ulrich (2003): "Fiskalische Dezentralisierung und Wirtschaftswachstum in "reichen" OECD-Ländern: Gibt es ein Optimum?" in: Wochenbericht des DIW Berlin(23/2003), pp. 375-382.

Wetzel, Deborah and Dunn, Jonathan (2001): "Decentralization in the Transition Economies: Challenges and the Road Ahead", in: World Bank Working Paper 25132. Washington, D.C., World Bank.

Wildasin, David E. (1998): "Fiscal Aspects of of Evolving Federations: Issues for Policy Research", in: World Bank Policy Research Paper 1884. Washington, D.C., World Bank.

World Bank (2000): "Making Transition Work for Everyone: Poverty and Inequality in Europe and Central Asia", in: World Bank Publication 20920. Washington, D.C.

World Bank (2007): "WDI Online Database", The World Bank Group, https://publications.worldbank.org/WDI/, found 23/03/2007.

II. POLAND'S SYSTEM OF INTERGOVERNMENTAL FISCAL RELATIONS

DECONCENTRATION, DECENTRALIZATION, FEDERALISM: TERMS AND DEFINITIONS IN THE POLISH LITERATURE

MAGDALENA GODEK*
RADOSŁAW WITCZAK**
TOMASZ URYSZEK***

The aim of this article is to outline the various views on deconcentration, decentralization, federalism, self–reliance, and autonomy presented in the Polish literature, stressing the advantages and disadvantages of decentralization. It should help to work out the common glossary of the notions understood similarly and accepted by Polish and Anglo-Saxon scientists.

1   Introduction

The notions and interpretations associated with deconcentration, decentralization, federalism, self–reliance, and autonomy are not only based on different definitions within the Polish literature, but the understanding of these terms by Polish authors also differs from the Anglo-Saxon point of view. The definitions of deconcentration will be analyzed in Section 2. The views on decentralization, federalism, self–reliance, and autonomy presented in the Polish literature will be discussed in more detail in Section 3.

*   Ph.D. student, Chair of Finance and Banking, University of Łódz
**   Ph.D. student, Chair of Finance and Banking, University of Łódz
*** Assistant, Chair of Finance and Banking, University of Łódz

The differences between the Anglo-Saxon and the Polish literature mostly derive from the two different ways of viewing the origin of the state.[1] In unitary countries like Poland, central authority was the creator of the state system. Originally it possessed all the decision-making power. It was the central authority which initiated the (re-) establishment of local entities. The central government decided about the range and the shape of autonomy of sub-national levels.

In federal states like Germany, historically independent entities (local regions, provinces) continued to exist and retained their autonomy to a certain extent. Local associations were created in a historical process. They derived from primitive communities built up in order to protect their common interests.[2]

For this reason Polish literature interprets the notions related to the process of decentralization from the perspective of a unitary country, where federalism is regarded as the last stage of the process of decentralization (i.e. a fully decentralized system). The assumption made in the Polish literature about unitary countries is that the central government does not permit the local authorities to reach a degree of autonomy as extensive as in a federal system.

To make the existing differences between the Polish and the Anglo-Saxon perspectives more clear it is necessary to trace back and analyze the reforms that took place in Poland after 1989. One of their aims was the transformation from the centrally-planned administration to a unitary but more decentralized state. These changes were implemented in a very short period. That is why there was not time for a deep discussion on the shape of the reforms. In most cases the legislators relied on the experiences of the western countries, and by doing so it was evident that decentralization was necessary. The biggest question was how to finance the tasks delegated to lower levels of administration. This problem was very important as the Polish state already showed huge deficits and the legislators were afraid that an increase of financial autonomy of local entities would aggravate the situation. There was an apprehension that due to the lack of financial sources the local governments would borrow money from banks and financial markets, which could cause the overall deficit to rise.

The essential fact was that the local levels were not taken into consideration during the discussion about further economic reforms. The debates concerned only the national

---

[1] The whole country, like Poland, Germany; see Glossary (State, in the following, has two different meanings: state as "nation state", i.e. the country as a whole, in a political sense; and state – like the German Bundeslaender – as a part of a federal state.)

[2] Sochacka-Krysiak K., Finanse..., op. cit., p.14

aspects of the reforms and their aims for the state policy. So the reforms concerning the tax system, health, social system etc., and of public finances were made as if the system were still centralized. The local governments did not take part in taking these decisions.

As the process of transformation of local administration was so spontaneous and dynamic, Poland stopped at the stage of a partly decentralized structure. When we start to describe this process we should pay attention to the theoretical background Polish reformers referred to before the transformation. It should be underlined, however, that in the Polish literature there are no clear-cut notions describing the process of transferring decision-making power concerning tasks, expenditures, and financial sources from the central to the lower levels.

The Polish literature distinguishes between deconcentration and decentralization within the transformation process. According to this distinction, deconcentration as well as decentralization can be considered from two different points of view: dynamic and static. The first point of view indicates that deconcentration and decentralization must be understood as processes which last for a certain period of time. Deconcentration and decentralization can also be considered as statuses. In this case we can say, for example, that the system of local administration or revenue collection is partly or entirely deconcentrated or decentralized. The Polish approach towards federalism is quite special because federalism is understood as the status of an entire decentralization of decision-making authority. Also, the understanding of autonomy is specific because autonomy equals independence.

2 Deconcentration in the Polish Literature

There are no diverging definitions of deconcentration in the Polish literature. Deconcentration is the first stage of the process of the transition of the state sector. Deconcentration means that administrative rights, which were initially executed by the central government, are transferred to other, subordinated governmental institutions or levels. Nevertheless, because of incomplete directives, the subordinate governmental institutions gain some discretionary decision-making power (scope). In other words, deconcentration is understood as a mere "technical" process of passing on some administrative authority to lower government levels.[3]

Deconcentration means transferring administrative rights of making decisions within a given framework about tasks, expenditures, and financial means to subordinated, centrally guided and controlled governmental institutions or levels. Deconcentration tries to achieve several aims:

- bringing the administrative process closer to the needs of the local population,

- reducing costs of goods and services delivered by the government by transferring administrative competences to more specialized institutions,

- reducing bureaucracy in management processes.

Deconcentration does not involve a process of political changes, as for example the representation of citizens and parties in the governing process of the subordinated level. Gajl views deconcentration as a positive process, because in the short run it is easier to conduct than decentralization.[4] Deconcentration decreases the concentration of state activities.

Deconcentration can, in other words, be understood as a transfer of administrative competences within the same management system, with the lower levels hierarchically subordinated to the central level. The tasks of the medium and lower levels are limited to the execution of the central government decision. The right to take political decisions (e.g. planning and distribution of financial means for public tasks) remains at the central level. Thus the process of deconcentration does not include the transfer of political rights to local communities. Nevertheless, in many cases, the right to execute orders leaves some scope for local communities' own decisions.

---

[3]   Gajl N., Finanse i gospodarka lokalna na świecie, Warszawa, PWN, 1993, p.15, based on Starościak J., Prawo administracyjne, Warszawa 1997, p.65. The following example should bring the problem of deconcentration in Poland closer to the readers: The Ministry of Culture transferred the management of theatres to the voivodship leader (vojevoda). The transfer of such administrative competences could also comprise the decision-making authority over the budget for theatres.

[4]   Gajl N., Finanse..., p.17

3   Decentralization in the Polish Literature

3.1   AUTONOMY AND SELF-RELIANCE IN THE DECENTRALIZATION PROCESS

Autonomy and "self-reliance" (which are not synonymous)[5] often appear in the definitions of decentralization. The interpretations of autonomy and self-reliance which can be found in the Polish literature differ from those offered in the Anglo-Saxon literature, especially because the differences between autonomy and "self-reliance" are important for Polish scientists. These differences also help to understand the Polish approach to the decentralization process. In particular, the notion of autonomy is understood differently from the Anglo-Saxon literature.

Autonomy

The notion of autonomy in Poland does not only differ from the Anglo-Saxon view, it is also understood differently by the Polish scientists. Gliniecka and Darwiło, in accordance with others authors, define autonomy in a broad sense as the absolute independence of the local level from the central authority.[6] This implies that local governments have no relations with the central state. In fact, it leads to the liquidation of the country and the creation of new central states.

The definition given by Kosek-Wojnar and Surówka is narrower. According to them, autonomy necessarily includes three aspects: the political, the financial, and the organizational autonomy. Political autonomy means the transfer of legislative power to the local governments. Financial autonomy involves the separation between local and central sources of revenue. In unitary countries, the central government transfers the right to attain own revenue sources to local governments. This means that the decision-making on taxes is transferred from the central level to subordinate units, giving the local governments the right to decide about tax bases and tax rates. Organizational autonomy stands for full independence of the local administration from the central one. Every form of redistribution (e.g. grants) causes some degree of dependence from the central level[7], which prevents full autonomy. From this definition we can conclude that a totally autonomous local authority has the power to decide

---

5   Kornberger-Sokołowska E., Decentralizacja finansów publicznych a samodzielność finansowa jednostek samorządu terytorialnego, Liber, Warszawa 2001, p. 39

6   Darwiło A, Gliniecka J., Finanse gmin, Wydawnictwo Uniwersytetu Gdańskiego, Gdańsk 1997, p.80

7   Kosek-Wojnar M., Surówka K., Finanse samorządu terytorialnego, p.22

about expenditures as well as revenues and the right to cause budget deficits. In contradiction to other Polish authors, Kosek-Wojnar and Surówka do not equate autonomy with independence. Local governments are still part of the central state. For them the process of decentralization can lead to autonomy.

Most Polish scientists do not support such an understanding of autonomy. They underline that autonomy always means independence. That is why Polish authors conclude that full autonomy is impossible to achieve in Poland because local authorities in unitary countries are always a part of the governing structure. They cannot be totally independent because local governments are always controlled by the central level to some extent. Moreover, according to Sochacka-Krysiak local governments in all modern states are strongly interrelated with the central state because they are established due to the will of the central decision-making authorities, even against the free decision of the members of the local community. The central government, by passing legislation concerning the local sector, decides about the scope of competences and financial sources for local entities. Furthermore, legal acts define the methods of controlling these entities. Kulesza also emphasizes that reforms concerning decentralization should not "have any autonomic contexts". In other words, such reforms cannot lead to the independence of local governments.

For Polish scientists, the unity of the country is a great achievement. Poland learned from history that its strength lies in the unity of the country. So for the Poles, the unity of the country and of its administration is a good too precious to be endangered in any way, especially in the twentieth century during which it has already been necessary to unify the structure of Poland twice. For this reason the notion of "autonomy" is rarely used in describing decentralization efforts. From the Polish point of view the local entities should not be autonomic but should be self-reliant.

The conceptions of autonomy presented above show that autonomy equals independence for the majority of Polish scientists. Such a definition goes too far because the notion of autonomy is narrower than independence, and there can be different degrees of autonomy. Fear of losing the country's unity slows down and even stops the process of decentralization in Poland, as any kind or degree of autonomy is seen as dangerous.

Self-Reliance

Due to the fact that autonomy is understood as independence, Polish scientists typically use the term self-reliance to describe the process of decentralization. However, there are again various concepts of self-reliance in the Polish literature. In Poland, self-reliance is often defined as a situation (the status) in which the local authorities are not hierarchically subordinated to the central level, but are obliged to obey the rules established within the existing legal framework. They are controlled by central authorities, but only within the system of law. "Self-reliance" comprises legal personality, financial self-reliance, and the range of competences.[8]

One of the fundamental features of self-reliant local governments is to give them legal personality.[9] In this case local authorities become the subject of public law, although they remain in a defined relation to the state.[10] As the result of assuming a legal personality local governments obtain the right to actively take part in economic processes (market economy, economic life). As a consequence they can participate in economic exchange (e.g. conclude contracts), pursue economic activities (e.g. establish enterprises)[11], and collect money from the financial markets. It should be stressed that the legal personality of local governments has a specific character (e.g. the rules concerning the liquidation of legal persons do not apply to local authorities).

Financial self-reliance is understood differently by the Polish scientists. In contrast to the majority of Polish scientists, Kosek-Wojnar and Surówka define financial self-reliance as absolute financial independence of local authorities from the central government. This view is based on local revenue autonomy of local governments. The local authorities should have their own taxes with the right to determine tax bases and tax rates. The central government cannot interfere in financial decisions of local authorities. But the concept of Kosek-Wojnar and Surówka does not give any suggestions, which specific types of revenues should be assigned to which governmental level. Every kind of vertical redistribution (e.g. grants) is understood as a form of dependence from the central government and is a limitation of local self-reliance.[12] Supporters of this thesis usually equate financial self-reliance with self-financing. Generally, this point of view is considered as an anachronism because block grants, for example, create only little dependence from the central government.[13]

Piotrowska-Marczak therefore defines financial self-reliance as the possibility for local authorities to establish the hierarchy and the scope of their own tasks as well as the expenditures necessary to fulfill these tasks.[14] In contrast to Kosek-Wojnar and Surówka financial self-reliance does not exclude supporting local revenues by central

8   Sochacka-Krysiak K., Finanse lokalne, Poltext, Warszawa 1993 p. 80

9   Kosek-Wojnar M., Surówka K., Finanse..., op. cit. p.26

10   Piotrowska-Marczak K., Finanse ..., op. cit., p. 14

11   Gajl N., op.cit., s. 13

12   Kosek-Wojnar M., Surówka K., Finanse..., op. cit.

13   Sochacka-Krysiak K., Finanse..., op. cit., p. 22

14   Piotrowska-Marczak, K., Finanse ..., op. cit., p. 19

grants. In other words, such an interpretation of financial self-reliance does not mean the necessity of creating own revenues but the possibility to allocate them, even if the funds come from the central state budget. Thus the notions of self-reliance and self-financing are not synonymous.[15] Walasik, departing from Piotrowska-Marczak's definition, adds that the availability of sufficient funds is a necessary condition for the "budgetary autonomy"[16] of local authorities.[17]

We would like to underline that the level of financial self-reliance depends on the degree of the share of own revenues in total local revenues. Own revenues should be mainly guaranteed by own local taxes, with local levels able to decide on tax rates and tax bases. In such a case the local authority becomes independent of the financial sources of the central government and can actively create its own expenditure policy.

Self-reliance can be classified in different ways. Following Piotrowksa-Marczak, there is revenue-related self-reliance, expenditure-related self-reliance and mixed self-reliance. Revenue-related self-reliance stands for the possibilities and options of the local level to gather revenues from various sources and by various methods. Expenditure-related self-reliance is understood as the freedom to decide about the use of financial means. Mixed self-reliance concerns both the access to ones own revenues and the rights to spend them at ones own will.[18]

3.2 DIFFERENT CONCEPTS OF DECENTRALIZATION IN THE POLISH LITERATURE

In comparison to deconcentration, decentralization goes further. It includes the transfer of political power as well as financial sources and property to local entities. There are different views on decentralization in the Polish literature. It is defined from a broad and a narrow point of view, with the narrower definition again divided into three groups.

According to Kornberger-Sokołowska, decentralization covers a multi-dimensional background. In this broad understanding, decentralization cannot only be defined as a transfer of competences and financial means to local authorities. Therefore, the developing, expanding and strengthening of every element concerning organization,

---

[15]   Piotrowska-Marczak K., Finanse ..., op. cit., p. 19.

[16]   The author uses the notion of budgetary autonomy instead of financial self-reliance.

[17]   Walasik A., Teoretyczne zagadnienia decentralizacji decyzji w zakresie polityki podatkowej, Samorząd terytorialny nr.1-2, 1998, p.33

[18]   Piotrowska-Marczak K., Finanse lokalne w Polsce, PWN, Warszawa 1997, p.19

Deconcentration, Decentralization, Federalism: Terms and Definitions

task competences and finances on the local level should be treated as a symptom of decentralization of public administration.[19] So, every kind of transferring any organizational and financial rights is considered to be the premise of decentralization.

Gajl proposes a narrower and more precise definition of decentralization. The process of decentralization includes four aspects: (1) the transfer of competences from the central to the subnational authorities, (2) the use of local property and legal competences by local governments which guarantee their independence, (3) a sufficient level of own financial sources, (4) the right to elect independent represent-tatives of the local authorities by citizens[20]. In contrast to Kornberger-Sokołowska, Gajl requires the four aspects to be realized simultaneously.

Definitions of decentralization in a narrow interpretation can be divided into three groups. The first one concentrates on the role of independent local authorities, the second one underlines the importance of competences, the third one stresses financial self-reliance.

1. According to Borodo, decentralization of tasks and competences of public finance is a consequence of administrative decentralization. Financial decentralization cannot be achieved in an organizational void. In order to transfer tasks and competences to local levels it is necessary to establish independent local administration first.[21] In short, decentralization can be interpreted as a transfer of local administration management to local authorities elected by the local community. These authorities represent local interests and are self-reliant.

2. Owsiak and Kosek-Wojnar believe that the division of competences and tasks between local and central authorities plays a decisive role in the creation of a system of public finance as well as in its decentralization. They assume that the local entities are already established and a transfer of competences is essential for the process of decentralization. This transfer should be based on the subsidiarity principle which requires that all public tasks should be fulfilled on the lowest possible governmental level.[22] Consequently, the responsibility should depend on the competences of the particular level of administration and the efficiency of the

[19] Kornberger- Sokołowska E., Decentralizacja..., op. cit. p.14-15

[20] Gajl N., Finanse..., op. cit., p. 12

[21] Borodo A., Samorząd terytorialny. System prawnofinansowy, PWN, Warszawa 2000, s. 34-35

[22] Kosek-Wojnar M, Surówka K., Finanse..., op. cit., p.17, Owsiak S., Finanse publiczne. Teoria i praktyka, PWN, Warszawa 1999, p. 114

system. The subsidiarity principle is the basis for the division of tasks between different levels of government.

For Gaudemet and Molinier decentralization is an illusion if the local community does not possess real financial self-reliance[23] even if it has broad legal competences. There is no decentralization as long as the local authority does not have its own revenue sources. It cannot make any decision on expenditures without the authorization of central level. Moreover, the local government loses its self-reliance when the obligatory expenditures become too high. So the real indicator of decentralization seems to be the autonomy of local finance.[24]

3. Gliniecka, Darwiłło, Gilowska support a similar opinion that transferring competences without the availability of sufficient funds makes self-reliance illusory. On the other hand, giving the funds without rights to decide how to spend them does not bring self-reliance either. Moreover, there is no convergence between theory and practice in some countries. Officially, financial self-reliance is a legal principle set down in the Polish constitution. In Poland however, local governments are not granted the financial means necessary to fulfill the tasks which are assigned to them by the central level.[25] For this reason Gilowska believes that decentralization of public finance should comprise four aspects:[26]

• transfer of the power to collect the necessary resources

• transfer of the right to have these funds in ones own budget

• transfer of the right to decide about the expenditures

• transfer of the right to make budgetary deficits

All definitions mentioned above are based on the assumption that the necessary condition of decentralization is the establishment of independent authorities chosen in direct democratic local elections. Nevertheless, the existing definitions of decentralization can be divided into two main groups. In the first one decentralization starts with the transfer of competences. In the second group the process of

---

[23] The translator from French into Polish used the phrase "financial autonomy" which is in fact equal to self-reliance used in the Polish literature.

[24] Gaudemet P. M., Molinier, J. op. cit., p. 131

[25] Gliniecka J., Zasady polskiego prawa dochodów samorządu terytorialnego, Oficyna Wydawnicza BRANTA, Bydgoszcz 2001, p.22

[26] Gilowska Z. Konsolidacja i decentralizacja finansów publicznych, Uniwersytet Warszawski 2000, p. 62

decentralization takes place when not only competences but also funds are transmitted to the local levels.

From our point of view the preconditions for decentralization are free, direct, democratic, local elections. The process of decentralization starts the moment decision-making competences concerning tasks, expenditures and revenues are transferred from the central authority to lower administration entities. The local authorities receive the right to make decisions concerning certain tasks independent of the central government. There are competences whose accomplishment does not need financial resources (e.g. the right to give the permission to organize public events like the "Love Parade"). In the case of tasks which require funds we cannot talk about a decentralization of competences if their transfer has not been accompanied by sufficient financial means.

3.3 DEFINITIONS OF FEDERALISM FROM THE POLISH POINT OF VIEW

In Poland there is no in depth discussion and wide literature concerning federalism. The main reason for the lack of interest in federalism in Poland is the assumption that the federal state is already and definitively decentralized. According to Polish scientists there is no need to decentralize a federal system. Nevertheless, in the following, we will give a short survey of the Polish literature's perspective on federalism.

Polish scientists interpret federalism differently, i.e. from the unitary and the federal point of view. This divergence derives from differing origins of the state. In some (unitary) countries, the central authority has taken all the decision-making power. In other (federal) states historically independent entities (local regions, provinces) retained their autonomy. Local associations were created independent of the creation of state structures. They derived from primitive communities built up in order to protect their common interests.[27] In the first ones, federalism is the most advanced form of decentralization. In the second ones, federalism is the manifestation of centralism.[28] Thus, in unitary states, federalism can only be achieved as a result of decentralization. In practice this process can be observed very rarely (in Europe only Belgium has come through it). In the Polish literature, federalism is considered as a way of forming a federation from originally independent local entities. In this definition federalism

---

[27] Sochacka-Krysiak K., Finanse..., op. cit., p.14

[28] Saint-Ouen F., Podział..., op. cit., p. 3-7

preserves the autonomy of the members of the federation and acts as a defense against the central power.[29]

According to Saint-Ouen, federalism seems to be an art of managing "complexity". It is based on two main principles: subsidiarity and decentralization.[30] Competences of public administration in the federal system are built up vertically from the bottom to the top. This means that public tasks should be executed at the lowest possible level. They are allowed to be transferred to the higher level only if they cannot be efficiently carried out at the lower level.[31] Thus the federal system of local competences is based on the principle of subsidiarity. Generally, in countries with a federal structure there are a number of nation-wide tasks which have been transferred into the hands of the central authority. Numerous competences are assigned to the particular members of the federation.

According to Gajl, in a federal country autonomy of local authorities is given at the constitutional, jurisdictional and administrative level. Every member of the federation can have its own constitution and administration. Besides, the rights of inhabitants are guaranteed by a local system of courts.[32]

In Poland federalism is only seen as a status after full decentralization, not as a process. It is assumed that the federal state is always decentralized in every aspect (political, judiciary, financial). This opinion goes too far, although federal countries are decentralized in political and judiciary respects. Regarding the fiscal decentralization, we find that unitary countries (e.g. Sweden) can be more decentralized than federal countries.

4   Advantages and Disadvantages of Decentralization

Decentralization as a process and as a status has a number of advantages and disadvantages. The advantages which are presented in the Polish literature can be classified into two groups: those increasing the efficiency of allocation and those

---

[29]   ibid., p. 3-7

[30]   Saint-Ouen F., Podział władzy w demokracji europejskiej, Samorząd Terytorialny 6/1991, p.3

[31]   see: Kornberger-Sokołowska E., Decentralizacja ..., op. cit. p.12

[32]   Gajl N., Finanse..., p.18-19

improving the transparency of the policy-making process. Advantages which increase the efficiency of allocation are the following:

- A decentralized system allows a more rational management of public finance. The costs of tasks fulfilled by the local government are lower than the ones arising when being carried out by the central level. The waste of public funds diminishes if they are managed at the local level. The administration does not have to achieve optimal profits or fight for a better position on the market. The only thing counting for the administration is the electorate's opinion. When the administration is decentralized it is easier to identify the politicians and bureaucrats responsibility for taking financial decisions.

- Due to decentralization, local governments get the possibility to pursue their own tax policy, taking into consideration the specific local conditions.

- At the same time, decentralization of revenues and incomes allow to directly link the cost and benefits of providing public goods and services. Local governments are regarded as being able to identify the local needs and find the most rational ways to satisfy them, taking into consideration the hierarchy of those needs.

- In a centralized system the information is sent from the highest level to the bottom within the central system. In a decentralized system the information circulates between the local authorities and the citizens before making the final decision. That may help to increase the correspondence between citizens' preferences and political decisions by giving the citizens the possibility to influence the decisions. Their preferences are taken into consideration.

- In a centralized system the central authority possesses a wide range of competences which may cause the loss of control over particular matters and its own activity.

- Decentralization of competences allows decisions to be taken faster as compared to a centralized system, and the necessary information is gathered without considerable time lags.

Advantages which improve the transparency of the policy-making process:

- The democratic election of local authorities is the foundation of a democratic society. It supports the construction of democracy and increases the involvement of citizens in public affairs. It results in improved control of local administration activity by the local community.

- Decentralization permits citizens to better control expenditures and their realization because it brings the financial decisions closer to the local communities. It is difficult to bring the responsible politicians or bureaucrats at the central level to account for their mistakes. So the decentralization results in a more just system.

Simultaneously, decentralization has several disadvantages. They are considered from three points of view: The unity of the country, redistribution and efficiency. For the unity of the country decentralization can have the following disadvantages:

• Decentralization results in spreading both state power and public funds.[33] It weakens the central state and can lead to independence movements.

• The existence of contradictory interests causes conflicts between local communities.[34] For example, the competition between local entities concerning foreign investments may cause conflicts which may decrease the unity of Poland.

• Decentralization can cause the domination of local interests over the national ones.[35]

As far as redistribution is concerned, decentralization may deepen economic differences between local entities.[36] Without an equalization system, the regions with better economic, social and geographical conditions will always have better possibilities to develop.

Decentralization can also influence the efficiency of the system. It carries the peril of the abuse of power for particular interests (i.e. corruption).[37] In the case of Poland, democracy is not developed enough. The citizens do not feel able to influence the activity of local authority. This enables the creation of informal relations between politicians and bureaucrats.

5 Conclusions

To sum up, the notions, definitions, as well as the whole theory of deconcentration, decentralization and federalism have already been covered, although in different depth, in the recent Polish literature. The review of this literature allows us to draw some conclusions:

1. The Polish authors present the statuses and processes of the transformation of intergovernmental relations as illustrated in Figure II - 1. In the Polish literature

---

[33] Kosek-Wojnar M., Surówka K., Finanse..., op. cit., p. 19

[34] ibid. p. 18

[35] ibid. p. 18

[36] ibid. p. 18

[37] Jastrzębska M., Decentralizacja ..., op. cit, p. 17

there is no sole fixed definition of decentralization. It is important to stress this fact because the Polish constitution includes the guaranty of decentralization of public finance but, as the notion is not precisely defined, the central state can always be reluctant to transfer its power concerning the sources of revenues (including taxes) to local governments

Figure II - 1: **Statuses and processes of the transformation of intergovernmental relations presented in the Polish literate**

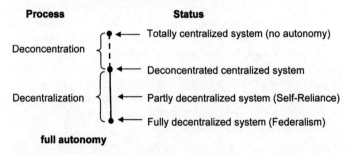

Process   **Status**

Deconcentration Totally centralized system (no autonomy)

Deconcentrated centralized system

Decentralization Partly decentralized system (Self-Reliance)

Fully decentralized system (Federalism)

full autonomy

Source: authors' own elaborations

2. The theoretical foundations of the definitions of deconcentration, decentralization and federalism are considered from the viewpoint of a unitary country. Deconcentration is regarded as a process separated from decentralization. Deconcentration is understood as the transfer of administrative rights which were initially controlled by the central government to other, subordinated governmental institutions or levels. It is understood as a mere "technical" process of passing on some administrative authority to lower, centrally controlled government levels.

In the Polish literature there is no sole fixed definition of decentralization. It is important to stress this fact because the Polish constitution includes the guaranty of decentralization of public finance but, as the notion is not precisely defined, the central state can always be reluctant to transfer its power concerning the sources of revenues (including taxes) to local governments

For us, the process of decentralization starts with the transfer of competences from the central level to local governments (elected in free democratic elections). In other words, decentralization begins when the local authorities receive the right to make independent decisions in the field of their own tasks, which have been transferred to them from the central government. One should remember that the accomplishment of some competences does not require financial resources. In the case of tasks which require funds we can talk about decentralization concerning these competences only if their transfer has been accompanied by adequate financial means. In the Polish literature a federal system is understood as a fully decentralized one. In our opinion such an attitude does not reflect reality. The degree of decentralization in federal countries can vary enormously. Federalism does not mean full decentralization.

The theoretical considerations of deconcentration, decentralization and federalism in the Polish literature are limited to very general definitions. These definitions are often not supported by economic theories. The arguments for decentralization and the disadvantages related to this process are presented without a previous deductive analysis. The pros and cons of decentralization are not backed by any economic theoreical background. Such an attitude results from the genesis of the transformation process in Poland, which started in 1989. Before the political changes in 1989 any discussion on decentralization was limited by the communist authority. After the fall of the totalitarian system lots of reforms concerning economic and social aspects (introduction of a market economy, monetary policy, social policy, tax system, social insurance, and health system) were conducted and that is why the discussion concerning the decentralization faded into the background.

It is important to pay attention to the fact that the reforms concerning, for example, the tax system or the health system were conducted separately without a general outlook on the whole public finance system (including the influence on the local system). The different governments wanted to introduce the reforms of the local administration as fast as possible. They referred to the experiences of the western countries. It was just assumed that decentralization of Poland is necessary.

Most Polish authors agree that in the Polish economy, which is still in the transformation process, deconcentration and decentralization is advisable. However, the scope of the changes is still a topic for discussion. Besides, the Polish attitude towards the notion of autonomy reveals a strong fear of the loss of independence; this slows down the process of decentralization. Decentralization and federalism are understood differently in the Polish literature. Therefore, it seems to be advisable to find common features for these notions.

ANALYSIS AND EVALUATION OF THE POLISH FISCAL SYSTEM –
THE TASK AND EXPENDITURE SIDE

LARS PONTERLITSCHEK

1 Introduction

Prior to 1989, Poland had a unitary and centralized system of government with lower tiers having little independent revenue or expenditure autonomy. The lower tiers of government were merely a part of the centralized state administration. Poland has since reformed its fiscal constitution, reorganized its structure of local governments by re-establishing the local self-government, and decentralized many public functions in order to make the government more responsive to its citizens. Lower tiers have gained significant decision-making powers, but the basic guideline to assign a dominant role to the central government has been retained. The following analysis of the Polish fiscal system will focus on the reforms of expenditure assignment in the period of 1989 to 2004. In a first step, the legal framework relevant for the distribution of public tasks among the different levels of government will be described. Then an overview of the process of decentralization of public tasks to the local government units will be given. After that the current expenditure assignment will be analyzed, before we identify problems associated with the current system and derive some proposals for reforms.

2 Expenditure Assignment in Poland

2.1 LEGAL FRAMEWORK

2.1.1 Changes in Poland's Territorial Structure as a Basis for Decentralization

After the Second World War, Poland was divided according to the three-level administrative structure effective during the inter-war period. The country's territory was divided into 17 voivodships, five cities with voivodship status, 330 poviats (counties) and, on the lowest level, 704 cities and 2,993 gminas (communes). In January 1955, gminas were dissolved and replaced by 8,790 gromadas. Between 1955 and 1972 there was an intensive reduction in the number of gromadas, accompanied by a tendency to create new poviats. At the end of 1972, there were 390 poviats (75 of which were cities with poviat status) and 4,315 gromadas. On January 1st, 1973, gromadas were dissolved and replaced by 2,365 gminas. On June 1st, 1975, poviats were dissolved, and the existing voivodships and cities with voivodship status were replaced by 49 voivodships.

As state[1] institutions, these 49 regions were purely administrative agencies of the central government until the 1999 reforms. They did not have their own budgets. Their budgets were part of the state budget which was composed of the central budget, voivodships' budgets, and local budgets. Elected bodies of the regions existed only formally because the election procedures did not meet democratic standards. On the local level, only gminas existed, but they did not have significant authority or autonomy either. For example, they had no right to possess their own property as they were merely units of the state administration. Before 1990, municipal property could not exist separately from state property and local budgets were treated as part of central government finance. There was no discretion in local revenue raising or in local expenditure decisions.

In 1990, independent and democratically elected municipal governments (gminas) were established by granting them legal status. During this process, gminas took over a major part of the state property and their budgets were separated from the state budget. In 1999, the territorial layout of the country was changed again. Sixteen self-governing voivodships became part of the "territorial self-government", i.e. they became the highest tier of local government. On the regional level, the Poland of today has a complicated dual structure: The voivodship councils are elected by the voivodships' inhabitants. Executive bodies – the voivodships' boards – are elected by these councils. The heads of these boards are the Voivodship Marshals. Voivodships have concurrent local and state administrations. The voivodships' local administration carries out self-government and also some state tasks but there are also state tasks fulfilled within the voivodships by the state administration. The head of the state administration at voivodship level, the "Voivod", is appointed by the Prime Minister. Thus the Voivod represents the national government at the regional level. Additionally, 314 counties (poviats) were re-established (they had existed between the end of World War II and 1975). At the same time, different tasks were decentralized to the newly created local governments.

---

[1]   "State" always refers to the central government's units.

A gmina is a self-governing community comprising the residents of the gmina and its territory. The gmina fulfils public duties in its own name and under its own responsibility, it has a legal identity and its self-governance is subject to legal protection. The basic bodies of a gmina are the gmina council and the mayor, both elected by its residents. The council has the constitutive and controlling power while the mayor represents the executive body in a gmina and is the head of the local administration. The capital, Warsaw, is a city with poviat rights and consists of eleven gminas.

Table II - 1 shows that Poland's structure is characterized by many small gminas. Approx. 66 % of the gminas have less than 10,000 inhabitants. Altogether, 307 of the 2,478 gminas are categorized as urban, 1,592 as rural, and 579 as urban-rural gminas.[2]

The poviat, being the mid-level unit of local self-government, covers the areas of adjacent gminas or the whole area of a city with the status of a poviat. The poviat bodies include the poviat council and governing board. Similar to gmina councils and voivodship assemblies, the poviat council is elected by all residents by direct election. The number of council members depends on the size of the poviat. The governing board of the poviat is elected by the poviat council.

Table II - 1: Structure of Polish gminas

Number of inhabitants	Number of municipalities	Proportion of municipalities (%)	Proportion of the whole population in munici-palities within the population range (%)
5,000	613	24.7	6.2
5,000 – 9,999	1,030	41.6	19.3
10,000 – 39,999	707	28.5	3.9
40,000 – 99,999	89	3.4	13.5
>100,000	39	1.6	29.1

Source: GUS (2005), pp. 143-144.

The voivodship is a unit of local self-government – a regional self-governing community and the largest unit of the basic territorial division of the Polish state. The Act on Voivodship Self-government provides for the fact that the scope of powers of a voivodship is without prejudice to the self-governing nature of any poviat or gmina, and

---

[2]   GUS (2005), p. 71.

no body of voivodship self-government may exercise control or supervision over poviat or gmina bodies, nor are they higher instance bodies in administrative proceedings. Voivodship self-government bodies include the voivodship assembly (sejmik), elected in direct elections, which is the constitutive and control body, and the voivodship governing board (executive body) which is appointed by the assembly.

Local officials at all subnational levels are elected by direct universal selection. They establish legislative and supervisory bodies: councils in gminas and poviats and local assemblies in voivodships. Executive bodies elected by the councils/assemblies are boards headed by a wojt or mayor (president) in gminas, a starosta in poviats and a marshal in voivodships.

Figure II - 2: Structure of the general government

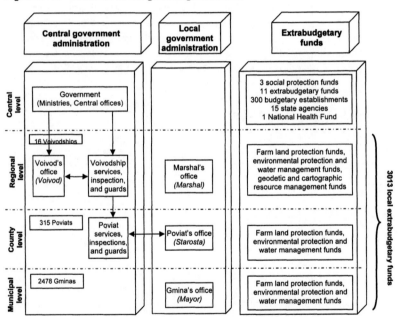

Source: Own elaboration following Burns and Yoo (2002), p. 21.

2.1.2 Composition of the General Government

The general government in Poland consists of the central (state) government, local governments, and social security funds. There are different forms of organization of institutions both in the state and local sector. The most important institutions are: local budgetary entities, budgetary establishments, auxiliary units of budgetary entities, state education institutions, state agencies, state and local institutions of culture, state and local medical care institutions, and various extrabudgetary funds:[3]

The budgetary entities' expenditure is covered from the state budget or the local government units' budgets. All other establishments or units should not be financed from the budgets, but from their own incomes, i.e. sales revenues or contributions. In reality, however, they often receive transfers from the state or local budgets.

Figure II - 3 shows that the state budget represents 40% of general government expenditure, while the extrabudgetary funds account for another 40%. Expenditures from subnational governments' budgets make up for 19% of general government expenditures.

Figure II - 3: General government's expenditure shares by level of government, 2004

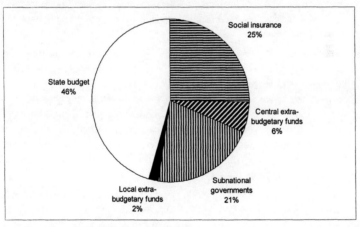

Source: {GUS, 2005 #179}, pp. 627-642.

---

[3]   Cf. GUS (2003), p. 532.

Extrabudgetary funds[4] finance a considerable part of government activities in Poland, but only a small portion of their activities is recorded in the state budget. A trend towards substantially downsizing the general government sector could not be witnessed since 1990. The share of total public expenditure of the general government in GDP amounted to 42.0% in 2004 compared to 45.1% in 1990. The central state budget expenditures in GDP on the other hand declined from 34.6% in 1990 to 21.4% in 2004. This downward trend reflects the decentralization process of public finances, especially after the local governments took over full responsibility for primary education in 1996. Consequently, the share of local government expenditures in GDP increased from 5.5% in 1991 to 10.6% in 2005.

2.2 REFORMS OF EXPENDITURE ASSIGNMENTS

2.2.1 Decentralization of Public Tasks to Local Governments

In the times of communism, nearly all public tasks in Poland were executed by the central government or its agencies. During the transition process that started in 1989, many reforms of the fiscal system were introduced and in doing so many tasks were decentralized to lower levels of government. Therein, Poland followed the theoretically derived insight that public tasks aimed at satisfying local needs should be performed by units of the local government.

In 1989, Poland inherited a centralized system in which old and mostly ineffective state-owned enterprises delivered local services. These state enterprises were typically responsible for an extremely heterogeneous bundle of functions. The finances of these enterprises were extremely unclear and characterized by large amounts of cross subsidization. In the following years, state-owned enterprises were either transferred into budgetary units or it was attempted to introduce market solutions to local service delivery by privatizing or transferring state-owned enterprises into commercial companies. Privatization and deregulation also helped to reduce the central government's scope of authority.

The Local Self-government Act of 1990 transferred a number of important public functions to the lower tiers of government. The act assigned gminas full responsibility for public transport, water supply and sewage treatment, solid waste collection and

---

[4]   The most important extrabudgetary funds, the social insurance fund, the farmers' insurance fund, the labor fund, and the national health fund are discussed in detail in the text "Social Security System in Poland, Description and Analysis of the Current System".

disposal, energy and heating systems, municipal cemeteries and libraries. Varying degrees of responsibility were also assigned to them for health and social welfare services, land use and spatial planning, environmental protection, fire prevention and public order.[5] Of the latter group, some services were assigned as own functions, while others were considered delegated functions. Gminas were also assigned responsibility for pre-school and primary education.

The responsibilities of the local self-government units can be divided into duties which are their own responsibility and into responsibilities delegated by statutes and by the central government administration. Own tasks can be of obligatory or facultative character and should be financed from the local governments' own revenues, whereas delegated tasks are usually financed from specific grants, transferred by the central government.[6] During the decentralization process, more and more public tasks became the duty of the local self-governments. In the beginning, only few tasks were decentralized, because there was concern as to whether the communes were really able to execute their duties. For example, it took a period of five years until the gminas finally took over the responsibility for running the primary schools, which they did successfully from 1996 onwards. In 1997, a new constitution came into force, in which the *principle of subsidiarity* was formally declared as one of the principles of democracy in Poland.

After the (re-)establishment of poviats and voivodships as tiers of the local government in 1999, the self-government units[7] perform nearly all public tasks in such fields as:

- primary and secondary schools,
- culture,
- social aid,
- municipal services,
- social dwelling construction,
- roads (approx. 95% of the roads are maintained by local governments),
- kindergartens and day nurseries.

---

[5]   Cf. Levitas, T. (1999), p. 11.

[6]   Cf. OECD (2001a), pp. 50-51.

[7]   I.e. gminas, poviats, cities with poviat rights, and voivodships.

Table II - 2 illustrates the process of decentralization, considering as examples tasks such as health care, education, and social security and welfare. While typical central tasks, like national defense, have always been executed exclusively by the central government (CG), the aforementioned duties were gradually shifted from being the central government's task to becoming the responsibilities of the local governments (LG). Especially in the field of education, we can observe the shift of expenditures toward the local level:

Table II - 2: Distribution of consolidated expenditure in selected sectors, 1995-2002

	1995		1999		2002	
	CG	LG	CG	LG	CG	LG
National Defense	100.0%	-	100.0%	-	100.0%	-
Health Care	89.8%	10.2%	9.8%	90.2%	64.5%	35.5%
Education	65.5%	34.5%	28.8%	71.2%	22.0%	78.0%
Social security and welfare	96.1%	3.9%	93.3%	6.7%	87.5%	12.5%

Source: Central Statistical Office, various years.

The decentralization process of some important tasks to subnational governments will now be discussed in more detail:

Education

Especially the decentralization efforts in the field of education brought about enormous expenditures for the local governments. As shown in table II - 3, there has been a fundamental change in the division of public expenditures on education between the central and local governments. Education duties have become the most important tasks fulfilled by the units of local self-government. Obligatory own tasks of gminas in this field comprise the establishing and operation of public kindergartens and primary schools. The decentralization of primary education was already decided in 1990 under the Local Government Act. The responsibility for primary education, however, was initially made voluntary until 1994 and then extended to 1996 because of resistance from the Teachers Union, the Ministry of Education and from rural gminas.[8] Thus the process of primary education reform took six years. The gminas finally assumed full

[8]   Cf. Levitas, T. (1999), p. 11.

responsibility for primary education, i.e. ownership and management of all primary schools, in 1996:

Table II - 3: Changes in the structure of primary education

Primary schools	School year				
managed by	1989/90	1991/92	1994/95	1997/98	1999/00
Central administration	20,391	19,295	13,999	763	48
Gminas	-	986	5,779	18,713	17,314

Source: REGULSKI (2003), p. 107.

Figure II - 4 shows that total public expenditure on education has been rather stable during the decentralization process, whereas the direct state expenditures have declined to nearly 0% of GDP until 1999. On the other hand, educational grants – which are a part of the general subsidy, as we shall later see – have risen significantly from 1992 onwards.

Figure II - 4: Shares of central government expenditure on education (in % of GDP)

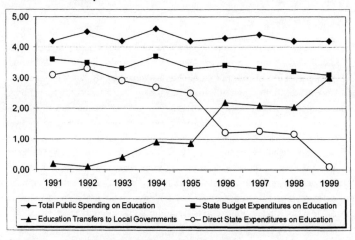

Source: Levitas and Herczynski (2001), p. 20.

At the same time, gminas' expenditures on education have risen dramatically from less than 1% in 1990 to more than 4% of GDP in 1999. Gminas' spending on education is financed to a large extent from the educational part of unconditional grants received from the central government, but also from their own revenues, as shown in the following graph:

Figure II - 5:   Shares of local governments' expenditure on education (in % of GDP)

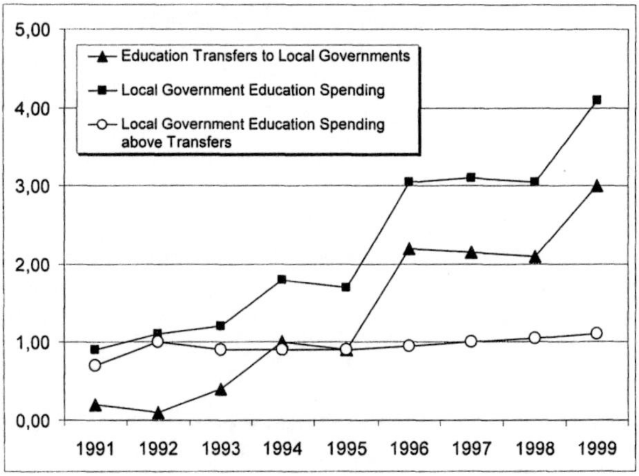

Source: LEVITAS and HERCZYNSKI (2001), p. 20.

In the 1999/2000 school year, primary education was reformed again. Instead of 8-year primary schools, 6-year primary and 3-year lower secondary schools were established, which are the responsibility of the municipal level as their own obligatory tasks. The then newly created poviats assumed responsibility for higher secondary schools, vocational schools, and special schools. Poviats and gminas are obliged to provide wages for the teachers in schools managed under their responsibility and have to cover all other costs of running the schools. Voivodships have since been in charge of the establishing and operation of public educational institutions and teacher training colleges as their own tasks. Public tertiary education at the university level (including the maintenance and payment of wages) remained the duty of the central government. The central government remained responsible for developing the curriculum of all public schools and for setting pedagogical standards for primary and secondary education.

Social security services

Social security services are provided by all three tiers of local government in cooperation with social organizations, the Catholic Church, foundations and associations. The most important part of such tasks is performed by the gminas. Their own tasks in this field are the management of social security centers, giving and paying of relief. Obligatory own tasks include the management of centers for homeless people and community centers for children. Duties delegated to gminas include all tasks arising from central government programs of social security services, which are established to protect people's living standards and the giving and paying of permanent relief and social pensions.

Transport, traffic

From 1999 onwards, voivodships have been responsible for regional roads, poviats for county roads, and gminas for municipal roads. In cities with poviat status, all public roads – national, regional, county, and municipal – are administered by the mayors of these cities (excluding highways and express national roads). The central government remains responsible for national roads and highways.

Health care

During the 1990s the health care system in Poland was free for citizens. In practice that meant that medical services were almost exclusively provided by the state's health care institutions financed directly from the state budget. The health care system survived the first ten years of transformation (1989-1998) in almost unchanged form.

The only fundamental change which took place during this period was the transfer of the substantial number of health care institutions to the local governments. At the beginning, this transfer was executed on the basis of individual agreements between the state administration and municipalities. Nevertheless, it did not change the way the health care system functioned.

The health care reform introduced in 1999 consisted in the transformation of health care institutions into 16 regional health funds and one national Health Fund for Uniformed Services. This reform was characterized by two important changes: (1) health funds were established as contracting units and payment agencies, (2) the public health care institutions were transformed into independent self-financing units. The 1999 reform, however, failed to fulfil the expectations connected with the improvement of health care functioning, nor did it achieve the expected financial effects. At the same time public expenditures for health care have risen substantially – according to GIME calculations in 1999, public expenditure for health care was 22% larger than in 1998. In 2000 the outlays for health care amounted to about PLN 30 billion, i.e. they constituted 10% of all public expenditure.

Table II - 4: State budget expenditure (in m PLN)

	1995	%	1999	%	2003	%
TOTAL	91,170	100.0	138,401	100.0	189.154	100,0
Allocations and subsidies	**31,657**	**34.7**	**72,879**	**52.7**	**105.176**	**55,6**
of which:						
Allocations to social insurance fund	6,000	6.6	9,459	6.8	28,265	14.9
Allocations to pension fund	6,102	6.7	12,891	9.3	15,014	7.9
Allocations to labor fund	-		-		3,944	2.1
Appropriated allocations for local self-government entities	3,568	3.9	11,548	8.3	10,276	5.4
General subsidies for local self-government entities	2,939	3.2	22,122	16.0	31,731	16.8
of which for educational tasks			16,551	12.0	24,321	12.9
Benefits for natural persons	**7,875**	**8.6**	**11,861**	**8.6**	**15,853**	**8.4**
Current expenditure of budgetary entities	**31,135**	**34.2**	**25,810**	**18.6**	**34,200**	**18.1**
of which:						
Wages and salaries	14,789	16.2	11,001	7.9	17,245	9.1
Contributions to compulsory social security and the Labor Fund	5,122	5.6	1,672	1.2	3,095	1.6
Public debt servicing	**14,360**	**15.8**	**18,778**	**13.6**	**24,051**	**12.7**
Property expenditure - investment expenditure[*]	**4,127**	**4.5**	**7,389**	**5.3**	**8,526**	**4.5**

Source: GUS (various years)

The main health care task of gminas was to organize the access to basic, non-specialist health care services. In the 1990s gminas took over non-specialist ambulatories from the state administration. Poviats had to organize the access to specialist services (ambulatory and hospital). In 1999 poviats took over hospitals and specialist ambulatories from the state administration. At this time voivodships took over more specialist hospitals with regional importance. Whilst privatization of ambulatories is popular, privatization of hospitals on poviat and voivodship levels is quite uncommon. Big debts, an active medical workers' union and a strong medical lobby in poviats and voivodships discourage private owners from investing in public hospitals.

On April 1st, 2003 the 17 health funds were replaced by one National Health Fund (NHF). Thus health care was re-centralized. The NHF consists of the main office and 16 regional branches. Members of the NHF council are appointed by the Prime Minister.

Table II - 5: Expenditure assignment – current status

Task	Gminas	Poviats	Voivod-ships	Central government (incl. Voivod)
Education:				
Curriculum for schools				X
Preschool and primary education	X			
Lower secondary education	X			
Higher secondary education		X		
Special secondary schools		X		
Tertiary education			X (vocational)	X (Universities)
Health Care:				
Public health and health protection	X	X	X	X
Hospitals		X	X	X
Social welfare:				
Nurseries and kindergartens	X			
Welfare homes		X	X	
Social services for individuals	X	X		
Social housing	X			
Unemployment		X	X	
Public utilities:				
Water supply	X			
Sewage	X			
Electricity	X			
Gas	X			
Central heating	X			

(continued): Expenditure assignment – current status

Culture:				
Theaters, museums, librarie	X	X	X	X
Parks	X			
Maintenance of buildings for cultural events	X			
Heritage conservation	X	X	X	

Task	Gminas	Poviats	Voivodships	Central government (incl. Voivod)
Environment, public sanitation:				
Waste collection and disposal	X			
Street cleaning	X			
Cemeteries	X			
Environmental protection	X	X	X	X
Natural / technological hazards			X	
Transport, traffic:				
Roads	X	X	X	X
Street lighting	X			
Public transport	X			
Railways			X	X
Urban Development:				
Town planning	X			
Regional/spatial planning		X	X	
Local economic development	X			
Tourism	X		X	X
General administration:				
Administrative functions (licences, etc.)	X	X	X	X
Other state administrative functions (electoral register, etc.)	X	X	X	
Police	X	X (state police)	X (state police)	X (state police)
Fire brigades		X	X	X
Consumer protection		X	X	
Fuel and Energy				X
National Defense				X

2.2.2 Changes in the State Budget Expenditures

At the beginning of the 1990s the two largest expenditure items of the central government were current expenditures of budgetary units, which consisted predominantly of wages and salaries, and social insurance contributions for public sector employees.[9] This changed noticeably during the decentralization process. The share of current expenditures declined significantly from nearly 60% in 1991 to 18% in 2003. The share of allocations to the social security system rose from 15% in 1991 to 25% in 2003, making it the largest item of the central government expenditures in 2003. The transfers to local governments have become a third very important item, which accounted for 22% of all state budget expenditures in 2003.

The share of investment expenditures in Poland fluctuates around 5% of the total state expenditures. Poland has the lowest expenditures for research and development and higher education[10] of all OECD countries.[11] Also, investment in physical infrastructure, especially roads, is rather low compared to other OECD countries.

2.3 CURRENT EXPENDITURE ASSIGNMENT IN POLAND

Generally, the tasks of the local self-government units can be divided into duties which are their own responsibility, and responsibilities delegated by the central government administration. Own tasks are financed from the local governments' own revenues and unconditional grants, whereas delegated tasks are usually financed from specific grants transferred by the central government.[12] Table II - 5 gives an overview of the current expenditure assignment among the different layers of government in Poland: This assignment of expenditures leads to the following distribution of budgetary expenditure between the central and the subnational governments[13]:

Table II - 6 shows that the central government still executes nearly 70% of all budgetary expenditures in Poland. It is exclusively responsible for national defense, compulsory social security, public debt servicing, and higher education. It illustrates

---

[9] Cf. Rapacki, R. (2002), pp. 344-345.

[10] Both together are called "investment in knowledge" by the OECD

[11] Cf. OECD Factbook 2005.

[12] Cf. OECD (2001a), pp. 50-51.

[13] The terms "subnational governments" and "local governments" are used interchangeably. They always comprise gminas, cities with poviat status, poviats, and voivodships.

that the extrabudgetary funds associated with the central government have very large budgets. Expenditures of state appropriated funds amounted to 135 bn PLN in 2004. Thus the central government still has the dominant role in Poland's public finance.

Table II - 6: Distribution of consolidated budgetary expenditure, 2004

	Total	Sub-national	Central	Sub-national	Central
		(in m PLN)		(in % of total expenditures)	
Total expenditure	**289,085**	**91,387**	**197,698**	**31.6**	**68.4**
of which:					
Agriculture and hunting	8,140	1,970	6,170	24.2	75.8
Transport, telecommunication	17,129	11,604	5,525	67.7	32.3
Dwelling economy	4,451	2,792	1,659	62.7	37.3
Public administration	17,080	9,033	8,047	52.9	47.1
National defense	11,027	0	11,027	0.0	100.0
Compulsory social security	48,483	0	48,483	0.0	100.0
Public debt servicing	22,674	0	22,674	0.0	100.0
Education	34,718	33,420	1,298	96.3	3.7
Educational care	2,964	2,691	273	90.8	9.2
Higher education	8,867	0	8,867	0.0	100.0
Health care	5,942	2,107	3,835	35.5	64.5
Social welfare	29,243	12,539	16,704	42.9	57.1
Culture, national heritage	4,059	2,997	1,062	73.8	26.2
Municipal economy and environmental protection	5,701	5,248	453	92.1	7.9

Source: GUS (2005), pp. 630 and 636.

Table II - 7: Expenditure of state appropriated funds (in m PLN)

		Expenditure
TOTAL	1995	54,366
	2004	**135,097**
Social insurance fund		108,658
Pension fund		15,963
Labor fund		9,142
Alimony fund		608
Administrative fund		479
Other funds		247

Source: GUS (2005), p. 633.

Local governments have the main responsibility for tasks such as transport and communication, lower education, and municipal economy and environmental protection. The expenditures of the subnational governments are distributed between the different types of local governments in the following way:

Table II - 8: Local self-government units' expenditure, 2004 (in m PLN)

Total expenditure	91,387	100%
Gminas*	40,942	44,80%
Cities with poviat status	32,137	35,17%
Poviats	12,445	13,62%
Voivodships	5,864	6,42%

Excluding expenditure of gminas which are also cities with poviat status.

Source: GUS (2005), p. 635

It is obvious that the main expenditures at the local level are executed by gminas and gminas that are cities with poviat status. The voivodships only spend 6.4 % of all local outlays. Table II - 9 illustrates the expenditure shares of the whole local government level in Poland as well as the expenditure shares of gminas, cities with poviat status, poviats, and voivodships.

Table II - 9: Local government expenditure shares (in m PLN), 2004

Type of expenditure	total	Gmi-nas	Cities with Poviat Status	Poviats	Voivod-ships
TOTAL expenditures	91,387	40,942	32,137	12,445	5,864
of which:					
Education	36.6%	42.7%	34.1%	36.2%	8.3%
Social welfare	13.7%	13.9%	13.4%	19.2%	2.7%
Transport and communication	12.7%	7.0%	16.9%	9.7%	35.5%
Public Administration	9.9%	11.6%	7.4%	12.1%	7.0%
Municipal economy and environmental protection	5.7%	8.4%	5.5%	0.1%	0.5%
Culture and national heritage	3.3%	2.8%	3.1%	0.5%	13.1%
Dwelling economy	3.1%	2.7%	5.0%	0.4%	0.5%
Educational Care	2.9%	1.3%	3.4%	8.1%	1.3%
Health care	2.3%	0.9%	1.9%	4.9%	8.9%
Agriculture and hunting	2.2%	3.1%	0.1%	0.2%	10.6%
Physical education and sport	1.5%	1.9%	1.6%	0.2%	1.3%
Tourism	0.1%	0.1%	0.1%	0.0%	0.1%

Source: {GUS, 2005 #179}, p. 636

The most important tasks of the whole local level are education, including educational care (39.5 % of all expenditures), social welfare (13.7 %), and transport and communication (12.7 %). We can further see that the most important tasks of the gminas are the field of education (approx. 44% of their total expenditures), social welfare, public administration, as well as municipal economy and environmental protection. Cities with poviat status have their main expenditures on education, transport and telecommunications, and social welfare. Poviats spend most on education, social welfare, public administration, and transport and telecommunication. The situation on the voivodship level is quite different from that of the smaller local governments. The primary function of the regional governments is not, as with gminas and poviats, the delivery of public services. Instead, their primary responsibility lies in developing and implementing regional development plans (economic development and infrastructure), which were regarded as crucial for Poland in order to be able to absorb European Union's financial support through structural and cohesion funds. Voivodships' most important expenditures are in the fields of transport and telecommunication, followed by culture and national heritage, agriculture and hunting, and health care.

The central government's expenditures by division are shown in table II - 10. The central government's highest expenditures are in the fields of compulsory social security, public debt servicing, social welfare, national defense, and public safety.

Table II - 10: State budget expenditure by type of expenditure (in m PLN)

Type of expenditure	2004
TOTAL	197,698.0
of which:	
Dwelling economy	1,659.0
Public administration	8,047.0
National defense	11,027.0
Compulsory social security	48,483.0
Public safety and fire care	9,085.0
Administration of justice	6,432.0
Public debt servicing	22,674.0
Education	1,298.0
Higher education	8,867.0
Health care	3,835.0
Social welfare	16,704.0
Culture and national heritage	1,062.0
Physical education and sport	195,0

Source: {GUS, 2005 #179}, p. 630.

Of special importance are capital investment-related expenditures which account for a significant portion of total expenditures. Capital expenditures of Poland's local governments represented approximately 60% of total capital expenditures in the public sector. This means that local governments are major capital investors in that sector, unlike the central government sector, which focuses primarily on current expenditures. Each year, local capital investments accounted for at least 15% of total expenditures incurred at that specific level (see table II - 11) while at the central level they represented only around 4%.

Table II - 11: Investment share in total expenditures by level of government

	1994	1996	1998	1999	2000	2001	2002	2003
All levels	22.5%	22.0%	22.4%	18.7%	17.4%	16.7%	15.9%	15.2%
Gminas	22.5%	22.0%	22.4%	21.9%	20.6%	19.1%	18.4%	16.9%
Cities with poviat rights				17.2%	16.1%	15.3%	14.8%	12.7%
Poviats				6.5%	7.5%	8.8%	7.8%	8.8%
Voivodships				31.7%	28.7%	27.8%	28.7%	32.8%

Source: KOPANSKA (2005), p. 15.

Such a huge capital investment effort by local governments is associated with serious underdevelopment of the municipal infrastructure inherited from the past. Due to the magnitude of existing needs, the amount allocated to capital projects is relatively stable in Poland, unlike in developed countries, where local capital budgets tend to fluctuate. However, the share of capital expenditures in total local expenditures decreased over the examined years (see table II - 12):

Table II - 12: Capital expenditure of local governments by sector (in %)

	Agri-culture	Trans-port	Municipal economy	Housing	Edu-cation	Health	Other
1997	8.5	4.3	53.1	7.4	15.3	2.1	9.4
1998	6.9	4.6	53.8	7.4	15.1	2.2	10.0
1999	8.0	17.9	35.2	6.7	14.1	7.5	10.7
2000	6.6	22.8	31.7	5.7	14.8	7.5	10.8
2001	6.6	31.6	19.0	5.8	16.1	8.1	12.9

Source: KOPANSKA (2005), p. 23.

Voivodships have the highest shares of capital investment, while poviats have the lowest share. The following table illustrates the changes over the last years concerning the economic sectors in which investments were made. Obviously, there has been a shift of capital expenditures from investments in municipal economy to the transport sector.

Finally, some data which show the expenditure situation in Poland in comparison with other OECD countries is presented in table II – 13 and table II - 14. The tables show that Poland has above average expenditure for social security, while health expenditures, investment in knowledge, and expenditure for education are among the lowest compared to other OECD member states.

Table II - 13: Public expenditure for selected tasks as a percentage of GDP

	Social security (2001)	Health care (2003)	Investment in knowledge (1999)
Australia	18.00	9.3	3.9
Austria	25.96	7.6	3.8
Belgium	27.23	9.6	4.3
Canada	17.81	9.9	5.4
Czech Republic	20.09	7.5	3.3
Denmark	29.22	n.a.	5.0
Finland	24.80	7.4	5.8
France	28.45	10.1	4.3
Germany	27.39	11.1	4.4
Greece	24.34	9.9	1.6
Hungary	20.07	7.8	2.7
Ireland	13.75	7.3	2.9
Italy	24.45	8.4	2.1
Japan	16.89	n.a.	4.6
Korea	6.12	n.a.	5.0
Mexico	11.83	n.a.	1.8
The Netherlands	21.75	9.8	4.5
Norway	23.90	10.3	3.9
Poland	**23.03**	**6.0**	**2.0**
Portugal	21.10	9.6	1.9
Slovak Republic	17.90	5.9	2.3
Spain	19.57	7.7	2.2
Sweden	28.92	9.2	6.5
Switzerland	26.41	11.5	5.0
United Kingdom	21.82	7.7	4.1
United States	14.78	15.0	6.2
OECD total	**21.20**	**9.0**	**3.8**

Source: OECD (2005), pp. 8-9; OECD Factbook 2005:
          http://www.sourceoecd.org/factbook

Table II - 14: Expenditure on education by level (in USD by PPP exchange rates)

	Expenditure per student 2001	
	Primary, secondary and post-secondary non-tertiary education	Tertiary
Australia	6,063	12,688
Austria	7,852	11,274
Belgium	6,781	11,589
Czech Republic	2,819	5,555
Denmark	7,865	14,280
Finland	5,733	10,981
France	6,783	8,837
Germany	6,055	10,504
Greece	3,475	4,280
Hungary	2,677	7,122
Iceland	6,892	7,782
Ireland	4,397	10,003
Italy	7,714	8,347
Japan	6,179	11,164
Korea	4,406	6,618
Luxembourg	11,091	-
Mexico	1,575	4,341
Netherlands	5,654	12,974
Norway	8,109	13,189
Poland	**2,396**	**3,579**
Portugal	5,065	5,199
Slovak Republic	1,681	5,285
Spain	4,870	7,455
Sweden	6,372	15,188
Switzerland	8,844	20,230
United Kingdom	5,324	10,753
United States	8,144	22,234
Average	**5,734**	**10,056**

Source: OECD Factbook 2005, http://www.sourceoecd.org/factbook

2.4 BIBLIOGRAPHY

Burns, Andrew and Yoo, Kwang-Yeol (2002): "Public Expenditure Management in Poland", OECD Economics Department Working Papers No. 346,

GUS (2003): "Statistical Yearbook of the Republic of Poland".

GUS (2005): "Statistical Yearbook of the Republic of Poland".

Kopanska, Agnieszka (2005): "The Problems of Developing the Municipal Debt Market in Poland", in: NISPAcee occasional papers VI(3), pp. 11-24.

Levitas, Tony (1999): "The Political Economy of Fiscal Decentralization and Local Government Finance Reform in Poland 1989-99". Washington, The Urban Institute.

Levitas, Tony and Herczynski, Jan (2001): "Decentralization, Local Governments and Education Reform in Post-Communist Poland", The Open Society Institute's Local Government Initiative Program.

OECD (2001a): "Fiscal Design Across Levels of Government - Year 2000 Surveys. Country Report: Poland". Paris.

OECD (2005): "OECD in Figures - Statistics on the Member Countries".

Rapacki, Ryszard (2002): "Public Expenditure in Poland: Major Trends, Challenges and Policy Concerns", in: Post-Communist Economies 14(3), pp. 341-357.

Regulski, Jerzy (2003): "Local Government Reform in Poland: An Insider's Story", Budapest, Local Government and Public Service Reform Initiative, Open Society Institute.

SOCIAL SECURITY SYSTEM IN POLAND - DESCRIPTION AND ANALYSIS OF THE CURRENT SYSTEM

LARS PONTERLITSCHEK

1 The Polish Social Security System

Since the 1st of January 1999, Poland has been establishing a reformed social security system which comprises the fields of pensions, sickness and maternity, accidents at work and occupational diseases, family allowances, social assistance, unemployment, and health care. Rules on eligibility and amount of benefits have been changed within the new social insurance scheme. The new system is organized as follows:

Figure II - 6: Organization of the Polish Social Security System

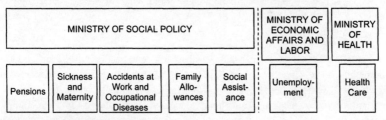

Source: ZUS (2005), p. 6.

The tasks in the sphere of social security are exercised by different institutions: the Social Insurance Institution (Zakład Ubezpieczeń Społecznych, ZUS), the Agricultural Social Insurance Institution (Kasy Rolniczego Ubezpieczenia Społecznego, KRUS), the National Health Fund, and different open pension funds. The main administrative element of the reformed social security system is ZUS. It determines the right to pensions and pays pensions to approx. 7.2 million people. It also determines the right to and pays sickness, maternity, or family allowances, etc. ZUS also assesses and collects the contributions to the health insurance and the labor fund, and transfers them to the relevant institutions, i.e. the National Health Fund and the Ministry of Economic Affairs and Labor.

The Polish social insurance system managed by ZUS covers inter alia old-age pension insurance, disability and survivors' pension insurance, sickness insurance, and work accident insurance. The following contributions are paid for the different types of insurances:

Table II - 15: Contributions to the different social security insurances in Poland

Type of insurance	Total contribution (% of gross salary)	Contribution of insured person	Contribution of employer
Social insurance			
Old-age pension of which:	19.52	9.76	9.76
first pillar	12.22	2.46	9.76
second pillar	7.30	7.30	0.00
Pensions (disability pensions, survivors' pensions, death grants)	13.00	6.50	6.50
Sickness insurance	2.45	2.45	
Work accident insurance	from 0.97 to 3.86		from 0.97 to 3.86[a]
Labor fund (unemployment)	2.45		2.45
Health insurance	8.50	8.50[b]	

[a] Depending on the assessed degree of risk and the number of workers.
[b] The contribution is deductible from the amount of due personal income tax (7.75 %) and from incomes after taxation (0.75 %).

Source: ZUS (2005), p. 20.

For old-age, disability, and survivors' pensions, the contributions are divided equally between the employer and the employee at 16.26 %. Only the employee pays sickness contributions, while the employer alone has to pay the contributions to the work accident insurance. Including labor fund contributions, the 'payroll tax' in Poland is between 38.39 and 41.28 % (depending on the contribution rate of the work accident insurance).

2   Types of Social Insurances in Poland

2.1 PENSIONS

The social insurance fund (SIF) was established in 1999 and is an appropriated state fund managed by ZUS. The SIF covers old-age pensions, disability pensions, and survivors' pensions. Moreover, sickness and maternity allowances are paid from this fund. The main source of financing benefits from social insurance are contributions paid by employers and employees, which amount to approx. 70 % of revenues (cf. table II - 16). Expenditures on pensions are by far the most important benefits paid out by the SIF:

Table II - 16: Revenues and expenditure of the Social Insurance Fund (SIF)

	2004 (m PLN)
TOTAL REVENUES	**107,713.3**
Revenues from contributions	73,392.6
Non-contributory revenues	34,320.7
State budget allocation	22,959.2
Other incomes	11,361.5
TOTAL EXPENDITURE	**107,567.7**
Cash benefits of which:	104,381.0
Old-age pension fund	58,006.5
Disability and survivors' pension fund	37,416.5
Sickness fund	4,748.9
Work accident fund	4,209.1
Pension prevention	79.8
Deduction for ZUS current operation and other expenditure	3,106.5

Source: ZUS (2005), pp. 22-24.

2.1.1 Old-age Pensions

As from the 1st of January 1999 an important reform of the old-age pension system came into force. Before this reform, Poland had a 'pay-as-you-go' (PAYG) pension system that was not divided into different risk categories, with contributions paid only by employers (45 % of wage[1]). The reform of the old-age pension system was necessary after the old system became too expensive. Moreover, the legal retirement age of 65 years for men and 60 years for women was counteracted by various possibilities for early retirement, which resulted in actual average retirement ages of 59 years for men and 54 years for women. The new system is based on close correlation between actually paid contribution and benefit amount. It also limits possibilities for early retirement and creates incentives for working until the legal retirement is reached.

In 1999, a multipillar system was implemented. The following table highlights the most important changes in the Polish old-age pension system:

---

[1] Cf. Golinowska, S., et al. (2003), p. 42.

Table II - 17: Comparison of the old and new old-age pension system

	Old system	New system
Contributor	Employer	Both employer and employee
Financing	Pay-as-you-go	Multipillar system with combined PAYG and funded pillars
Pension base	10-year average earnings	Lifetime earnings
Pension age	Various early retirement possibilities. Actual rates: 59 for men, 54 for women	65 for men, 60 for women for nearly all workers

Source: CHLON-DOMINCZAK (2002), p. 118.

The first pillar of the new pension system – managed by ZUS – consists of 'pay-as-you-go' contributions paid to the public pension fund. Each employed person gets an individual account in which the contributions are recorded and benefits calculated according to the number of years they worked and the size of the contributions (the so-called 'notional defined contribution', NDC[2]). A closer link between contributions paid and benefits has been realized with the implementation of the NDC system. The contributions to this first pillar represent 12.22% of gross salary.

The second pillar – managed by private institutions, i.e. open pension funds – is a fully funded scheme in which the contributions are invested in private pension funds selected by the individual employee. Contributions of this second pillar represent 7.3% of gross salary. The contributions to these two pillars are made before tax and income tax will have to be paid on the benefits received. These two pillars are mandatory, but there is also a voluntary, state-aided third pillar, in which each individual can make contributions to occupational pension funds. It is aimed at ensuring above-standard old-age benefits for an additional contribution. Contributions to the third pillar are made individually after tax, but the benefits from such an investment are exempt from income tax. The new system became obligatory for persons born after the 31st of December 1968. Persons born between 1949 and 1969 still have to pay contributions to the first (old) pay-as-you-go system, but were allowed the right to decide whether they want to participate in the second, funded, pillar until the end of 1999. Persons born before the 1st of January 1949 stayed with the old pay-as-you-go-system.

---

[2] NDC systems have been implemented in many East European transition economies (cf. Müller, K. (2003), pp. 555 et seqq.). An NDC scheme bases benefits entirely on contributions paid during working life while pension benefits are paid out of current contributions as in a conventional PAYG system. For a comprehensive description of NDC systems, cf. Börsch-Supan, A. (2003), pp. 7 et seqq.

Table II - 18: The three pillars of the old-age pension system

	First pillar	Second pillar	Third pillar
System management	Public	private	private
Participation in the system	compulsory	compulsory	voluntary
Financing	pay-as-you-go	funded	funded
Calculation of benefit amount	defined contribution system	defined contribution system	defined contribution system
Social objective	Determined basic level of benefits	determined basic level of benefits	higher standard of benefits

Source: ZUS (2005), p. 34.

2.1.2 Disability and Survivors' Pensions

The disability pension is granted to insured persons who are incapable of work (total or partial disability) and have completed at least 5 years of insurance during the last 10 years. The share of disability pensions in Poland's pension portfolio is approx. 29.5 %.[3] In contrast to old-age pensions, the disability pension system has remained unchanged.

Survivors' pensions are paid to widows/widowers and orphans or other persons who received financial support from the deceased employee. This type of pension accounts for approx. 17.6 % of all pensions paid by ZUS.[4]

2.2 SICKNESS AND WORK ACCIDENT BENEFITS

In Poland, sickness benefits for the first 33 days are paid by employers and afterwards by the sickness fund. Benefits are 80 % for up to 90 days and then 100 % of average earnings during the preceding 6 months.

In case of work injury that leads to temporary disability, 100 % of average earnings during the preceding 6 months are paid from the first day of incapacity. For a permanent disability to work, benefits are paid depending on the average national salary, the insured's income, the insured's contribution years, et al.

---

[3]   Cf. ZUS (2005), p. 36.

[4]   Cf. ZUS (2005), p. 37.

2.3 SOCIAL INSURANCE FOR FARMERS

A specific feature of the Polish social insurance system is the existence of a separate insurance scheme for farmers managed by the Agricultural Social Insurance Institution (KRUS). It covers more than 1.5 million persons who receive cash benefits from pension insurance (old age, disability, and survivors') as well as from work accident, sickness, and maternity insurance. The system is partly financed from farmers' contributions and to a large extent from state budget allocations. Expenditures on tasks executed by KRUS amounted to 16.3 billion PLN in 2004, of which 83.4 % represented expenditure on farmers' pensions. Revenues from farmers' contributions only covered 7.9 % of pension expenditures. The rest had to be transferred from the state budget.

2.4 HEALTH INSURANCE

Another specific feature of the Polish social security system is the separation of sickness insurance (within ZUS) from health insurance. Sickness insurance provides cash benefits in respect of sickness and maternity, while health insurance is a system that provides benefits of preventive, diagnostic, therapeutical, or rehabilitation character.

The health care system has twice been substantially reformed since 1999. First, 16 regional health insurance funds and one branch fund for uniform services of national range were created in 1999. On the 1st of April 2003, the 16 regional funds were replaced by one National Health Fund which has 16 regional branch offices.[5]

The main source of financing health care are contributions to the health insurance. Contributions amount to 8.5 % of gross salary and are deductible from PIT. They are collected by ZUS and then transferred to the National Health Fund. For the non-working population (unemployed, children, students, etc.) and for individual farmers, contributions are financed by the state budget.

---

[5] Cf. my text on expenditure assignment for further information on health care in Poland.

Table II - 19: Budgets of Health Funds and National Health Fund (NHF), 1999 - 2004, in m PLN

	2000	2001	2002	2003 Health Funds	2003 NHF	2003 Total	2004 NHF
	Health Funds	Health Funds	Health Funds				
Total revenue	**24,955.4**	**28,929.2**	**30,557.2**	**7,560.4**	**22,011.2**	**29,571.7**	**31,745.0**
Contribution from the insured	93.8%	92.8%	86.6%	92.3%	99.0%	97.2%	98.5%
Appropriated allocations from state budget on health care state programs	0.2%	0.0%	0.1%	0.0%	0.2%	0.2%	0.1%
Revenue from interregional equalization	4.1%	4.0%	4.6%	4.9%	0.0%	1.2%	0.0%
Other operating revenue	0.8%	1.9%	8.2%	2.7%	0.7%	1.2%	1.2%
Financial revenue	1.1%	1.3%	0.6%	0.2%	0.2%	0.2%	0.2%
Total expenditure	**24,716.7**	**28,482.0**	**31,211.2**	**7,693.5**	**22,534.5**	**30,228.0**	**31,089.6**
Write-off on the reserve fund	0.9%	1.0%	0.7%	0.8%	0.0%	0.2%	0.0%
Write-off on the Health Funds Association	0.0%	0.0%	0.0%	0.0%	0.0%	0.0%	0.0%
Expenditure on interregional equalization	4.2%	3.7%	4.3%	4.8%	0.0%	1.2%	0.0%
Expenditure on medical services for the insured	92.8%	92.3%	91.2%	92.1%	97.9%	96.4%	98.1%
Expenditure on state health care programs	0.2%	0.0%	0.1%	0.0%	0.2%	0.2%	0.1%
Expenditure on Health Funds own health care programs	0.3%	0.5%	0.7%	0.2%	0.2%	0.2%	0.0%
Administrative costs	1.3%	1.3%	1.0%	1.1%	1.0%	1.0%	1.0%
Other operating costs	0.2%	1.2%	2.0%	1.0%	0.6%	0.7%	0.7%
Financial costs	0.1%	0.0%	0.0%	0.1%	0.1%	0.1%	0.1%
Outcome	**238.7**	**447.2**	**-654.1**	**-133.1**	**-523.2**	**-656.4**	**655.4**

Source: Ministry of Health, GIME.

2.5 UNEMPLOYMENT INSURANCE

Unemployment benefits are paid to persons who lost their jobs for a period of six, twelve, or 18 months, depending on the unemployment rate in the poviat where the unemployed person lives, the personal situation, and the age of the unemployed.[1]

Benefits from the unemployment insurance are financed from compulsory contributions by the employers (2.45 % of gross salary), which make up for 80 % of Labor Fund incomes, an allocation from the state budget (15 %), and other incomes (5 %).

3 Problems of the Social Security System

3.1 EXPENSIVENESS OF THE SYSTEM

In comparison with East European transition countries social security was very expensive in Poland before the reform of 1999. Table II - 20 shows that Poland had much higher expenditures on social security and welfare than other transition countries at the end of the 1990s:

Table II - 20: Expenditure on social security and welfare in Eastern Europe

Poland		East-European 9[*]	
Average (5 year) 1995-1999		Average (5 year) 1995-1999	
% of GDP	% of total expenditure	% of GDP	% of total expenditure
19.2	50.2	12.21	34.04

[*] East-European 9 includes Bulgaria, Czech Republic, Estonia, Hungary, Latvia, Lithuania, Romania, Slovakia, Slovenia, but excludes Poland.

Source: World Bank (2006).

In comparison with OECD[2] countries, Poland also had above-average public expenditures on social security: Poland spent 22.8 % of GDP on social security in

---

[1]   Cf. ZUS (2005), p. 60.

[2]   Unfortunately, OECD databases only provide data on social expenditures until 2001. Therefore, first a comparison of Poland with OECD countries and an assessment of the Polish situation before the 1999 reforms will be made. Afterwards, the development of the relevant figures for Poland after the 1999 reforms will be presented with the help of OECD and Eurostat data, which are available for East European countries from 2000 onwards, in order to evaluate the success of the reforms. Note that OECD and Eurostat use slightly differing classifications and calculation methods.

1998, while the average of all OECD countries was at 21 % of GDP.[3] The following tables illustrate the situation in Poland in comparison with other OECD member countries:

Table II - 21: Total public social expenditure[4] in selected OECD countries (in % of GDP)

	1990	1995	2000	2001
Australia	14.2	17.8	18.6	18.0
Austria	24.1	26.6	26.0	26.0
Belgium	26.9	28.1	26.7	27.2
Canada	18.6	19.6	17.3	17.8
Czech Republic	17.0	18.9	20.3	20.1
Denmark	29.3	32.4	28.9	29.2
Finland	24.8	31.1	24.5	24.8
France	26.6	29.2	28.3	28.5
Germany	22.8	27.5	27.2	27.4
Hungary	NA	NA	20.0	20.1
Italy	23.3	23.0	24.1	24.4
Netherlands	27.6	25.6	21.8	21.8
New Zealand	21.9	18.9	19.2	18.5
Norway	24.7	26.0	23.0	23.9
Poland	**15.5**	**23.8**	**21.9**	**23.0**
Portugal	13.9	18.0	20.5	21.1
Slovak Republic	NA	19.2	18.3	17.9
Spain	19.5	21.4	19.9	19.6
Sweden	30.8	33.0	28.6	28.9
Switzerland	17.9	23.9	25.4	26.4
United Kingdom	19.5	23.0	21.7	21.8
United States	13.4	15.5	14.2	14.8
OECD Average	19.1	21.4	20.7	21.1

Source: OECD (2004), Social Expenditure Database (http://www.oecd.org/els/social/expenditure).

---

[3]   Cf. OECD (2001b).

[4]   Includes old-age, survivors, incapacity related, health, family, active labor market, unemployment, housing, and other benefits.

Table II - 22: Expenditure on old age in selected OECD countries (in % of GDP)

	1990	1995	2000	2001
Australia	3.3	4.7	5.3	4.7
Austria	9.6	10.4	10.5	10.7
Belgium	7.6	8.5	8.5	8.7
Canada	4.2	4.9	4.7	4.8
Czech Republic	5.6	5.5	6.8	6.7
Denmark	8.6	9.6	8.3	8.3
Finland	7.1	8.6	7.6	7.9
France	9.3	10.7	10.6	10.6
Germany	9.9	11.1	11.5	11.7
Hungary	NA	NA	7.8	8.0
Italy	9.6	10.7	11.2	11.3
Netherlands	7.8	7.0	6.4	6.4
New Zealand	7.3	5.6	5.0	4.7
Norway	7.2	7.1	6.5	6.8
Poland	*4.3*	*8.0*	*8.1*	*8.5*
Portugal	4.4	6.4	7.5	7.9
Slovak Republic	NA	6.2	6.7	6.7
Spain	7.4	8.4	8.5	8.3
Sweden	8.7	9.9	9.2	9.2
Switzerland	8.2	10.5	11.4	11.8
United Kingdom	7.2	8.0	8.2	8.1
United States	5.2	5.4	5.2	5.3
OECD Average	**6.3**	**7.2**	**7.4**	**7.6**

Source: OECD (2004), Social Expenditure Database
(http://www.oecd.org/els/social/expenditure).

Table II - 23: Expenditure on incapacity related benefits[5] in selected OECD countries (in % of GDP)

	1990	1995	2000	2001
Australia	1.9	2.3	2.3	2.3
Austria	2.1	2.5	2.6	2.5
Belgium	3.2	3.4	3.2	3.3
Canada	1.1	1.0	0.8	0.8
Czech Republic	2.5	2.7	3.0	3.0
Denmark	3.3	3.7	3.7	3.9
Finland	4.3	5.1	3.9	3.9
France	2.5	2.1	2.1	2.1
Germany	1.8	2.2	2.3	2.3
Hungary	NA	NA	2.6	2.7
Italy	2.7	2.4	2.2	2.1
Netherlands	6.9	5.3	4.1	4.1
New Zealand	3.0	2.8	2.8	2.8
Norway	4.8	4.7	4.7	4.8
Poland	*3.5*	*6.0*	*5.5*	*5.5*
Portugal	2.5	2.5	2.5	2.5
Slovak Republic	NA	2.3	2.4	2.3
Spain	2.3	2.6	2.4	2.4
Sweden	5.6	5.1	4.8	5.2
Switzerland	2.3	3.1	3.6	3.8
United Kingdom	2.1	2.8	2.5	2.5
United States	1.0	1.2	1.1	1.1
OECD Average	**2.5**	**2.7**	**2.5**	**2.6**

Source: OECD (2004), Social Expenditure Database
(http://www.oecd.org/els/social/expenditure).

---

[5]   Includes disability, occupational injury and disease, and sickness benefits.

Table II - 24: Expenditure on survivors in selected OECD countries (in % of GDP)

	1990	1995	2000	2001
Australia	0.3	0.3	0.2	0.2
Austria	2.9	2.9	2.7	2.7
Belgium	2.9	2.9	2.7	2.6
Canada	0.4	0.5	0.4	0.4
Czech Republic	0.9	0.8	0.9	0.9
Denmark	0.0	0.0	0.0	0.0
Finland	1.0	1.1	0.9	1.0
France	1.7	1.7	1.5	1.5
Germany	0.5	0.5	0.4	0.4
Hungary	NA	NA	0.3	0.3
Italy	2.4	2.6	2.6	2.6
Netherlands	1.2	1.0	0.7	0.7
New Zealand	0.2	0.1	0.1	0.1
Norway	0.4	0.4	0.3	0.3
Poland	*1.1*	*2.0*	*2.0*	*2.1*
Portugal	1.0	1.3	1.4	1.5
Slovak Republic	NA	0.4	0.2	0.2
Spain	0.9	0.9	0.6	0.6
Sweden	0.7	0.7	0.6	0.6
Switzerland	1.1	1.4	1.5	1.6
United Kingdom	0.6	0.7	0.7	0.6
United States	0.9	1.0	0.8	0.8
OECD Average	**1.0**	**1.0**	**1.0**	**1.0**

Source: OECD (2004), Social Expenditure Database
(http://www.oecd.org/els/social/expenditure).

Table II - 25: Expenditure on health in selected OECD countries (in % of GDP)

	1990	1995	2000	2001
Australia	5.2	5.5	6.2	6.2
Austria	5.2	5.8	5.4	5.2
Belgium	6.6	6.0	6.2	6.4
Canada	6.7	6.5	6.4	6.7
Czech Republic	4.9	6.8	6.5	6.7
Denmark	7.0	6.8	6.9	7.1
Finland	6.3	5.7	5.0	5.3
France	6.6	7.3	7.1	7.2
Germany	6.5	8.1	7.9	8.0
Hungary	NA	6.3	5.0	5.1
Italy	6.4	5.3	6.0	6.3
Netherlands	5.4	6.0	5.5	5.7
New Zealand	5.7	5.6	6.1	6.1
Norway	6.4	6.7	6.5	6.8
Poland	*4.6*	*4.2*	*4.0*	*4.4*
Portugal	4.1	5.1	6.2	6.3
Slovak Republic	NA	5.8	4.9	5.0
Spain	5.3	5.5	5.3	5.4
Sweden	7.5	7.1	7.1	7.4
Switzerland	4.5	5.4	5.9	6.4
United Kingdom	5.0	5.8	5.8	6.1
United States	4.8	6.1	5.9	6.2
OECD Average	**5.2**	**5.6**	**5.7**	**5.9**

Source: OECD (2004), Social Expenditure Database
(http://www.oecd.org/els/social/expenditure).

Table II - 26: Expenditure on unemployment in selected OECD countries (in % of GDP)

	1990	1995	2000	2001
Australia	1.1	1.2	1.0	1.0
Austria	0.8	1.1	0.7	0.8
Belgium	2.6	2.7	2.2	2.2
Canada	1.9	1.3	0.7	0.8
Czech Republic	NA	0.1	0.3	0.2
Denmark	4.3	4.4	3.0	3.0
Finland	1.1	3.9	2.1	2.0
France	1.8	1.8	1.6	1.6
Germany	0.7	1.5	1.2	1.2
Hungary	NA	0.9	0.5	0.4
Italy	0.8	1.0	0.6	0.6
Netherlands	2.5	2.9	1.3	1.3
New Zealand	1.9	1.2	1.4	1.1
Norway	1.1	1.1	0.4	0.4
Poland	*0.0*	*1.7*	*0.8*	*1.0*
Portugal	0.4	0.9	0.9	0.9
Slovak Republic	NA	0.4	0.8	0.5
Spain	2.3	2.3	1.3	1.3
Sweden	0.9	2.1	1.3	1.0
Switzerland	0.1	1.0	0.5	0.5
United Kingdom	0.7	0.9	0.3	0.3
United States	0.4	0.3	0.2	0.3
OECD Average	**1.2**	**1.5**	**0.9**	**0.9**

Source: OECD (2004), Social Expenditure Database
(http://www.oecd.org/els/social/expenditure).

As the tables above show, Poland was above the OECD average values in all categories except for unemployment benefits and health care at the end of the 1990s. Especially Poland's share of incapacity related benefits in GDP are the highest among the observed countries. Also the number of disability pensioners is very high. Furthermore, during the 1990s, the number of sickness days rose steadily.[1]

The old pension system especially implied the following problems which endangered its sustainability:

- low effective retirement ages,

- excessively liberal disability criteria,

- high replacement ratios,

- large redistributive components in the pension formula, and

- excessive privileges for some categories of workers.

The reforms of 1999 were executed in order to resolve these problems. Positive aspects of these reforms are:

- Through the implementation of the multipillar system (partly on pay-as-you-go and partly on funding), a risk diversification was introduced to the old-age pension system because its development now depends partly on the labor market and partly on the capital market.

- The new system strengthens self responsibility and self provision of each individual. This becomes especially evident by regarding the voluntary third pillar.

- The stricter link between contributions paid and pension amount creates incentives for people to stay longer in employment.

- Eligibility to early retirement was hampered.

The reformed old-age pension system with its public-private mix substantially reduced retirement pensions (see section II 3.2), but left disability pensions unchanged. Although we can observe rising expenditures for disability pensions, the problem of the high expenditures in this field has not been tackled in the 1999 reforms. This might favor those workers who become disabled in comparison with workers with similar earnings and career histories but no disability. Inequities between disability and old-age pensions would be the result of such a development. Concerning the high expenditures for sickness benefits, the reforms of 1999 included control over doctors and a system

---

[1]   Cf. World Bank (2003), p. 50.

of monitoring sick pay prescriptions, which reduced sickness days significantly. Nonetheless, the number of sick days in Poland is still above OECD average and benefits remained rather generous in comparison with other OECD members.

Consequently, Poland has a rather expensive social security system – even after the reforms. Table II - 27 displays the development of expenditure on pensions since the year 2000. It shows that Poland has rising expenditures on pensions after the reform and that the country has much higher expenditures on pensions in relation to GDP than the other new East European EU members:

Table II - 27: Expenditure on pensions⁺ in the EU (in % of GDP)

	2000	2001	2002	2003
Czech Republic	8.7	8.7	8.9	8.8
Estonia	6.9	6.2	6.1	6.3
Latria	9.6	8.6	8.3	7.5
Lithuania	7.8	7.3	7.0	6.8
Hungary	8.7	8.9	9.0	9.3
Poland	*13.0*	*13.9*	*14.2*	*14.3*
Slovenia	11.4	11.5	11.7	11.2
Slovakia	7.5	7.5	7.5	7.5
EU-25 Average	**12.5**	**12.5**	**12.4**	**12.6**

⁺ The 'pensions' aggregate comprises the following social benefits: disability pension, early-retirement due to reduced capacity to work, old-age pension, anticipated old-age pension, partial pension, survivors' pension, early-retirement benefit for labour market reasons.

Source: EUROSTAT (2006), http://ec.europa.eu/eurostat.

Table II - 28 shows that since 2000 expenditures on old-age pensions in relation to GDP have increased in Poland. Thus we can assume that the introduction of the three-pillar system was not successful in terms of limiting public expenditures in this field. But this before-after analysis is just an indication for this thesis. We do not have reliable data for a with-and-without analysis of the reform.

Table II - 28: Expenditures on old-age pensions in the EU (in % of GDP)

	2000	2001	2002	2003
Czech Republic	6.9	6.8	7.0	7.0
Estonia	5.8	4.5	4.5	4.6
Latria	7.8	7.0	6.7	6.2
Lithuania	6.6	6.2	5.9	5.6
Hungary	5.9	5.9	6.0	6.1
Poland	**7.9**	**8.5**	**8.7**	**8.7**
Slovenia	7.5	7.6	7.7	7.7
Slovakia	6.2	6.3	6.4	6.4
EU-25 Average	**9.5**	**9.5**	**9.4**	**9.6**

Source: EUROSTAT (2006), http://ec.europa.eu/eurostat

3.2   OTHER PROBLEMS

First of all, the introduction of fully funded pillars to the old-age pension systems brought about high implementation costs in Poland. The costs of the pension reform have been estimated to 0.8 % of the GDP in 1999, 1.4 % of GDP in 2000, 1.8 % of GDP in 2001, 2.2 % of GDP in 2002 and 1.8 % of GDP in the years 2003-2004.[2] It is estimated that the cumulated costs of the system change will amount to 100 % of the Polish GDP until 2050.[3]

One result of the old-age pension reform is that the pension risk for younger generations has been shifted entirely to individuals by combining the private pillar with the introduction of "notionally defined contribution accounts" in the PAYG system. Now, the (future) amount of benefits highly depends on the situation of the capital market. First simulations of benefit amounts for birth groups 1949-1974 display a dramatic decline of replacement ratios from currently up to 65 % to only 40 % of salary in case of retirement at age 65.[4] At the same time, redistribution toward low-income earners

---

[2]   Cf. Golinowska, S., et al. (2003), p. 45.

[3]   Cf. Müller, K. (2003), p. 560.

[4]   Cf. Chlon-Dominczak, A. (2002), p. 128.

inherent to the former old-age pension system has been substantially limited with the implementation of the NDC scheme.

Gender equality is a problem in the Polish social security system. The different retirement ages for men and women were left unchanged during the reforms. Given the NDC pension scheme, the lower legal retirement age for women will lead to much lower pensions for them.

A problem which has not been addressed in the reforms is the existence of special pension systems for farmers. Poland is the only transition country with a separate system of social insurance for farmers. The benefits paid out by KRUS are almost entirely financed through state budget subsidies. Farmers were excluded from the reforms due to political reasons (lobbying). There are a large number of small farms which generate very low incomes. This limits the possibility for higher contributions. On the other hand, even large farmers pay rather low contributions compared to employees outside the agricultural sector who have similar incomes. Moreover they are exempt from PIT. Altogether, the system of social insurance for farmers is closer to a social assistance system than to a social insurance system.

Also the existence of separate sickness and health insurance systems has not been addressed in the 1999 reforms. Additionally, compared to other OECD countries, Poland has very high marginal contribution rates to the social security system[5], leading to an increased cost of labor.

---

[5]   Cf. OECD (2006), Tables III.1 and III.2.

4 Bibliography

Börsch-Supan, Axel (2003): "What are NDC Pension Systems? What Do They Bring to Reform Strategies?" Discussion Paper Series of the Mannheim Research Institute for the Economics of Aging, 42-2003, Mannheim.

Chlon-Dominczak, Agnieszka (2002): "The Polish Pension Reform of 1999", in: Fultz, Elaine: Pension Reform in Central and Eastern Europe. Vol 1: Restructuring with Privatization: Case Studies of Hungary and Poland. Geneva, ILO-CEET. pp. 95-205.

Eurostat (2006): "European Union Statistics", http://ec.europa.eu/eurostat, found 26/06/2006.

Golinowska, Stanislawa, Pietka, Katarzyna, Sowada, Christoph and Zukowski, Maciej (2003): "Study on the Social Protection Systems in the 13 Applicant Countries. Poland Country Study, carried out for the European Commission by GVG", GVG, http://ec.europa.eu/employment_social/ social_protection/docs/poland_final.pdf, found 07/07/2006.

Müller, Katharina (2003): "Die Rentenreformen in den mittel- und osteuropäischen EU-Beitrittsländern", in: Vierteljahreshefte zur Wirtschaftsforschung 72(4), pp. 551-564.

OECD (2001b): "Social Expenditure Database", http://www.sourceoecd.org, found 13/06/2006.

OECD (2004): "Social Expenditure Database", http://www.oecd.org/els/ social/ expenditure, found 28/06/2006.

OECD (2006): "OECD Tax Database", OECD, Internet: http://www.oecd.org/ document/60/0,2340,en_2649_34897_1942460_1_1_1_1,00.html, found 23/06/2006.

World Bank (2003): "Poland - Toward a Fiscal Framework for Growth", in: World Bank Report No. 25033-POL. Washington, D.C.

World Bank (2006): "Public Spending Cross Country Data", http://web.worldbank.org / WBSITE/EXTERNAL/TOPICS/ EXTPUBLIC SECTORANDGOVERNANCE/EXTPUBLICFINANCE/0,,contentMDK:20240133~ menuPK:2083280~pagePK:148956~piPK:216618~theSitePK:1339564,00.html, found 19/05/2006.

ZUS (2005): "Social Insurance in Poland", http://www.zus.pl/english/english.pdf, found 10/05/2006.

REVENUE ASSIGNMENT IN POLAND

RADOSŁAW WITCZAK[*]

The aim of this article is to present the system of the Polish local finances and different governmental institutions influencing them. The stress is put on the tax assignment between central government and local authorities. It should help to prepare acceptable solutions for the improvement of the system of local finances in Poland. The basis for the evaluation of the current tax assignment schemes are the theoretical principles established by the theory of fiscal federalism.

The first task is to describe and evaluate the degree of decentralization in Poland with respect to the structure of central and local governments. This will be done in section 1. In section 2 we will try to identify the influence of the social insurance system on local authorities in Poland. Section 3 will describe and evaluate the tax assignment in Poland.

1   Governmental Institutions in Poland

The layers of government in Poland can be broken down into three groups: central government, local authorities and social security institutions. The characteristics of central government institutions and local authorities in Poland will be presented in this part of the article. The question to be answered in this section is to what extent Poland has decentralized its structure of government.

1.1   CENTRAL GOVERNMENT IN POLAND

During the time of communism the role of the central government in Poland was almost omnipotent. The central authority was responsible for nearly everything. All governmental tasks were centrally planned and controlled. After the collapse of communism in 1989, Poland introduced a number of far-reaching social and economic reforms. These changes also included the redesign of the governmental system. The

---

[*]   Doctor, Institute of Finance, Banking and Insurance, University of Łódz,

question of this part is to what extent the central authorities have been decentralized or only deconcentrated.

The central government institutions consist of legislative and executive power. The structure of general government in Poland is presented in table II - 29.[1]

Table II - 29: The structure of central government in Poland

Level	legislation power	executive power
central state	Parliament (*Sejm & Senat*)	President, government, agencies subordinated to the Parliament,
assigned		Voivod, regional state agencies

Source: own elaboration

In Poland, the legislative power belongs to the parliament. Parliament consists of two chambers: the lower house called Sejm and the higher one called Senat. The members of the Sejm are elected in proportional elections under the condition that their party gets at least 5% of votes in the whole country. The election districts do not match the division into communes or poviats. The members of the Senat are elected in majority elections. The election districts generally correspond (with some exceptions) to the former division into 49 voivodships before the administrative reform in 1999. [2]

The right to propose new acts can be exercised by the members of the Sejm, the government, the president, the Senat or by groups of citizens. After adoption by the Sejm, bills are sent to the Senat. The Senat can reject the act or may suggest any amendments, which can be rejected again by the Sejm.[3]

The Sejm approves the Prime Minister appointed by the President but it can also propose its own candidate under certain circumstances. [4]

---

[1]   The system of judiciary power (which is independent from the central government, but under the control of the government and the president) is excluded due to the fact that the justice system is not a core of fiscal federalism

[2]   Constitution of the Republic of Poland of 4-2-1997; act of 4-12-2004 Election Ordinance to Sejm and Senat (Dz. U. 2004, No. 46, Poz. 499).

[3]   Constitution of the Republic of Poland of 4-2-1997.

[4]   Constitution of the Republic of Poland of 4-2-1997.

The next central government institution in Poland is the President. The President belongs to the executive power. He is elected directly. The scope of his rights is not very wide. In some situations he appoints the Prime Minister who is approved by the Sejm. Under particular conditions he may dissolve the parliament. He can veto almost any act passed by the parliament with the exception of the state budget act. The Sejm can reject a presidential veto with 3/5 majority.[5]

In addition to the President, the executive body is the Council of Ministers (the government), acting as a collective body. The Prime Minister has a strong position, which is very similar to the chancellor in Germany. He proposes the candidates for the different ministerial offices. He appoints the candidates for the majority of directors of central institutions. He also appoints the Voivods.[6] The Voivods represent the central government in voivodships. They are in charge of the central administration in the voivodships apart from "special administration", which, for example, comprises police or tax administration, which are controlled by the responsible minister. The main role of the Voivod is to coordinate central government policy on the regional level. The Voivod is also the supervising body of the subnational governments.[7] The regional audit chamber controls the financial activity of the local governments, supervises the legality, and gives opinions. Some executive institutions, like the Supreme Chamber of Control[8], are controlled by the Sejm.

1.2 LOCAL AUTHORITIES IN POLAND

In Poland, local authority is based on a three-tier division: gminas (communes), poviats (counties), and voivodships (provinces/regions). Two new sub-national levels - poviats and voivodships - were only established in 1999.

With regard to the electoral law applied when the council of a commune is elected, two types of communes can be distinguished: rural communes and urban communes. In the rural communes the council of the commune is elected following the majority principle. This kind of communes comprises several villages or small cities. In urban

---

[5]   Constitution of the Republic of Poland of 4-2-1997.

[6]   Constitution of the Republic of Poland of 4-2-1997.

[7]   The act of 6-5-1998 on the governmental administration in voivodship Dz.U. 1998 No 91 Poz. 577.

[8]   Bałaban, A. Rada Ministrów. Organizacja i funkcjonowanie, Zakamycze 2002; J. Glumińska- Pawlic, K. Sawicka, Budżet jednostki samorządu terytorialnego, Zielona Góra 2002.

communes (which can include not only the city itself but some villages as well) the council of the commune is elected according to the proportional representation principle.[9] In both types of communes the council of the commune is a controlling body. It has the same competences in all types of communes including the approval of the budget or the right to sell property of the commune.[10]

The executive power in a commune is wielded by the wójt (in rural communes) or the burmistrz – mayor in cities or president in some more important cities.[11] The executive power of all types of communes is elected by direct majority voting. The executive body of a commune has some decision-making competences like giving permission for the building of a house. It has the right to decide about the hiring of staff for the local administration. Some of its decisions, for example concerning finance and property, have to be approved by the commune's council.[12]

Some of the cities are equipped with more responsibilities. They are called cities with poviat rights. They combine both the tasks and the incomes of communes and poviats. The biggest cities (all capitals of voivodships and some other cities) have the statuses of cities with poviat rights. The city council is elected by proportional voting. It approves the budget or allows the sale of city property. The executive power of a city with poviat rights is in charge of all local administration.

The next level of subnational authorities is the poviat. A poviat comprises several communes. The council of a poviat is elected by proportional voting. It has decision-making powers and is a controlling body. The council of a poviat has the rights, for example, to approve the budget or to allow sale of poviat property.[13]

The executive power of a poviat is wielded by the board of the poviat with the starosta as chairman. The starosta is in charge of the whole poviat administration and has some decision making power. He is elected by the council of a poviat.

---

[9] Act of 7-16-1998 Election Ordinance to Councils of Communes, Poviats, Voivodships Dz.U. 1998 No 95 P. 602; Act of 6-20-2002 on the direct election of wójt, major and president Dz.U. 2002 No 113 P 984.

[10] Act of 3-8-1990 on local governments Dz.U. 1990 No 16 Poz. 95.

[11] According to the act of 3-8-1990 on local governments Dz.U. 1990 No 16 Poz. 95 the mayor has the title of president in cities with more than 100,000 inhabitants, and towns in which the president of the executive power had this title before the implementation of this act.

[12] The act of 3-8-1990 on local governments Dz.U. 1990 No 16 Poz. 95; H. Izdebski, Samorząd terytorialny. Podstawy ustroju i działalności, Warszawa 2001.

[13] Act of 6-5-1998 on poviat authorities Dz.U. 1998 No 91 Poz. 578.

The third tier of local authority is the voivodship. The council of the voivodship is elected by proportional voting. It has decision making powers and is a controlling body. The council of the voivodship elects the marshal of the voivodship as the chairman of the board of the poviat who has the executive power[14].

Poland has three levels of local governments. There are 2478 communes, including 65 cities with poviat rights, 314 poviats, and 16 voivodships.[15] They are politically independent from the central government. The Prime Minister and the Voivod monitor the activities of local governments for conformity with the law.

The central government can only suspend the subnational governments in a situation where there is a violation of the law (i.e. the exceeding of debt limits). The legal status of communes is the strongest because their existence as local governments is established in the Polish constitution.[16] The existence of local governments on the level of poviat and voivodship can be changed by an act passed by the parliament.

According to the Polish constitution, Poland is a unitary country. The central government has been partly deconcentrated. If we look at the structure of the central and the local governments we see that Poland is a decentralized country with respect to political aspects. According to the definition of a federal state given by Rosen Poland is even a federal state.[17]

2 The Relations between the Social Security System and Local Authorities in Poland

The way of financing the social security system can influence local finances. The needs to finance the social security system can be an obstacle to shifting sources from the central budget into local finances. In this section we will try to indicate the connection between the social security system and local finances in Poland.

The social security system in Poland comprises five kinds of branches:

- old age pension,
- disability and survivors pension,

---

[14] Act from 5.06.1998 on voivodship authorities Dz.U. 1998 No 91 Poz. 576.

[15] http://www.mswia.gov.pl/.

[16] See art. 163 of the Polish Constitution.

[17] Rosen, Harvey S. (2002): "Public Finance", 6th ed., Boston

- work accident,

- sickness,

- health.

Health insurance is completely separated from the other kinds of social insurances which are managed by the Social Insurance Fund. Health insurance is a system of benefits of preventive, diagnostic, therapeutical and rehabilitative character and is managed by the Health Insurance Fund.

The old age pension system concerns only getting a pension when reaching retirement age. In the case of women the retirement age is 60 years, for men it is 65 years. Due to many early retirement possibilities, the average age of retiring persons is less than the given limits.

The disability and survivors pension systems have to intervene in cases of a steady or a long time inability to work due to an accident or health problems. In such cases, the insured person gets the pension independent of his or her age.[18]

The work accident insurance system is associated with the steady or partial inability to work caused by work accidents. In contrast to the disability and survivors insurance system the insured person does not have to meet any conditions (like the time of insurance) to receive benefits.[19]

The sickness insurance system concerns the short time inability to work due to illness. Sickness benefits shall partly compensate for salary losses. The sickness insurance is not associated with getting services from the public health system.[20]

The system of financing the old age pension, disability and survivors pension, work accident and sickness insurance is organized differently for farmers and other insured persons.[21]

The social insurance system for farmers is managed by the Agriculture Social Insurance Fund. The contributions fixed for farmers are very low. They cover only a small part of the payments for the farmers. So the Funds of Farmers Social Insurance receives grants from the central state budget which amounted to above 93% of all incomes in 2003.[22]

---

[18] Salwa Z. Prawo pracy i ubezpieczeń społecznych, Warszawa : LexisNexis, 2004.

[19] Krajewski, A., Ubezpieczenia społeczne, Warszawa 2003.

[20] Salwa Z. Prawo pracy i ubezpieczeń społecznych, Warszawa : LexisNexis, 2004.

[21] Jastrzębska, J., Ubezpieczenia społeczne i zdrowotne w rolnictwie, Lublin : IMW, 2003

[22] Ministry of Finance, Sprawozdania z wykonania budżetu państwa za rok 2003, .p. 293

The old age pension, disability, and survivors pensions, as well as work accident and sickness insurances for other insured persons are appropriated funds.[23] They are managed by a special institution – the Social Insurance Fund which is accountable to the Prime Minister. The parliamentary control of these funds is limited, although they receive some grants (especially the old age pension and pension funds insurance have too little sources from contributions compared to their expenditures on benefits). In some situations the insurance is mandatory (for example, business activity, work). Only in some cases (for example, Ph.D. study) it is voluntary. The insured person has to pay contributions that differ for each kind of insurance.[24] The base for calculating the amount of benefits is gross wage with some exemptions.

For the old age pension system the contributions are collected from the employer, including both his own contribution and that of the employee. The contribution amounts to 9.76% each. The base for calculating the contribution are the gross wages (with some elements of wages as exceptions which are not included in the base). The contribution rate for the disability and survivors pension system amounts to 6.5% for both employer and employee. The contribution to the work accident insurance is only paid by the employer. The rate depends on the kind of business activity and the number of employee accidents. For the year 2006 the rate varies between 0.86% and 3.86%. Contributions to sickness insurance are paid only by the insured person and amounts to 2.45%.

The last branch of the social security system is the health insurance.[25] The health insurance system is associated with benefits of preventive, diagnostic, therapeutical and rehabilitative character. In some cases (for example, medical care for children) medical help does not depend on the contribution, thus it is in part a kind of social security policy. In 2006 the contribution rate to health insurance amounted to 8.75%. This rate will increase to 9% over the next years. Health insurance is handled by the National Health Fund, which now controls the health insurance system. The National Health Fund is directly subordinated to the government. The regional assigns of the National Health Fund sign contracts with hospitals concerning the number of medical services and the conditions of payment for them. In this way they decide about the scope of health treatment. Some of the hospitals are owned by different levels of local authorities. We have to point out that the basis for payroll taxes is already heavily

---

[23] See art. act of 10-13-1998 on the social security system Dz. U. 1998 No 137 Poz. 887

[24] Garbiec, R., System ubezpieczeń społecznych, Wydaw. Wydziału Zarządzania Politechniki Częstochowskiej, Częstochowa 2003

[25] Health insurance is regarded as a kind of social insurance, see R. Musgrave, P. Musgrave, Public Finance in Theory and Practice, 1973, p. 347

exploited to finance social security systems. In spite of the high social insurance contributions the revenues of social insurance institutions from this source are not sufficient to cover all expenditures. The grants from the central budget amounted to a share of 14.94% in 2003 of the overall revenues of the social insurance institutions.[26] Therefore a decrease of the level of social security contributions is very difficult to implement.

The social insurance system is generally independent from the local governments in Poland. Only in the case of financing medical services it influences the local finances, especially the expenditures for fulfilling the health tasks of sub-national authorities.

3 Revenues of Government Levels in Poland

According to the principles of the theory of fiscal federalism the main sources of income for both the central and subnational governments ought to be taxes and user charges.[27] A proper local tax is defined as one that is assessed by a local government, at rates decided on by that government, collected by that government, and whose revenues accrue to that government.[28] The way of administrating taxes in Poland will be described in section 3.1. The tax assignments among governmental levels in Poland will be discussed in section 3.2.

3.1 TAX ADMINISTRATION IN POLAND

The revenue of both the central and the local levels are influenced by tax administration and the way of tax collection. We will discuss whether the Polish tax system is ready for the implementation of proper local taxes. The Polish tax administration is divided into tow separate groups: tax revenue administration and fiscal control.[29]

---

[26]   The author's own calculations, based on Ministry of Finance, Sprawozdanie z wykonania budżetu państwa za rok 2003, p. 219

[27]   See L. Ponterlitschek, Theory of Fiscal Federalism, in : Editor's Volume "Poland on its way to a federal state?"

[28]   See L. Ponterlitschek, Theory of Fiscal Federalism, in : Editor's Volume "Poland on its way to a federal state?".

[29]   Kulicki, J., Kontrola Skarbowa, Dom Wydawniczy ABC, Warszawa 2000.

The tax revenue administration collects taxes and may take certain decisions concerning the taxpayers. It has the authority to diminish the tax amount in individual cases. The tax revenue administration consists of the central and the local tax administration.[30] The central tax administration is responsible for the collection and administration of all central taxes and some local taxes. It is subordinated to the Ministry of Finance. Their officials are regarded to be not as well qualified as the staff employed in fiscal control.[31] The local tax administration has its own structure, which is independent from the central tax administration. It is responsible for the executive power of each level of subnational government. In fact, a local tax administration exists only in communes. An open question is whether the officials of this administration are prepared very well for controlling taxes. This plays an important role in Poland where tax evasion is at a high level.[32] The poviats and voivodships do not have their own tax administrations because they do not receive any taxes.

Fiscal control is responsible for the control of taxpayers (including local taxes). It is accountable to the Ministry of Finance, so in practice fiscal control concentrates on controlling central taxes.[33]

The regulations concerning the question which level of government decides on the design of taxes will be explained in part 2.2.

3.2 TAX ASSIGNMENT IN POLAND

The assigning of taxes to different levels of government in Poland will be discussed in this section. User charges[34] are included in this discussion.[35] Taxes and user charges can be divided into three groups: local taxes and user charges, shared taxes, central taxes. They play an important role in the revenues of local governments (see Table II - 30).

---

[30]   Kulicki, J., Kontrola Skarbowa, Dom Wydawniczy ABC, Warszawa 2000

[31]   Kuzińska, H., Osiem grzechów głównych, Rzeczpospolita, December 15-16, 2001; D. Szubielska, Kontrole: podatkowa i skarbowa – istotne wątpliwości, Przegląd Podatkowy 7/2002

[32]   See Ministry of Finance, Biała Księga Podatków, Biuletyn Skarbowy 5/1998, pp. 16-17.

[33]   Kuzińska, H., Osiem grzechów głównych, Rzeczpospolita, Decemeber 15-16, 2001.

[34]   "user charges" is used as a generic term for all kinds of charges, fees, and duties.

[35]   See L. Ponterlitschek, Theory of Fiscal Federalism, in : Editor's Volume "Poland on its way to a federal state?"

Table II - 30: Revenues of the subnational governments (in m PLN) in 2004

Type of revenue	Gminas	Poviats	Voivodships
Own revenues	**39,513.9**	**3,070.1**	**4,116.7**
Share in income from CIT	1,462.2	94.3	3,368.6
Share in income from PIT	13,263.1	1,288.3	527.4
Agricultural tax	921.8		
Tax on real estate	10,953.6		
Forest tax	118.7		
Tax on means of transport	616.3		
Tax paid by small firms in the form of tax card	131.3		
Tax on inheritances and gifts	218.9		
Tax on civil law transactions	1,053.0		
Stamp duty	575.1		
Other fees	2,473.2	817.0	27.7
Revenue from property	3,556.8	220.0	56.1
Other own revenue	4,169.8	650.6	136.9
Conditional grants	**8,525.2**	**3,025.2**	**1,559.0**
Unconditional grants	**23,683.9**	**6,340.3**	**1,290.0**
Revenue from the EU	**339.2**	**35.7**	**4.5**
Total	**72,062.2**	**12,471.3**	**6,970.2**

Source: Ministry of Finance, http://www. mf.gov.pl

3.2.1 Local Taxes and User Charges

In this section we will present the elements of the local taxes' parameters. Following this, we will discuss whether the taxes that are used as local taxes in Poland are "good" local taxes according to the theoretical literature. We will try to identify to what extent local governments in Poland have autonomy concerning tax base and tax rate. All local taxes in Poland are only levied at the communal level. There are no local taxes at the level of voivodships or poviats. Local taxes can be broken down into: property taxes, business taxes, sales taxes, other taxes and user charges (fees).

3.2.1.1   Property Taxes

Property taxes are considered to be typical local taxes. Property taxes in Poland include real estate tax, agriculture tax, forest tax, inheritance and donations tax, and the tax on means of transport.

The real estate tax is levied on buildings and land. It is a source-based tax. The tax base is the surface of real estates. In some cases the tax base for the real estate tax is the value of the real estate. The tax rate depends on the kind of property (houses, non-residential buildings, land). The maximum tax rates for each tax subject are established at the central level by the parliament. Due to inflation the maximum tax rates can increase every year. Until 2002 communes had the right to reduce the tax rate but only to half the level of the maximum rate. From 2003 onwards they can establish the tax rate from zero to the maximum level. Communes can vary the tax rates in respect to the area. There are some exemptions, which were set by the parliament. Communes can widen the exemptions, but they are not able to disregard the exemptions established by the parliament. This tax is collected by the local tax administration. [36]

Currently there are discussions concerning the imposing of the real estate tax value in Poland. There are two problems which make a quick implementation of the real estate tax value difficult. The first one is the lack of lists of real estate in Poland. The second concerns the way in which the value of real-estate should be calculated. Due to these problems, the Ministry of Finance plans to introduce the real estate tax value no earlier than in 2007. [37]

The real estate tax is a typical property tax. It should be assigned to the local level because the tax subject is immobile and the revenues are stable. However, local authorities should have the right to vary the tax rate without any limits set by the central government. [38]

The next property tax is the agriculture tax. The agriculture tax is imposed on land associated with agricultural activity. The central parliament sets the tax base. The tax base is the so-called "countable surface of area", but only for bigger areas (i.e. more than one real or one countable hectare together); for smaller pieces the base is their real surface. That tax is a source-based tax. The countable surface of area is a specific established measure. It depends on the real surface of the agricultural area, the type of soil, the kind of agricultural activity, and the commune in which the agriculture area is situated. The countable surface of area reflects the productive capability of the agricultural activity. The maximum tax rate is set by the parliament but the communes can establish the tax rate at a lower level. There are some exemptions, which were

---

[36] Act of 1-12.1991r. on local taxes and fees (Dz. U. z 1991r. No 9 P. 31 z późn. zm.), Etel, L., Podatek od nieruchomości, rolny, leśny, C. H. Beck, Warszawa 2005, pp. 31-346.

[37] The real-estate tax, Conference at Centrum Dokumentacji i Studiów Podatkowych, Łódź 2003.

[38] See L. Ponterlitschek, Theory of Fiscal Federalism, in : Editor's Volume "Poland on its way to a federal state?".

also set by the parliament. Communes can widen the exemptions but they cannot eliminate the exemptions established by the parliament. The agriculture tax is collected by the local tax administration.[39]

The agriculture tax is also a typical property tax. The tax is imposed on the immobile property and such taxes should therefore be assigned to the local authorities. The question arises if local authorities should have the right to impose their own tax rates without regarding the limits imposed by the central government.[40]

The forest tax is imposed on forest areas. It is a typical property tax. The parliament sets the tax base and the maximum level of the tax rate. Communes can reduce the tax rate or add more exemptions. It is a source-based tax. The forest tax is collected by the local tax administration.[41] Due to fact that this tax is levied on immobile property, it should be assigned to the local level as is done in Poland.[42]

Another type of the communes' revenue is the donation and inheritance tax. Tax base and tax rates are established by the parliament. Exemptions and progressive bracket rates are applied. This tax is collected by the central tax administration. For some subjects of this tax it is a residence-based tax. For others it is a source-based tax. The central tax administration passes the revenue from this tax to the communes. The rules of transferring the revenues depend on the tax subject.[43] The donation and inheritance tax can be classified as a property tax. It should be generally assigned to the local authorities which should have influence on both tax base and tax rates. Due to the fact that it is imposed on mobile property it can be administrated by the central government.[44] In Poland, local governments have no influence on any of the tax parameters

The tax on means of transport can be classified as a property tax. It is imposed on lorries, buses and other kinds of vehicles. It is a residence-based tax. The tax base is established by the parliament. The commune decides about the tax rate but within the

---

[39] Brzeziński, B., Wstęp do nauki prawa podatkowego, Dom Organizatora, Toruń 2001, p. 58.

[40] Hanusz, A., Czerski, P., Gminne podatki i opłaty budżetowe, Zakamycze 2004, pp. 53-78.

[41] Mastalski, R., Prawo podatkowe II – część szczegółowa, Warszawa 1998, p. 358.

[42] see L. Ponterlitschek, Theory of Fiscal Federalism, in : Editor's Volume "Poland on its way to a federal state?".

[43] Gliniecka, J. Zasady polskiego prawa dochodów samorządu terytorialnego, Oficyna Wydawnicza Branta, 2001 pp. 47-48.

[44] see L. Ponterlitschek, Theory of Fiscal Federalism, in : Editor's Volume "Poland on its way to a federal state?".

limits set by the parliament. The tax on means of transport is collected by the local tax administration.[45] The tax on means of transport is also a good local tax and insofar appropriate for the use at regional or local level. [46] The question arises whether local authorities should have the right to impose their own tax rates without any limits from the central government.

3.2.1.2   Business Taxes

Business taxes can be assigned to the local levels. In Poland, there are the following local business taxes: the chart tax and the market charge.

The chart tax is a kind of lump sum income tax. It is a source-based tax. It is imposed on incomes from specific kinds of small-business activity. The parliament decides about tax base and tax rates. The tax base is the estimated income of the firm. The tax rate depends on the type of business activity, the place where business activity is conducted and the size of this activity. It is mainly measured by the number of employees. The chart tax is collected by the central tax administration.[47]

In theory there is no agreement on the imposition of such taxes. Bird thinks that subnational taxation of corporate income should be avoided. According to McLure local governments can impose business taxes.[48] Concerning Poland we have to point out that corporations can do business in more than one local jurisdiction. But the Polish chart tax does not have a formula to divide a corporation's income among different jurisdictions. Local governments have no influence on any of the tax parameters. Such a tax is more similar to a shared tax, but the local governments have a 100% share in tax revenues collected by the central authority.

The market charge is another kind of business tax. Although the name is 'market charge' it has all the parameters characteristic of a tax and is in fact a kind of lump sum tax. This tax also belongs to local business taxes. Sole tax base is the fact of an existing business activity concerning the sale of goods on the markets. It is paid independent of the fees for the right to sell on the market. The tax base does not

---

[45]   Etel, L., Zmiany zasad opodatkowania środków transportowych, Przegląd Podatkowy, 2/2002, pp. 44-48.

[46]   see L. Ponterlitschek, Theory of Fiscal Federalism, in : Editor's Volume "Poland on its way to a federal state?"

[47]   Łukowicz, A. Karta podatkowa w 2003 r., Difin, Warszawa 2003.

[48]   see L. Ponterlitschek, Theory of Fiscal Federalism, in : Editor's Volume "Poland on its way to a federal state?".

depend on the amount of profit or turnover. It is a source-based tax. The tax base is established by the parliament. The commune decides about the tax rate but within the limits set by the parliament. The tax rate is flat and is the same for all firms selling on the market. The market charge is collected by the local tax administration.[49] According to theory, the local authorities can levy such taxes. [50]

3.2.1.3   Other Taxes

Other taxes are the tax on civil law transactions, the resort duty, and the dog tax.

The tax on civil law transactions concerns non-business transactions signed by individuals who are not liable for VAT. It is imposed on different contracts like sale or loan contracts. However, in some cases it concerns contracts involved with business activity like the setting up of corporations. The parliament sets down the tax base and tax rates. The tax rates are flat and their level depends on the type of the tax subject. The tax on civil law transactions is collected by the central tax administration. For some subjects of this tax it is a residence-based tax. For others it is a source-based tax.[51] To some degree the tax on civil law transactions can be classified as a general sales tax. The assignment of this tax corresponds to the theory. It should be levied and administrated by the central government, as is done in Poland.[52] It is similar to a shared tax where the local governments receive a 100% share of the revenues collected by the central authority.

The next tax is the resort duty.[53] In spite of its name the resort duty has all parameters characteristic for a tax. It is imposed on tourists coming to specific resort communes. The tax base is established by the parliament. The central government (voivod) decides on the communes which can implement this tax. The commune decides about the tax rate but within the limits set by the parliament. The resort duty is collected by

---

[49]   Hanusz, A., Czerski, P., Gminne podatki i opłaty budżetowe, Zakamycze 2004, pp. 209-217.

[50]   See L. Ponterlitschek, Theory of Fiscal Federalism, in : Editor's Volume "Poland on its way to a federal state?".

[51]   Zdanowicz, J., Podatek od czynności cywilnoprawnych. Opłata skarobowa, C. H. Beck, Warszawa, 2004, p.23-123.

[52]   See L. Ponterlitschek, Theory of Fiscal Federalism, in : Editor's Volume "Poland on its way to a federal state?".

[53]   Although the name is 'place charge' it has all the elements of construction characteristic for a tax

the local tax administration. [54] It is a source-based tax. It is a kind of a lump sum tax and its assignment corresponds with the theory. The next local tax is the dog tax. It is a residence-based tax. Tax base and the maximum tax rate of the dog tax are established by the parliament. The tax rate is flat. The commune can set the tax rate up to the maximum limit and can establish its own exemptions. The dog tax is paid to the local tax administration. [55] A dog tax is a good local tax because tax subjects are immobile, the revenues are stable and it corresponds to the pay-as-you-use-principle: local government incur costs due to the existence of dogs (for example, the cleaning of roads).

3.2.1.4 User Charges

User charges can be levied at all levels of government. Some of the most important local charges are: exploitation duty, stamp duty, administration fee, real-estate fee.

Until 2001, the exploitation fee had all elements of a tax. It was imposed on the production of minerals. Tax base was a corporation's turnover. Tax base and tax rates were established by the parliament and the Ministry of Finance. The tax rate was flat. This tax was collected by the local tax administration. The local authorities had no influence on either tax base or tax rate. [56] It was a source-based tax. The exploitation fee could be classified as business tax. Since the changes to the law in 2001 it is more similar to a typical user charge. Turnover is not the tax base anymore, but the kind of exploited minerals like sand, silver. Parliament and the Ministry of Finance still establish the tax base and tax rates, but it is collected by the local tax administration. [57]

Stamp duty is imposed on individuals when receiving public services like the issuing of officials documents. Duty base and duty rates are established by the parliament. It is collected by the local tax administration. It is a source-based charge. [58]

The administration fee can be imposed for administrative functions of the communes if those functions are not financed by funds from the central government. The council of

---

[54] Hanusz, A., Czerski, P., Gminne podatki i opłaty budżetowe, Zakamycze 2004, pp. 217-221.

[55] Act of 1-12-1991r. on local taxes and fees (Dz. U. z 1991r. No 9 P. 31 z późn. zm.)

[56] Bordo, A., Finanse Publiczne RP, Bydgoszcz 2000, pp. 149-151;

[57] Hanusz, A., Czerski, P., Gminne podatki i opłaty budżetowe, Zakamycze 2004, pp. 226-230.

[58] Zdanowicz, J., Podatek od czynności cywilnoprawnych. Opłata skarobowa, C. H. Beck, Warszawa, 2004, pp. 123-181.

communes can set down the subject, the base and the rate. The parliament establishes the limits for this charge. The administrative fee is collected by the local tax administration. It is a source-based charge.[59]

The real-estate fee is imposed on those real estates the value of which has grown in association with infrastructure investments made by the commune. The commune establishes the charge base and the rate of the fee.[60]

All presented user charges are used at the level of local authorities as they realize the benefit principle for public services.

3.2.1.5   The Role of Local Taxes and User Charges for Local Governments

Only communes and cities with poviat rights have some revenues from local taxes and user charges. The degree of autonomy is different for the individual taxes. With respect to some taxes like real estate tax, agriculture tax, forest tax, the tax on means of transport, and the dog tax local authorities have an influence on tax base and on tax rate. However, communes and cities with poviat rights cannot set the tax base entirely independent from the central government.

For some taxes the local governments can set their own tax rates only within limits given by the parliament: this is true for the tax on means of transport, the market charge, and the resort duty.

For some taxes communes and cities with poviat rights cannot influence any of the tax parameters. They do not even collect these taxes. Among these taxes are: the donation and inheritance tax, the tax on civil law transactions, the chart tax, and the exploitation duty. Such taxes are more similar to shared taxes where the local governments get a 100% share of the revenues collected by the central authority.

In order to evaluate the degree of fiscal autonomy of local governments in Poland we should not include these taxes and user charges into their own revenues, because they are entirely controlled by the central government.

---

[59]   Hanusz, A., Czerski, P., Gminne podatki i opłaty budżetowe, Zakamycze 2004, pp. 203-209.

[60]   Hanusz, A., Czerski, P., Gminne podatki i opłaty budżetowe, Zakamycze 2004, pp. 221-226.

3.2.2 Tax-sharing Arrangements in Poland

Shares in taxes collected by the central government are another revenue source for local governments. Two taxes are shared between the central and sub-national governments: the corporate income tax and the personal income tax.

3.2.2.1   Tax-sharing Arrangements for the Corporate Income Tax

Tax base and tax rate of the corporate income tax is established by the parliament. The tax rate is flat at 19 %. The corporate income tax is collected by the central tax administration.[61] According to theory, this tax should be assigned to the central government but can be shared with different levels of governments.[62]

The revenues from this tax flow to those subnational governments in whose domains the seat of a company is situated. If corporations have divisions in other jurisdictions the revenues are divided between the different local authorities. The base for this division is the number of employees.[63]

The shares of corporate income tax differ dependent on the levels of local authorities. After the reforms in the financial system, which were implemented in 2004, shares were altered as well.

In the years 1999 to 2003 the communes received a share of 5%, voivodships a share of 1%. [64]

From 2004 onwards, the communes receive a share of 6.71%, poviats get a share of 1.4 % and voivodships a share of 15.9%.[65]

The increase of the overall shares of local governments in corporate income tax suggests a growth of local revenues.

---

[61]   Marciniuk, J. Podatek dochodowy od osób prawnych. Rok 2004, Beck, 2004

[62]   See L. Ponterlitschek, Theory of Fiscal Federalism, in : Editor's Volume "Poland on its way to a federal state?".

[63]   Rozporządzenie Ministra Finansów z dnia 23 grudnia 2003 roku w sprawie rozliczeń dochodów z tytułu udziału jednostek samorządu tertytorialnego we wpływach z podatku dochodowego od osób prawnych Dz.U. 2003 No 224 P. 2228

[64]   Act of 11-26-1998 r. on Revenues of subnational governments in the years 1999 and 2000, Dz.U. 1998 No 150 P. 983.

[65]   Act of 11-13-2003 r. on Revenues of subnational governments, Dz.U. 2003 No 203 P. 1966.

However, the increase of revenues for local governments may not be as substantial. It has been at least partly compensated by the reduction of the tax rate from 34% in 1999 to 19% in 2004.

3.2.2.2 Tax-sharing Arrangements for the Personal Income Tax

The next shared tax is the personal income tax. It also comprises the payroll tax. Tax bases and tax rate of the personal income tax are established by the parliament. In principle the tax schedule is progressive, however for some subjects the tax rate is flat (it concerns, for example, the incomes from business activity). The local governments have no influence on the level of the tax rate. The personal income tax is collected by the central tax administration. [66]

The assigning of the personal income tax to the central government is due to the fact that the central government can use a progressive income tax for redistribution and stabilization purposes. Therefore, the personal income tax in Poland is collected by the central tax administration. But a certain share is allocated to the local governments. Base for the distribution among the different jurisdictions is the amount of income tax collected by the central tax authority from taxpayers living in the area of the local government two years before the establishment of the shares. [67]

In the reforms implemented in 2004 the shares of subnational authorities were changed as well.

In the years 1999 to 2003 communes had a share of 27.6 %, poviats received a share of 2.5 % and voivodships a share of 1.5 %. [68]

From 2004 onwards communes receive 39.34 %, poviats get 10.25 % (except for 2004 during which the share were diminished to 8.42 %) and voivodships receive 1.6 % of the total personal income tax revenues. [69]

Under the circumstances described in Article 89 communes receive a share of 39.34% in the revenues from personal income tax. In reality this share will be much smaller for some communes for many years. In 2004 the share in the revenue from personal

---

[66] Marciniuk, J. Podatek dochodowy od osób fizycznych. Rok 2004, Beck, 2004.

[67] Art. of 11-13-2003 r. on Revenues of subnational governments, Dz.U. 2003 No 203 P. 1966.

[68] Act of 11-26-1998 r. on Revenues of subnational governments in the years 1999 and 2000, Dz.U. 1998 No 150 P. 983.

[69] Berezowska, E. Skutki zmian w ustawie o dochodach jednostek samorządu terytorialnego, in Finansowanie jednostek samorządu terytorialnego, Poznań 2004, p. 23.

income tax received by communes amounted to 35.7%. In the next years this share will be calculated for communes according to the following formula:[70]

$S = [0.3934 - 0.0381 \times (NIHSC_b / NIHSC_{2003})] \times 100\%$

in which:

S   -   the share of communes in the overall revenues from personal income tax

$NIHSC_b$ -   the number of inhabitants admitted to the houses of social care before the 1st of January 2004 according to the state on the 30th of June of the base year

$NIHSC_{2003}$ -   the number of inhabitants admitted to the houses of social care before the 1st of January 2004 according to the state on the 31st of June 2003

This formula implies that for some communes the shares will be smaller than 39.34% over the next years. The second part of the formula makes the shares dependent on the number of inhabitants admitted to the houses of social care.

3.2.3 Central Government Taxes

In addition to revenues form shared taxes, there are also several taxes which are exclusively assigned to the central level: VAT, business taxes, excise taxes, lump sum income tax on priests.

The design of VAT in Poland corresponds to the requirements specified in the EU VAT Directives. The normal VAT rate is 22%, the reduced rates amount to 7 % and 3% respectively (only for some period of time), and the exemption with the right to get back the tax collected in previous phases of purchase. Only parliament can decide about tax rates and exemptions. The central tax administration is responsible for the collection of the VAT.[71] The revenues from this tax are exclusively assigned to the central level. In the early 1990s local authorities received a share of the revenues from this tax but due to fiscal problems of the central budget VAT was turned into an exclusive central tax.

There are two business taxes assigned to the central authority: the lump sum income tax on business activity and the tax on games and mutual betting.

The lump sum income tax on business activity concerns small and medium business. Tax base (sales based on business activity) and tax rates are established by the

---

[70]   See, Biuletyn Finansów Publicznych, IBGR. 1/2004, p. 98.

[71]   Zubrzycki, J., Leksykon VAT 2005.

parliament. The tax rates are flat. The lump sum income tax on business activity is collected by the central tax administration. This tax is a residence-based tax.[72] In theory such taxes can be administrated by central governments or subnational authorities.

The tax on games and mutual betting is levied on incomes from games of chance. Tax base and tax rate are established by the parliament. The tax rate is flat. The central tax administration collects this tax. This kind of taxes can be assigned not only to the central authorities but to the subnational governments as well.

In Poland, excise taxes are imposed on the production or selling of specific products. Tax base and tax rates are established by the parliament. The level of tax rates depends on the type of products which are subject to the tax. The tax rate is flat. Excise taxes are collected by the central tax administration.

According to theory it is considered to give local authorities the right to impose such taxes. It is believed that subnational governments can administer excise taxes. They could levy excise taxes as destination-based taxes.[73] However, excise taxes in Poland are mainly imposed on the production. Insofar, the producers of taxable goods are the taxpayers. Thus it is a source tax and that is why it is assigned to the central authority.

In Poland, there is a lump sum income tax on priests. The revenues flow to the central government. Tax base and tax rates are established by the parliament. The tax rate depends on the function of the priest and the number of believers. This tax is collected by the central tax administration.[74]

---

[72] Huchla A., Zryczałtowany podatek dochodowy komentarz, Warszawa 2000.

[73] See L. Ponterlitschek, Theory of Fiscal Federalism, in : Editor's Volume "Poland on its way to a federal state?".

[74] Act of 11-20-1998. on lump sum income tax on some revenues received by physical persons. (Dz. U. z 1998 nr 144 poz. 930 z późn. zm.).

INTERGOVERNMENTAL TRANSFERS IN POLAND – LEGAL FRAMEWORK

TOMASZ URYSZEK AND LARS PONTERLITSCHEK

1 Intergovernmental Grants in Poland – Current Regulations

Since the beginning of 2004, a new Act on the Revenues of the Local Governments is in force. The new act was adopted on the 13th of November 2003. The intention of this act was to support the process of further decentralization and to increase local governments' own revenues of. Not only tasks but also financial means to finance them should be decentralized. The new act is intended to increase the responsibility of the local governments for the financial means received from the central budget. The most important changes brought about by the new Act on the Revenues of Local Governments are connected with changes in financing some own and delegated tasks co-financed by the state budget. In the old system, these tasks were financed by conditional grants, now they are fulfilled by local governments as their own tasks. This change in the competences of some tasks had an influence on the size of conditional grants. Moreover, higher shares of local governments in central taxes and a new construction of the unconditional grants were introduced. The basic, compensatory, and road parts of the general subsidies were abolished and replaced by newly designed types of unconditional grants.

Own revenues and unconditional grants are supposed to be the most important revenue sources of local governments. Conditional grants should only be a supplemental source of local incomes. Such an approach seems to follow the theory of fiscal federalism. However, the definition of "own revenues" does not correspond with that of "own incomes", according to the new Act on the Revenues of Local Governments, which includes (among others) the shared taxes.

According to the new act, the revenue sources of local governments are divided into:

- own revenues,

- unconditional grants (called 'general subsidies' in Polish laws and statistics[1]),
- conditional grants (called 'appropriated allocations' in Polish laws and statistics) from the central budget.

Table II - 31: Territorial self-governments' revenues (in m PLN) in 2005

Type of revenue	Gminas	%	Cities with poviat status	%	Poviats	%	Voivod ships	%
Own revenue	20,588	44.94	23,379	64.5	3,738	27.2	4,417	62.5
Appropriated allocations	7,433	16.22	3,961	10.9	3,046	22.1	1,128	16.0
General subsidies from the state budget	16,080	35.10	8,325	23.0	6,699	48.7	1,351	19.1
Revenue from non-budgetary sources	1,742	3,80	605	1.7	280	2.0	170	2.4
Total	45,813	100.0	36,270	100.0	13,763	100.0	7,066	100.0

Source: GUS (2006), pp. 429-430, own calculations.

The new act significantly changed the sources of revenues of the local governments. The current situation will be outlined in the following.

1.1 UNCONDITIONAL GRANTS

In table II - 31 we can see that large unconditional grants are given for the financing of local governments in Poland. Nearly one third of all revenues of local governments consist of unconditional grants. The share of general subsidies is even higher for gminas and poviats where they constitute 35 % and 49 % of all revenues respectively. The relative importance of these grants for cities with poviat status and voivodships, where they only constitute 23 % and 19 % of their total revenues, is considerably smaller.

The general subsidies are divided into different parts, which take into account the financial needs and partly the financial capacities of the local governments. Since 2004, the road part, basic part, and compensatory part are abolished. The equalizing part still exists, but the labels of the particular parts of this grant as well as the

---

[1]   Both notions will be used in the text.

calculation method used for these parts were changed in the new transfer scheme. A supplement was installed to compensate local governments which lost revenue due to the 2003 Act on Revenue of Territorial Self-governments. Currently, the following types of unconditional grants are transferred from the state budget to the local governments:

Table II - 32: The structure of unconditional grants

Unconditional grants	Local government		
	Gminas	Poviats	Voivodships
Educational part	+	+	+
Equalizing part	+	+	+
Balancing part	+	+	–
Regional part	–	–	+

Table II - 33: Breakdown of the general subsidies

GENERAL SUBSIDIES	2005 (in m PLN)	%
Total	32,455.7	100.0%
Educational part	**26,097.4**	**80.4%**
for gminas (excl. cities with poviat status)	12,139.5	
for cities with poviat status	7,851.2	
for poviats	5,542.2	
for voivodships	564.5	
Compensatory part (discontinued)	**11.8**	**0.0%**
for gminas (excl. cities with poviat status)	7.3	
for cities with poviat status	4.5	
Equalizing part	**4,731.5**	**14.6%**
for gminas (excl. cities with poviat status)	3,609.8	
for cities with poviat status	45.5	
for poviats	637.2	
for voivodships	439.0	
Balancing part	**909.7**	**2.8%**
for gminas (excl. cities with poviat status)	304.1	
for cities with poviat status	210.8	
for poviats	394.8	
Regional part for voivodships	**314.5**	**1.0%**
Supplement to general subsidies	**390.9**	**1.2%**
for gminas (excl. cities with poviat status)	19.6	
for cities with poviat status	213.5	
for poviats	125.3	
for voivodships	32.5	

Source: MINISTRY OF FINANCE (2007).

147

1.1.1 The Educational Part of the Unconditional Grants

The educational part of the unconditional grants is transferred to all types of local governments. It is by far the most important part of the unconditional grants, amounting to 80 % of all unconditional grants given to the local governments, as shown in table II - 33.

The total amount of the educational part to be distributed among the local governments is set down by the law on the state budget as "not less than in the previous year", which gives the local governments some planning reliability. The educational part of the general subsidies is calculated uniformly for all three levels of local government according to the following formulas:

(0.1)
$$s_i = S \times \frac{u_i}{U}$$

where:

s_i – educational part of the general subsidies for the i-th local self-government entity;

S – total distributable amount of the educational part of the general subsidies;

u_i – "converted" number of pupils in the i-th local self-government entity;

U – "converted" number of pupils in Poland.

The converted number of pupils in the i-th self-government entity (u_i) is calculated as:

(0.2)
$$u_i = d_i \times \sum_{k=1}^{39} n_{ik} \times P_{ik}$$

where:

d_i – "cost-coefficient" for the i-th self-government entity;

n_{ik} – number of pupils in the k-th category of pupils;

P_k – conversion coefficients, reflecting the different per capita costs of the individual educational tasks.

The coefficient d_i reflects the higher per capita cost of educational services in rural areas and is supposed to encourage the self-government entities to employ better qualified teachers. For the i-th self-government entity the coefficient d_i is calculated as follows:

(0.3)
$$d_i = \frac{\sum_{k=1}^{4} \omega_k \times T_{ik}}{\sum_{k=1}^{4} \omega_k \times T_k^*} \cdot \left(1 + 0.12 \times \frac{p_{iR}}{p_i}\right)$$

where:

ω_k – average wage of teachers in the k-th qualification group (k = 1,2,3,4);

T_{ik} – number of teachers in the k-th qualification group (k = 1,2,3,4) in the i-th self-government entity;

T_k^* – number of teachers in the k-th qualification group (k = 1,2,3,4) in Poland;

p_{iR} – number of pupils in rural schools in the i-th self-government entity;

p_i – number of pupils in schools in the i-th self-government entity.

As can be seen in the formulas above, the calculation of the educational part of the unconditional grant is very complex in Poland. One example of the exorbitant complexity are the 39 categories of pupils in formula (0.2) which grew from one category in 1996 to 39 categories over the last years. Examples of these categories (= educational tasks) are:

standard primary town schools for children, P = 1.0;

5.   standard primary "rural schools" for children, P = 1.38;

6.   secondary schools for children, P = 1.08;

7.   classes for handicapped children, P = 1.8, etc.

Another example of the complexity are the four different qualification groups of teachers in formula (0.3) which influence the size of the grant. There are various factors which determine the amount of the educational part given to the local governments. The most important factors are the number of pupils, the share of pupils that are located in rural areas in the total number of pupils in the self-government entity, the number and formal qualification of teachers employed by the government entity, and the type of school.

1.1.2 The Equalizing Part of the Unconditional Grants

The second important part of the general subsidies is the equalizing part which makes up for 14.5 % of all unconditional grants. This part was introduced in order to equalize the big differences between the revenues of the individual local governments. The equalizing part is transferred from the state budget to all types of local governments. Different calculation methods are applied for the three levels of local government:

1.1.2.1   Equalizing Part for Gminas

The equalizing part is split into a *basic amount* and a *completing amount*.

The basic amount

This amount is received by gminas in which the G indicator is lower than 92% of the Gg indicator:

$$G < 92 \text{ \% } Gg$$

where:

$$G = \frac{TR_g}{L_g}$$

TR_g – Tax revenues of the gmina in the year before the base year which, according to the legal acts, consist of real estate tax, agricultural tax, forest tax, the tax on means of transport, other local taxes and charges as well as the shares in PIT and CIT.

L_g – The number of inhabitants of the gmina on the 31st of December of the year before the base year.

The base year is the year before the current fiscal year.

$$Gg = \frac{TTR_g}{TL_g}$$

TTR_g – Total tax revenues of all gminas in the year before the base year.

TLg – Total number of inhabitants of the whole country on the 31st of December of the year before the base year.

Thus, the basic amount is given to gminas that have less than 92 % of the average fiscal capacity from the own revenues of all gminas. The amount that the gmina receives as the basic amount of the equalizing part of the unconditional grant depends on the difference between the G and Gg indicators. However, depending on the size of this difference, the calculation methods differ. There are three calculation methods which are applied:

If G ≤ 40% Gg:
Basic amount = $[(0.4 \times Gg - G) \times 0.9 + 0.4075 \times Gg] \times L_g$

If 40% Gg < G ≤ 75% Gg:
Basic amount = $[(0.75 \times Gg - G) \times 0.8 + 0.1275 \times Gg] \times L_g$

If 75% Gg < G < 92% Gg:
Basic amount = $[(0.92 \times Gg - G) \times 0.75] \times L_g$

The completing amount

This amount is given to gminas in which the population density is below the population density in Poland, but it is only available for gminas whose fiscal capacity does not exceed 150% of the average fiscal capacity of all gminas (G > 1.5×Gg). The sum that a gmina receives from the state budget is calculated as follows:

$$\text{Completing amount} = 0.17 \times Gg \times \frac{AD_c - AD_g}{AD_c} \times L_g$$

where:

AD_c – Population density in the whole country,

AD_g – Population density in the individual gmina.

The population density is defined as the number of inhabitants per 1 km^2.

1.1.2.2 Equalizing Part for Poviats

The allocation of the basic amount of the equalizing part is less complex for poviats as only one formula is used, irrespective of the size of the underprovision with tax revenues. This is different to the situation in gminas in which the size of the tax revenue gap has an influence on the design of the grant.

The basic amount

The basic amount is transferred to poviats in which the P indicator is smaller than the Pp indicator (P < Pp).

$$P = \frac{\text{tax revenues of the poviat in the year before the base year}}{\text{number of inhabitants in the poviat}}$$

$$Pp = \frac{\text{total sum of tax revenues of all poviats in the year before the base year}}{\text{number of inhabitants in the whole country}}$$

Thus, the basic amount is given to poviats which have per capita tax revenues below average. Tax revenues of the poviats, according to the Act on the Revenues of Local Governments, are their shares in the central taxes (PIT and CIT).

The sum of the basic amount is calculated as follows:

Basic amount = $0.88 \times (Pp - P) \times L_p$

where L_p is the number of inhabitants in the individual poviat.

After receiving the basic amount of the equalizing part, 88 % of the poor poviats' fiscal gap (Pp – P) is filled.

The completing amount

This amount is received by poviats with above average unemployment rates. It is given to poviats if the value of the b indicator is higher than 1.1 (b > 1.1).

$$b = \frac{\text{unemployment rate in the poviat (B)}}{\text{unemployment rate in the whole country (Bb)}}$$

The rate of unemployment is calculated by the statistical office.

The sum of this amount given to a poviat depends on the extent of the unemployment and is calculated in the following way:

If $1.1 < b \leq 1.25$:

Completing amount = $(b - 1.1) \times 0.1 \times Pp \times L_p$

If $1.25 < b \leq 1.40$:

Completing amount = $0.25 \times Pp \times (b - 1.25) + 0.015 \times Pp \times L_p$

If $b > 1.40$:

Completing amount = $0.4 \times Pp \times (b - 1.40) + 0.0525 \times Pp \times L_p$

1.1.2.3   Equalizing Part for Voivodships

Similar to the equalizing part for poviats, the basic amount given to the voivodships is granted uniformly, irrespective of the degree of the underprovision with tax revenues.

The basic amount

The basic amount is given to voivodships in which the W indicator is smaller than the Ww indicator (W < Ww), i.e. to voivodships that have below average per capita tax incomes from shared taxes:

$$W = \frac{\text{tax revenues of the individual voivodship in the year before the base year}}{\text{number of inhabitants in the voivodship}}$$

$$Ww = \frac{\text{tax revenues of all voivodships in the year before the base year}}{\text{number of inhabitants in the whole country}}$$

A voivodship's tax revenue consists solely of its share in the central PIT and CIT.

The basic amount is then calculated as follows:

Basic amount = $0.7 (Ww - W) \times L_v$

where L_v is the number of inhabitants of the individual voivodship.

Thus, after equalization 70 % of each voivodship's fiscal gap (Ww − W) is filled.

The completing amount

The completing amount is granted to voivodships in which the number of inhabitants is less than 3,000,000 people (L_v < 3,000,000). The amount given to the individual voivodships differs in dependency on the number of inhabitants in these voivodships[2]:

a) If $L_v \leq 2,000,000$:

$$\text{Completing amount} = 0.09 \times Ww \times \left(2,000,000 + \frac{L_v - 1,000,000}{2}\right)$$

b) If $2,000,000 < L_v \leq 2,500,000$:

$$\text{Completing amount} = 0.09 \times Ww \times \left(2,500,000 + \frac{L_v - 2,000,000}{2}\right)$$

c) If $2,500,000 < L_v \leq 3,000,000$:

$$\text{Completing amount} = 0.09 \times Ww \times \left(2,750,000 + \frac{L_v - 2,500,000}{2}\right)$$

The completing amount is not given to voivodships which have tax revenues that exceed 110 % of the average tax income of all voivodships ($W > 1.1 \times Ww$).

1.1.3 The Balancing Part of the Unconditional Grants

The balancing part is only granted to gminas and poviats. The total amount to be distributed is financed by contributions of wealthy gminas and poviats to the state budget (see section II 1.1.5). The algorithm to calculate the amount of the grant is annually set down by the Minister of Finance. In general, the distribution of the grant depends on the gminas' expenditures for social welfare and on the poviats' expenditures for social welfare, road infrastructure, and their general financial situation. Details of the distribution of this part of the general subsidies change yearly and are therefore not presented here.

---

[2] Note: The following formulas are written like this in the relevant law. All three formulas are identical and can be written as $0.09 \times Ww \times (1,500,00 + 0.5 \times L_v)$.

1.1.4 The Regional Part of the Unconditional Grants

The regional part is exclusively granted to voivodships. The total distributable amount of this part consists of contributions of wealthy voivodships to the state budget. There are five different criteria for receiving the regional part:

- 20 % of the total amount of the regional part is divided between the voivodships in which the rate of unemployment exceeds 110 % of the average rate of unemployment in Poland.

- Another 40% are divided between the voivodships in which the surface of the voivodship roads per capita is higher than the average surface of the voivodships' roads per capita in the country. The calculation of the sums given to the individual voivodships is quite complicated in both cases mentioned above.

- Another 10 % of the total sum of the regional part is given to those voivodships in which GDP per capita is below 75 % of average GDP per capita in Poland.

- The remaining 30 % of the total amount of the regional part of the grant is divided between the voivodships because of the changes in the way of financing the tasks.

- The algorithm to calculate the amount of the grant is annually set down by the Minister of Finance and is therefore not presented here.

1.1.5 Transfers from the Local Governments to the State Budget

As already mentioned, the balancing part and the regional part of the general subsidies are financed from transfers by the wealthy local governments to the state budget. There exist different regulations for the respective local levels which are explained in the following.

1.1.5.1 Transfers to the State Budget from Gminas

Gminas with per capita tax revenues that exceed 150 % of the average tax revenues of all gminas ($G > 1.5 \times Gg$) have to pay a part of the surplus to the state budget in the form of compulsory contributions. There exist three brackets for the calculation of these payments:

If $1.5 \times Gg < G \leq 2 \times Gg$:

Contribution = $0.2 \times (G - 1.5 \times Gg) \times L_g$

If $2 \times Gg < G \le 3 \times Gg$:

Contribution $= [0.1 \times Gg + 0.25 \times (G - 2 \times Gg)] \times L_g$

If $G > 3 \times Gg$:

Contribution $= [0.35 \times Gg + 0.3 \times (G - 3 \times Gg)] \times L_g$

1.1.5.2 Transfers to the State Budget from Poviats

Poviats whose tax revenues exceed 110 % of the average tax revenues of all poviats ($P > 1.1 \times Pp$) have to make contributions to the state budget. Again, three tax revenue brackets exist. The associated contributions are calculated as follows:

If $1.1 \times Pp < P \le 1.2 \times Pp$:

Contribution $= 0.8 \times (P - 1.1 \times Pp) \times L_p$

If $1.2 \times Pp < P \le 1.25 \times Pp$:

Contribution $= 0.08 \times Pp + 0.95 \times (P - 1.2 \times Pp) \times L_p$

If $P > 1.25 \times Pp$:

Contribution $= 0.1275 \times Pp + 0.98 \times (P - 1.25 \times Pp) \times L_p$

1.1.5.3 Transfers to the State Budget from Voivodships

Also voivodships which do not receive the basic amount of the equalizing grant because their tax revenues exceed 110 % of all voivodships' average tax revenues ($W > 1.1 \times Ww$) have to pay compulsory contributions to the state budget. In case of the voivodships, only two tax income brackets are applied for the calculation of their contribution:

If $1.1 \times Ww < W \le 1.7 \times Ww$

Contribution $= 0.8 \times (W - 1.1 \times Ww) \times L_v$

If $W > 1.7 \times Ww$

Contribution $= [0.48 \times Ww + 0.95 \times (W - 1.7 \times Ww)] \times L_v$

1.2 CONDITIONAL GRANTS

In 2004 there was a change in the competences with regard to several tasks; which were transferred from being central tasks which were delegated to local governments to become the local governments' own tasks. Before 2004, these tasks used to be delegated tasks; which consequently were financed by conditional grants. After becoming the local governments' own tasks, these tasks are now financed by higher shares in PIT and CIT. This change in competences reduced the relative importance of conditional grants for the financial situation of local governments, especially for poviats and voivodships.

According to the new Act on the Revenues of Territorial Self-governments, local governments can receive conditional grants from the state budget, from appropriated funds, or from other local governments. Allocations transferred from the state budget can be given for financing three types of tasks:

1. tasks delegated to local governments by law,

2. tasks delegated through contracts, and

3. the local governments' own tasks.

In general, the tasks delegated from the central government or by the other local governments should be financed with conditional grants sufficient for the execution of the transferred tasks.

Furthermore, conditional grants can be given for the local governments' own tasks such as regional development, investment in the field of education, or support of education in rural areas (including grants and financial help for youth in rural areas). In these cases, up to 50 % of total expenditures planned by the local government can be co-financed by the central government for the particular investment. Thus part of the conditional grants transferred to local governments is designed as matching grants in order to foster capital investment expenditures. The remaining 50 % should be financed by the local government's own sources, otherwise a part of the received grant has to be paid back to the state budget. This part is determined as the difference between the received amount of the specific grant and the value of own financial sources involved in financing the task. It can be written as follows:

$A = B + C$

where:

A — financial sources necessary to finance the particular task planned by the local government

B — own financial means of the local government; $B \geq 50\% A$,

C — conditional grant; $C \leq 50\% A$.

If $B < 50\% A$: the local government has to pay the money back to the central budget. This negative grant (D) is calculated as follows:

$D = C - B$ and $B < 50\% A$

Apart from the abovementioned criteria for the co-financing of certain tasks, there are no regulations concerning eligibility, maximum amount of allocations, procedures for applying for such transfers, selection criteria and so forth. This means that criteria are discretionary and depend on political decisions.

According to the Act on the Revenues of Local Governments, local authorities can also receive conditional grants to finance their own tasks included in the so-called Voivodship Contract, which is defined in the Act on the Principles of the Support for Regional Development. This contract is a kind of agreement between the central government (represented by the Voivods as the representatives of the central government in the individual voivodships) and the local government council, which covers tasks that were transferred from the central level to the local governments. These tasks should be compatible with the existing strategy of regional development. These contracts were intended as a form of financing tasks connected with the regional development.

2 Intergovernmental Grants in Selected Local Governments[3]

In order to give an impression of the changes in financing Polish local governments resulting from the 2004 reforms, the revenue structure of four selected local governments (one voivodship, two poviats, and one gmina) will be presented exemplarily in this section. Therefore, the shares of conditional and unconditional grants in total revenues of selected Polish local governments are shown.

2.1 THE REVENUE STRUCTURE OF THE LOCAL GOVERNMENT OF THE ŁÓDŹ VOIVODSHIP[4]

The revenue structure of the local government of the Łódź Voivodship is presented below. The most important revenue source for the Łódź Voivodship in 2003 were conditional grants. The changes that took place in 2004 altered this situation. The share of conditional grants decreased to 58 % of its 2003 value. The absolute value of educational grants slightly increased while the equalizing grants increased by more

---

[3] The data for his section were obtained directly from the particular local authorities.

[4] The Łódź Voivodship (or: lodzkie voivodship, Łódź Voivodship; in Polish called "województwo łódzkie") is the voivodship whose capital is Łódź. The name "the Łódź Voivodship" or "the Lódz voivodship" is its official English name (source: www.lodzkie.pl).

than 250 %. The relative importance of unconditional grants for the financial situation of the voivodship decreased because in the meantime the most important revenue source of the Łódź Voivodship are shared taxes, particularly shares in the corporate income tax.

Table II - 34: Intergovernmental grants in total revenues of the local government of the Łódź Voivodship

	2003		2004		2004/2003
	in PLN	in % of total revenues	in PLN	in % of total revenues	Dynamics
TOTAL REVENUES	209,487,157	100.00%	323,573,193	100.00%	154.46%
of which:					
Unconditional grants	83,680,879	39.95%	87,315,804	26.98%	104.34%
of which:					
Educational part	31,152,461	14.87%	33,122,390	10.24%	106.32%
Equalizing part	19,259,510	9.19%	52,293,414	16.16%	271.52%
Road part	33,268,908	15.88%	---	---	---
Supplement to the unconditional grant to finance investments started before 1 Jan. 1999	---	---	1,900,000	0.59%	---
Conditional grants	88,321,428	42.16%	51,436 092	15.90%	58.24%

Source: Authors' own elaboration.

As can be seen in Figure II - 7, the changes in the structure of revenues of this local government seem to go in the right direction. The plunge of conditional grants in the structure of revenues of the Łódź Voivodship is indisputably favorable. The conditional grants were replaced by other sources of revenues ("the rest" mainly consists of shared taxes), which can be spent on the tasks assigned by the individual local government (instead of conditional grants, which can only be spent on the specific given task). However, it is still an open question whether the increase in shared taxes can be interpreted as a rise in the independence of the local government.

Figure II - 7: Changes in the revenue structure of the local government of the Łódź Voivodship

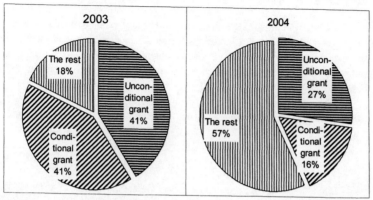

Source: Authors' own elaboration.

Figure II - 8: Structure and changes of the unconditional grant in the local government of the Łódź Voivodship

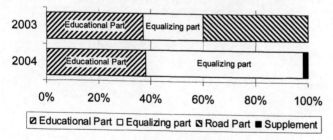

*) Supplement to the unconditional grant to finance investment started before 1-1-1999

Source: Authors' own elaboration.

The largest part of the unconditional grant in the Łódź Voivodship has been the educational part in 2003 which, however, can be spent for any task the local government chooses. In 2004, the equalizing part plays a more important role.

2.2 THE REVENUE STRUCTURE OF THE LOCAL GOVERNMENT OF THE ZGIERSKI POVIAT[5]

Zgierski Poviat is a poviat near the city of Łódź. The structure of its revenues is shown below. The table shows that total revenues increased although both unconditional and conditional grants decreased from 2003 to 2004. Table II - 35 gives the explanation for this: there has been a significant increase in the shared taxes which accrue to the poviat level in 2004.

Table II - 35: The share of intergovernmental grants in total revenues of the Zgierski Poviat

	2003		2004		2004/2003
	in PLN	in % of total revenues	in PLN	in % of total revenues	Dynamics
TOTAL REVENUES	64,956,372	100.00%	72,059,872	100.00%	110.94%
of which:					
Unconditional grants	33,566,213	51.68%	32,328,614	44.86%	96.31%
of which:					
Educational part	26,583,240	40.92%	27,298,111	37.88%	102.69%
Equalizing part	2,101,990	3.24%	3,024,232	4.20%	143.87%
Road part	4,880,983	7.51%	---	---	---
Balancing part	---		1,584,938	2.20%	
Supplement to the unconditional grant to finance investment started before 1 Jan. 1999	---	---	421,333	0.58%	---
Conditional grants	23,350,839	35.95%	19,119,666	26.53%	81.88%

Source: Authors' own elaboration.

---

5   Zgierski Poviat (in Polish: "poviat zgierski") is a poviat whose capital is Zgierz.

Figure II - 9: Changes in the revenue structure in the Zgierski Poviat

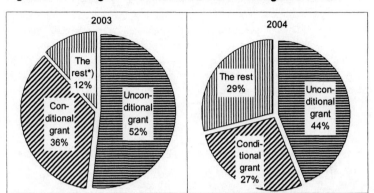

*) "the rest" means the own revenues according to the Polish legal acts. However, "the rest" does not only include local taxes and charges but also shared taxes. So, according to fiscal federalism theory the rest stands for more than own revenues.

Source: Authors' own elaboration.

As indicated in Figure II - 10, the structure of unconditional grants changed as a result of the reform. This change is shown below.

Figure II - 10: Structure and changes of unconditional grants in the Zgierski Poviat

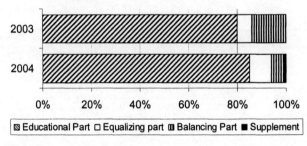

*) Supplement to the unconditional grant to finance investment started before 1 Jan. 1999

Source: Authors' own elaboration.

To some extent the changes in the structure of revenues and of unconditional grants are similar to those presented for the Łódź Voivodship. The decrease of conditional grants in the structure of revenues of the Zgierski Poviat is very optimistic. Similar to the situation of the local government of the Łódź Voivodship, conditional grants were replaced by other sources of revenues. These revenues can be used according to the decisions of the local government (instead of conditional grants, which can only be spent on the specific, indicated task). So, the local government becomes more responsible for task assignment within its territory. However, as poviats (similar to voivodships) are not allowed to impose their own taxes in Poland, they are still mainly financed from the state budget.

2.3 THE REVENUE STRUCTURE OF THE LOCAL GOVERNMENT OF THE PABIANICKI POVIAT[6]

The Pabianicki Poviat, similar to the Zgierski one, is a poviat near the city of Łódź. The structure of its revenues is shown below. In Pabianicki Poviat we find a very similar situation to that described for Zgierski Poviat. Total revenues increased due to a tremendous increase in own revenues from 2 % to 20 % of total revenues, while the revenues from grants decreased.

Table II - 36: The share of intergovernmental grants in total revenues of the Pabianicki Poviat

	2003		2004		2004/2003
	in PLN	in % of total revenues	in PLN	in % of total revenues	Dynamics
total revenues	41,924,351	100.00%	43,988,493	100.00%	104.92%
of which:					
unconditional grants	22,434,621	53.51%	20,176,758	45.87%	89.94%
conditional grants	18,505,027	44.14%	14,801,023	33.65%	79.98%
the rest	984,703	2.35%	9,010,712	20.48%	915.07%

Source: Authors' own elaboration.

---

[6]   Pabianicki Poviat (in Polish: "poviat pabianicki") is a poviat whose capital is Pabianice

Figure II - 11: Changes in the revenue structure in the Pabianicki Poviat

Source: Authors' own elaboration

As a result of the 2004 reform, this poviat started to finance a significant number of tasks from sources other than intergovernmental grants.

2.4   THE REVENUE STRUCTURE OF THE LOCAL GOVERNMENT OF THE GMINA PIĄTNICA

The revenue structure of this gmina is presented below.

Table II - 37: The share of intergovernmental grants in total revenues of the gmina of Piątnica

	2003		2004		2004 / 2003
	in PLN	in % of total revenues	in PLN	in % of total revenues	Dynamics
TOTAL REVENUES	13,829,373	100.00%	15,914,891	100.00%	115.08%
of which:					
Unconditional grants	8,404,539	60.77%	9,380,278	58.94%	111.61%
Conditional grants	1,139,763	8.24%	1,342,582	8.44%	117.79%
The rest	4,285,071	30.99%	5,192,031	32.62%	121.17%

Source: Authors' own elaboration.

Figure II - 12:   **Changes in the revenue structure in the gmina of Piątnica**

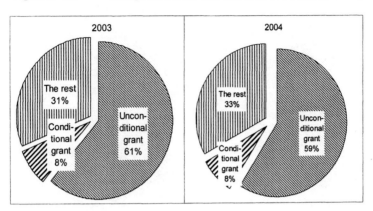

Source: Authors' own elaboration.

In contrast to the local governments presented above, the revenue structure of this gmina did not change significantly. However, the starting point for this gmina was not so bad. The share of conditional grants was small and this gmina used a lot of other revenues (including its own and shared taxes).

Apart from the (favorable) changes in the structure of the revenues of local governments it should be underlined that the financial means of the particular levels of local authorities are insufficient to finance the necessary tasks. The tasks are "underfinanced" and they are often executed at low standards.

3   Bibliography

GUS (2006): "Concise Statistical Yearbook of Poland", GUS,
        http://www.stat.gov.pl/english/opracowania_zbiorcze/maly_rocznik_stat/2006/10_
        chapters.pdf, found 31/07/2006.

Ministry of Finance (2007): "SPRAWOZDANIA BUDŻETOWE", http://www.mf.gov.pl
        /index.php?wysw=4&sgl=2&dzial=229, found 15/01/2007.

THE SELF-GOVERNMENT UNITS IN POLAND
FINANCIAL DATA

MARTA MACKIEWICZ,
ELŻBIETA MALINOWSKA-MISIĄG,
MARCIN TOMALAK

1 Revenue of the Territorial Self-Government Units

1.1 REVENUE OF ALL TSGs

The territorial self-government units' revenue consists of own revenues, general subsidies, and appropriated allocations from the state budget.

Own revenues of territorial self-government entities comprise:

- revenue from shares in corporate and personal income taxes,
- receipts from taxes established and collected on the basis of separate acts, i.e.: the tax on real estate, the agricultural tax, the tax on transport means, the tax on inheritance and gifts, the forest tax, the tax on civil law transaction,
- receipts from fees established and collected on the basis of separate acts,
- revenue from property of local self-government,
- other income, such as administrative fees, local fees, interest of funds.

General subsidies and allocations from the state budget will be described later.

Revenues of TSG are mainly own revenues – their share in the total revenue structure has even increased since 2003. Table II - 38 and Figure II - 13 describe this development.

Table II - 38: Revenue of territorial self-government entities from 1999 – 2005

Specification	1999	2000	2001	2002	2003	2004	2005
	10^6 PLN						
Total revenue	64,877.5	72,609.5	79,594.7	80,033.9	79,140.4	91,504.0	102,911.9
Own revenue	28,398.8	30,289.8	32,508.5	33,540.6	34,463.5	47,080.3	54,889.0
of which:							
share in taxes state budget's revenue	10,137.1	9,996.4	10,240.6	10,294.4	10,304.4	20,003.9	22,789.2
tax on real estate	5,943.9	6,644.1	8,504.9	9,768.3	10,123.3	10,953.5	11,668.6
revenue from property	4,272.5	5,051.4	3,296.2	3,115.2	3,359.5	3,832.9	4,334.1
Allocations	14,362.3	16,461.7	17,656.2	16,792.8	12,948.4	13,109.5	15,567.1
of which:							
from state budget	13,026.0	14,767.1	16,403.8	15,593.3	11,851.5	11,657.2	13,921.3
General subsidies	22,116.4	25,858.0	29,430.0	29,700.5	31,728.5	31,314.2	32,455.7

Source: Ministry of Finance and Statistical Yearbooks of the Republic of Poland, Central Statistical Office, Warsaw

Figure II - 13: Structure of the TSG revenue, 1999 – 2005

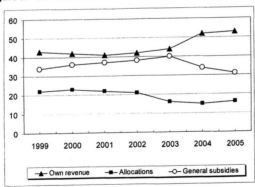

Source: Ministry of Finance and Statistical Yearbooks of the Republic of Poland, Central Statistical Office, Warsaw

The highest revenues are realised by gminas and cities with poviat status. In 2005, gminas' own revenues were PLN 22.3 billion, and the general subsidies from the state budget PLN 16.1 billion. In the cities with poviat status those proportions were shaped differently: own income was PLN 24.0 billion, and general subsidies PLN 8.3 billion.

1.2 THE REVENUES OF GMINAS

The major part of gminas' revenues are shares in tax revenues of the state budget in PIT and CIT. These shares are classified as own revenues of gminas, even though gminas do not have the right to decide about tax rates and exemptions. Gminas obtain the full amount of 7 *local taxes*, as well as the stamp duty, the marketplace charge, the local charge, the administrative charge and the charge for exploitation of mineral resources.

Table II - 39: Revenue of territorial self-government entities in 2005

Specification	Gminas[1]	Cities with poviat status	Poviats	Voivodships
		10^6 PLN		
Total revenue	**45,813.2**	**36,269.8**	**13,762.7**	**7,066.2**
Own revenue	22,300.5	23,983.9	4,017.7	4,587.0
Share in taxes state budget's revenue	6,712.7	10,244.3	1,895.7	3,936.5
Tax on real estate	6,994.9	4,673.7		
Revenue from property	1,622.4	2,437.5	210.5	63.6
Appropriated allocations	7,432.4	3,960.5	3,045.5	1,128.8
of which:				
– from the state budget	6,887.8	3,651.7	2,481.3	900.4
General subsidies from state budget	16,080.3	8,325.5	6,699.5	1,350.5

Source: Ministry of Finance

[1] Cities with poviat status not included

Table II - 40: Gminas'[1] revenue structure, 1999 – 2005

Specification	1999	2000	2001	2002	2003	2004	2005
				%			
Total							
Own revenue	52.6	50.9	50.3	49.9	51.2	55.3	56.4
General subsidies	32.1	32.8	35.0	35.2	37.8	32.9	29.7
Appropriated allocations	15.4	16.3	14.6	14.9	11.0	11.8	13.9
from the state budget	14.5	15.1	13.5	13.9	10.2	10.8	12.8
from appropriated funds	0.4	0.4	0.5	0.5	0.6	0.6	0.8

[1] Cities with poviat status included

Source: Ministry of Finance, authors' own calculations

Since 2004 there has been a decrease of the general subsidies' share in gminas' total revenue. The tendency to enlarge the general subsidies' share, visible since 1999, was stopped henceforth. The decline of the general subsidies' share does not originate from the limitation of that source of revenue, but is caused by extremely high own revenues.

Table II - 41: Revenue of gminas[2] by voivodships in 2004

Voivodships	Total	Own revenue	General subsidies	Appropriated allocations
		10^6 PLN		
Poland	**40,308.5**	**18,732.0**	**15,821.2**	**5,755.3**
Dolnośląskie	3,557.8	2,035.4	1,017.7	504.7
Kujawsko-Pomorskie	2,026.1	833.1	860.6	332.4
Lubelskie	2,409.5	831.3	1,211.3	366.9
Lubuskie	1,271.3	599.6	448.1	223.6
Łódzkie	2,627.1	1,280.2	991.7	355.2
Małopolskie	3,467.1	1,395.4	1,583.9	487.8
Mazowieckie	4,795.5	2,400.1	1,839.1	556.3
Opolskie	1,386.9	726.4	489.0	171.5
Podkarpackie	2,657.6	966.5	1,281.6	409.5
Podlaskie	1,160.7	447.6	551.7	161.4
Pomorskie	2,280.6	1,035.0	880.8	364.8
Śląskie	3,138.7	1,813.2	962.4	363.1
Świętokrzyskie	1,630.2	650.2	721.1	258.9
Warmińsko-Mazurskie	1,844.6	760.5	748.4	335.7
Wielkopolskie	4,016.5	1,938.0	1,563.8	514.7
Zachodniopomorskie	2,038.3	1,019.7	669.9	348.7

Source: authors ' own calculations based on Central Statistical Office (GUS) data

[2]   Cities with poviat status not included

In 2004, the largest total revenues were realised by the gminas from Mazowieckie and Wielkopolskie voivodships, but the largest own revenues by gminas from Mazowieckie and Dolnośląskie. Most of the general subsidies go to gminas from Mazowieckie, Małopolskie and Wielkopolskie voivodships.

The average revenues of gminas (including cities with poviats rights) per capita in 2004 were 1,591 PLN. Distribution of the revenues among the voivodships was not very different - in the "richest" voivodship (Zachodniopomorskie) the revenues of gminas per capita were only by 21.6% higher than in the "poorest" (Lubelskie). In 2004, the largest total revenues were realised by the gminas from

Table II - 42: Revenue of gminas* by voivodships in 2004, per capita

Voivodships	Total	Own revenue	General subsidies	Appropriated allocations
	PLN			
Poland (total)	**1,591.2**	**739.4**	**624.5**	**227.2**
Dolnośląskie	1,722.9	985.7	492.8	244.4
Kujawsko-Pomorskie	1,595.6	656.1	677.8	261.8
Lubelskie	1,470.1	507.2	739.1	223.9
Lubuskie	1,662.5	784.1	586.0	292.4
Łódzkie	1,557.0	758.7	587.7	210.5
Małopolskie	1,510.4	607.9	690.0	212.5
Mazowieckie	1,619.1	810.4	620.9	187.8
Opolskie	1,499.3	785.3	528.6	185.4
Podkarpackie	1,499.1	545.2	722.9	231.0
Podlaskie	1,489.5	574.4	708.0	207.1
Pomorskie	1,704.0	773.3	658.1	272.6
Śląskie	1,603.0	926.1	491.5	185.4
Świętokrzyskie	1,509.1	601.9	667.6	239.7
Warmińsko-Mazurskie	1,636.3	674.6	663.9	297.8
Wielkopolskie	1,584.3	764.4	616.8	203.0
Zachodniopomorskie	1,798.2	899.6	591.0	307.6

(* Cities with poviat status not included)

Source: authors' own calculations based on Central Statistical Office (GUS) data

Table II - 43: Poviats' revenue structure, 1999 – 2005

Specification	1999	2000	2001	2002	2003	2004	2005
	%						
Own revenue	6.2	7.9	8.6	10.8	11.3	24.9	29.2
General subsidies	44.4	47.7	46.3	47.0	56.1	50.8	48.7
Appropriated allocations	49.4	44.4	45.1	42.3	32.6	24.3	22.1
- from the state budget	48.5	43.7	44.1	41.0	31.3	22.6	18.0
- from appropriated funds	0.2	0.2	0.3	0.4	0.5	0.5	0.6

Source: Ministry of Finance, authors' own calculations

Table II - 44: Revenue of poviats and cities with poviat status by voivodships in 2004

Voivodships	Total	Own revenue	General subsidies	Appropriated allocations
	10^6 PLN			
Poland (total)	**44,225.1**	**23,136.2**	**14,203.0**	**6,885.9**
Dolnośląskie	3,314.0	1,750.5	1,041.1	522.4
Kujawsko-Pomorskie	2,321.7	1,071.4	842.8	407.5
Lubelskie	1,946.1	724.0	859.2	362.9
Lubuskie	953.7	371.5	392.4	189.8
Łódzkie	2,772.5	1,396.1	862.0	514.4
Małopolskie	3,244.1	1,600.8	1,133.0	510.3
Mazowieckie	8,597.5	5,893.9	1,779.9	923.7
Opolskie	774.0	321.9	300.2	151.9
Podkarpackie	1,592.4	524.4	737.1	330.9
Podlaskie	1,279.3	495.7	537.9	245.7
Pomorskie	2,895.0	1,683.6	839.1	372.3
Śląskie	7,035.8	3,973.5	2,022.0	1,040.3
Świętokrzyskie	1,012.8	341.8	442.8	228.2
Warmińsko-Mazurskie	1,372.9	511.8	568.0	293.1
Wielkopolskie	3,294.9	1,658.0	1,186.9	450.0
Zachodniopomorskie	1,818.4	817.2	658.5	342.7

Source: Authors' own calculations based on Central Statistical Office (GUS) data

1.3 REVENUES OF POVIATS

Until the end of 2003 poviats were predominantly financed by transfers from the state budget, especially by general subsidies. When the new law on the self-government units' revenue came into force, the share of own revenues in total revenue increased – as can be seen in table II - 43– from 11.3% to 24.9% in 2004 and to 29.2% in 2005.

In 2004, more than one third of total poviats revenues were realised by poviats from two voivodships: Mazowieckie and Śląskie. The share of own revenues in these two voivodships was even higher – 42.6%.

In 2004, the average revenue per capita in poviats and in cities with poviats status was PLN 1,158. The biggest revenues per capita were in Mazowieckie and Śląskie. In Mazowieckie voivodship own revenues were nearly twice as high as Poland's average own revenues.

Table II - 45: Revenue of poviats and cities with poviat status by voivodships in 2004, per capita

Voivodships	Total	Own revenue	General subsidies	Appropriated allocations
		per capita, PLN		
Poland (total)	**1,745.8**	**913.3**	**560.7**	**271.8**
Dolnośląskie	1,604.9	847.7	504.2	253.0
Kujawsko-Pomorskie	1,828.4	843.8	663.7	320.9
Lubelskie	1,187.4	441.7	524.2	221.4
Lubuskie	1,247.2	485.8	513.2	248.2
Łódzkie	1,643.1	827.4	510.9	304.9
Małopolskie	1,413.2	697.4	493.6	222.3
Mazowieckie	2,902.8	1.990.0	601.0	311.9
Opolskie	836.7	348.0	324.5	164.2
Podkarpackie	898.2	295.8	415.8	186.7
Podlaskie	1,641.7	636.1	690.3	315.3
Pomorskie	2,163.1	1.257.9	627.0	278.2
Śląskie	3,593.4	2.029.4	1.032.7	531.3
Świętokrzyskie	937.6	316.4	409.9	211.3
Warmińsko-Mazurskie	1,217.9	454.0	503.9	260.0
Wielkopolskie	1,299.7	654.0	468.2	177.5
Zachodniopomorskie	1,604.2	720.9	580.9	302.3

Source: authors' own calculations based on Central Statistical Office (GUS) data

1.4 REVENUES OF VOIVODSHIPS

Between 1999 and 2003, the bulk of the voivodships' revenues were constituted by transfers from the state budget. Appropriated allocations had a higher share in revenue, however, general subsidies had a noteworthy percentage in it too.

Till the end of 2003, voivodships' own revenues constituted (with 16%) a much smaller share of the total revenue than transfers. During three years of the new decade a share of own revenue in a total revenue did not even reach its level of the years 1999 – 2000. Relatively small revenues from PIT and CIT, as well as financing new tasks using appropriated allocations, increased the dependency of voivodships on the state budget. A breakthrough came in 2004 when, due to a growth of shares of voivodships in the revenues from PIT and CIT, own revenues constituted more than half of their total revenues.

Table II - 46: Voivodships' revenue structure, 1999 – 2005

Specification	1999	2000	2001	2002	2003	2004	2005
Own revenue	18.0	16.0	13.4	15.7	15.9	59.1	64.9
General subsidies	34.7	37.8	34.4	35.8	33.1	18.5	19.1
Appropriated allocations	47.3	46.2	52.2	48.5	51.0	22.4	16.0
from the state budget	43.9	41.4	47.5	42.1	45.0	18.6	12.7
from appropriated funds	0.1	0.4	1.2	1.7	1.6	0.9	0.8

Source: Ministry of Finance, authors' own calculations

Figure II - 14: Share of the self-government units' own revenues, 1990 – 2005

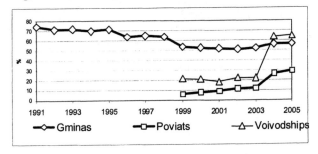

Source: Ministry of Finance, authors' own calculations

The revenues of voivodships are very diverse. The regions characterised by the highest revenue are Mazowieckie and Ślaskie. In 2004, the revenues of Podlaskie voivodship were almost 10 times smaller than those of Mazowieckie.

Table II - 47: Revenues of voivodships in 2004

Voivodships	Total	Own revenue	General subsidies	Appropriated allocations
	10^6 PLN			
Poland (total)	**6,970.3**	**4121.2**	**1,290.0**	**1,559.1**
Dolnośląskie	483.3	291.5	100.7	91.1
Kujawsko-Pomorskie	330.9	159.8	87.9	83.2
Lubelskie	325.5	110.2	127.3	88.0
Lubuskie	215.3	81.6	78.2	55.5
Łódzkie	325.1	188.9	87.3	48.9
Małopolskie	486.1	275.7	76.3	134.1
Mazowieckie	1,481.9	1328.7	57.1	96.1
Opolskie	163.1	73.9	52.6	36.6
Podkarpackie	344.5	130.0	114.9	99.6
Podlaskie	172.9	69.8	66.8	36.3
Pomorskie	378.1	238.4	54.4	85.3
Śląskie	1,016.2	529.4	85.3	401.5
Świętokrzyskie	200.5	67.1	61.2	72.2
Warmińsko-Mazurskie	253.9	87.3	79.0	87.6
Wielkopolskie	538.5	385.5	49.1	103.9
Zachodniopomorskie	254.6	103.6	112.0	39.0

Source: Central Statistical Office (GUS) data

Until the end of 2003 the per capita revenues of voivodships were more diverse than the revenue of poviats. That was caused by the higher share of own revenues in the total revenue and a smaller dependency of the voivodship on state budget transfers. In 2004, a new voivodship revenue system was enforced, which tended to flatten per capita revenues in particular voivodships. As a result, the voivodships' situation became similar to that of poviats.

In 2004, three voivodships (Mazowieckie, Śląskie, Lubuskie) realised bigger revenues per capita than the average of all voivodships. The smallest revenue was noted in Łódzkie voivodship.

Table II - 48: Revenues of voivodships in 2004, per capita

Voivodships	Total	Own revenue	General subsidies	Appropriated allocations
	per capita, PLN			
Poland (total)	182.6	107.9	33.8	40.8
Dolnośląskie	166.9	100.7	34.8	31.5
Kujawsko-Pomorskie	160.0	77.3	42.5	40.2
Lubelskie	148.8	50.4	58.2	40.2
Lubuskie	213.3	80.9	77.5	55.0
Łódzkie	125.4	72.9	33.7	18.9
Małopolskie	149.3	84.7	23.4	41.2
Mazowieckie	288.3	258.5	11.1	18.7
Opolskie	154.8	70.1	49.9	34.7
Podkarpackie	164.3	62.0	54.8	47.5
Podlaskie	143.6	58.0	55.5	30.1
Pomorskie	172.5	108.7	24.8	38.9
Śląskie	215.9	112.5	18.1	85.3
Świętokrzyskie	155.4	52.0	47.4	56.0
Warmińsko-Mazurskie	177.8	61.1	55.3	61.3
Wielkopolskie	160.2	114.7	14.6	30.9
Zachodniopomorskie	150.1	61.1	66.0	23.0

Source: authors' own calculations based on Central Statistical Office (GUS) data

1.5 REVENUES OF EXTRABUDGETARY ENTITIES

The most important extra-budgetary entities of the self-governmental sector are the budgetary establishments. They still receive support from the budgets of territorial self-government entities. The highest allocations are received by budgetary establishments of cities with poviat status. The total allocations for self-governmental budgetary establishments in 2004 was PLN 2.2 billion (25.9% of their total revenue).

From 1999 – 2004 special funds of budgetary entities were quite a significant part of the TSG extra-budgetary economy. In 2005, the form of special funds of budgetary entities was abolished and replaced – in the self-governmental sector – by own revenues' accounts of budgetary entities.

Table II - 49: Revenues of budgetary establishments, special funds and auxiliary units of territorial self-government budgetary entities, 1999 – 2004

Specification	1999	2000	2001	2002	2003	2004
	10^6 PLN					
Budgetary establishments						
Revenue	11,651.7	9,847.7	9,590.3	10,025.2	8,538.5	8,428.5
of which: allocations from the TSG budgets	3,437.2	1,944.0	1,969.5	2,079.3	2,031.8	2,185.2
Special funds						
Revenue	1,106.8	1,307.3	1,352.5	1,352.5	1,275.5	1,304.4
of which: allocations from the TSG budgets	0.0	8.4	1.6	1.8	0.4	0.6
Auxiliary units						
Revenue	443.2	472.9	512.8	531.0	506.9	495.3
of which: allocations from the TSG budgets	18.5	20.3	22.6	20.7	18.1	21.1

Source: Statistical Yearbooks of the Republic of Poland. Central Statistical Office. Warsaw

From 1999 – 2004 the share of allocations from the TSG budgets in the auxiliary units' revenue was about 4%.

Another form of the extra-budgetary economy are the appropriated funds. Self-governmental appropriated funds are:

- environmental protection and water management funds.
- geodetic and cartographic resource management funds.
- agricultural land protection funds.

Table II - 50: Revenues of local appropriated funds, 1999 – 2004

Specification	1999	2000	2001	2002	2003	2004
	10^6 PLN					
Total revenue	**662.9**	**853.9**	**735.5**	**1.048.6**	**957.8**	**951.5**
of which:						
sale of products and services	92.1	123.1	118.8	137.8	174.0	175.2
allocations from the TSG budgets	1.3	1.7	12.2	8.1	7.7	5.0

Source: Statistical Yearbooks of the Republic of Poland. Central Statistical Office. Warsaw

Their total revenue in 2004 was nearly PLN 1 billion – most of it was realised by environmental protection and water management funds. Self-governmental appropriated funds receive very small transfers from the TSG budgets.

Table II - 51: Expenditures of territorial self-government entities by type of expenditure, 1999 – 2004

Specification	1999	2000	2001	2002	2003	2004
	\multicolumn{6}{c}{10^6 PLN}					
1	2	3	4	5	6	7
Total expenditures	65,845.9	75,746.8	82,734.3	83,181.8	80,954.3	91,386.8
Allocations	6,243.0	5,749.0	6,608.6	6,689.7	6,781.4	7,573.3
Benefits for natural persons	4,988.7	5,593.2	6,418.4	6,843.6	6,284.5	8,692.5
Current expenditure of budgetary entities *of which:*	41,580.3	50,241.0	52,919.3	53,864.8	53,228.3	57,186.3
wages and salaries	22,363.6	27,766.4	29,654.3	29,918.5	29,426.4	30,864.8
contributions to compulsory social security and Labour Fund	4,332.0	5,095.8	5,509.2	5,497.8	5,734.8	6,020.9
purchase of materials and services	13,016.7	14,915.2	15,688.9	16,347.9	15,957.5	17,545.3
Property expenditure	12,562.3	13,532.0	14,071.4	13,529.3	12,570.4	15,188.7
Others	471.6	631.6	2,716.6	2,254.4	2,089.7	2,746.0
	\multicolumn{6}{c}{%%}					
Total expenditures	100.0	100.0	100.0	100.0	100.0	100.0
Allocations	9.5	7.6	8.0	8.0	8.4	8.3
Benefits for natural persons	7.6	7.4	7.8	8.2	7.8	9.5
Current expenditure of budgetary entities *of which:*	63.1	66.3	64.0	64.8	65.8	62.6
wages and salaries	0.0	0.0	0.0	0.0	0.0	0.0
contributions to compulsory social security and Labour Fund	34.0	36.7	35.8	36.0	36.3	33.8
purchase of materials and services	6.6	6.7	6.7	6.6	7.1	6.6
Property expenditure	0.0	0.0	0.0	0.0	0.0	0.0
Others	19.8	19.7	19.0	19.7	19.7	19.2

Source: Statistical Yearbooks of the Republic of Poland, Central Statistical Office, Warsaw

2 Expenditures of the Self-Government Units

2.1 EXPENDITURES OF ALL SELF-GOVERNMENT UNITS

Expenditures of territorial self-government entities are predominantly current expenditures of budgetary entities. From 1999 – 2004 it was PLN 51.5 billion on average, which constituted 64.4% of the total self-governmental spending.

As we can see, the majority of expenditures comprise wages and salaries with contribution to the compulsory social security and the Labour Fund. The second biggest type of expenditures were property expenditures – 16.6% of total expenditures in 2004. The purchase of materials and services was the second largest item in 2004. Allocations constituted 8.3% of total expenditures in the presented period and benefits for natural persons 8.1%.

In each type of self-government entities, the current expenditures of budgetary entities constitute the largest part of the total expenditures. However, the share varies between the types of local self-government entities – from 30.4% in voivodship budgets to 78.1% in poviat budgets. The differences in shares of specified types of expenditure are significant, especially if we compare budgets of voivodships and poviats, e.g. the share of property expenditure amounts to almost 1/3 of total expenditures in voivodships while it constitutes only 10% of poviats' expenditures. Allocations constitute 29% of voivodships' total expenditures and 5% of poviats' expenditures.

In spite of the significant share of current expenditures in the total expenditures in all types of entities, the share of investment spending is much higher than in the central budget.

The differences in the nature of tasks of self-government levels are reflected in the structure of property expenditures and current expenditures. The table below shows the shares in 2005. In comparison to 2004 the share of property expenditure is 1.2 points higher. Only in voivodships property expenditures constitute a significant part (34%), in other types of self-government entities this kind of expenditure is rather low.

Expenditures of gminas and cities with poviat status were predominantly expenses for education. Gminas and cities with poviat status, responsible for the upkeep of primary and lower secondary schools (*gimnazjum*), distribute most of their resources for that purpose. Poviats are responsible for the maintenance of higher secondary schools (*liceum*). In the case of voivodships the major part of the expenditure is distributed to transport and communication.

Table II - 52: Expenditures of territorial self-government entities by type of expenditures in 2004

Specification	Total	Gminas	Cities with poviat status	Poviats	Voivodships
			10^6 PLN		
1	2	3	4	5	6
Total expenditures	91,386.8	40,941.8	32,136.7	12,444.7	5,863.6
Allocations	7,573.3	2,060.2	3,209.1	589.3	1,714.7
Benefits for natural persons	8,692.5	5,233.3	2,728.4	688.4	42.4
Current expenditure of budgetary entities	57,186.3	25,617.8	20,070.4	9,715.7	1,782.4
of which:					
wages and salaries	30,864.8	14,184.8	10,126.1	5,795.2	758.7
contributions to compulsory social security and Labour Fund	6,020.9	2,916.7	1,914.7	1,042.1	147.4
purchase of materials and services	17,545.3	7,375.4	7,138.3	2,220.9	810.7
Property expenditure	15,188.7	7,471.9	4,709.6	1,265.5	1,741.7
Others	2,746.0	558.6	1,419.2	185.8	582.4
			%%		
Total expenditure	100.0	100.0	100.0	100.0	100.0
Allocations	8.3	5.0	10.0	4.7	29.2
Benefits for natural persons	9.5	12.8	8.5	5.5	0.7
Current expenditure of budgetary entities	62.6	62.6	62.5	78.1	30.4
of which:					
wages and salaries	33.8	34.6	31.5	46.6	12.9
contributions to compulsory social security and Labour Fund	6.6	7.1	6.0	8.4	2.5
purchase of materials and services	0.0	0.0	0.0	0.0	0.0
Property expenditure	19.2	18.0	22.2	17.8	13.8
Others	16.6	18.3	14.7	10.2	29.7

Source: Statistical Yearbook of the Republic of Poland 2005, Central Statistical Office, Warsaw 2005

Table II - 53: Expenditures of territorial self-government entities in 2005

Specification	Total	Gminas	Cities with poviat status	Poviats	Voivodships
	10^6 PLN				
1	2	3	4	5	6
Total expenditures	103,807.1	45,837.5	3,6491.2	13,890.9	7,587.5
of which:					
Property expenditures	18,430.4	8,349.4	5,890.5	1,621.3	2,569.2
Current expenditures	85,376.7	37,488.1	30,600.8	12,269.6	5,018.3
	%				
Total expenditures	100.0	100.0	100.0	100.0	100.0
Property expenditures	17.8	18.2	16.1	11.7	33.9
Current expenditures	82.2	81.8	83.9	88.3	66.1

Source: Ministry of Finance

Gminas spent about 44% of total expenditures in the self-government sector. Together with cities with poviat status the share was as high as 79%. It reflects the role of this type of entities. The expenditures of voivodships constituted only 7.3% of total expenditures but the share of its property expenditures was higher – almost 14% of total property expenditures in all types of entities. Conversely, the share of poviats' budgets in total expenditures constitutes only 13.4% and the share of property expenditures is much lower – 5.9% only. Tables concerning the expenditures of local self government by division can be found in Appendix 1.

The reform introduced in 2004 has particularly influenced the expenditure structure of the voivodships. For example, in Mazowieckie voivodship the share of allocations increased, which is the consequence of higher surplus payments to the state budget. The second reason is the wider range of cooperation with private sector institutions providing public services. The differences in allocations per capita by voivodships are high and amount to 199%.

Table II - 54: Expenditures of local self-government entities by function in 2004

Specification	Total	Gminas	Cities with poviat status	Poviats	Voivodships
	10⁶ PLN				
1	2	3	4	5	6
Total expenditures	**91,386.8**	**40,941.8**	**32,136.7**	**12,444.7**	**5,863.6**
of which:					
education	33,419.7	17,469.8	10,960.6	4,504.7	484.6
social welfare	12,539.3	5,680.9	4,310.1	2,388.8	159.5
transport and communication	11,604.2	2,871.5	5,438.8	1,212.6	2,081.3
public administration	9,033.5	4,745.4	2,372.6	1,507.7	407.8
education care	2,690.9	519.8	1,081.8	1,010.6	78.7
municipal economy and environmental protection	5,248.1	3,428.6	1,782.3	8.7	28.5
					%
Total expenditures	100.0	100.0	100.0	100.0	100.0
of which:					
education	36.6	42.7	34.1	36.2	8.3
social welfare	13.7	13.9	13.4	19.2	2.7
transport and communication	12.7	7.0	16.9	9.7	35.5
public administration	9.9	11.6	7.4	12.1	7.0
education care	2.9	1.3	3.4	8.1	1.3
municipal economy and environmental protection	5.7	8.4	5.5	0.1	0.5

Source: Statistical Yearbooks of the Republic of Poland 2005, Central Statistical Office, Warsaw 2005

Table II - 55: Expenditures of local self-government entities in 2005

Specification	Total	Gminas	Cities with poviat status	Poviats	Voivodships
	\multicolumn{5}{c}{10^6 PLN}				
1	2	3	4	5	6
Total expenditures	**103,807.1**	**45,837.5**	**36,491.2**	**13,890.9**	**7,587.5**
of which:					
Property expenditure	18,430.4	8,349.4	5,890.5	1,621.3	2,569.2
investment expenditure	17,750.0	8,218.8	5,537.6	1,609.2	2,384.5
Current expenditure	85,376.7	37,488.1	30,600.8	12,269.6	5,018.3
wages and salaries	32,389.1	14,801.0	10,670.4	6,044.0	873.7
contributions to compulsory funds	6,782.7	3,079.5	2,146.8	1,386.3	170.1
allocations	6,069.8	1,341.3	2,596.8	750.8	1,381.0
debt servicing	996.8	345.5	500.7	115.3	35.2
of which: guarantees and bail bonds	41.8	9.5	2.7	23.8	5.8
other expenditure	39,138.3	17,920.7	14,686.1	3,973.1	2,558.4
	\multicolumn{5}{c}{%}				
Total expenditures	**100.0**	**100.0**	**100.0**	**100.0**	**100.0**
of which:					
Property expenditure	17.8	18.2	16.1	11.7	33.9
investment expenditure	17.1	17.9	15.2	11.6	31.4
Current expenditure	82.2	81.8	83.9	88.3	66.1
wages and salaries	31.2	32.3	29.2	43.5	11.5
contributions to compulsory funds	6.5	6.7	5.9	10.0	2.2
allocations	5.8	2.9	7.1	5.4	18.2
debt servicing	1.0	0.8	1.4	0.8	0.5
of which: guarantees and bail bonds	0.0	0.0	0.0	0.2	0.1
other expenditure	37.7	39.1	40.2	28.6	33.7

Source: Ministry of Finance

The wider range of tasks in social welfare caused an increase in the benefits for natural persons, but its dynamic (per capita) varies among voivodships, e.g. in Lubelskie there was a 27% increase while in Dolnośląskie and Pomorskie it was 44% compared with 2003. The difference in expenditures on benefits for natural persons[3] per capita is also high.

2.2 EXPENDITURE STRUCTURE OF GMINAS

The gminas have spent 40.9 billion PLN in 2004, which corresponds to 44.8% of the total expenditures of self-government entities. In the gminas' expenditures, as opposed to the voivodships, the highest gap of 352% can be observed in benefits for natural persons per capita. With up to 200% the difference is much lower in the case of current expenditures and property expenditures.

The highest property expenditures per capita can be observed in two voivodships: Swiętokrzyskie and Podkarpackie, which are among the poorest and, from an economic point of view, worst performing voivodships.

2.3 EXPENDITURE STRUCTURE OF POVIATS AND CITIES WITH POVIAT STATUS

Poviats and cities with poviats rights spent 44.6 billion PLN in 2004 which corresponds to 48.8% of the total expenditure of self-government entities. The poviats' expenditures alone constituted 13.6% of the total amount. In the case of poviats and cities with poviat status, the dispersal between voivodships is even stronger. Especially if we take property expenditures into consideration. The highest value (Mazowieckie) in comparison with the lowest value (Opolskie) amounted to 506%. Opposed to gminas' budgets, the highest property expenditures in the case of poviats and cities with poviat status can be observed in the best performing voivodships Mazowieckie and Śląskie.

---

[3] e.g. social benefits, child benefits, grants and scholarships

Table II - 56: Budgets of self-government entities by voivodships in 2004

Voivodships	Total	Allocations	Benefits for natural persons	Current expenditure of budgetary entities	Property expenditure
			10^6 PLN		
Poland (total)	**91,386.8**	**7,573.3**	**8,692.5**	**57,186.3**	**15,188.8**
Dolnośląskie	7,273.5	613.0	706.2	4,559.9	1,151.3
Kujawsko-Pomorskie	4,623.6	396.1	592.9	2,958.3	601.5
Lubelskie	4,734.0	363.6	472.1	3,076.2	735.7
Lubuskie	2,445.9	227.9	303.0	1,490.7	397.5
Łódzkie	5,700.1	435.5	559.7	3,668.2	910.8
Małopolskie	7,397.9	606.8	595.9	4,718.2	1,321.3
Mazowieckie	14,928.9	1,172.9	948.5	8,941.7	2,702.7
Opolskie	2,333.8	158.7	229.5	1,595.8	318.1
Podkarpackie	4,677.7	355.9	462.8	2,990.6	812.5
Podlaskie	2,690.2	276.1	255.4	1,616.0	503.3
Pomorskie	5,444.9	418.8	565.2	3,498.4	849.7
Śląskie	10,815.0	1,007.6	988.4	6,530.7	1,970.4
Świętokrzyskie	2,866.6	170.1	288.7	1,826.8	549.1
Wrmińsko-Mazurskie	3,526.7	271.8	448.0	2,199.8	545.4
Wielkopolskie	7,794.6	652.5	770.3	4,984.4	1,248.1
Zachodniopomorskie	4,133.4	445.9	506.2	2,530.2	571.2
			per capita in PLN		
Pland (total)	2,393.6	198.4	227.7	1,497.8	397.8
Dolnośląskie	2,511.8	211.7	243.9	1,574.7	397.6
Kujawsko-Pomorskie	2,236.3	191.6	286.8	1,430.9	290.9
Lubelskie	2,163.7	166.2	215.8	1,406.0	336.3
Lubuskie	2,423.6	225.8	300.2	1,477.1	393.9
Łódzkie	2,198.6	168.0	215.9	1,414.9	351.3
Małopolskie	2,271.9	186.4	183.0	1,449.0	405.8
Mazowieckie	2,904.7	228.2	184.6	1,739.8	525.9
Opolskie	2,214.9	150.6	217.8	1,514.5	301.9
Podkarpackie	2,230.3	169.7	220.7	1,425.9	387.4
Podlaskie	2,234.4	229.3	212.1	1,342.2	418.0
Pomorskie	2,483.5	191.0	257.8	1,595.7	387.6
Śląskie	2,297.3	214.0	209.9	1,387.2	418.5
Świętokrzyskie	2,221.8	131.8	223.8	1,415.9	425.6
Warmińsko-Mazurskie	2,469.0	190.3	313.6	1,540.1	381.8
Wielkopolskie	2,318.4	194.1	229.1	1,482.6	371.2
Zachodniopomorskie	2,437.6	263.0	298.5	1,492.1	336.9

Source: Statistical Yearbook of the Republic of Poland 2005, Central Statistical Office, Warsaw 2005

Table II - 57: Budgets of gminas* by voivodships in 2004

Voivodships	Total	Allo-cations	Benefits for natural persons	Current expenditure of budgetary entities	Property expen-diture
			10^6 PLN		
Poland (total)	**40,941.8**	**2,060.2**	**5,233.3**	**25,617.8**	**7,471.9**
Dolnośląskie	3,570.9	249.2	483.6	2,121.7	626.4
Kujawsko-Pomorskie	2,027.7	70.1	336.1	1,316.5	285.8
Lubelskie	2,450.0	125.2	297.8	1,576.0	429.0
Lubuskie	1,294.7	81.3	212.5	767.6	219.8
Łódzkie	2,606.4	102.0	315.7	1,641.7	494.7
Małopolskie	3,572.7	182.5	377.5	2,315.5	652.2
Mazowieckie	4,878.5	203.9	501.8	3,075.2	1,031.4
Opolskie	1,411.6	79.7	174.8	924.4	217.9
Podkarpackie	2,731.9	127.4	344.8	1,728.7	505.4
Podlaskie	1,176.1	51.4	135.5	752.6	228.1
Pomorskie	2,346.2	106.4	352.8	1,441.1	420.2
Śląskie	3,202.6	155.6	307.5	2,050.6	637.9
Świętokrzyskie	1,681.4	71.0	209.6	1,031.7	352.7
Warmińsko-Mazurskie	1,874.3	92.4	328.7	1,155.4	277.3
Wielkopolskie	4,052.5	204.2	526.6	2,541.4	727.8
Zachodniopomorskie	2,064.1	157.9	328.1	1,177.7	365.1
			per capita in PLN		
Poland (total)	**1,072.3**	**54.0**	**137.1**	**671.0**	**195.7**
Dolnośląskie	1,233.2	86.1	167.0	732.7	216.3
Kujawsko-Pomorskie	980.7	33.9	162.6	636.8	138.2
Lubelskie	1,119.8	57.2	136.1	720.3	196.1
Lubuskie	1,282.9	80.6	210.6	760.6	217.8
Łódzkie	1,005.3	39.3	121.8	633.2	190.8
Małopolskie	1,097.2	56.0	115.9	711.1	200.3
Mazowieckie	949.2	39.7	97.6	598.3	200.7
Opolskie	1,339.7	75.6	165.9	877.3	206.8
Podkarpackie	1,302.6	60.7	164.4	824.2	241.0
Podlaskie	976.8	42.7	112.5	625.1	189.5
Pomorskie	1,070.2	48.5	160.9	657.3	191.7
Śląskie	680.3	33.1	65.3	435.6	135.5
Świętokrzyskie	1,303.2	55.0	162.5	799.6	273.4
Warmińsko-Mazurskie	1,312.2	64.7	230.1	808.9	194.1
Wielkopolskie	1,205.4	60.7	156.6	755.9	216.5
Zachodniopomorskie	1,217.3	93.1	193.5	694.5	215.3

Source: Statistical Yearbook of the Republic of Poland 2005, Central Statistical Office, Warsaw 2005
* = cities with poviat status not included.

The Self-Government Units in Poland

Table II - 58: Expenditure of poviats and cities with poviat status by voivodships in 2004

Voivodships	Total	Allocations	Benefits for natural persons	Current expenditure of budgetary entities	Property expenditure
			10^6 PLN		
Poland (total)	**44,581.4**	**3,798.4**	**3,416.8**	**29,786.1**	**5,975.2**
Dolnośląskie	3,285.9	217.0	219.7	2,303.8	434.1
Kujawsko-Pomorskie	2,310.2	220.2	253.5	1,552.4	235.0
Lubelskie	1,948.8	144.1	172.2	1,364.4	215.9
Lubuskie	958.3	89.4	89.7	652.2	116.2
Łódzkie	2,831.6	236.3	242.3	1,930.4	361.5
Małopolskie	3,401.5	305.1	215.6	2,280.0	511.6
Mazowieckie	8,972.4	748.4	443.3	5,635.5	1,460.5
Opolskie	764.4	42.0	53.8	596.2	59.2
Podkarpackie	1,625.9	132.8	116.6	1,150.5	204.6
Podlaskie	1,343.0	171.1	118.7	799.6	233.5
Pomorskie	2,782.8	210.7	210.7	1,955.2	330.4
Śląskie	6,823.8	637.4	675.6	4,315.7	947.1
Świętokrzyskie	1,005.3	68.8	78.3	724.6	121.4
Warmińsko-Mazurskie	1,396.1	101.5	118.0	961.7	178.4
Wielkopolskie	3,297.2	266.8	233.8	2,314.5	397.6
Zachodniopomorskie	1,834.3	206.9	175.2	1,249.3	168.2
			per capita in PLN		
Poland (total)	**1,167.7**	**99.5**	**89.5**	**780.1**	**156.5**
Dolnośląskie	1,134.8	74.9	75.9	795.6	149.9
Kujawsko-Pomorskie	1,117.4	106.5	122.6	750.9	113.7
Lubelskie	890.7	65.9	78.7	623.6	98.7
Lubuskie	949.6	88.6	88.9	646.3	115.1
Łódzkie	1,092.2	91.1	93.5	744.6	139.4
Małopolskie	1,044.6	93.7	66.2	700.2	157.1
Mazowieckie	1,745.8	145.6	86.3	1,096.5	284.2
Opolskie	725.4	39.9	51.1	565.8	56.2
Podkarpackie	775.2	63.3	55.6	548.6	97.6
Podlaskie	1,115.4	142.1	98.6	664.1	193.9
Pomorskie	1,269.3	96.1	96.1	891.8	150.7
Śląskie	1,449.5	135.4	143.5	916.7	201.2
Świętokrzyskie	779.2	53.3	60.7	561.6	94.1
Warmińsko-Mazurskie	977.4	71.1	82.6	673.3	124.9
Wielkopolskie	980.7	79.4	69.5	688.4	118.3
Zachodniopomorskie	1,081.7	122.0	103.3	736.7	99.2

Source: Statistical Yearbook of the Republic of Poland 2005, Central Statistical Office, Warsaw 2005

Table II - 59: Budgets of voivodships by voivodships in 2004

Voivodships	Total	Allocations	Benefits for natural persons	Current expenditure of budgetary entities	Property expenditure
			10^6 PLN		
Poland (total)	**5,863.6**	**1,714.7**	**42.4**	**1,782.4**	**1,741.7**
Dolnośląskie	416.7	146.8	2.9	134.4	90.8
Kujawsko-Pomorskie	285.7	105.8	3.3	89.4	80.7
Lubelskie	335.2	94.3	2.1	135.8	90.8
Lubuskie	192.9	57.2	0.8	70.9	61.5
Łódzkie	262.1	97.2	1.7	96.1	54.6
Małopolskie	423.7	119.2	2.8	122.7	157.5
Mazowieckie	1,078.0	220.6	3.4	231.0	210.8
Opolskie	157.8	37.0	0.9	75.2	41.0
Podkarpackie	319.9	95.7	1.4	111.4	102.5
Podlaskie	171.1	53.6	1.2	63.8	41.7
Pomorskie	315.9	101.7	1.7	102.1	99.1
Śląskie	788.6	214.6	5.3	164.4	385.4
Świętokrzyskie	179.9	30.3	0.8	70.5	75.0
Warmińsko-Mazurskie	256.3	77.9	1.3	82.7	89.7
Wielkopolskie	444.9	181.5	9.9	128.5	122.7
Zachodniopomorskie	235.0	81.1	2.9	103.2	37.9
			per capita in PLN		
Poland (total)	153.6	44.9	1.1	46.7	45.6
Dolnośląskie	143.9	50.7	1.0	46.4	31.4
Kujawsko-Pomorskie	138.2	51.2	1.6	43.2	39.0
Lubelskie	153.2	43.1	1.0	62.1	41.5
Lubuskie	191.1	56.7	0.8	70.3	60.9
Łódzkie	101.1	37.5	0.7	37.1	21.1
Małopolskie	130.1	36.6	0.9	37.7	48.4
Mazowieckie	209.7	42.9	0.7	44.9	41.0
Opolskie	149.8	35.1	0.9	71.4	38.9
Podkarpackie	152.5	45.6	0.7	53.1	48.9
Podlaskie	142.1	44.5	1.0	53.0	34.6
Pomorskie	144.1	46.4	0.8	46.6	45.2
Śląskie	167.5	45.6	1.1	34.9	81.9
Świętokrzyskie	139.4	23.5	0.6	54.6	58.1
Warmińsko-Mazurskie	179.4	54.5	0.9	57.9	62.8
Wielkopolskie	132.3	54.0	2.9	38.2	36.5
Zachodniopomorskie	138.6	47.8	1.7	60.9	22.4

Source: Statistical Yearbook of the Republic of Poland 2005, Central Statistical Office, Warsaw 2005

2.4 EXPENDITURE STRUCTURE OF VOIVODSHIPS

Voivodships spent 5.9 billion PLN in 2004, which corresponds to 6.4% of the total expenditures of self-government entities. The expenditures per capita are quite low: the average for Poland is 154.6 PLN of which 44.9 were spent on allocations, 46.7 were current expenditures, and 45.6 were spent on investment. Only 1.1 PLN were destined for benefits for natural persons. The dispersal of total expenditure figures per capita between voivodships exceeds 200% and reaches the highest number in the case of benefits for natural persons.

- Total grants for local self government entities in 2005 amounted to PLN 11.2 billion (without the targeted reserve), of which the grant for current expenditure amounted to PLN 11 billion. Grants for delegated tasks in 2005 constituted:
- 78% of total grants for gminas,
- 57% of total grants for poviats,
- 42% of total grants for voivodships.

Table II - 60: Grants for delegated tasks

Specification	Gminas	Poviats	Voivodships
	10^6 PLN		
Total grants of which	9,364.9	3,694.6	913.6
grants for delegated tasks	7,346.5	2,103.5	380.4

Source: Supreme Chamber of Control

If we assumed that the grants for delegated tasks is equivalent to the expenditures on delegated tasks, it would constitute about 10.8% of the total expenditures and 10.1% in gminas, 16.9% in poviats, and 6.5% in voivodships.

Contrary to the state extra-budgetary economy, the most important extra-budgetary entities of the self-governmental sector are the budgetary enterprises. They still receive support from the budgets of territorial self-government entities. The self-governmental extra-budgetary economy entities spent a total of PLN 13.2 billion in 1999. During the next three years this amount gradually decreased to approximately PLN 11.7 billion and in 2004 the expenditures amounted to a mere PLN 8.1 billion.

Table II - 61: Expenditures of budgetary establishments, special funds and auxiliary units of territorial self-government budgetary entities, 1999 – 2004

Specification	1999	2000	2001	2002	2003	2004
	10^6 PLN					
1	2	3	4	5	6	7
Budgetary establishments						
Expenditures	11,530.6	9,830.6	9,602.3	10,031.7	8,246.5	8,095.3
Surplus payment to the TSG budgets	70.5	53.2	31.4	31.6	31.3	47.9
Special funds						
Expenditures	1,074.0	1,282.6	1,303.6	1,320.1	1,225.1	1,285.8
Auxiliary units						
Expenditures	439.7	474.9	501.3	527.0	501.3	486.2
Payment of profits to the TSG budgets	3.2	3.2	4.0	4.3	5.5	5.4

Source: Statistical Yearbooks of the Republic of Poland, Central Statistical Office, Warsaw

Self-governmental appropriated funds expenditures in 2004 amounted to PLN 983.6 million. Almost the whole amount was spent on environmental protection and water management.

Table II - 62: Expenditures of local appropriated funds, 1999 – 2003

Specification	1999	2000	2001	2002	2003	2004
	10^6 PLN					
1	2	3	4	5	6	7
Total expenditure	**511.1**	**794.0**	**750.9**	**1,041.1**	**940.7**	**983.6**
of which:						
materials and services	172.9	277.2	276.2	380.4	370.1	397.4
allocations	0.6	13.6	118.6	197.1	200.6	225.8

Source: Statistical Yearbooks of the Republic of Poland, Central Statistical Office, Warsaw

Table II - 63: Internal general government's transfers in 2003

To \ From	SBU	TSG units	SIF	ASIF	Labour Fund	Uni-versities	Others	Total
								mln PLN
1	2	3	4	5	6	7	8	9
State budgetary units (SBU)	13.6	304.4	0.0	0.0	0.0	0.0	560.9	878.9
TSG units	43,866.1	524.5	0.0	0.0	0.0	0.0	382.9	44,773.5
State extra-budgetary units	50.1	0.0	0.0	0.0	0.0	0.0	0.0	50.1
Local extra-budgetary units	0.0	2,156.1	0.0	0.0	0.0	0.0	0.0	2,156.1
Social Insurance Fund (SIF)	31,117.7	5,043.8	0.0	24.0	1,137.7	1,194.8	1,027.9	39,545.9
Agricultural Social Insurance Funds (ASIF)	15,049.0	0.0	0.0	0.0	0.6	0.0	62.7	15,112.3
State Fund for Rehabilitation of Disabled Persons	52.2	17.5	0.0	0.0	0.0	0.0	24.2	93.9
Labour Fund	4,171.4	691.0	0.0	3.3	0.0	163.7	338.9	5,368.3
Alimony Fund	1,468.9	0.0	0.0	0.0	0.0	0.0	0.0	1,468.9
Voivodship's Environm.Protection and Water Management Fund	0.0	0.0	0.0	0.0	0.0	0.0	133.4	133.4
Health Funds	228.1	408.3	0.0	1,460.3	0.0	0.0	367.6	2,464.3
Social Insurance Institution	52.6	0.0	1,879.4	13.8	27.3	0.0	94.9	2,068.0
Agency for Restructuring and Modernisation of Agriculture	1,681.2	0.0	0.0	0.0	0.0	0.0	0.0	1,681.2
State Treasury Agricultural Property Agency	0.2	0.0	0.0	0.0	0.0	0.0	0.0	0.2
Universities	5,823.5	7.0	0.0	0.0	0.0	0.0	0.0	5,830.5
Cultural institutions	321.5	0.0	0.0	0.0	0.0	0.0	0.0	321.5
together	103,896.1	9,152.6	1,879.4	1,501.4	1,165.6	1,358.5	2,993.4	121,947.0

Source: GIME's own calculations

3 Transfers Between the Local Budgets and the State Budget

Public institutions are mutually linked by many financial relations. There is an inter-relation network in the general government. In some cases contributions to the social insurance funds are the only transfers which link an institution to other units in the public sector. However, there are also many entities which are almost completely dependent on internal transfers from other public institutions.

The most important public institutions in the transfer process are state budget, territorial self-government entities and two insurance funds (Social Insurance Fund and Agricultural Social Insurance Fund). The Labor Fund and universities have minor importance in the transfer system. Transfers to social insurance funds – employer's contributions – result from the social protection rules and are not an element of our research. Transfers between the state and the territorial self-government are a crucial part of the political system. Directions and categories of vertical transfers between the state and the local governments are the main topic of this chapter.

Public funds flow in both directions between the state and the territorial self-government. These vertical transfers are equivalent to 36.2% of all internal public sector transfers[4]. The territorial self-governments transfer money to the state budget as a part of horizontal equalization (rich territorial self-government entities transfer money to poorer ones via the state budget) but this is not a very strong instrument. Transfers from the state budget to local entities are 144 times higher than those in the opposite direction. A lot of public resources are collected by the state as its own revenue, although eventually they finance self-government expenditure. In rural and urban areas the difference in the fiscal capacity is so significant that it is not possible to create one tax revenue system without an extensive system of transfers.

3.1 TRANSFERS BETWEEN THE STATE BUDGET AND BUDGETS OF TSGs

Territorial self-governments are the main beneficiary of transfers from the state budget. These transfers bear both supportive and appropriated characteristics. The Polish Constitution divides budgetary transfers into appropriated allocations and general subsidies. The main difference is that appropriated allocations are assigned to cover

---

[4]   Other important transfers are contributions to Social Insurance Fund (32.4% of public transfers) and Agricultural Social Insurance Fund (12.4%).

expenditure on activities appointed by the state administration, while general subsidies have supportive character, without pressing self-government units to define the purpose of expenditures.

Table II - 64: The general subsidies from the state budget, 1999 – 2005

Specification	1999	2000	2001	2002	2003	2004	2005
				10^6 PLN			
General subsidies	22,116.5	25,858.0	29,432.3	29,701.2	31,728.6	31,314.2	32,455.7
Basic part	1,449.3	1,771.0	1,851.8	2,112.3	2,179.8	–	–
Educaional part	16,537.2	19,367.4	22,117.7	22,318.2	24,320.9	25,082.8	26,097.4
Compensatory part	1,415.9	1,743.1	2,084.6	2,022.7	1,869.4	109.7	11.8
Road part	2,075.7	2,316.0	2,674.6	2,567.5	2,657.9	–	–
Equalizing part	638.5	660.6	703.6	680.5	700.6	4,531.0	4,731.5
Balancing part	–	–	–	–	–	707.2	909.7
Regional part	–	–	–	–	–	299.7	314.5
Supplement	–	–	–	–	–	583.8	390.9
				%			
General subsidies	100.0	100.0	100.0	100.0	100.0	100.0	100.0
Basic part	6.6	6.8	6.3	7.1	6.9	–	–
Educational part	74.8	74.9	75.1	75.1	76.7	80.1	80.4
Compensatory part	6.4	6.7	7.1	6.8	5.9	0.4	0.0
Road part	9.4	9.0	9.1	8.6	8.4	–	–
Equalizing part	2.9	2.6	2.4	2.3	2.2	14.5	14.6
Balancing part	–	–	–	–	–	2.3	2.8
Regional part	–	–	–	–	–	1.0	1.0
Supplement	–	–	–	–	–	1.9	1.2
				Previous year = 100			
General subsidies	x	116.9	113.8	100.9	106.8	98.7	103.6
Basic part	x	122.2	104.6	114.1	103.2	–	–
Educational part	x	117.1	114.2	100.9	109.0	103.1	104.0
Compensatory part	x	123.1	119.6	97.0	92.4	5.9	10.8
Road part	x	111.6	115.5	96.0	103.5	–	–
Equalizing part	x	103.5	106.5	96.7	103.0	646.7	104.4
Balancing part	x	–	–	–	–	–	128.6
Regional part	x	–	–	–	–	–	105.0
Supplement	x	–	–	–	–	–	67.0

Source: Ministry of Finance, GIME's own calculations

The decentralization of public funds requires more fiscal power for the self-government. Recent changes in the self-government revenue structure go into the right direction, although it does not mean that transfers have been limited. Between 1999 and 2005, the TSGs' own revenues increased by 87%. At the same time transfers from the state budget to the TSGs increased by 29%. Growth of transfers was caused by higher general subsidies. In 2005, general subsidies amounted to PLN 32.5 billion, while in 1999 they were only PLN 22.1 billion. There was nearly a 50% growth of general subsidies during six years.

Figure II - 15: Territorial self-government expenditure on education and educational part of general subsidies from 1999 – 2003, according to TSG category

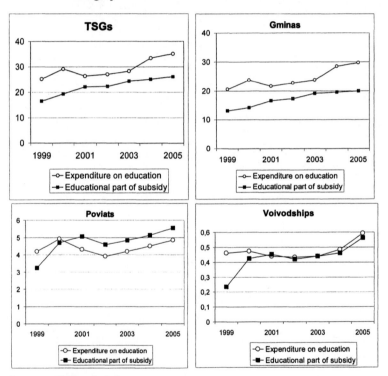

Source: GIMA calculations

3.1.1 General Subsidies

The abolition of the basic, compensatory, and road part did not change the total value of the subsidies. In place of abolished parts the Sejm introduced new subsidy parts: balancing (for gminas and poviats), regional (for voivodships) and supplements (for entities which lost some revenue due to the 2003 Act on the Revenue of Territorial Self-Government Entities).

The educational part is the most significant part of general subsidies. From 1999 – 2003 the educational part constituted 75.5% of the general subsidies. After the 2003 reform, the share of this part has even risen to more than 80% of the subsidies. This part is received by each TSG entity, since all TSG entities finance schools and other educational activities. Factors affecting the division of the educational part are: the number of pupils, location (rural, urban), its specific characteristics ("common" schools, sport-oriented schools, schools for handicapped or for national minorities), and execution of the tasks which exceed ordinary school activities.

Nevertheless the amount of the educational part remains insufficient to cover all the expenditure on educational activities. From 1999 – 2003 total TSG expenditures on educational tasks exceeded the educational part by PLN 31 billion. From 2001 – 2003 the average gap between the TSGs' expenditure on educational tasks and the educational part of general subsidies amounted to a level of PLN 4.3 billion (19% of expenditure on education). In 2004 and 2005 the gap was even bigger. Standards of education financing set by the state are not adequate to the needs. Actually, TSG entities have to participate in education financing if they want to meet modern standards. The function of the educational part is difficult to explain when the gap between transfers and needs expands permanently.

Replacing the educational part of the subsidies with own revenues would be crucial for further decentralisation. It is impossible to do this without a big reform of the tax system and self-government revenue system. Expenditures on education absorb about 34% of all self-government expenditures. That is why there should be a concept of replacing the educational part of the subsidies with own revenues. We should accept the idea of dividing the gminas' revenue system into a few separate systems which would be adequate to the fiscal capacity of big cities, smaller towns and rural regions. In a uniform system of revenues the discrepancies in the fiscal capacity of gminas is too large to replace the subsidies with their own revenues. The establishing of three different systems of revenues for gminas with similar fiscal capacity (big cities, towns and rural gminas) would create conditions for an abolition of the educational part of the subsidies and the increase of the gminas' share in taxes, without expansion of the equalizing transfers.

The big gap between the expenditures on education and the educational part of the subsidies is mainly the problem of gminas. Over the last years a stagnation or very little growth in the educational part of the subsidies could be observed. Meanwhile, expenditures on education have grown very quickly, as gminas tried to invest in this field as well as in broadening the range of extra-time activities for pupils. From 2003 – 2005 the gap doubled in cities with poviat rights and in urban-rural gminas. In other urban gminas the increase was even higher, in rural gminas slightly lower.

The self-governments have relatively little influence on the cost reduction in education, because the state administration sets rules for the system of teachers' employment and makes decisions about establishing and shutting-down schools. Moreover, the teachers' remuneration system is strictly regulated by the Teacher's Charter passed by the Sejm.

Table II - 65: Educational part of the general subsidies, 1999 – 2005

Specification	1999	2000	2001	2002	2003	2004	2005
	10^6 PLN						
Total	16,537.2	19,367.4	22,117.7	22,318.2	24,320.9	25,082.8	26,097.4
Gminas	13,060.1	14,254.1	16,603.0	17,314.6	19,047.1	19,483.3	19,990.7
Poviats	3,241.7	4,688.9	5,061.9	4,583.2	4,833.9	5,138.3	5,542.2
Voivodships	235.4	424.4	452.8	420.4	440.0	461.2	564.5

Source: Ministry of Finance, www.mf.gov.pl

3.1.2 Appropriated Allocations

Appropriated allocations are the second main category of transfers from the state budget to the TSG. They were created to support the execution of certain tasks. The share of the appropriated allocations in the TSGs' total revenue is significantly smaller than the general subsidies' share. From 1999 – 2002 appropriated allocations were equivalent to 21 – 23% of the TSGs' total revenue.

In voivodships and especially in poviats, allocations constituted approximately half of the total revenue. From 1999 – 2002 the police were financed by poviats which received allocations from the state budget to finance these tasks. Since 2003 the police, guards, and inspection have again been financed directly by the state administration, so the share of the appropriated allocations in poviats' revenues decreased correspondingly. In gminas, appropriated allocations played a less significant role.

Figure II - 16: Territorial self-government expenditure on education and educational part of general subsidies from 1999 – 2003, by TSC categories

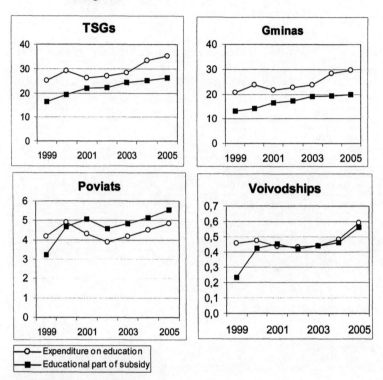

Source: GIME calculations

In 2004, some tasks (e.g. maintenance of social care homes, the establishing and maintenance of family support centers, maintenance of regional social aid institutions, financial help for surrogate families, maintenance of orphanages, financing of allowances in public transport fares) and corresponding resources were passed to the self-government units. Before that, these tasks had been financed by appropriated allocations from the state budget and delegated to self governments. Since 2004 they have been the TSGs' own tasks, which are financed by an increased TSG share in PIT and CIT. As a result of the changes, the share of appropriated allocations from the state budget decreased to 13.0% of the TSGs' total revenue in 2004 and to 13.5% in 2005.

Table II - 66: Appropriated allocations from the state budget to TSGs, 1999 – 2005

Specification	1999	2000	2001	2002	2003	2004	2005
	10^6 PLN						
Total	13,726.4	15,526.4	16,588.0	15,730.3	11,985.4	11,928.4	13,921.3
On tasks delegated by law	7,814.1	8,839.4	10,872.6	9,999.9	6,509.8	8,044.2	9,837.5
Current tasks	7,765.3	8,491.1	10,599.5	9,729.1	6,098.7	7,562.0	9,590.3
Investment tasks	48.9	348.2	273.1	270.8	411.2	482.3	247.2
On tasks delegated by contracts	700.5	759.3	184.5	137.0	133.9	271.2	229.7
Current tasks	303.3	647.9	117.4	101.3	118.3	190.2	152.5
Investment tasks	397.2	111.4	67.1	35.7	15.5	81.0	77.2
On own tasks	5,211.8	5,927.7	5,530.9	5,593.4	5,341.7	3,613.0	3,854.1
Current tasks	3,500.9	4,102.6	3,728.5	4,087.2	3,959.1	2,450.4	2,931.0
Investment tasks	1,710.9	1,825.0	1,802.4	1,506.1	1,382.6	1,162.5	923.1

Source: Ministry of Finance, www.mf.gov.pl

The appropriated allocations for the TSGs include

- grants from the state budget,
- grants from appropriated funds,
- grants from other TSGs.

The largest part of appropriated allocations is transferred from the state budget, but its share in revenue is much smaller now than it was in 1999. The share of allocations from other TSG entities is quite small, but it has increased, as the cooperation between self-government entities has been tightened. The share of allocations from appropriated funds is the smallest but the most stable.

There are three groups of appropriated allocations from the state budget:

- allocations to finance the state (central) administration tasks delegated by law,
- allocations to finance part of the TSGs' own tasks,
- allocations to finance the state (central) administration tasks delegated by contracts.

Table II - 67: Appropriated allocations as a share in TSGs' total revenue, 1999 – 2005

Specification	1999	2000	2001	2002	2003	2004	2005
	% of total revenue						
Total revenue	100.0	100.0	100.0	100.0	100.0	100.0	100.0
1. Appropriated allocations	22.1	22.7	22.2	21.0	16.4	14.3	15.1
1.1. From the state budget	21.2	21.4	20.8	19.7	15.1	13.0	13.5
on tasks delegated by the law	12.0	12.2	13.7	12.5	8.2	8.8	9.6
on tasks delegated by contracts	1.1	1.0	0.2	0.2	0.2	0.3	0.2
on own tasks	8.0	8.2	6.9	7.0	6.7	3.9	3.7
1.2. From other TSGs	0.6	0.9	0.8	0.8	0.6	0.7	1.0
1.3. From appropriated funds	0.4	0.4	0.5	0.5	0.6	0.6	0.6
2. Other revenue	77.9	77.3	77.8	79.0	83.6	85.7	84.9

Source: Ministry of Finance, www.mf.gov.pl

The first group has a compulsory character. The self-government is obligated to execute these tasks according to the corresponding regulations, which simultaneously define the appropriated allocations as the source of financing it.

The TSGs can apply to the state administration for co-financing of some of the TSGs' own tasks by allocations. The state administration considers the applications within the framework of the amounts foreseen in the Budget Act.

The third group of allocations from the state budget is handed out on the basis of optional agreements between the state administration and TSGs. The state budgetary units can contract with the TSGs with regard to the execution of state tasks, but when the conditions seem to be disadvantageous to a TSG it may refuse to sign the contract.

The reforms which have been accomplished so far resulted in a transfer of competences for some local-oriented tasks to the TSGs. But the process of transferring public revenues to the TSGs was much slower. According to the TSGs' 2004 data, transfers from the state budgetconstituted 47.3% of the TSGs' total revenue. Consequently, the share of state transfers has remained very large.

Figure II - 17: TSGs' own revenue, general subsidies and appropriated allocations, 1999 – 2005

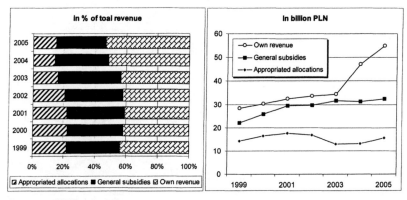

Source: GIME calculations

Figure II - 18: TSGs' compulsory transfers to the state budget, 1999 – 2005

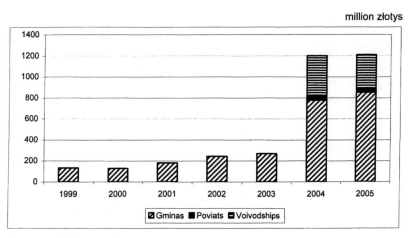

Source: GIME calculations

Within the equalization system there are also transfers from the TSGs to the state budget. Gminas with a tax revenue *per capita* exceeding 150% of the average tax revenue have to make compulsory transfers to the state budget. These transfers increase the balancing part of subsidies. One can say that gminas with their tax revenue exceeding 150% of the average gmina tax revenue *per capita* have to pay a specific kind of revenue tax. Revenues over 150% of the average were "taxed" at a 20% rate, revenues over 200% of the average at a 25% rate, and revenues over 300% of the average at a 30% rate.

Since 2004, poviats and voivodships have been included in the system of compulsory transfers to the state budget. Both kinds of self-government entities have been governed by more restrictive rules than gminas, which have the same rates and ceiling limits as before. Poviats and voivodships are obliged to transfer money to the state budget, if their tax revenue exceeds 110% of the average revenue of all poviats and voivodships respectively.

3.2 TRANSFERS TO GMINAS

3.2.1 General Subsidies

Due to their revenue *per capita* gminas are much more diversified than poviats and voivodships. In addition, gminas with the highest tax revenues make compulsory transfers to the state budget, but still their transfer rate is much lower than in other categories of the TSG. The general subsidies from the state budget are the main instrument of revenue equalization. After the 2003 reform, these subsidies have reduced the diversification of revenues because poorer gminas have received higher subsidies *per capita* than richer ones.

The paradox of the equalization system is that the state takes money from reach gminas as an obligatory contribution and simultaneously grants them the educational part of the subsidies and appropriated allocations. Before the 2003 reform, the own revenues *per capita* were more equal for both rich and poor gminas, so the effect of equalization was not as strong as it is now. The general subsidies for gminas have risen by more than 47% between 1999 and 2005. The educational part increased the most. The increase in salaries of teachers, who are still one of the worst remunerated groups in Poland, led to the higher educational part of the subsidies for gminas.

The 2003 act on the TSG revenue resulted in a reduction of those subsidies which were replaced by the increase in own revenues. The decrease was not very significant, because 82% of the subsidies were consumed by the educational part, which remained unchanged. Other parts of subsidies decreased by 15% in 2004. In 2005, the general subsidies for gminas returned to the path of growth as they increased by 3.0% since 2004. The educational part increased by 2.6% and other parts increased by 5.1%.

Table II - 68: The general subsidies for gminas, 1999 – 2005

Specification	1999	2000	2001	2002	2003	2004	2005
	10^6 PLN						
General subsidies	16,604.2	18,469.1	21,346.2	22,227.7	23,981.7	23,683.9	24,405.8
Basic part	1,449.3	1,771.0	1,851.8	2,112.3	2,179.8	x	x
Educational part	13,060.1	14,254.1	16,603.0	17,314.6	19,047.1	19,483.3	19,990.7
Compensatory part	1,415.9	1,743.1	2,084.6	2,022.7	1,869.4	109.7	11.8
Road part	585.6	601.7	709.9	683.7	788.1	x	x
Equalizing part	93.4	99.3	96.9	94.4	97.4	3,396.8	3,655.3
Balancing part	x	x	x	x	x	304.4	514.9
Supplement	x	x	x	x	x	389.7	233.1

Source: Ministry of Finance, www.mf.gov.pl

Table II - 69: Appropriated allocations from the state budget to gminas, 1999 – 2005

Specification	1999	2000	2001	2002	2003	2004	2005
	10^6 PLN						
Total	7,507.5	8,507.9	8,211.1	8,752.8	6,458.7	7,815.6	10,539.5
On tasks delegated by the law	5,005.3	5,413.7	5,857.2	6,094.3	4,153.1	6,130.3	8,119.9
Current tasks	4,988.1	5,357.9	5,802.7	6,046.4	4,110.8	6,065.1	8,069.0
Investment tasks	17.1	55.8	54.5	47.9	42.3	65.2	51.0
On tasks delegated by contracts	242.8	277.5	146.8	120.1	110.6	64.1	92.1
Current tasks	184.5	192.3	90.2	87.5	100.9	55.3	64.2
Investment tasks	58.4	85.2	56.5	32.6	9.7	8.8	27.9
On own tasks	2,259.4	2,816.7	2,207.1	2,538.4	2,195.1	1,621.2	2,327.5
Current tasks	1,503.5	1,982.1	1,523.0	1,811.5	1,668.9	1,097.2	1,890.4
Investment tasks	755.9	834.6	684.1	726.9	526.1	524.0	437.1

Source: Ministry of Finance, www.mf.gov.pl

3.2.2 Appropriated Allocations

The 2003 reform of the TSG revenues did not decrease the value of appropriated allocations from the state budget to gminas. In comparison with allocations transferred to gminas in 2003, revenue from this source even increased by 21% in 2004.

In 2005, the increase of appropriated allocations from the state budget was even higher (35%). Gminas were given new social security tasks financed from the state budget. In the upcoming years the share of budgetary transfers will still remain at the same level, because of a significant inflow of EU resources.

Table II - 70: The gminas revenue structure, 1999 – 2005

Specification	1999	2000	2001	2002	2003	2004	2005
	% of total revenue						
Total revenue	**100.0**	**100.0**	**100.0**	**100.0**	**100.0**	**100.0**	**100.0**
1. Own revenue and transfers from the EU	**52.6**	**50.9**	**50.3**	**49.9**	**51.2**	**55.3**	**56.4**
2. General subsidies	**32.1**	**32.8**	**35.0**	**35.2**	**37.8**	**32.9**	**29.7**
2.1. Educational part	25.2	25.3	27.2	27.4	30.0	27.0	24.4
2.2. Other parts	6.8	7.5	7.8	7.8	7.8	5.8	5.4
3. Appropriated allocations	**15.4**	**16.3**	**14.6**	**14.9**	**11.0**	**11.8**	**13.9**
3.1. From the state budget	14.5	15.1	13.5	13.9	10.2	10.8	12.8
on tasks delegated by law	*9.7*	*9.6*	*9.6*	*9.7*	*6.5*	*8.5*	*9.9*
on tasks delegated by contracts	*0.5*	*0.5*	*0.2*	*0.2*	*0.2*	*0.1*	*0.1*
on own tasks	*4.4*	*5.0*	*3.6*	*4.0*	*3.5*	*2.2*	*2.8*
3.2. From other TSGs	0.4	0.8	0.7	0.5	0.3	0.4	0.4
3.3. From appropriated funds	0.4	0.4	0.5	0.5	0.6	0.6	0.6

Source: Ministry of Finance, www.mf.gov.pl

3.2.3 Redistributional Effects of Transfer Payments

The share of own revenues in the gminas' total revenue decreased between 1999 and 2003. At the same time, further tasks were transferred to gminas without supplying them with additional sources of own revenues at the same time. In 2002, the share of their own revenues in total revenues dropped below 50%. This happened for the first time in many years. At last, some changes were made in 2003 when the Sejm passed the new act on the TSG revenues. From 2004 – 2005, the share of gminas own revenue increased to 55 – 56% of the total revenue due to the higher share in PIT and CIT and newly introduced revenues from the administration of state property by gminas.

From 2004 – 2005, there was a decrease of general subsidies' share in the gminas revenue structure. Henceforth, the tendency to raise the general subsidies' share was stopped. But the decline of the general subsidies' share in the revenue structure was not caused by a limitation of that source of revenues, but because of the extremely high own revenues, especially tax revenues.

Figure II - 19: Own revenues, general subsidies and appropriated allocations for gminas, 1999 – 2005

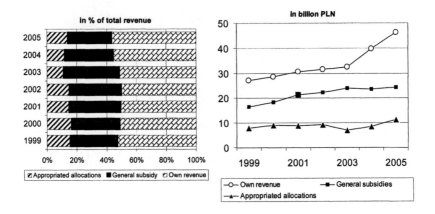

Source: GIME calculations

After the 2003 reform, there was no significant change to the transferring of resources from gminas with fiscal revenues exceeding 150% of average potential revenues *per capita* to the state budget and from the state budget to gminas with potential revenues lower than 92% of the average. The potential tax revenues are calculated as the sum of actual tax revenues and revenues lost due to given allowances and non-maximum tax rates. The following chart presents the effect of financial equalization caused both by the equalizing part of the subsidies and by compulsory transfers from gminas to the state budget.

Fiscal capacity (potential tax revenues) is shown on the horizontal scale. Revenues increased by the equalizing part of subsidies and decreased by compulsory transfers from gminas to the state budget are shown on the vertical scale. The revenues after equalization are higher than the potential tax revenues (positive effect of equalization) when their fiscal capacity is lower than 92% of the average. When potential tax revenues exceed 150% of the average, the revenues after equalization are lower than their fiscal capacity.

Figure II - 20: Gminas' potential tax revenues and equalization effects of the equalizing part of subsidies and compulsory transfers from gminas

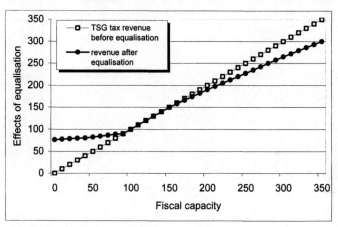

Source: GIME's own calculations

Transfers from the state budget to the gminas are much more significant in the revenue equalization system. In 2005, deviation from the average decreased from -72% to -11% after transfers to entities with the lowest revenue (1st decile group of tax revenue *per capita*). At the same time the dominance of the richest gminas from the 10th group of tax revenue *per capita* decreased. The coefficient of variation was reduced from 113% of the tax revenues (strong asymmetry) to 30% of the revenues including transfers.

The category of gminas is a more significant factor in the revenue dispersion than territorial factors. In 2005, rural gminas achieved tax revenues which were 39% lower than the average. Transfers from the state budget to rural gminas were high enough to overtake urban-rural gminas after equalization. The difference between cities with poviat rights and rural gminas decreased from 147% to 35% of the revenue *per capita*.

Table II - 71: Gminas' tax revenue and budgetary transfers in 2005

Specification	Revenue per capita			Deviation from the average		
	TR^1	TT^2	TR + TT^3	TR^1	TT^2	TR + TT^3
	PLN			%%		
Poland	**849.9**	**894.2**	**1,744.1**	**0.0**	**0.0**	**0.0**
Gminas by decile group of tax revenue per capita						
I	235.0	1,309.8	1,544.8	-72.3	**46.5**	-11.4
II	303.8	1,230.7	1,534.5	-64.3	37.6	-12.0
III	349.1	1,173.9	1,523.0	-58.9	31.3	-12.7
IV	398.3	1,128.6	1,526.9	-53.1	26.2	-12.5
V	449.7	1,075.9	1,525.6	-47.1	20.3	-12.5
VI	507.8	987.5	1,495.3	-40.3	10.4	-14.3
VII	576.2	899.4	1,475.6	-32.2	0.6	-15.4
VIII	668.7	752.1	1,420.8	-21.3	-15.9	-18.5
IX	807.9	810.3	1,618.2	-4.9	-9.4	-7.2
X	1,328.9	782.2	2,111.0	56.4	-12.5	21.0
Gminas by category						
Cities with poviat status	1,271.9	879.2	2,151.1	49.7	-1.7	23.3
Other urban gminas	804.1	649.7	1,453.7	-5.4	-27.3	-16.6
Urban-rural gminas	669.7	860.5	1,530.3	-21.2	-3.8	-12.3
Rural gminas	515.6	1,078.5	1,594.0	-39.3	20.6	-8.6
Gminas by voivodship						
Dolnośląskie	902.9	766.6	1,669.5	6.2	-14.3	-4.3
Kujawsko-pomorskie	754.9	1,019.8	1,774.8	-11.2	14.1	1.8
Lubelskie	572.9	1,035.2	1,608.1	-32.6	15.8	-7.8
Lubuskie	738.1	972.4	1,710.5	-13.2	8.7	-1.9
Łódzkie	784.8	832.1	1,617.0	-7.7	-6.9	-7.3
Małopolskie	704.3	973.7	1,678.0	-17.1	8.9	-3.8
Mazowieckie	1,282.8	736.4	2,019.2	50.9	-17.6	15.8
Opolskie	774.6	789.9	1,564.5	-8.9	-11.7	-10.3
Podkarpackie	557.9	1,095.8	1,653.6	-34.4	22.5	-5.2
Podlaskie	649.0	1,037.8	1,686.8	-23.6	16.1	-3.3
Pomorskie	870.5	910.6	1,781.1	2.4	1.8	2.1
Śląskie	977.8	804.2	1,782.0	15.0	-10.1	2.2
Świętokrzyskie	594.6	985.4	1,580.0	-30.0	10.2	-9.4
Warmińsko-mazurskie	665.6	1,059.1	1,724.7	-21.7	18.4	-1.1
Wielkopolskie	874.1	876.2	1,750.3	2.8	-2.0	0.4
Zachodniopomorskie	831.6	919.9	1,751.4	-2.2	2.9	0.4

1 TR – tax revenue (categories defined in the Act on the Self-Government Revenue as gminas' tax revenues)
2 TT – net total transfers with the state budget (transfers from the state budget to gminas and obligatory contribution from gminas to the state budget)3 TR + TT – tax revenue and net total transfers with the state budget (transfers from the state budget to gminas and obligatory contribution from gminas to the state budget)

Source: GIME calculations

Dispersion between gminas from rich and poor voivodships (territorial dispersion) is not as significant as dispersion between different categories. Gminas of Podkarpackie, Lubelskie and Świętokrzyskie have the lowest fiscal capacity in Poland. On the other hand, the equalization effect as a consequence of fiscal transfers is so strong that, finally, gminas of Podkarpackie have higher revenues than gminas of voivodships with bigger fiscal capacity before equalization, like Łódzkie and Opolskie.

Between 1999 and 2005, the gminas' revenue structure remained nearly unchanged. Gminas were given higher share in PIT and CIT, but at the same time the subsidies and appropriated allocations were increased, too. The state budget still plays a dominant role in collecting funds for gminas. The expectations connected with the new act on self-government revenues remained unfulfilled and the process of revenue deconcentration was stopped.

The situation concerning autonomy in the execution of tasks is similar. In the 1990s, gminas were given many important local tasks to be executed on their own responsibility, but since 1999 there has been stagnation in this field. In 2003, some social care activities were transferred to gminas as their own tasks. After that, the central government was reluctant to transfer responsibilities and funds to gminas. New local tasks like payments of family benefits and charges to farmers' petrol have been delegated to gminas and financed by the appropriated allocations from the state budget. The second aspect of limitation directly concerns overregulation by the law. Gminas are bound by too many regulations in major fields like education or spatial planning, which block expected reforms and limit autonomy of these units.

3.3 TRANSFERS TO POVIATS

The poviats' revenue *per capita* is less diverse than the revenue of gminas. Until the end of 2003, poviats were financed predominantly by transfers from the state budget. The poviats' system of transfers was designed not to diversify revenue of entities. In 2004, the new poviats revenue system was introduced. Appropriated allocations were reduced by 19% and the poviats share in income taxes increased. Transfers from the state budget fell down from 87% of the total revenue in 2003 to 73% in 2004 and 67% in 2005. Even though the first step towards fiscal independency of poviats was made, these entities have remained highly dependent on the state budget. Transfers still play a dominant role in the poviats' revenue system.

3.3.1 General Subsidies

Revenues from the general subsidies for poviats were raised by 43% between 1999 and 2003. As in gminas, the high increase was an effect of teachers' salaries, which raised the educational part of subsidies by 49%. The 2003 reform did not affect the value of the subsidies for poviats. The subsidies remained the dominant category of revenues, representing nearly half of the poviats' total revenues. In 2005, the general subsidies increased by nearly 6%, mainly as an effect of the 8% growth in the educational part of the grants. The share of the educational part in the subsidies was even bigger (83%) than in 2000 (78%).

Table II - 72: Poviats revenue structure, 1999 – 2005

Specification	1999	2000	2001	2002	2003	2004	2005
	% of total revenue						
Total revenue	**100.0**	**100.0**	**100.0**	**100.0**	**100.0**	**100.0**	**100.0**
1. Own revenue and transfers from the EU	**6.2**	**7.9**	**8.6**	**10.8**	**11.3**	**24.9**	**29.2**
2. General subsidies	**44.4**	**47.7**	**46.3**	**47.0**	**56.1**	**50.8**	**48.7**
2.1. Educational part	32.9	37.3	36.1	36.1	43.5	41.2	40.3
2.2. Other parts	11.5	10.4	10.3	10.9	12.6	9.6	8.4
3. Appropriated allocations	**49.4**	**44.4**	**45.1**	**42.3**	**32.6**	**24.3**	**22.1**
3.1. From the state budget	48.5	43.7	44.1	41.0	31.3	22.6	18.0
on tasks delegated by the law	*28.5*	*24.5*	*28.0*	*24.2*	*12.6*	*10.3*	*9.7*
on tasks delegated by contracts	*0.1*	*3.4*	*0.1*	*0.1*	*0.1*	*0.2*	*0.2*
on own tasks	*19.9*	*15.8*	*16.0*	*16.7*	*18.6*	*12.1*	*8.2*
3.2. From other TSGs	0.7	0.5	0.6	0.9	0.8	1.2	3.5
3.3. From appropriated funds	0.2	0.2	0.3	0.4	0.5	0.5	0.6

Source: Ministry of Finance, www.mf.gov.pl

Table II - 73: The general subsidies for poviats, 1999 – 2005

Specification	1999	2000	2001	2002	2003	2004	2005
	10^6 PLN						
General subsidies	4,371.6	5,988.5	6,503.9	5,962.6	6,236.5	6,340.3	6,699.5
Educational part	3,241.7	4,688.9	5,061.9	4,583.2	4,833.9	5,138.3	5,542.2
Road part	817.2	966.2	1,092.4	1,037.5	1,051.8	–	–
Equalizing part	312.7	333.4	349.6	341.9	350.8	634.9	637.2
Balancing part	–	–	–	–	–	402.8	394.8
Supplement	–	–	–	–	–	164.2	125.3

Source: Ministry of Finance, www.mf.gov.pl

Table II - 74: Appropriated allocations from the state budget to poviats, 1999 – 2005

Specification	1999	2000	2001	2002	2003	2004	2005
	10^6 PLN						
Total	4,774.6	5,486.6	6,191.8	5,203.4	3,474.3	2,819.3	2,481.3
On tasks delegated by law	2,801.8	3,071.8	3,932.7	3,073.5	1,395.9	1,283.9	1,328.5
Current tasks	2,770.5	3,029.1	3,898.1	3,044.9	1,364.8	1,223.6	1,264.4
Investment tasks	31.3	42.6	34.7	28.6	31.1	60.3	64.2
On tasks delegated by contracts	14.0	432.4	10.0	11.9	11.2	20.2	26.3
Current tasks	13.9	432.4	9.3	10.1	11.1	19.1	23.8
Investment tasks	0.1	0.0	0.6	1.8	0.1	1.1	2.5
On own tasks	1,958.8	1,982.4	2,249.1	2,118.0	2,067.2	1,515.2	1,126.5
Current tasks	1,518.5	1,532.9	1,747.8	1,813.0	1,795.4	1,288.8	931.7
Investment tasks	440.3	449.4	501.4	305.0	271.8	226.4	194.7

Source: Ministry of Finance, www.mf.gov.pl

3.3.2 Appropriated Allocations

In the first few years after the establishing of poviats, appropriated allocations played a dominant role in the poviat revenue system. The share of appropriate allocations from the state budget was higher than 40% of the poviats' total revenue. In 2003, poviats lost police financing (and the adequate part of the appropriated allocations) on behalf of the state administration. The share of allocations in total revenues fell down to 31%. In 2004, the amount of allocations from the state budget to poviats was cut down by 19% and in 2005 there was another reduction by 12%. Between 1999 and 2005, appropriated allocations from the state budget to poviats dropped by 48%. The reduction concerned both allocations on tasks delegated by the law and own tasks of poviats.

The chart below shows the structure and amounts of revenues split between three major categories from 1999 – 2005. On the right we see that in the case of poviats appropriated allocations have been substituted by their own revenue. Since 2003, the process of substitution has become more intensive. Meanwhile, the 2003 reform had very little influence on the share of general subsidies in the total revenue. In 2005, the share of subsidies was similar to the figure reported for 2003.

Figure II - 21: Own revenue, general subsidies and appropriated allocations in poviats, 1999 – 2005

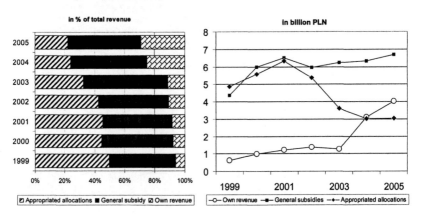

Source: GIME's own calculations

3.3.3 Redistributional Effects of Transfer Payments

In 2004, appropriated allocations were partially replaced by shares in PIT and CIT. It resulted in particular poviats having significantly higher revenues than before, whilst some poviats with smaller economic capabilities lost a lot due to the change. In order to limit the diversification, poviats with higher fiscal capacity have been obliged to transfer an extensive part of surplus to the state budget and the poorer entities were granted the equalizing part of subsidies from the state budget. All entities with tax revenues *per capita* exceeding 110% of the average have to pay a major part of the surplus to the state budget. The transfer rate is 80% of the surplus over 110% of the average, 95% of the surplus over 120% of the average and 98% (!) of the surplus over 125% of the average. Meanwhile, poviats with revenues *per capita* lower than the average benefit from large equalizing transfers, equal to 88% of the difference between the average and their tax revenue *per capita*.

Figure II - 22: Poviat tax revenue before and after equalization

in percent of average potential revenue

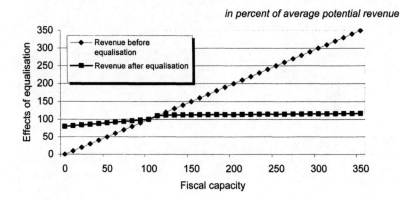

Source: GIME calculations

The system of revenue equalization is very strong. Tax revenues *per capita* are highly diverse. In 2005, the average poviats' tax revenues *per capita* were equivalent to PLN 69 with a coefficient of variation of 43%. The divergence of revenues due to fiscal capacity was highly reduced after financial equalization. After we add the equalizing part of the subsidies and subtract the obligatory contribution to the state budget, the average revenues *per capita* increase to PLN 97 and the coefficient of variation decreases to 8%! It shows that fiscal capacity is not very important for poviats, as it is balanced by strong revenue equalization.

Table II - 75: Poviats' tax revenue and effects of budgetary transfers

Specification	Revenue per capita			Deviation from the average		
	TR^1	$TR + ET^2$	$TR + TT^3$	TR^1	$TR + ET^2$	$TR + TT^3$
	PLN			%%		
Poland	**74.8**	**98.3**	**435.3**	**0.0**	**0.0**	**0.0**
	Poviat with					
highest tax revenues	279.0	191.0	496.7	273.2	94.4	14.1
lowest tax revenues	31.5	75.5	289.6	-57.8	-23.2	-33.5
	Poviats by voivodship					
Dolnośląskie	87.7	108.1	478.7	17.3	10.0	10.0
Kujawsko-pomorskie	61.2	94.3	422.8	-18.1	-4.1	-2.8
Lubelskie	50.0	83.1	421.7	-33.2	-15.4	-3.1
Lubuskie	69.5	101.9	478.4	-7.0	3.8	9.9
Łódzkie	73.3	94.1	429.5	-1.9	-4.3	-1.3
Małopolskie	68.7	92.2	383.6	-8.1	-6.2	-11.9
Mazowieckie	101.1	109.2	424.1	35.2	11.1	-2.6
Opolskie	74.3	98.7	429.5	-0.6	0.5	-1.3
Podkarpackie	56.2	87.4	406.5	-24.8	-11.0	-6.6
Podlaskie	52.9	87.4	423.7	-29.2	-11.0	-2.7
Pomorskie	70.3	96.6	466.6	-6.0	-1.7	7.2
Śląskie	105.0	109.5	386.9	40.5	11.4	-11.1
Świętokrzyskie	56.9	88.6	462.4	-23.9	-9.8	6.2
Warmińsko-mazurskie	59.6	100.8	521.0	-20.3	2.6	19.7
Wielkopolskie	80.3	99.5	431.4	7.4	1.3	-0.9
Zachodnio-pomorskie	68.0	104.4	504.7	-9.1	6.2	16.0

1 TR – tax revenue

2 TR+ET – tax revenue and equalizing transfers with the state budget (transfers from the state budget to poviats and obligatory contribution from poviats to the state budget)

3 TR + TT – tax revenue and total transfers with the state budget (transfers from the state budget to poviats and obligatory contribution from poviats to the state budget)

Source: GIME calculations

Revenue equalization is only a small part of the transfers between poviats and the state budget. The share of revenue equalization in total transfers is 7%. Much bigger funds are transferred, as the educational part of the subsidies and appropriated allocations. The average poviat transfers *per capita* are four times higher than the tax revenues after equalization. Thus poviat revenues are mainly determined by transfers connected with expenditures and not the tax revenue nor revenue equalization transfers. After one adds up tax revenues and total transfers between poviats and the state budget, the average poviat revenues per capita increase to PLN 452 and the coefficient of variation is 22%.

In he poviat with the highest fiscal capacity – Poviat Piaseczyński – transfers reduce the advantage in tax revenues *per capita* from 273% above the average to 14%. Both transfer categories – revenue equalization and the connection with expenditures – have the same effect on revenues decreasing this advantage. In the poviat with the lowest tax revenues – Poviat Łomżyński – transfers have more diverse effects. The revenue equalization transfers reduce the gap between the average poviat tax revenues and tax revenues of Poviat Łomżyński from 58% to 23% below the average. However, the effect of transfers connected with expenditures is negative and Poviat Łomżyński's revenues, including total transfers, are nearly 34% lower than the average.

The tax revenues of poviats of different voivodships are not very diversified. In 2005, the coefficient of variation was 23% for poviat tax revenues *per capita* by voivodship. After the revenue equalization transfers, the coefficient of variation decreased to 8% and hardly changed when other transfers were included. The effect of a decrease in poviat revenue diversification both after equalization transfers and other transfers only affected seven voivodships. In Małopolskie, the relation of poviat tax revenues to the average poviat tax revenues per capita was -8.1%. As a result of transfers, the relation decreased to 11.9%. Sometimes transfers radically changed the fiscal power of poviats. Entities from Śląskie had a 40.5% advantage in tax revenues *per capita* above the average. After transfers, the relation of Śląskie poviat's revenues to the average was reduced to -11.1%! However, poviats of Warmińsko-Mazurskie had tax revenues *per capita* which were -20.3% lower than the average. As a result of the transfers, their revenues exceeded the average by 19.7%.

Changes in the revenue structure has not improved the autonomy of poviats. Administration service and colleges are strictly regulated by the law and roads governed by poviats are underfinanced so the real autonomy in poviat decision-making is limited. The problem of poviat autonomy is the legal system which defines poviats as institutions providing administration services. With these responsibilities, poviats do not need a lot of autonomy. Moreover, it should be reconsidered whether institutions with such a range of competencies need to act as separate self-government units.

3.4 TRANSFERS TO VOIVODSHIPS

Until the end of 2003, the *per capita* revenue of voivodships was more diversified than the revenue of poviats. This was caused by the higher share of own revenues in total revenues and the lower dependency of the voivodship on state budget transfers. In 2004, a new voivodship revenue system was enforced, tending to flatten the *per capita* revenue between voivodships. As a result, the situation of voivodships became similar to that of poviats.

Between 1999 and 2003, a major part of the voivodships revenues were constituted by transfers from the state budget. Appropriated allocations had the biggest share in revenues; however, general subsidies also made up a noteworthy percentage of it (33-38%). At that time, the general subsidies increased by 32%. As opposed to gminas and poviats, the educational part did not dominate the subsidies structure for voivodships, as the road part was more important. During that period, total revenues from the road part were twice as big as transfers from the educational part. The majority of regional educational tasks are not administered by voivodships, but by the state administration. Although voivodships execute many public tasks, like road construction and maintenance or the financing of regional public institutions, the implementation of a regional policy without influence on the educational system is difficult to achieve. The main problem is that in many cases voivodships only execute tasks which are decided about by the central government.

Table II - 76: The general subsidies for voivodships, 1999 – 2005

Specification	1999	2000	2001	2002	2003	2004	2005
	10^6 *PLN*						
General subsidies	1,140.6	1,400.4	1,582.2	1,510.3	1,510.4	,290.0	,350.5
Educational part	235.4	424.4	452.8	420.4	440.0	461.2	564.5
Road part	672.9	748.2	872.4	846.4	818.0	x	x
Equalizing part	232.4	227.9	257.1	243.5	252.5	499.3	439.0
Regional part	x	x	x	x	x	299.7	314.5
Supplement	x	x	x	x	x	29.9	32.5

Source: Ministry of Finance, www.mf.gov.pl

3.4.1 General Subsidies

The abolition of the road part had a much stronger influence on voivodships than on poviats. In 2004, the subsidies decreased by nearly 15%. The share of the educational part has grown constantly, but the educational part does not have such a high share in subsidies as to be able to balance a negative trend in other parts of the subsidies for voivodships. In 1999 it was 21% of the subsidies and in 2005 the educational part was equivalent to 42% of the subsidies.

Table II - 77: Appropriated allocations from the state budget to voivodships, 1999 – 2005

Specification	1999	2000	2001	2002	2003	2004	2005
	10^6 PLN						
Total	1,444.3	1,531.9	2,185.0	1,774.1	2,052.4	1,293.5	900.4
On tasks delegated by the law	7.1	353.9	1,082.6	832.1	960.8	629.9	389.0
Current tasks	6.7	104.1	898.7	637.8	623.1	273.2	257.0
Investment tasks	0.4	249.8	183.9	194.2	337.7	356.8	132.0
On tasks delegated by contracts	443.7	49.4	27.8	5.1	12.1	187.0	111.3
Current tasks	104.9	23.2	17.8	3.7	6.4	115.8	64.6
Investment tasks	338.7	26.2	10.0	1.3	5.7	71.1	46.7
On own tasks	993.5	1,128.6	1074.7	937.0	1079.5	476.5	400.1
Current tasks	478.9	587.6	457.7	462.8	494.8	64.4	108.9
Investment tasks	514.7	541.0	616.9	474.2	584.7	412.1	291.2

Source: Ministry of Finance, www.mf.gov.pl

3.4.2 Appropriated Allocations

In 2004, voivodships' revenues from appropriated allocations reached the amount of 1999. However, the structure of allocations has changed. The allocations from the state budget were 10% smaller than in 1999, but there was an increase in grants transferred from other TSG entities and from appropriated funds. The 2003 reform resulted in a significant downsizing of the state budget grants on tasks delegated by the law, as well as the voivodships' own tasks. The decrease of these transfers was compensated by the higher share of voivodships in PIT and CIT. In 2005, appropriated allocations from the state budget were equivalent to 62% of those of 1999.

3.4.3 Redistributional Effects of Transfer Payments

Changes in the structure of the voivodships' revenue occurred discontinuously. From 1999 – 2005, the revenues from appropriated allocations were very unstable. As an effect of the 2003 reform, the share of appropriated allocations decreased from 51% in 2003 to 22% in 2004 and 16% in 2005. The share of general subsidies was reduced as well. In 2003, general subsidies for voivodships were equivalent to 33% of the total revenue but after one year they decreased to 19%.

In voivodships, the financial equalization of tax revenue *per capita* is quite significant. The divergence of revenue due to fiscal capacity is highly reduced after financial equalization. In 2005, the standard deviation in the voivodship tax revenue *per capita* was equivalent to PLN 50 and the coefficient of variation was 58%. After we add the equalizing part of the subsidies and subtract the obligatory contribution to the state budget, standard deviation reduces to PLN 31 and the coefficient of variation is 32%.

Figure II - 23: Own revenue, general subsidies and appropriated allocations: in voivodships, 1999 – 2005

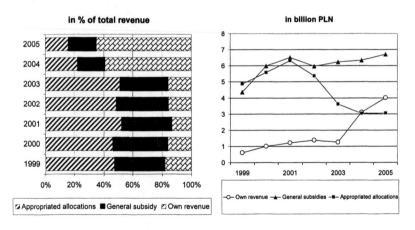

Source: GIME's own calculations

Table II - 78: Voivodships' tax revenue and effects of budgetary transfers

Specification	Revenue per capita			Deviation from the average		
	TR^1	$TR + ET^2$	$TR + TT^3$	TR^1	$TR + ET^2$	$TR + TT^3$
	PLN			%%		
Poland	**103.2**	**114.7**	**149.8**	**0.0**	**0.0**	**0.0**
Dolnośląskie	108.4	119.4	160.0	5.1	4.2	6.8
Kujawsko-pomorskie	68.2	81.9	128.1	-33.9	-28.6	-14.5
Lubelskie	50.9	74.4	116.9	-50.7	-35.1	-22.0
Lubuskie	71.7	91.6	161.5	-30.5	-20.1	7.8
Łódzkie	70.7	85.9	107.7	-31.5	-25.1	-28.1
Małopolskie	65.2	76.8	102.2	-36.8	-33.0	-31.8
Mazowieckie	254.3	194.1	276.9	146.5	69.3	84.8
Opolskie	111.5	135.8	175.4	8.0	18.4	17.1
Podkarpackie	55.2	80.0	119.9	-46.5	-30.2	-20.0
Podlaskie	52.6	78.0	116.7	-49.0	-31.9	-22.1
Pomorskie	85.0	89.3	129.6	-17.6	-22.1	-13.5
Śląskie	106.9	108.1	139.0	3.7	-5.7	-7.3
Świętokrzyskie	51.0	78.0	107.1	-50.6	-32.0	-28.5
Warmińsko-mazurskie	56.7	81.6	135.9	-45.0	-28.8	-9.3
Wielkopolskie	106.1	106.1	134.8	2.9	-7.5	-10.1
Zachodniopomorskie	61.2	81.0	138.8	-40.7	-29.4	-7.4

1 TR – tax revenue

2 TR+ET – tax revenue and equalizing transfers with the state budget (transfers from the state budget to voivodships and obligatory contribution from voivodships to the state budget)

3 TR + TT – tax revenue and total transfers with the state budget (transfers from the state budget to voivodships and obligatory contribution from voivodships to the state budget)

Source: GIME calculationsThe voivodship with the highest fiscal capacity –

Mazowieckie – achieved a 2.4-times higher tax revenue *per capita* than the average of all voivodships and a 5-times higher revenue than the entity with the smallest capacity – Lubelskie. Mazowieckie transferred 24% of its tax revenues as an obligatory contribution to the state budget for the regional part of the general subsidies for voivodships. The second voivodship which had to pay the contribution – Pomorskie – was charged a very limited value (about 2% of the tax revenue). More equality in the voivodships' revenues is a direct effect of fiscal equalization (both equalizing part of the general subsidies as revenue and obligatory contributions to the state budget as expenditure). After equalization, Mazowieckie's revenue *per capita* (tax revenue less obligatory contribution to the state budget) was 67% higher than the average and 2.6-times higher than the revenue of Lubelskie.

The advantage of Mazowieckie has increased after including other transfers from the state budget. Sometimes the fiscal effect of other transfers counteracts the effect of equalizing transfers, as in Łódzkie, where equalization brought a relatively high amount of revenues, while other transfers were so small that the deviation of Łódzkie's revenue to the mean was similar before and after the transfers including the state budget.

The system of transfers discriminated two quite rich voivodships – Śląskie and Wielkopolskie. Their tax revenue *per capita* was above average for voivodships. After equalization, their revenue decreased below the average. Transferring other parts of the subsidies and appropriated allocations from the state budget even worsened the relative situation of these voivodships.

Figure II - 24: Voivodships', poviats' and gminas' tax revenues before and after equalization

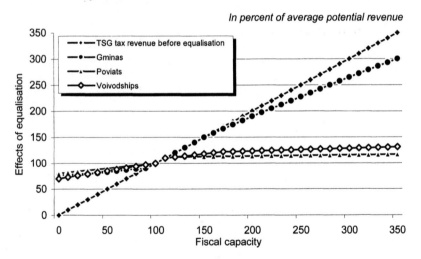

Source: Public Finance Bulletin GIME, 1(9)/2004, p. 116

3.5 EQUALIZATION EFFECTS OF THE DIFFERENT TSGS IN COMPARISON

However, every category of TSGs is subject to equalizing revenues and the scale of the process is different. Poviats have the least diverse budgets. The voivodships' revenue is slightly more diversified, whilst among gminas the system of transfers is effective only in case of entities with low *per capita* revenue.

The effect of equalization transfers is often limited due to the negative effect of other transfers which increase disparities in revenues. This problem is especially important in gminas and poviats where other transfers sometimes result in increasing revenue disparities. Equalization transfers and other transfers are not interrelated with each other and the joint revenue effect is accidental. The lack of interrelation between transfers results in an excessive share of the state budget in the creation of self-government revenues. The rich entities, which transfer money to the state budget in the revenue equalization system, get money back, as, for example, the educational part of the subsidies or appropriated allocations. The problem is that self-governments took over some public tasks but were not granted adequate own revenues. As a result, the state budget still finances many local and regional tasks. This is the most important objective of transfers. Revenue equalization is less crucial.

4   Tables

Table II - 79: Expenditure of self-government entities by division and types of self-government entity in 2004

Division	Total	Voivodships	Poviats	Gminas
		per capita in PLN		
Total	**2,393.6**	**153.6**	**491.3**	**1,914.0**
Agriculture and hunting	51.6	16.3	1.0	34.7
Forestry	1.6	0.0	1.8	0.4
Manufacturing	3.0	2.9	0.0	0.1
Energy, gas and water supply	6.2	0.0	0.0	6.2
Trade	0.3	0.0	0.0	0.3
Transport and telecommunication	303.9	54.5	47.9	217.7
Tourism	1.9	0.2	0.1	1.6
Dwelling economy	73.1	0.8	1.9	71.0
Service activity	14.0	1.4	4.2	9.8
Information technology	0.2	0.0	0.0	0.2
Public administration	236.6	10.7	59.5	186.4
Offices of supreme administration	1.9	0.0	0.0	1.9
National defense	0.0	0.0	0.0	0.0
Public safety and fire care	53.6	0.1	29.3	34.1
Revenue from legal persons, natural persons and other entities	3.5	0.0	0.1	3.4
Public debt servicing	23.9	0.9	3.8	20.5
Different settlements	33.1	10.0	1.8	22.0
Education	875.3	12.7	177.8	744.6
Higher education	1.0	0.5	0.2	0.4
Health care	55.2	13.6	23.9	25.7
Social assistance	306.5	0.6	80.6	252.4
Other tasks in the sphere of social policy	21.9	3.6	13.7	9.3
Educational care	70.5	2.1	39.9	42.0
Municipal economy and environmental protection	137.5	0.7	0.3	136.5
Culture and national heritage	78.5	20.1	2.4	56.8
Botanic and zoological gardens, natural areas and protected areas	2.0	0.0	0.0	2.0
Physical education and sports	36.6	1.9	0.9	34.0
				Cont.

continued

Division	Cities with poviat status	Other urban gminas	Urban-rural gminas	Rural gminas
	%			
Total	**100.0**	**100.0**	**100.0**	**100.0**
Agriculture and hunting	2.2	10.6	0.2	1.8
Forestry	0.1	0.0	0.4	0.0
Fishing	0.0	0.0	0.0	0.0
Mining and quarrying	0.0	0.0	0.0	0.0
Manufacturing	0.1	1.9	0.0	0.0
Energy manufacturing, gas and water supply	0.3	0.0	0.0	0.3
Trade	0.0	0.0	0.0	0.0
Hotels and restaurants	0.0	0.0	0.0	0.0
Transport and telecommunication	12.7	35.5	9.7	11.4
Tourism	0.1	0.1	0.0	0.1
Dwelling economy	3.1	0.5	0.4	3.7
Service activity	0.6	0.9	0.9	0.5
Information technology	0.0	0.0	0.0	0.0
Science	0.0	0.0	0.0	0.0
Public administration	9.9	7.0	12.1	9.7
Offices of supreme administration	0.1	0.0	0.0	0.1
Public safety and fire care	2.2	0.0	6.0	1.8
Revenue from legal persons, natural persons and other entities	0.1	0.0	0.0	0.2
Public debt servicing	1.0	0.6	0.8	1.1
Different settlements	1.4	6.5	0.4	1.1
Education	36.6	8.3	36.2	38.9
Higher education	0.0	0.3	0.0	0.0
Health care	2.3	8.9	4.9	1.3
Social assistance	12.8	0.4	16.4	13.2
Other tasks (sphere of social policy)	0.9	2.3	2.8	0.5
Educational care	2.9	1.3	8.1	2.2
Municipal economy and environmental protection	5.7	0.5	0.1	7.1
Culture and national heritage	3.3	13.1	0.5	3.0
Botanic and zoological gardens, natural areas and protected areas	0.1	0.0	0.0	0.1
Physical education and sports	1.5	1.3	0.2	1.8

Source: Authors' own calculation based on the data of the Ministry of Finance

Table II - 80: Expenditure of gminas by division in 2004

Division	Cities with poviat status	Other urban gminas	Urban-rural gminas	Rural gminas
	per capita in PLN			
Total	2,501,4	1,565,9	1,590,2	1,665,4
Agriculture and hunting	3,0	0,4	33,0	93,6
Forestry	0,4	0,1	0,4	0,4
Fishing	0,0	0,0	0,0	0,0
Mining and quarrying	0,0	0,0	0,0	0,0
Manufacturing	0,2	0,1	0,1	0,1
Energy gas and water supply	1,5	6,8	5,6	11,8
Trade	0,6	0,4	0,4	0,0
Hotels and restaurants	0,0	0,0	0,0	0,0
Transport, telecommunication	423,3	104,4	91,6	135,5
Tourism	1,3	1,5	2,3	1,4
Dwelling economy	125,7	87,4	39,3	21,1
Service activity	15,0	8,6	7,1	6,4
Information technology	0,4	0,2	0,1	0,1
Science	0,0	0,0	0,0	0,0
Public administration	184,7	163,9	176,4	209,3
Offices of supreme administration	1,6	1,7	2,0	2,2
National defense	0,0	0,0	0,0	0,0
Compulsory social security	0,0	0,0	0,0	0,0
Public safety and fire care	66,3	15,6	17,4	19,4
Administration of justice	0,0	0,0	0,0	0,0
Revenue from legal persons, natural persons, other entities	2,4	2,7	3,6	4,8
Public debt servicing	35,4	14,6	14,1	10,9
Different settlements	54,9	2,7	5,9	6,4
Education	853,1	587,8	682,8	753,4
Higher education	0,7	0,6	0,1	0,1
Health care	47,3	17,5	15,2	12,8
Social assistance	312,9	261,6	233,9	189,2
Other tasks (social policy)	22,6	5,6	2,5	0,8
Educational care	84,2	21,7	22,7	18,1
Municipal economy and environmental protection	138,7	149,2	151,5	114,7
Culture and national heritage	78,3	54,5	50,9	37,2
Botanic and zoological gardens, natural areas and protected areas	5,9	0,0	0,1	0,1
Physical education and sports	40,9	56,0	31,2	15,4

continued

Division	Cities with poviat status	Other urban gminas	Urban-rural gminas	Rural gminas
		%%		
Total	100.0	**100.0**	**100.0**	**100.0**
Agriculture and hunting	0,1	0,0	2,1	5,6
Forestry	0,0	0,0	0,0	0,0
Fishing	0,0	0,0	0,0	0,0
Mining and quarrying	0,0	0,0	0,0	0,0
Manufacturing	0,0	0,0	0,0	0,0
Energy gas and water supply	0,1	0,4	0,4	0,7
Trade	0,0	0,0	0,0	0,0
Hotels and restaurants	0,0	0,0	0,0	0,0
Transport, telecommunication	16,9	6,7	5,8	8,1
Tourism	0,1	0,1	0,1	0,1
Dwelling economy	5,0	5,6	2,5	1,3
Service activity	0,6	0,6	0,4	0,4
Information technology	0,0	0,0	0,0	0,0
Science	0,0	0,0	0,0	0,0
Public administration	7,4	10,5	11,1	12,6
Offices of supreme administration	0,1	0,1	0,1	0,1
National defense	0,0	0,0	0,0	0,0
Compulsory social security	0,0	0,0	0,0	0,0
Public safety and fire care	2,6	1,0	1,1	1,2
Administration of justice	0,0	0,0	0,0	0,0
Revenue from legal persons, natural persons, other entities	0,1	0,2	0,2	0,3
Public debt servicing	1,4	0,9	0,9	0,7
Different settlements	2,2	0,2	0,4	0,4
Education	34,1	37,5	42,9	45,2
Higher education	0,0	0,0	0,0	0,0
Health care	1,9	1,1	1,0	0,8
Social assistance	12,5	16,7	14,7	11,4
Other tasks (social policy)	0,9	0,4	0,2	0,0
Educational care	3,4	1,4	1,4	1,1
Municipal economy and environmental protection	5,5	9,5	9,5	6,9
Culture and national heritage	3,1	3,5	3,2	2,2
Botanic and zool. gardens, natural areas, protected areas	0,2	0,0	0,0	0,0
Physical education and sports	1,6	3,6	2,0	0,9

Source: Authors' own calculation based on the data of the Ministry of Finance

LIMITATIONS ON THE FISCAL POLICY OF A LOCAL GOVERNMENT[1]

PIOTR BURY[*]

1 Introduction

Decentralization means "the status or structure of the allocation of tasks, expenditures and revenues among the different levels of government" (static approach) or "a political process entailing a transfer of competencies or decision-making authority from the central level to sub-national levels of government" (dynamic approach; Ponterlitschek 2005: 2-3). Therefore, federalism can be understood as a synonym for decentralization or as the result of the decentralization process. The same applies to fiscal federalism, but since most public decisions refer to finance, either in terms of expenditures on public tasks or in terms of income to ensure the money for that, the adjective "fiscal" seems to be not so necessary.

The re-introduction of *gminas* in Poland in 1990 was the first step towards the decentralization of the country. Although two higher tiers of the local government (*powiats* and *voivodships*) were added in 1999, *gminas* are still the units best equipped with revenue sources and powers to decide about their income and spending. Deciding these matters rationally means to formulate and execute a local fiscal policy[2].

The fiscal policy of each local government is limited by various factors of general or specific nature. The first group results from the national law and is common for all local government units of the same tier within the country. The second consists of individual features, specific for each unit; they range from objective (like location, status, size) through mixed (economy and tax base) to subjective ones (local interests, attitude of

---

[1]   Based on Bury 1999; see also Bury, Oulasvirta 2004.

[*]   Institute of Economics, Świętokrzyska Academy, Poland

[2]   "Fiscal", esp. in Polish terms, can be misleading as it is commonly associated with taxing. Possibly better would be "financial" but in a wide sense, as it also contains the monetary policy and thus could not be adopted by local governments. In Polish literature this kind of – central and local – policy, which refers to public finance, is rather called a "budgetary" policy (see Weralski 1971; more about different approaches – see Bury 2002:29-30).

local officials etc.). These two types affect the local sub-policies concerning both expenditures and income[3]. It may be said that general limitations express the distance to full decentralization (fiscal federalism), while the specific ones reduce a local government's freedom irrespective of the former.

The paper consists of three sections. Two types of limitations, general and specific, are presented in Sections 2 and 3, respectively. The discussion is generally limited to *gminas*, mainly due to their basic role within the local government system and to quite a variety of revenue sources (it is the only tier that may levy local taxes and tax-character fees). Section 4 contains conclusions pointing eventually at the necessity of central government interference into the *gminas'* revenues.

2 General Limitations

National law creates a framework for any activity performed by all subjects on the state's territory. This refers to the local governments and their fiscal (and other) policies as well.

As far as expenditures are concerned, acts on the local government of each tier announce the lists of their obligatory tasks[4]. Although the list provided for *gminas* is not the longest one, it consists of tasks crucial for everyday life and development of local communities.

The mentioned list of tasks is very general and refers to all *gminas*, irrespective of their individual features. In practice, however, each particular task has to be seen as based on individual needs of and possibilities for each local government. For instance, one of the *gminas'* tasks is public transport; in small rural *gminas* this may be a bus line run by the national company or ceded to the inhabitants, in medium-sized urban *gminas* there may be a municipal bus company and in metropolises a city-owned limited company operating bus, tram or even an underground network with the necessary infrastructure. In any event, such a record of tasks in the national law forces a local government to act within particular fields, while simultaneously imposing a limitation on its expenditure policy.

---

[3] A similar situation occurs on the national level as a result of international agreements or obligations (e.g. imposed by the EU).

[4] See the three Acts on Local Government.

What is more, in many cases central legislation also provides detailed amounts of particular expenditures. This is, for instance, true in the case of education, which is the biggest burden on local budgets, with teachers' salaries not allowed to be lower than is fixed in the "Teacher's Chart".

On the other hand, national law also reduces the local governments' possibilities to gather money. In the case of the *gminas* this influence is expressed in:

- a detailed list of possible income sources;
- fixed (in some cases as maximum and minimum) rates of local taxes and fees;
- obligatory reductions and exemptions;
- a maximum level of the annual and total *gmina's* debt;
- limited powers of the local authority.

The first two limitations mean that the acts introducing different revenue sources fix the rates of each tax or fee, also providing a list of obligatory reductions and exemptions in each case[5]. Such solutions seriously reduce the *gminas'* possibilities of collecting money from local sources.

National law also controls the use of repayable sources, fixing percentage limits on a *gmina's* annual (15%) and total (60%) amount of debt in relation to its planned income. The annual limit may even be cut down to 12% (as today) together with additional restrictions when the total debt of the public finance sector is too big.

Besides all that, the *gminas* are equipped with powers that lead to a decrease in their direct income. First of all, they have a right to decide about rates which are lower than those fixed by the law. Then, in addition to the national ones, the *gminas* may introduce their own reductions and exemptions as well as postponements and remissions. Such actions may be, of course, elements of the particular *gmina's* development policy and decided to attract investors and new inhabitants so as to enlarge the local tax-base. On the other hand, however, no *gmina* could levy taxes above the fixed limits, even if those were considered as too low for local conditions.

And no tier of the local government is allowed to create its own sources of income in addition to the national list. Only the *gminas* have a little more freedom here, as their communities may decide about so-called self-taxation of inhabitants. It is a local tax which may be introduced only as a consequence of a local referendum. A first move may be made by either the *gmina's* council or a number of inhabitants, the purpose and

---

5   An impressive list is included in the tax on agriculture, with the negative effects being partly compensated (till the end of 2003) by the general grant.

terms have to be stated by the council, but eventually it is the people who make the decision. So, the legal procedure of doing this is rather complicated and – again – fixed by national law. In any event, self-taxation appears to by a quite uncommon source of revenue.

3   Specific Limitations

This group of limitations results from different kinds of features, each of them being specific for a local government unit and in a certain period of time. The biggest differences may be observed on the level of *gminas* and this type of units will be discussed further (larger units are more diversified inside but at the same time more similar to other units of the same level.)

From among many different specific features of the *gminas* the most important ones for fiscal policy seem to be the following:

- "natural" features (status, size, location, economy, tax base);
- the needs-to-funds relation (in space and time);
- the attitude of local officials;
- local interests (parties, pressure groups, strong individuals);
- awareness of reactions of the *gmina's* users.

3.1   "NATURAL" FEATURES

The first group consists of features which may be called immanent or "natural". They provide a standard set used to describe a *gmina* and are – at least for short periods – rather stable.

Status

There are 2478 *gminas* in Poland. Most of them are rural (ca. 1590), then mixed urban-rural (ca. 580) and urban (ca. 310)[6].

---

[6]   At the end of 2004; based on data of the Central Statistical Office and current changes (in general the total number remains stabile, while within the structure the rural ones lose for the benefit of mixed and urban ones).

Urban units of the local government need to be explained. The last group mentioned above consists of towns of different sizes (see below). Another 65 big towns are simultaneously local government units of the higher tier, so-called urban *powiats*, cities with *powiat* rights or – shortly – city-*powiats*[7]. As such, they have to fulfil tasks of a *gmina* as well as those of a *powiat* and collect money from sources provided for both tiers of local government. The largest unit of this kind is the capital Warsaw (until the last elections in October 2002 it was an obligatory municipal union of 11 urban *gminas*).

The status itself has no big influence on local finance. The most significant direct impact may be seen in the construction of the educational part of a general grant which is divided on the base of the weighted number of pupils. According to this, three pupils in a rural school make up an additional weighted pupil and consequently – an additional sum of money (see Bury, Swianiewicz 2003).

The status gives a brief information on what kind of a *gmina* it is and is a picture of the other features.

Size

This feature is usually expressed by the number of inhabitants or by the area of the territorial unit[8].

As far as the population is concerned, the smallest *gmina* has only 1.3 thousand inhabitants (Krynica Morska; urban), while in the biggest that number is about 1,677.8 thousand (Warsaw; also urban); their range differs by as much as 1291 times!

In terms of area, the smallest *gmina* only covers 3 square kilometres (Górowo Iławeckie; urban), while the largest covers as much as 635 square kilometres (Pisz; mixed). Here the difference is not quite as big but in any case it exceeds 210 times; the *gmina's* leader in Górowo may walk around it during a lunch-break, while in Pisz a whole day spent in a car would not be enough to visit each settlement.

The relative measure which combines the two is population density. In Polish *gminas* it varies from 5 persons per square kilometre (Lutowiska; rural) to about 4,500 (Świętochłowice; urban). The discrepancy for this measure is quite big and equals 900 times.

---

[7]   Urban *powiats* are towns with over 100,000 inhabitants plus those who, due to the administrative reform, lost their position as previous *voivodships'* capitals (except for three that did not agree to take this advantage, plus one which resigned recently).

[8]   Data below: middle of 2004; based on data of the Central Statistical Office.

All these differences influence the fiscal policy of each *gmina*. Let us start with its expenditure part. Generally, a smaller *gmina* has smaller tasks to take care of and it may even give up some if they are considered as not so important or impossible to run (as, for instance, in the case of local transport reported above). On the other hand, a small population number may also cause problems with running such municipal facilities – something which cannot be avoided - like, for example, primary schools. This is so because of fixed costs in the service apparatus which cannot be diminished in the short run. A disadvantage for small *gminas* is also the difficulty to utilize scale economies in many services, something that may result in higher unit costs in comparison with big ones. On the other hand, when the size of a *gmina* grows too much the advantage of scale economies shifts to a disadvantage. Many service costs behave like a U-shaped curve (Bennett 1980). Generally, these regularities are also true also for sparsely populated *gminas*, for instance: more smaller schools to avoid expensive commutation or relinquishment of some technical services like sewage collection systems.

The range of tasks, however, grows faster than the *gmina's* population itself, especially in towns. This is so because the bigger the town is, the more diversified and composed is the infrastructure it needs. Using again the example of public transport, a single bus line may be quite sufficient for a small town, while a bigger one would need a bus network. At a certain size a tram will appear more efficient means of transport. And in a metropolis all this will be completed with an underground. Similar gradation may be observed with regard to culture (from an amateur troupe via professional theatre, specialized scenes, up to the opera and ballet) and many other public facilities. Quite a part of these services is used by non-inhabitants, so the spillover effect appears. All this results in higher total per head costs of bigger *gminas*[9].

The features above also have an impact on the income side of the *gminas'* budgets. The size of population was a factor which decided about the amount of so-called proportional quota distributed among the *gminas* within the basic part of the general grant. Due to the algorithm the smallest *gminas* received much more than those of between 5,000 and 10,000 inhabitants, while bigger ones got only a little more (Uryszek 2005). In effect the smallest *gmina* had a coefficient of 3.85, while the largest had one of – only 1.23. From 2004 onwards, this proportional quota has ceased to exist. Instead, another one, based on population density, was introduced. It is granted to *gminas* with an index lower than average; the more sparsely populated a *gmina*, the more money it receives.

---

[9]   Some empirical examples cited in: Bury 1993.

Location

The statement of a fact that *gminas* occupy different parts of the country (plains, mountains, sea-shore, lakes-areas etc.) sounds trivial. But this fact has a great impact on the *gminas'* finances and relevant policies.

A small, sleepy seaside *gmina* "lives" in full swing for 2-3 months during the summer, provided the weather is good. During this period it has to serve (water, sewage, waste collection etc.) the number of people which even exceed its "normal", permanent population. This season is also an opportunity to gather extra money, although here the possibilities are much smaller than the needs. In fact, contrary to common opinions, *gminas* can directly receive very small amounts of money due to their recreational function (see below).

On the other hand, water-supply and sewage systems are relatively easy and cheap to build on the flat, sandy plains of central Poland. In the mountains, especially when considering the spread of small settlements, all this is much more difficult if not impossible. Another example may be that of taking pupils to school; relatively easy in lowlands with a dense network of roads but troublesome in the mountains where roads must follow the valleys.

Economy

In part, this feature results from the former ones. This is not always true, but in fact the status of a *gmina* reflects its economy. The traditionally typical function of towns is as a home to industry, while for rural areas it is –agriculture and forestry. In general, the industry is more "productive" with regard to local budgets. In Poland it delivers the money from the property tax and – very important in some mining *gminas* – the exploitation fee. In addition, the people working there guarantee their home local governments an inflow of a part of their personal income tax. Until the end of 2003 this share was 27.6% in general and for some *gminas* with coal-[mines it was 32.6]%. For 2004 it was as much as 35.72% for all units; from then on the individual coefficient for each *gmina* is calculated, up to the ceiling of, eventually, 39.34%. Also, a share in the corporate income tax flows back – proportionally – to those *gminas* where these people work: from 2004 as much as 6.71%, before – 5%. Agriculture and especially forestry, due to very low tax-rates as well as numerous exemptions and reductions, only deliver small amounts of money to the local budgets. Only in a few *gminas* with very good soils the tax on agriculture may be more efficient than the property tax.

The location factor has a direct impact on some kinds of business. Seaside *gminas* are the only places for sea ports, shipyards and fishery. The sea-shore and mountains may be intensively used for recreation and tourism. Many traditionally poor *gminas* located at the country borders seized the opportunity and became huge market centres for citizens from neighbouring countries. Such business replenishes local budgets with the market fee, which – unlike the exploitation fee – does not deprive the *gmina* of a right to receive the equalizing part of a general grant.

Another kind of business related to location is recreation. It becomes more and more popular and some *gminas* have chosen it as their leading function. From the point of view of local budget income, however, recreation is not a productive function. In towns, an important source may be the property tax levied on recreational grounds and facilities. In rural areas, however, these possibilities are much smaller, despite of the fact that big, well known recreational centres are usually urban centres as well. Renting rooms in private homes, something that is typical in the countryside, is not treated as a business activity in the law on property tax. Landlords (everywhere) can pay the lump-sum income tax towards the local budget if they decide to choose that form of taxation (other forms are the revenue sources of the central budget).

Despite of the fact that some kinds of businesses may be very tax-productive, it is better for a *gmina* not to rely upon one sector but to have a mixture of activities to be more resistant to fluctuations in the economy.

Local tax base

Each government should adjust its fiscal policy to the actual tax base, which, to a great extent, is decided by the kind and condition of the local economy. Local tax bases have a twofold impact on local fiscal policies. Economic status of firms and inhabitants delimit the *gmina's* possibilities of collecting money from taxes and fees as well as from user charges. On the other hand, poorer local governments need more money to secure public services which may be not necessary at all in wealthy *gminas*.

A poor local tax base, together with bigger needs of such local governments, argue for intergovernmental grants as being necessary too in order to assure the desirable level of basic public services in each *gmina*.

3.2 THE NEEDS-TO-FUNDS RELATION

This limitation varies both in space and in time. The *gminas* have, of course, different needs and different possibilities to meet and to finance those. The second element of this relation may be easily expressed by the richest and the poorest local governments.

In Poland this discrepancy is quite big: for instance, the total budget income per capita in 1995 was 65 times higher in the rural *gmina* of Kleszczów than in the rural *gmina* of Zakrzew. For the so-called *gminas'* own income (i.e. without general and specific grants and other external sources) that factor is much bigger: in the same year 1995

Kleszczów (again) had as much as 437 times more income per inhabitant than Lipnica Wielka (rural). These differences significantly dropped in 1996 but then grew again. In 2004 Kleszczów gathered in total "only" 34 times more money than the rural *gmina* of Tomaszów Lubelski, while for the *gminas'* own income that discrepancy was 196 times (the poorest being the rural *gmina* of Dzwola).

But also in very similar *gminas* whose situation is financially stabile, this relation may suddenly appear as unfavourable for one of them. The reason may be, for instance, an urgent repair of a roof on a local school or of a bridge on a local road. This relation will change for the same *gmina* in the next budget, when the necessary works are finished. Another example, not as easy to cope with for a small *gmina*, would be the sudden bankruptcy of a big firm, meaning a breakdown of the local tax base.

Another problem may result from a standard size (or a module) of a public facility. In many cases it is impossible to, step by step, satisfy the growing local demand for a public service. It is common practice to wait until the demand is high enough, with the quality of services offered by the existing facilities deteriorating, and to then finance a new module which in turn will not be used to the full for a time.

3.3 ATTITUDE OF LOCAL OFFICIALS

This limitation means a collection of many features connected with the local authority, i.e. a *gmina's* leader and council members, as well as the staff of local administration. Among these features are, for example, the following ones: the attitude to the posts occupied within the authority and to the related duties, ideas about the *gmina's* functioning and growth, identification with local affairs, opening up to new ideas and readiness to cope with parochialism, understanding of the *gmina's* problems in wider social and economic contexts, looking for outer investors and funds offered by the EU etc.

All the above mentioned features eventually influence the *gmina's* position and wealth. There are a number of examples of *gminas* with relatively poor conditions, which do quite well thanks to their competent authorities and – on the other hand – an even bigger number of *gminas* with better potential, which, nevertheless, are not doing anything except waiting for the central government's help in form of general and specific grants.

3.4 LOCAL INTERESTS

First of all, it should be stressed that it is the local level at which local interests could be specified and considered.

General interests of a *gmina* should, of course, be represented by its elected authorities. This is not always so, however, especially since after the last elections in 2002 a *gmina's* leader and the majority in the local council may come from different political corners. But even if a consensus is achieved on this level, there may be individuals or groups not satisfied with the official policies and/or trying to win as much as possible for themselves. They may represent, for example, a political party of the opposition (or even the one in power!), pressure groups like the local fire-brigade, church or women's organizations but also – in small *gminas* –strong individuals like a parish-priest or a businessman who offers several dozens of jobs.

Many of such conflicts, derived from limited money at local disposal, could be avoided if the budget were bigger. There are, however, other local resources like the area necessary for development, which cannot be expanded all that easily (or at all).

Accidental and superficial observations seem to prove that demands of inhabitants are rather expressed in defence of existing facilities (a small local school or a bus-stop), while official bodies direct their actions toward creating something new for the local community.

In both cases the demands to spend public money for this or that activity, if expressed early enough, may help to prepare a more effective local budget. On the other hand, when submitted for the current year, they might cause tensions and cuts in other sectors. In each case such actions limit the fiscal policy of the local government.

3.5 AWARENESS OF REACTIONS OF THE GMINA'S USERS

The last limitation discussed here is the local authority's awareness of reactions of the *gmina's* users in response to, on the one hand, public financial burden (hereafter tax) and, on the other, an offer of public services (hereafter service) in this *gmina*. The *gmina's* users are first of all households and firms located in this *gmina*, but also the subjects who are there accidentally (e.g. on holiday or just a stopping by) or – as potential ones – considering this *gmina* as a possible place to settle down.

The reactions in those cases in which the relation between the local public burden and services[10] is considered as not satisfactory, may be charcterized as follows:[11]

tax/service-behavioural;

tax/service-developmental;

tax/service-locational.

When compared with the other, the first type of reaction may be called a passive one. Although a household or a firm is not satisfied with the tax-to-service relation it decides to endure it by changing its own habits: reducing its demand for public services, decreasing its consumption, agreeing with less interest in business, spending additional money for privatised services that used to be public, etc.

The second type of reaction is a dynamic one. It is the user's action towards a decrease in the local financial burden and/or towards an increase in the offer of the *gmina's* services. In the case of both kinds of actions, people and firms can act directly or use the intervention of councillors or other persons (see the previous section).

The third kind of reaction is just an escape: people and firms move to those *gminas* where they consider the discussed relation as better for them.

Each of these three types of user reactions may occur separately or in a discretionary sequence from the "behavioural" down to the "locational".

The users' reactions are considered here as their potential behaviour, so they can influence a local government's fiscal policy in advance and only when the local government is aware of them. And any sensible government should foresee and thoroughly consider all possible consequences of its decisions, here – in the sphere of local fiscal need and public services. The actual reactions themselves, when they happen, also become limitations, but then the succession is reversed: the eventual response of the local government will be forced and related to the current budget (with possible issues for the future, long-term fiscal policy).

The first reaction (behavioural) may be considered by a local government as not that important and may eventually be neglected. It can admittedly already end like this, but quite possibly may be continued by the second or the third type of reaction. The second (developmental) reaction may be treated by an arrogant authority as a

---

[10] Rosen (2002) calls it "tax-welfare package" (after Ponterlitschek 2005).

[11] Based on the idea presented by McLoughlin (1969) in relation to the places or transportation channels.

nuisance but for a sensible one it would be a valuable symptom of public discontent and an impulse for changes in the local fiscal policy.

The worst, however, would be the reaction of the third type (locational). The decision to change the place of living or of one's business activity is not easy, so the reasons for doing so must be really significant. And when once decided and executed, such a change is rather irreversible and can have an additional effect by encouraging those who still hesitate to follow the pioneers.

The loss of a number of inhabitants or firms will put less pressure on the local government's activities, but at the same time will result in a smaller income flowing into the local budget. And such a *gmina* may even need relatively more money, because it is not always possible to cut its expenditures in the rate corresponding with the decrease in the number of tax payers and their public service needs (see section II 3.2). The "escape result" may be, however, an intended effect of the local policy; getting rid of, for instance, strong polluters or unemployed and other poor people may eventually be positive.

Of course, the tax-to-service relation is not the only and not the most significant one which prevails in deciding about the reactions above, especially those which end with the change of location[12], but possibly its role will grow, as it can be observed in better developed countries (also on the national level: exotic citizenships of some rich Europeans or so-called cheap flags seem to be good examples here).

4   Conclusions: The Need for Central Government Interference

In the previous sections, different factors which limit each local government's freedom in deciding about local revenues and – to a smaller extent – expenditures were presented. One group of these limitations results from the decisions made at the national level. In general, local budgets' income sources provided by the central legislation lead to huge discrepancies between *gminas* in their own revenue per capita.

Even if the wealth or poverty of individuals seems to be accepted and justified in the market economy, this is not so in the case of local governments. Each of them has to fulfil a set of necessary public services according to fixed standards. And what is more – the demand for these services is usually bigger in poorer *gminas*. Therefore, they

---

[12]   See Rhode, Strumpf (2003: 1649), after Ponterlitschek (2005).

need more money. To receive more money could be achieved by granting local governments new sources of incomes of their own and/or suppression of limitations imposed by the national legislation.

Even if the general limitations could be removed at all, each *gmina* would still face a set of individual ones. First of all, there are big differences in economic potential between regions in Poland[13]. They are much bigger as far as *gminas* are concerned. New sources of income would then, of course, be welcome but not so much for *gminas* with a poor economic base. Especially the assignment of occasionally proposed new shares in the central taxes, like VAT or excise, would for sure increase each local government's revenue but at the same time would deepen the discrepancies between them in the category of their own income.

Thus the general conclusion is that intergovernmental help is inevitable. The current Polish system of the general grant to some extent equalizes the big differences between the *gminas'* incomes. It provides both vertical and horizontal equalization. The latter, however, is rather limited: first, as far as the obligatory payments are concerned, to relatively rich *gminas*; secondly, the amount of money which remains after excluding the payments is still very high in comparison with the poorer ones. In any event, the new system is somewhat better than the previous one.

---

[13] See Mackiewicz, M.; Malinowska-Misiąg, E.; Misiąg, W. and Tomalak, M. (2005).

5 References

Bennett, R.J. (1980): The Geography of Public Finance, London.

Bury, P. (1993): "Oceny with planowaniu urbanistycznym a gospodarność with rozwoju miast" (Evaluation in Town Planning and the Economics of Urban Development), University of Łódź, Łódź.

Bury, P. (1999): "Ograniczenia polityki dochodowej gmin" (Limitations on the Revenue Policy of Gminas), in: Obrębalski M. (ed.): Gospodarka lokalna with teorii in with praktyce, "Prace Naukowe", No.807, AE, Wrocław, pp.54-65.

Bury, P. (2002): "Finanse lokalne z elementami finansów państwa" (Local Government Finance with Elements of Central Government Finance), Kielce.

Bury, P. and Oulasvirta, L. (2004): "A Framework for the Fiscal Policy of a Local Government", "Working Papers", No.39, Glasgow Caledonian University, June.

Bury, P. and Swianiewicz, P. (2003): "Grant Transfers and Financial Supervision over Local Governments in Poland", "Working Papers", No.37, Glasgow Caledonian University, November.

Mackiewicz, M.; Malinowska-Misiąg, E.; Misiąg, W. and Tomalak, M. (2005): "Interregional and Intergovernmental Transfers in the Polish General Government Sector 1999-2003", IBnGR (GIME), Gdańsk, VW-Project.

McLoughlin, J.B. (1969): "Urban & Regional Planning. A Systems Approach", London.

Ponterlitschek, L. (2005): "The Theory of Fiscal Federalism", ZEU J-L University of Giessen, VW-Project.

Rhode, P.W. and Strumpf, K.S. (2003): "Assessing the Importance of Tiebout Shorting: Local Heterogeneity from 1850 to 1990", American Economic Review, No.93(5), December, pp.1648-1677.

Rosen, H.S. (2002): "Public Finance", Boston.

Uryszek, T. (2005): "Intergovernmental Grants in Poland", University of Łódź, VW-Project.

Weralski, M. (1971): "Polityka budżetowa" (Budgetary Policy), Warszawa.

Ustawa z dnia 5 czerwca 1998 r. of samorządzie województwa (Act on Local Government of *Voivodship* Level), DzU 2001, No.142, item 1590.

Ustawa z dnia 8 marca 1990 r. of samorządzie gminnym (Act on Local Government of *Gmina* Level),, DzU 2001, No.142, item 1591.

Ustawa z dnia 5 czerwca 1998 r. of samorządzie powiatowym (Act on Local Government of *Powiat* Level), DzU 2001, No.142, item 1592.

III. SELECTED TOPICS OF GERMANY'S SYSTEM OF INTERGOVERNMENTAL FISCAL RELATIONS

THE FEDERAL FINANCIAL EQUALISATION SYSTEM IN GERMANY

ANDREAS KIENEMUND

The Federal Republic of Germany is a federal state comprising the Federal Government and 16 federal states (Länder). In the structure of the German state, the Länder represent an independent level of government endowed with its own rights and obligations. According to the constitutional rules on public finance, the municipalities are deemed to be part of the Länder. In order for the Länder, as independent constituent states, to fulfil the tasks allotted to them under the Constitution (which is called the Grundgesetz or Basic Law in Germany), they need adequate financial resources. The Länder must also have free and independent control over these resources.

Germany's fiscal system is characterised by far-reaching mechanisms that attempt to harmonise federal structures. The Constitution itself stipulates detailed principles for the distribution of tax revenues between the Federal Government and the Länder, as well as among the Länder themselves. The German Constitution as a whole is geared towards the principle of maintaining equivalent living conditions for the entire population. This principle also influences the realm of federal fiscal relations.

Germany's constitution guarantees that both the Federal Government and the Länder receive appropriate levels of funding. The procedural regulations in this regard can be divided into four phases:

1. First, the entire tax revenue is distributed to the two levels of government – namely the Federal Government and all Länder – and the municipalities receive a supplementary grant of revenue (vertical distribution).

2. Next, the total Länder portion of tax revenue is assigned among the various Länder (horizontal distribution).

3. In a third stage, there is equalisation between poor Länder and rich Länder (financial equalisation among the Länder).

4.   In addition, poor Länder also receive funds from the Federal Government (supplementary federal grants).

The details of the individual stages are subject to simple legal regulations in the Constitution.

Other countries with federal systems have regulated fiscal relations to a much lesser degree in their constitutions. Instead, they have opted for statutory laws or contractual arrangements.

1   Vertical Distribution of Tax Revenue

The Constitution jointly allocates several particularly important taxes to the Federal Government, Länder and, to a degree, the municipalities. According to the Constitution, either the Federal Government, the Länder or the municipalities are entitled to the remaining types of tax in full.

Income tax, corporation tax and VAT are divided between the Federal Government and the Länder as a whole. The municipalities are entitled to a share of the income tax and VAT. These taxes are therefore referred to as joint taxes. The Federal Government receives 42.5% of the income tax, 50% of the corporation tax and, from 2007 onwards, in the region of 55 % of VAT (up from around 53 % of VAT in 2006). The revenue accruing to the Länder is 42.5% of the income tax, 50% of the corporation tax and, as of 2007, around 43% of VAT (down from about 45% of VAT in 2006). At present, 15% of the income tax and around 2% of VAT go to the municipalities.

Of all the types of tax, income tax and VAT generate by far the most revenue. The distribution of these major taxes between the Federal Government and the Länder is the principal reason for the close interconnection of public finances at the different levels of government. It entails both levels of government being equally affected by fluctuations in the levels of revenue over time. This mechanism helps to prevent disagreements on tax distribution. Since amendments to a federal tax law may also influence the level of tax revenue accruing to both the Federal Government and the Länder, such amendments require the consent of the Federal Council (Bundesrat, the legislative chamber representing the Länder).

The Federal Government receives all the revenues from federal taxes. The majority of the excise duties (such as mineral oil duty and tobacco duty) as well as the insurance tax are federal taxes. The Länder are entitled to receive all of the revenue from Länder taxes. These include the inheritance tax, the motor vehicle tax, most types of transactions taxes (in particular, the real property transfer tax) as well as some other types of taxes that generate small amounts of revenue. The municipalities receive the revenues from the trade tax, the real property tax as well as the local excise taxes. The Federal Government and the Länder receive a share of the trade tax receipts through an apportionment.

2 Horizontal Distribution of Tax Revenue

At the second stage, the tax revenue belonging to the Länder as a whole is distributed among the individual Länder. Apart from VAT, the individual Länder are in principle entitled to the tax revenue which is collected by the revenue authorities on their territory (principle of local revenue).

In the case of income tax and corporation tax, the principle of local revenue is corrected by special regulations, or what is referred to as allotment. With regard to income tax, this means that in the end every Land receives approximately those tax revenues that are collected for the income of its inhabitants inside or outside of its territory. Companies pay corporation tax centrally. In line with the principle of allotment, this tax is distributed to all states in which a company maintains a place of business.

VAT is not distributed according to the principle of local revenue. A part of the Länder share of VAT, but not more than 25%, goes as a supplementary portion to those Länder whose receipts from the income tax, the corporation tax and the Land taxes per capita are lower than the per capita average of all Länder. This partially, but by no means fully, closes the gap between the tax revenue of the fiscally weak Länder and the Länder average. The exact amount of the VAT supplementary portions depends on the amount by which the per capita tax revenue of a Land falls below the average per capita tax receipts for all Länder. A linear-progressive topping-up schedule is used to calculate the exact amount of the VAT supplementary portions.

The remainder of the Länder share of VAT, at least 75%, is distributed according to the number of inhabitants.

The distribution of VAT is thus, in itself, a first form of financial equalisation, because its purpose and effect is to harmonise the tax receipts of the Länder. It massively increases the amount of tax revenue that financially weak Länder receive.

3   Financial Equalisation among the Länder

The system of financial equalisation among the Länder further reduces the differences in receipts among themr. Poor Länder receive adjustment payments. These payments have to be funded by the wealthy Länder. The system of financial equalisation among the Länder ensures that fiscally weak Länder also have adequate financial resources to fulfil their tasks and develop their sovereignty. An alignment of the Länder's revenue is intended to create and maintain equivalent living conditions for the entire population in all of Germany.

The financial equalisation among the Länder is not, on the other hand, intended to do away with their fiscal autonomy and sovereignty. This is why differences in receipts among the Länder are only reduced and not fully compensated.

The starting point for the financial equalisation among the Länder is the financial capacity per inhabitant of the various Länder. The financial capacity of a Land is the sum of its receipts and (64%) of the receipts of its municipalities.

The local authority revenues are taken into account when assessing financial capacity because the Länder are responsible for providing their municipalities with appropriate and adequate financial resources. Länder with financially strong municipalities are required to spend less of their own finances on the financial resources of their municipalities than Länder with financially weak municipalities.

In principle, all types of Länder and municipality revenues are taken into account when determining financial capacity. However, there are exceptions to this rule. This means that, ultimately, the tax revenues of the Länder and municipalities mainly flow into the financial equalisation among the Länder.

In principle, the system of financial equalisation among the Länder assumes that the financial requirement per inhabitant is the same in all the Länder. This assumption is not appropriate in the case of the Länder of Berlin, Bremen and Hamburg, which are city-states. The city-states are simultaneously both cities and Länder in their own right. They have a much higher financial requirement per inhabitant than the normal Länder. Therefore, for the purposes of the equalisation system, their populations are notionally increased by 35%. The three sparsely populated Länder of Brandenburg, Mecklenburg-Western Pomerania and Saxony-Anhalt also have a slightly higher financial requirement per inhabitant. Their populations are therefore slightly notionally increased for the purposes of the financial equalisation.

The exact size of the adjustment payments to a poor, fiscally weak Land, depends on the amount by which its financial capacity per (fictitious) inhabitant falls below the average financial capacity per inhabitant. The difference from the average is topped-up partially, but not completely. A linear-progressive topping-up schedule is used to calculate by how much the difference is topped-up.

Similarly, the size of the adjustment amounts which a rich, fiscally strong Land has to pay depends on the amount by which its per capita financial capacity exceeds the average fiscal capacity per inhabitant. The difference from the average is skimmed-off partially, but not completely. A linear-progressive skimming-off schedule is used, which is symmetrical to the topping-up schedule. To ensure that the sum of the adjustment amounts correspond with the sum of the adjustment payments, the adjustment amounts are either increased or decreased by a corresponding percentage.

The regulations are designed to ensure that in terms of financial capacity per inhabitant the order of the Länder does not change as a result of the financial equalisation among the Länder.

The system of financial equalisation among the Länder further reduces the differences in the levels of their financial resources. Take, for example, a fiscally weak Land with a financial capacity per capita that amounts to 70% or 90% of the average before financial equalisation. Once the financial equalisation system has been applied, this increases to 91% or 96% of the average. On the other hand, a fiscally strong Land with 110% or 120% of the average financial capacity per inhabitant before equalisation has between 104% and 106½% afterwards (see also the example given in table III - 1).

This far reaching system of financial equalisation among the Länder is subject to criticism, especially among the fiscally strong Länder. In the past, those have already taken this matter before the Federal Constitutional Court. By and large, the equalising effect of the system has diminished slightly over the course of time.

4   Supplementary Federal Grants

Supplementary federal grants are grants which the federal government makes to poor Länder to achieve financial equalisation among the Länder. These grants are uncommitted funds and serve to meet general financial requirements. There are two different kinds: general supplementary federal grants and supplementary federal grants for special needs.

General supplementary federal grants further reduce the gap between the average financial capacity per (fictitious) inhabitant and that of poor Länder, which still remains after financial equalisation among the Länder. General supplementary federal grants go to Länder whose financial capacity per inhabitant, after financial equalisation among the Länder, is less than 99.5% of average financial capacity per inhabitant. The shortfall is made up proportionally.

This means that a financially weak Land, whose financial capacity per inhabitant amounts to 70% or 90% of the average before financial equalisation among the Länder, has 97½% or 98½% of the average per capita financial capacity once equalisation and general supplementary federal grants have been applied (see also table III - 1). The difference from the average for the Länder is therefore considerably and clearly reduced overall.

Furthermore, supplementary federal grants for special needs are also granted. These serve to compensate individual poor Länder for special burdens they have to bear.

The special burdens merely provide the basis and reasons for granting supplementary federal grants for special needs. The funds are not legally tied to a specific purpose. The Länder receiving such federal grants for special needs bear sole responsibility for their use.

Table III - 1: Equalisation of the differences in financial capacity by applying the system of financial equalisation among the *Länder* and the general supplementary federal grants

Financial capacity per inhabitant before financial equalisation among the Länder as % of the average financial capacity per inhabitant	Financial capacity per inhabitant after financial equalisation among the Länder as % of the average financial capacity per inhabitant[1]	Financial capacity per inhabitant after financial equalisation among the Länder and the general supplementary federal grants as % of the average financial capacity per inhabitant
70	91	97½
80	93½	98
90	96	98½
100	100	
110	104	
120	106½	
130	109	

[1] Numbers for the rich Länder (financial capacity > 100%) neglect the (above mentioned) factor ensuring the correspondence of the adjustment payments with the adjustment amounts.

Currently, the eastern German Länder and Berlin receive special-need supplementary federal grants to build up their infrastructure, which is still comparatively underdeveloped as a result of the partitioning of Germany, and to compensate for the disproportionately weak financial capacity of their municipalities. At present, these funds amount to a total of € 10 billion annually and are therefore extremely important to the Länder that receive them. They form part of the Solidarpakt II (Solidarity Pact II), which is intended to rectify the consequences of the division of Germany. These supplementary federal grants for special needs will gradually be phased out by 2019.

In addition, the eastern German Länder receive special-need supplementary federal grants, worth a total of € 1 billion annually, to compensate for the special burdens placed on them by structural unemployment. These grants are limited until 2009. There will be a review in 2008 to identify whether they are still required above and beyond 2009.

Furthermore, small, poor Länder receive special-need supplementary grants, amounting to around € 517 million annually, to make up for their above-average administrative costs. Smaller Länder have higher administrative costs per inhabitant than larger Länder. This is because the fixed costs of administration in smaller Länder have to be divided between a smaller number of inhabitants. A review is held every five years to establish whether the preconditions for awarding these supplementary federal grants for special needs still exist.

4.1 CURRENT INITIATIVES TO REFORM THE FEDERAL SYSTEM

Over the past few years, Germany has seen an intensive debate about the reform of the country's federal order. The federal system has generally proven its value. In the course of time, however, substantial political overlaps have evolved between the Federal Government and the Länder, leading to lengthy and complex decision-making processes. Therefore, the aim has been to disentangle these overlaps and to ensure a more transparent allocation of responsibilities between levels of government.

To achieve this goal, the reform measures were separated into two packages. The first set of reforms was concluded by the summer of last year with the introduction of a law amending the Constitution on September 1, 2006. This first stage was devoted to an overall strengthening of responsibilities between the levels of government. The reform package included specific measures to:

- strengthen the legislative competence of the federal government in areas of national importance (for example the laws on weapons and explosives or the laws on nuclear energy);

- strengthen the legislative competence of the Länder in areas of regional importance (for example the regulation of the legal circumstances of a Land's own civil servants or the law of assembly);
- reduce the number of laws requiring the consent of the Bundesrat.

With regard to the financial relations between the Federal Government and the Länder, the reform of the federal system has:

- abolished all areas of joint financing that are not indispensable in providing uniform living conditions and coordinating national interests; all abolished areas of joint financing have been transferred to the sole competence of the Länder which receive adequate compensation from the Federal Government in turn;
- strengthened the tax autonomy of the Länder in the field of real property transfer tax;
- created a strong incentive for rigorous adherence by the Federal Government and the Länder to the European Stability and Growth Pact. The Constitution now clearly stipulates that both sides are responsible for adhering to the European rules. If Germany breaches the terms of the Pact and the Council of Ministers applies sanctions, the federal government will have to bear 65% and the Länder 35% of the stipulated amount.

It cannot yet be determined with any degree of precision, how successful these measures will be. From the Federal Government's perspective, the actual reduction in the number of laws requiring the consent of the Bundesrat will be the key measure of the success of the reform. This issue has been one of the cornerstones of the reform. With regard to the areas where the Länder have gained new legislative competences, practice will show how effectively and responsibly they will make use of their new power.

The federal financial equalisation system has not been included in the package of reforms for two reasons. First, the legislative framework – which has only recently entered into force – is designed to remain in place until 2019. Second, fiscal relations are such a complex subject matter (contested not only between the Federal Government and the Länder, but also among the poor and the rich Länder themselves) that the framers of the constitutional reform felt that the process stood a greater chance of success if the issues were divided up and fiscal relations were dealt with in a separate round. As a consequence, the first set of reforms only adopted selected measures in the field of fiscal relations, while the second step will be solely devoted to the reform of federal fiscal relations.

It is as yet too early to predict which reform measures will pass during the second round. A reform commission, established in December 2006, will produce different proposals over the upcoming months, which will then be discussed. Issues that will be of central importance during the second round of reform will certainly include the matter of strengthening the fiscal discipline of all levels of government, for example:

- by establishing a warning system to prevent budgetary crises on the part of the Federal Government or the Länder, or
- by tightening the conditions for public debts.

Another matter for reform may include the issue of granting greater levels of tax autonomy to the Länder, for example:

- by giving them legislative competence over certain taxes, or
- by granting them the right to stipulate regional collection rates with respect to certain taxes.

It is not possible to say whether such tax autonomy will go so far as to require a reform of the federal financial equalisation system. Considering the substantially divergent interests of the rich and the poor Länder, however, it seems unlikely that the federal financial equalisation system will be changed fundamentally in the course of the reform process.

THE LOCAL FISCAL CONSTITUTION IN GERMANY
– AN OVERVIEW

WOLFGANG SCHERF UND KAI HOFMANN

1   Introduction

The basic structure of the federalist system in Germany is laid out in the fiscal constitution, the primary legal source being the German constitution (Grundgesetz). In addition, many rules concerning the municipal level are settled in the constitutions of the German states (Laender). The fiscal constitution describes the assignment of tasks across different levels of government, the tax assignments and the basic tax sharing rules, and defines the aims of the fiscal equalization system. The public sector in Germany is subdivided into three levels of government: the federal level (Bund), the states (Laender) and the municipalities (including associations of local municipalities).

The Grundgesetz grants German municipalities the right to govern all issues of the local community in their own responsibility. These include, for example, the provision of communal streets, nurseries, primary education. Problems of regionally limited scope, which exceed the municipalities' field of responsibility but do not affect the country as a whole have to be dealt with by the Laender. The Laender thus act as intermediate local authorities. According to the German constitution, the Laender are responsible for all governmental tasks as long as the Bund is not explicitly given the responsibility. The Laender's tasks are concentrated in the fields of the educational system, police and public administration. The Bund is in charge of a number of tasks which affect the whole federal territory due to their nature (e.g. national defence, federal streets, currency policy). Moreover, it is responsible for the system of social insurance and stabilisation policy.

On the revenue side, the division of funds across different levels of government is dominated by a system of tax sharing. Despite all its weaknesses, this system can be interpreted as a solution which compromises between the requirements of a federal structure of state and a rational fiscal system.

Income tax (especially wage tax) and corporation tax account for more than 40% of the whole tax revenues, clearly indicating that the ability-to-pay principle plays a dominant role in German taxation. In addition, the value added tax contributes an additional 30% to total tax revenues. Next to these large taxes, there are special excise taxes (e.g.

tobacco tax, petroleum tax) and taxes on assets (e.g. tax on land and buildings, inheritance tax). The distribution of these taxes contains a vertical and a horizontal element. Each part of the tax revenue is assigned to a certain level. For example, the Bund decides about and collects 100 % of the petroleum tax and the tobacco tax. The Laender are entitled to all revenues from the motor vehicle tax, beer tax and inheritance tax. Municipal taxes are, in particular, the trade tax and real property tax.

The fiscally important taxes named above are all part of the system of tax sharing, which assigns each level a certain percentage of total revenues. In the past, especially the shares of the turnover tax for Bund and Laender have been adjusted to account for changes in the assignments of tasks. Municipalities and local authorities' associations are formally and legally regarded as part of the Laender. The Laender are responsible for providing adequate funding for the municipalities within their own regional system of fiscal equalization.

After assigning several taxes vertically and determining those of the federation, the shares of revenues assigned to Laender and municipalities must be distributed among the 16 German Laender and among the municipalities of a given Land respectively. The revenues from certain taxes collected within a Land or municipality, respectively, represent the starting point of their horizontal distribution. (For tax sharing and fiscal equalization among the German Laender, see the previous section of this book). Given this starting point, the distribution of funds is modified in a system of horizontal and vertical fiscal equalization which aims at achieving a more even distribution of fiscal means. This system is installed to promote the establishment of equal living conditions as demanded by the German constitution (Art. 72 (2) GG).

2   The Position of Municipalities within the System of Public Finance

The arrangement of the federal fiscal relations according to the constitution mainly regards the relationship between federation and Laender. At the same time, Art. 28 (2) GG (Volkmann, 2001) guarantees the right of municipal self-administration and Art. 106 (5)-(9) GG states that municipalities are entitled to the revenue of impersonal taxes (property tax and trade tax) and have a right to participate in the Laender's revenue from shared taxes.

2.1 THE PRINCIPLE OF SELF-ADMINISTRATION OF MUNICIPALITIES

According to Art. 28 (2) GG, municipalities have the right of "governing all affairs of local interest within the scope of law on their own responsibility". In particular cases, the field of activities which a singular municipality is responsible for depends on its structural conditions, especially the size of its population, the size of the municipal area, the economic structure and its fiscal capacity. Tasks which smaller municipalities may not be able to handle are often pursued as tasks of local importance in larger municipalities. Generally, municipalities may handle new tasks of local interest unless they are explicitly assigned to other institutions by law. At the same time, the restriction "within the scope of law" in Art. 28 (2) GG makes clear that this does not mean that municipalities are granted a fixed set of tasks which cannot be altered by laws on higher levels.

The most important characteristic of municipal self-administration is the right to decide autonomously about the realization of municipal tasks. Self-administration though does not only require a high degree of autonomy with respect to tasks, but also flexibility concerning expenditures and revenues. For this purpose Art. 28 (2) GG grants the municipalities the right to run independent budgets on their own responsibility and thereby have the right to decide where and how to spend their revenues. Again, however, this municipal self-administration has to account for a number of restrictions which derive from the "framework of laws". The laws mentioned here can refer to the general assignment of a task to the municipal level as well as the mode of realising a task of local relevance.

There are mainly two groups of tasks which can be distinguished: tasks of self-administration and externally defined tasks. Tasks of self-administration are performed by communes on their own responsibility. They are merely subject to legal supervision by national non-municipal institutions. These tasks can again be split into compulsory and voluntary tasks of self-administration. Regarding the first group, communes are legally obliged to perform the tasks, but in principle they are free to choose the mode of task-performance. For voluntary tasks of self-administration municipalities have the additional right to decide whether to take over the task or not.

Examples for voluntary tasks of self-administration are especially cultural and social institutions such as theatres, museums, welfare centres, but also regional business development schemes. Compulsory tasks of self-administration are particularly social welfare payments, primary schools, regional planning of construction work and sewage disposal. The increasing influence of the central government on the performance of tasks proves to be a problem as it undermines municipal autonomy. In many cases it has become largely impossible to distinguish compulsory tasks of self-administration tasks from delegated tasks.

Delegated tasks are performed by the municipalities on behalf of superordinate regional authorities. These tasks are governmental tasks which are delegated to the municipalities by the Bund or Land. Delegated tasks are assigned by law. The superordinate unit has a far reaching authority to issue directives, which may include detailed regulations, unless laws provide for other arrangements. At the same time, the municipalities are responsible for issues of personnel and organisation.

2.2 THE REVENUES OF MUNICIPALITIES

Municipalities may dispose of several sources of revenues to cover their expenditures. The total amount of municipal revenues (credit raising excluded) is at about € 144 billion in 2001. Taxes constitute the largest part of these revenues (34.1 %). Nearly the same amount is received in the form of grants (33 %). In addition, there are fees and (financial) contributions (31.1 %), gains from privatisation (4.8 %) and other revenues (15.1 %) which include revenue from local business activity and concession. The level of debt is, due to more restrictive regulations, of little importance (2.7 %).

Fees are levied for individual utilizations of certain communal services. They can be divided into price-resembling user fees (e.g. for waste and sewage disposal) and tax-resembling administration fees (for official acts). Contributions mainly take the form of local assessments which are levied to cover for costs of developing real estate, just as fee contributions are payments in exchange for special services received from the municipality. The main difference is that fee financed services can be apportioned to singular persons, whereas those services financed by contributions can only be apportioned to certain groups of users.

Fees and contributions are the municipalities' primary instruments of financing their expenditures. A rise of municipal property tax factors or of the deficits to cover expenditures is only tolerable if the possibilities to levy fees or contributions are widely exhausted (Färber, 2000: p. 85). Fees may not exceed production costs of the service provided. If this ceiling is reached, for instance in the sector of waste and sewage disposal, fees may not be raised to cross-subsidize other municipal services.

In contradiction to the tasks of the municipalities, which are only defined in a general sense, the German constitution specifies very precisely which kind of taxes are assigned to the municipalities (sovereignty of claiming tax revenue). According to Art. 106 (5) GG they receive a share of 15 % of the income tax (but not of the corporation tax) as well as a share of the VAT. Additionally, the municipalities are entitled to the revenues from business tax and real estate tax. For both taxes the tentative tax (tax base x basic federal tax rate) is defined in an identical fashion for all municipalities, but the individual municipalities have the right to apply a tax factor. Finally, municipalities and municipal associations are entitled to the revenue from local excise taxes, which are of minor fiscal importance.[1]

The municipal share of income tax accounted for 41.6 % of all tax revenues in 2001, thereby being the most important tax for municipalities. At present the municipalities receive 15 % of their Land's revenue of wage tax and the individual income tax, as well as 12 % of the tax revenue on interest incomes. The distribution of these tax shares between municipalities depends on the income tax revenue of their inhabitants. However, tax revenues are limited to taxable wages and personal incomes of not more than 50,000 Euro for singles and 100,000 Euro for couples. These limits cause municipalities with a high average income of their citizens to obtain less income tax than they would be entitled to according to the total local revenue.

Since 1998, the municipalities participate in the turnover tax with a share of 2.2 %. In 2001, these revenues added up to 5.5 % of total tax revenues on the municipal level. The current distribution to individual Laender as well as the distribution to the individual municipalities within the Laender is carried out by a complicated two-stage system.[2] From 2003 on, the distribution follows a standardized allocation formula, which is based on the regional/local number of employees who are subject to social insurance contributions (without government employees), fixed assets, inventories, salaries and wages paid by regional/local enterprises.

With respect to municipal autonomy, the trade tax is the most important municipal tax. The share of the trade tax revenue was 34.9 % in 2001. Nowadays only the taxable business profits generated in the business plants located within the municipality are taxed. These taxable business profits mainly consist of profits of the corresponding business plants plus some additions and minus some cutbacks. Furthermore, a tax-exemption of 24,500 € for natural persons and private partnerships is introduced. That

---

[1] For instance amusement tax, beverage tax, dog tax, second home tax, tax on hunting and fishing, pub licence tax, package tax.

[2] The share in the turnover tax was meant to compensate the abolishment of the trade tax on capital in 1998. As the trade tax on capital has not been levied in the former GDR Laender, it has not been possible to split the share in the turnover tax by a standard quota applying to the whole federal territory. The share in the turnover tax is divided between old (85%) and new (15%) Laender. The current distribution quota consists of the trade tax revenue, the number of employees subject to social insurance contributions and, for West Germany, the former revenue of the trade tax on capital.

means that the trade tax is mainly paid by incorporated firms and big non-incorporated enterprises.

The municipalities are allowed to apply an individual factor to the tentative tax. The latter is the product of the taxable business profits and the basic federal tax rate. If a firm entertains business plants in multiple municipalities, the tentative tax is split according to the wages. For corporations the basic federal rate amounts to 5 %. Non-incorporated firms face a progressive federal rate. The marginal tax rate starts at 1 % and reaches 5 % at a level of 60,000 €. The trade tax is counted as operating expenditure so it can be deducted from its own taxable base as well as from the taxable bases of the income- and corporation tax. To compensate for the preferential treatment of corporations by the tax reform 2002, non-incorporated firms are granted an additional tax exemption depending on their trade tax burden.

Besides the business tax the real estate tax is also counted as the second impersonal tax which municipalities have the right to collect. Similar to the trade tax, they are allowed to apply a municipal factor to a tentative tax which is defined in an identical fashion across Germany. Its share of the municipal tax revenue amounted to 16.5 % in 2001. Subject to taxation is the assessed value of domestic property, which is still based on the unit values calculated in 1964. The uniform applicable tax rate ranges from 0.26 % to 0.35 %, depending on the type of property.[3] On this calculated tentative tax the municipality applies its municipal factor for agricultural and forest property (real property tax A) and for factory premises and living premises (real property tax B) respectively. The municipal factor for real property tax A is normally significantly below the municipal factor for real property tax B.[4]

2.3 THE MUNICIPAL FISCAL EQUALIZATION SYSTEM

The municipal fiscal equalization system basically serves two functions. The fiscal function shall extend the financial capacity of the municipalities to an extent which enables them to perform their self-determined and externally defined tasks. The redistributive function intends to reduce inter-municipal differences in fiscal capacity if

---

[3]   In East Germany the assessed value for properety is based on the year 1935. With respect to the lower value assessments higher basic federal rates are applied (0,005% to 0,010%).

[4]   Because of the deficiencies of standard value assessment the current form of the real estate tax can hardly be justified. It could either be included in a municipal output tax or the tax base would have to be changes (i.e. real estate area, rents).

these differences have not been caused by autonomous decisions of the municipalities. Besides the two main functions the municipal fiscal equalization system also has to comply with and support the regional planning activities within a Land. Finally, the municipal fiscal equalization system can fulfil a stabilization function, provided that the Laender design the system in such a way that municipal revenues are stabilized across the business cycle.

Germany's municipal fiscal equalization system is arranged differently in different Laender. However, the following basic procedure applies to all Laender. The total funds used in the municipal fiscal equalization system constitute the total shared revenue fund. According to Art. 106 (7) GG the Laender are obliged to let their municipalities participate in the Laender's share of the income-, purchase- and corporation taxes (mandatory tax network). Moreover, the Laender may voluntarily direct the revenues from Laender taxes or from the Laenders' fiscal equalization system to the voluntary tax network. The degree to which these taxes are included in the tax network is determined by the Bundeslaender. It depends primarily on the distribution of tasks between Land and municipalities, but also on the degree to which the Land's government is "municipality-friendly".

The total shared revenue fund is used to pay unconditional and conditional grants. Conditional grants mainly consist of investment grants. In addition, expenses for delegated tasks are refunded. The funds for conditional grants are normally taken in advance from the fund of shared revenues. This leaves a reduced fund for unconditional grants (hereafter key fund).

Unconditional grants are the core of the municipal fiscal equalization system. Unconditional grants are meant to improve the municipalities' fiscal capacity in general. In addition, their allocation aims at reducing the disparities between municipalities with respect to their fiscal capacities. The allocation of unconditional grants to urban and rural districts follows the same pattern. The distribution of unconditional grants to the singular municipalities is based on the relation of their fiscal needs to their fiscal capacity.

Fiscal needs are measured on a per capita basis. In many cases, the indicator of fiscal needs (Bedarfsmesszahl, BMZ) depends on the size of a municipality. Consequently, the bigger a municipality is, the higher is the indicator of per capita fiscal needs. Laender which use such rules try to account for the fact that large municipalities usually provide additional infrastructure which is not provided by small municipalities but regularly used by the inhabitants of the latter. Sometimes, the costs arising due to crowding are used as an additional justification to deviate from the principle "inhabitant = inhabitant" (Scherf, 2000: pp. 153). Additionally, other indicators like the (relative) number of pupils, the presence of foreign soldiers etc are included to account for special types of needs.

The indicator of fiscal capacity (Steuerkraftmesszahl, SMZ) of a municipality is basically defined by the share the municipality receives from income tax, VAT, real estate tax, and trade tax. However, the indicator of fiscal capacity does not depend on effective but on standardized tax rates of the real estate and the trade tax. Thus it can be ensured that differences in municipal tax factors do not influence the amount of unconditional grants and thereby create an incentive for municipalities to set a certain (low) tax rate in order to receive more vertical transfers.

If the indicator of the fiscal needs of a municipality exceeds the tax capacity measure (BMZ > SMZ), the difference between the two is reduced by unconditional grants. Given the easiest case with a proportional compensation scheme and the compensation rate "a" we receive: SZ = a(BMZ - SMZ), where SZ is the amount of unconditional grants received (SZ = Schluesselzuweisung). In some cases, the compensation scheme guarantees a certain minimum fiscal capacity regardless of the compensation rate. If the tax capacity measure exceeds the fiscal burden measure (SMZ > BMZ), the municipality is called "abundant". An abundant municipality does not receive any unconditional grants. In some Laender, the surpluses are partially skimmed by a fiscal equalization assessment and transferred to the key fund.

The redistributional effects of the unconditional grants mainly depend on the sum available as key fund. If the sum is increased, non-abundant municipalities receive more means per capita. This reduces the disparity between fiscally weak and fiscally strong municipalities. In practice, the Laender differ in the way they define fiscal capacity and fiscal need as well as in the degree to which disparities between the two are compensated. When setting these parameters, the legislator must take into account that there exists a latent conflict between distributional aims on the one hand and fiscal autonomy for municipalities. In particular, the incentive for municipalities to increase their own fiscal capacity by cultivating and using their own tax base must not be destroyed by exceedingly generous compensation schemes.

2.4 TASKS AND REVENUES OF COUNTIES

In between a Land and its municipality there exists the intermediate level of counties. Some large cities are simultaneously municipality and county, but most counties are made up of groups of smaller municipalities. This raises the question of how local tasks are to be divided among municipalities and counties. The Grundgesetz explicitly grants counties the right of self-administration. At the same time, they are not granted any tasks by the constitution but have to fulfil tasks delegated by the Land as well as tasks of obligatory self-government as defined by law. With respect to voluntary self-government, the municipalities have the priority when it comes to taking on these tasks. The tasks may only be delegated to a county if this is absolutely necessary. This necessity is firstly recognized for tasks of supra-municipal tasks of integration, such as the construction of county roads, regional planning above the municipal level, environmental control and business development.

Second, the counties are given complementary tasks. These are tasks which, e.g. due to economies of scale, cannot be fulfilled efficiently by single, typically smaller municipalities. These complementary tasks include youth homes and homes for the elderly, specialized schools (e.g. for music) or public utility enterprises. The scope of county tasks does not necessarily cover all municipalities within one county. Due to differences in municipal structure, there is substantial diversity in the scope and degree of county activities between counties.

Third, counties may engage in compensating activities aimed at regional redistribution. The county's task is to reduce the disparity in local public services among municipalities and to possibly also reduce the differences in fiscal capacity beyond what the municipal fiscal equalisation has already achieved. While administrative support or support in form of personnel is unproblematic, there is a controversial debate concerning the legitimacy of additional financial support because this is feared to interfere with the fiscal equalisation systems and the aims pursued by them.

Counties do not have noteworthy own revenues. Their budget consists of fees and grants from the fiscal equalization system, wherein parts of the key funds are reserved for counties. In addition, the counties may collect a special county contribution which is paid by the municipalities. In most cases, the county levies an equal contribution rate on all the financial means of all municipalities (own taxes + unconditional transfers). The rate varies depending on the amount of tasks transferred to the counties. The special county contribution is the only disposable source of resources for the counties but at the same time means a direct and uncompensated reduction in municipal fiscal capacity. Therefore, the settlement of the contribution rate frequently is a heavily disputed matter.

Initially, the special county contribution was meant to be a minor instrument of financing county activities. However, they now account for 40 % of county revenues, thereby becoming the predominant source of funds. The increase was partly caused by the fact that the Laender have transferred an increasing number of tasks to the counties but failed to provide the corresponding financial resources. Thus the counties had to rely on increasing county contributions from the municipalities. This development adds to a number of other factors which, in the past, have reduced the fiscal autonomy of the municipal level.

3 Problems and Perspectives of Local Public Finance in Germany

The current system of local public finance has been subject to many controversial debates over the last two decades. The debate primarily focuses on the local trade tax and the extent to which it is suitable as a municipal tax. In recent years, the growing burden of municipal tasks and the simultaneous lack of sufficient financial means has caused a new controversy.

3.1 REFORM OF THE LOCAL TRADE TAX

The benefit received principle plays an important role in justifying local tax revenues. In line with this principle, the household-specific local infrastructure is largely financed by the municipal income tax share (Scherf, 2000: pp. 21; Scherf, 2002.). The local trade tax was originally justified by the same principle and was meant to represent a tax price, which local firms pay for the use of the specific infrastructure provided for them. By varying the factor by which the uniform tentative tax is multiplied, the municipality and the local firms can coordinate the supply and demand for specific local infrastructure (Wissenschaftlicher Beirat beim Bundesministerium der Finanzen, 1982: p. 33). The current trade tax does, however, not fulfil the requirements for a local tax. First, there are too many tax exemptions (e.g. for agriculture, forestry, free professionals) and for small enterprises (due to a large, general exemption). Thus the benefit received principle is violated. Together with the differences in industry structure, the tax exemptions cause large regional disparities in tax revenues which do not coincide with differences in economic activity. Thus the trade tax in its current form is unsuitable to ensure fiscal autonomy of municipalities. The fact that the trade tax is highly volatile across time and the business cycle causes further criticism. Given the tight restrictions on municipal deficits, the volatility in the municipalities' major tax base causes pro-cyclical fiscal behaviour by municipalities, especially in the domain of public investments. Finally, the fact that the trade tax is not refundable at the German border results in a substantial international competitive drawback for firms producing in Germany.

Given these shortcomings, the reform of the trade tax has been debated for a long time. Lately, municipalities have been granted a share of the overall turnover tax. However, they are not given the right to introduce a municipal tax factor. Thus this step cannot fully replace the trade tax because it does not allow municipal fiscal autonomy. Proposals to introduce local income and profit taxes would transfer tax revenues to those municipalities where employees and shareholders live rather than where the firm is located and where the local infrastructure is used (Bundesverband der deutschen

Industrie, Verband der chemischen Industrie, 2001.). This would massively reduce the incentives for municipalities to attract firms and foster local economic development. In addition, the local tax base would remain volatile.

On the other hand, a local tax on the real net output generated within the municipality (hereafter output tax) seems to be a suitable concept (Wissenschaftlicher Beirat beim Bundesministerium der Finanzen, 1982.). Its tax base captures the local business activities as a whole, including formerly exempted industries and firms. If agriculture and the housing sector are to be included, the commercial real property tax could be abolished. The output tax has a broad tax base and therefore only requires a moderate tax rate (e.g. 2.5 to 3.0 %). Municipalities can be given the right to apply a factor to the uniform tentative tax, thereby ensuring municipal fiscal autonomy. The real net output is a good proxy for the intensity with which firms use local infrastructure. Thus the output tax complies with the benefit received principle and allows firms and municipalities to coordinate the demand and supply of specific public infrastructure. In addition, the broad tax base reduces regional disparities in original tax revenues and consequently reduces the need for horizontal redistribution. Finally, the tax base is much more stable across the business cycle and hence prevents pro-cyclical behaviour. The output tax reduces the distortions to competition among different industries inherent to the current trade tax. In order to prevent competitive drawbacks on the international level, the firms can be allowed to deduct a "normalized" output tax burden from its turnover tax payments (Scherf, 2000: p. 32). In sum, the introduction of a municipal output tax seems a suitable reform which can solve most of the problems associated with the current trade tax and strengthen fiscal autonomy and the benefit received principle on the municipal level.

3.2 STRENGTHENING AND APPLYING THE PRINCIPLE OF CONNEC-TIVITY

In order to fulfil their tasks, municipalities need sufficient financial means. The definition of what is "sufficient" is disputed among Laender and municipalities. In general, both levels agree that the municipalities' right of self administration needs to be protected by ensuring that the financial capacities on the municipal level cover delegated tasks and the tasks of compulsory self-government. At the same time, they must be left some financial means to fulfil their tasks of voluntary self-government. This does, however, not mean that municipalities must be granted a fixed amount of resources regardless of the financial situations of Laender and the Bund. Instead, the fact that there is no hierarchy in tasks across different levels of government means that the municipalities have to account for their financial situations.

The principle of connectivity (Art. 104a (1) GG) applies largely to the relationship between Bund and Laender but only has very limited implications for the fiscal relationship between Bund, respectively Laender on the one and municipalities on the other side. It is important to note that the Bund is not allowed to circumvent the Laender and delegate tasks or transfer financial means directly to the municipalities. This step would violate the organisational sovereignty of the Laender. This in turn means that the municipalities can only turn to the Laender when demanding sufficient financial resources to fulfil delegated tasks and tasks of obligatory self-government. The constitutions of the Laender differ with respect to the degree to which they account for the principle of connectivity. Some constitutions state that the total fiscal capacities of the municipality must be sufficient to fulfil the different types of tasks. At the same time, they do not demand specific vertical transfers to cover delegated tasks and tasks of obligatory self-government. Other constitutions are somewhat stricter and demand that tasks may only be transferred if the question of how the extra costs are to be covered is solved simultaneously. However, the constitutions do not explicitly say that the means transferred together with the tasks must cover all costs. [And even in those cases where the principle of connectivity has been strengthened in recent constitutional reforms (e.g. Hesse), the stricter rules only apply to future changes in task assignments.]

In the past, Bund and Laender have repeatedly violated the principle of connectivity by transferring tasks to the municipal level without providing the necessary means. This does not only involve delegated tasks but also tasks of obligatory self-government. In the latter case, legislative changes by the Bund or Laender have substantially increased the costs of given tasks. Especially changes in the field of welfare benefits and child-care facilities, both carried out on the local level, have been criticized in this respect. Part of the problem, especially when it comes to task delegation on behalf of nationwide decisions, is caused by the way in which these are decided. The municipalities have no formal power in the corresponding decision making process but are represented by the Laender. These do not always appear to be acting in the interests of the municipalities.

In order to prevent these problems in the future, the principle of connectivity must be followed more closely. This in turn means that the level of government which decides about a certain task - rather than the one which carries it out - must be primarily responsible for providing the necessary means. In practice, of course, this rule creates its own problems because it is difficult to differentiate between expenditures which are essentially necessary to carry out the task at hand and those expenditures which result from the freedom of movement granted to the municipal level in fulfilling the task. In order to increase an efficient performance, the delegating level might set financial incentives for the administrating municipalities.

3.3 MEASURES TO STABILIZE THE FINANCIAL SITUATION OF MU-NICIPALITIES

The instability of revenues is a central problem of municipal finance. The first reason for this instability is the volatility of municipal taxes. Next to the extremely volatile trade tax, the revenues from the municipal share of income tax fluctuate with the tax base "income". This would not pose a central problem if the Laender adjusted vertical transfers to smoothen municipal revenues across time: In reality, however, the Laender mostly fail to do so. Instead, they pass on the cyclical fluctuations in their own revenues to the municipalities or even amplify them by reducing the funds in the fiscal equalization system.

Replacing the municipal trade tax by a local tax on real net output can be a first but important step to stabilize municipal revenues. This step would make the fiscal equalization system on the federal level easier because the participation of Bund and Laender in the municipal trade tax – an element which was alien to the system in the first place – would be obsolete. This would detangle the complicated system of tax sharing and would at the same time promote fiscal equivalence. A further stabilization of municipal revenues could be achieved by modifying the system of sharing income taxes. Instead of assessing the amount of revenues transferred to the municipal level as a fixed share of the annual total income tax revenues, it could be assessed using an average amount of revenues over many years. Of course, Bund and Laender would have to cope with stronger fluctuations but this would be in line with their responsibility for stabilizing the economy and their ability to run deficits.

In a next step, it may be interesting to give municipalities the right to impose a tax factor on local income taxes. The German Grundgesetz already covers this possibility (Art. 106 (5) GG). The purpose of this step would not be to solve the problem of financial means caused by insufficient transfers or other deficiencies of the current system. Instead, this would make it possible for the municipality to tailor the supply of local public goods and services according to the preferences of the resident population.

4 References

Bundesministerium für Wirtschaft und Finanzen (Hrsg.): Gutachten der Steuerreform-
kommission 1971, Schriftenreihe des Bundesministeriums der Finanzen, vol. 17,
Bonn, p. 915.Reformkommission Soziale Marktwirtschaft: Reform der Finanzverfassung, Bertelsmann Stiftung – Heinz Nixdorf Stiftung – Ludwig-Erhard-
Stiftung, 1998.

Färber, Gisela: Theorie und Praxis kommunaler Gebührenkalkulation, in: Andel,
Norbert (Hrsg.): Probleme der Kommunalfinanzen, Berlin, 2000, p. 85.

Haverkamp, Franz: Die Finanzbeziehungen zwischen Ländern und Gemeinden, in:
Arnold, Volker / Geske, Otto-Erich (Hrsg.): Öffentliche Finanzwirtschaft, München
1988, pp. 55 – 120.

Henneke, Hans-Günter: Die Kommunen in der Finanzverfassung des Bundes und der
Länder, 3. ed., Wiesbaden, 1998.

Karrenberg, Hanns / Münstermann, Engelbert: Gemeindefinanzbericht 2002,
Städtische Finanzen: Kollaps oder Reform!, in: der städtetag, vol. 4, 2002, p. 81.

Scherf, Wolfgang: Der Länderfinanzausgleich in Deutschland. Ungelöste Probleme und
Ansatzpunkte einer Reform, Frankfurt a.M., 2000.

Scherf, Wolfgang: Perspektiven der kommunalen Besteuerung, in: Andel, Norbert
(Hrsg.): Probleme der Kommunalfinanzen, Berlin, 2000, p. 21.

Scherf, Wolfgang: Ersatz der Gewerbesteuer durch eine anrechenbare
Wertschöpfungssteuer, in: Wirtschaftsdienst, vol. 10, 2002, pp. 603.

Volkmann, Uwe: Der Anspruch der Kommunen auf finanzielle Mindestausstattung, in:
Die Öffentliche Verwaltung (DÖV), Vol. 12, 2001, p. 500.

Wissenschaftlicher Beirat beim Bundesministerium der Finanzen, Gutachten zur
Reform der Gemeindesteuern in der Bundesrepublik Deutschland, Schriftenreihe
des Bundesministeriums der Finanzen, vol. 31, Bonn, 1982, p. 33.

Zimmermann, Horst: Kommunalfinanzen. Eine Einführung in die
finanzwissenschaftliche Analyse der kommunalen Finanzwirtschaft, Baden-
Baden, 1999.

Recent information on the development of the municipal budgets are to be found in the
municipal finance report which is released annually by the German Staedtetag. For
statistical information please refer to: Deutscher Staedtetag (editor), Statistisches
Jahrbuch der Gemeinden; www.staedtestatistik.de ; www.destatis.de.

UNEMPLOYMENT INSURANCE AND MICRO-LEVEL LABOR MARKET POLICY IN A FEDERAL STATE – THEORETICAL CONSIDERATIONS AND THE GERMAN EXPERIENCE

STEFAN SCHÄFER AND IVO BISCHOFF

1   Introduction

In the last decade, Germany has spent several hundred billion euros on active labor market policy. Given that the unemployment rate has not changed to the better but to the worse, the question of whether these funds have been used efficiently has become increasingly virulent. A large body of literature exists that evaluates the mix of instruments used by the German government and its agencies (e.g. Jacob/Kluve (2006), Büttner/Prey (1998)). Another branch of literature analyses the institutional framework of active labor market policy in Germany, in particular the distribution of tasks and funds across different levels of government (e.g. OECD (1998), Brinkmann (1998)). This paper belongs to the second branch of literature. It focuses on placement and training activities and their interrelations with the German unemployment insurance. The essential question is the following: Who should be in charge of training and placement of the long-term unemployed?

Section 2 starts out by briefly characterizing different training and placement policies. Next, it presents a very simple model in order to illustrate the effects of these policies. We differentiate between a central agency carrying out these activities and a decentralized solution in which a large number of autonomous regional agents are in charge of training and placement activities. The analysis will show that there are strong arguments for the decentralization of these activities. In section 3, we broaden the perspective by introducing the federal unemployment insurance into the model. This extended version of the original model is used to reassess the effects of decentralized training and placement policies. The analysis will show that the unemployment insurance causes spillovers which substantially reduce the efficiency of decentralized training and placement. Section 4 describes the institutional framework of labor market policy in Germany and analyzes it against the background of the theoretical considerations from the previous sections. It also points at potential improvements that could be made with regard to the allocation of tasks, competences and funds on different levels of government.

2 Training and Placement Activities in a Federalist System

2.1 INTRODUCING THE INSTRUMENTS

Training and Development Policies

In the western economies, unemployment statistics show a clear distinctive line between those people whose unemployment risk is low and those people who face a very high unemployment risk. This line has to do with the level and type of professional qualification. On the one side of the line are skilled and especially high-skilled employees. Their chance of becoming unemployed is not very high. Also, if they happen to lose their jobs, they find it comparatively easy to get a new job. Only a small percentage of them remains unemployed for a longer period of time. The group on the other side of the line consists primarily of low-skilled or unskilled workers. For them, it becomes increasingly difficult to find a permanent job. In most cases, it is necessary to considerably increase their level of qualification in order to place them on the labor market. In Germany, this unfortunately applies to a growing number of young people who are dropouts or whose skills are insufficient for vocational training. Training is also needed for those skilled employees whose specific skills are no longer in demand, e.g. because of structural changes in the industries in which they used to be employed (e.g. Hagedorn/Kaul (2002), Taheri (2000)).

In many cases, the unemployed themselves do not have the necessary financial means to pay for the training schemes. They also lack sufficient information with regard to their qualification options and labor market requirements. In order to reintegrate them in the labor market, they need some form of government support.

Placement of the Unemployed

In order to reduce the time span of unemployment, it is necessary to find an adequate position as quickly as possible. At the same time, firms which want to fill vacant positions are also interested in finding adequate personnel as quickly as possible. Unfortunately, there is a lack of reciprocal knowledge on the supply and demand side of the market. Therefore, matching job-seekers and job-offering firms is very time-consuming and expensive (e.g. Stigler (1962), Petrongolo/Pissarides (2001)). In order to reduce these costs, many countries have established special placement agencies. These help both parties to find the adequate position and the adequate employee respectively.

2.2 Federal Training and Placement

After having introduced the two instruments let us now return to the question posed at the beginning of the paper: Which level of government should be in charge of training and placement activities in a federalist state? This section will demonstrate the major aspects in a simple economic model. Let us assume that we have a very crude economy in which labor is the only source of income. Let us furthermore assume that every individual earns the same wage when employed. In this case individuals differ only with respect to the probability of having a job. Every individual j has an individual probability p_j to be employed; its probability to be unemployed is $(1-p_j)$.

The average employment probability is denoted p. This also represents the level of employment. Therefore $(1-p)$ is the unemployment rate. The total income generated in our economy is given by

$$Y^{tot} = p \cdot Y \tag{1}$$

where Y = income at full employment. (hereafter Y = 1)

Training and placement activities help the unemployed to find a job faster than they would have without these activities. Such measures increase the individual's p_j and thereby also the aggregate employment level p. At the same time, training and placement generate costs which have to be incurred by the employed. In order to cover those costs, the employed are taxed. For the sake of simplicity, let us assume a flat tax with tax rate t. The tax burden reduces the total income that is available for consumption:

$$Y^{net} = p \, (1 - t) \tag{2}$$

On the other hand, since the money collected via these taxes is used for training and placement, there is an increase in the employment level. For reasons of simplicity, let us assume that the employment rate p is a linear function of the tax rate t.

$$p = p_0 + \alpha t \tag{3}$$

The parameter p_0 denotes the level of employment which would occur without any training and placement activities. The productivity parameter α states to what extent the employment level rises if the tax rate is increased by one percent. p_0 and α are constants.

Substituting (3) into (2) leads to the total net income:

$$Y^{net} = (p_0 + \alpha t)(1 - t) \tag{4}$$

Thus the net income is a function of t (apart from the constants p_0 and a). By differentiating (4) with respect to t, we can identify the marginal increase in income resulting from an increase in t:

$$\frac{\delta Y_1^{net}}{\delta t} = \alpha - p_0 - 2\alpha t \tag{5}$$

Setting the derivative equal to 0 yields the income-maximizing tax rate $t^\cdot$.

$$t^\cdot = \frac{1}{2} - \frac{p_0}{2\alpha} \tag{6}$$

The corresponding optimal employment level is given by:

$$p^\cdot = p_0 + \alpha t^\cdot = \frac{(p_0 + \alpha)}{2} \tag{7}$$

The resulting net income is given by the following term:

$$Y^\cdot = \frac{1}{4}\left[2p_0 + \frac{(p_0)^2}{\alpha} + \alpha\right] \tag{8}$$

Taken for themselves, these results do not show too much. We will, however, return to them later when we compare this solution to a decentralized solution.

2.3 DECENTRALIZATION AND PRODUCTIVE EFFICIENCY IN TRAINING AND PLACEMENT

In order to design training and placement policies efficiently, a large amount of specific information has to be taken into account. First of all, information about the unemployed individual is required: Why did a particular person lose his job? What are his skills? If his skills do not meet the demand, what training scheme is suitable for him? Second, it is necessary to obtain information about the current labor market situation: Which positions are currently vacant? Third, specific information on the training opportunities is needed: Which training programs are available at the moment? What are the respective deadlines, requirements etc.? (e.g. Sen (1995),

In order to save costs, it is advisable to try to find a job or a training program offered in the home region of the unemployed. Government officials attending to the unemployed individual should therefore be informed about the training or job opportunities in the region of residence. In addition, they should be in close contact with the unemployed in order to be able to design a successful training and placement program (e.g. Boadway/Cuff (1999)).

Both requirements can only be met if the relevant government agencies have dependencies in all regions within the federation. Following this logic, there are two ways in which the training and placement agency can be designed:

First, there may be a very large institution with bureaus all over the country. This is the way the "Bundesanstalt für Arbeit" in Germany is organized. It has about 200 regional bureaus and a large central administration in Nuremberg. The regional bureaus have only very little autonomy. This bears the danger of creating a top-heavy bureaucratic monopoly which is highly immobile and at the same time causes massive overhead costs (Oates (1999), Mosley/Schütz/ Schmid (2003)).

We can save the largest part of these costs by following another, the second solution. According to this solution, training and placement activities are completely decentralized. Decentralization creates a large number of small and mobile regional agents. The regions decide autonomously which specific policies to apply. At the same time, these regional authorities need to be given incentives that ensure that the funds collected for training and placement are used efficiently. This in turn means that the taxes covering training and placement costs must be collected within the region itself. Furthermore, the regional level must have the right to set the tax rate. Given that the relevant information is only available on the regional level, only the regional government can set the optimal tax rate for the region. (e.g. Oates (1996), Salmon (1987))

Though regional authorities have better information than the central government, they are a far cry from being fully informed. Even they will find it difficult to identify the best training schemes and placement strategies. And they cannot be expected to be able to calculate an optimal tax rate the way we are able to in our simply modelled world. Instead, each regional authority will set a tax rate and design its policies based on the incomplete information available. Since different regions decide on the basis of different information, they can be expected to set different tax rates and use different instruments in their training and placement activities. Throughout the federation, many different solutions are therefore applied at the same time. Since the seminal work of Friedrich August von Hayek, the positive aspects of such a setting are widely acknowledged. The fact that many different solutions for one problem are tested at the same time enables agents to very quickly differentiate between good and bad solutions. At the same time, the negative effects of bad solutions do not affect all regions but are restricted to some. A region which applied bad solutions is provided with information about better solutions simply by looking at other, more successful regions. Since this information is also available to its residents, they can then demand that their regional government copy better solutions (Hirschman (1970), Bailey (1999)). Overall, decentralization thus promotes technical and organizational progress and furthermore spurs the diffusion of new, superior solutions (Sinn (1992), Voigt (1997)).

All of the above suggests that regional agencies are able to provide training and placement activities at a much lower cost than a large centralized bureaucracy would. Expressed in the terms of the simple model developed above, this means that if a decentralized organization provides training and placement activities, the parameter α will be substantially larger. To illustrate the effects of this decentralized solution, let us return to the model. Assume a representative region r whose regional government wants to maximize the net income earned within its region.

$$Y_r = p_r \, (1 - t_r) = (p_0 + a_r t_r) \, (1 - t_r) \tag{9}$$

Differentiating with respect to t_r leads to the following expression:

$$\frac{\delta Y_1^{net}}{\delta t_r} = \alpha_r - p_0 - 2\alpha_r \, t_r \tag{10}$$

The optimal tax rate is thus

$$t_r^* = \frac{1}{2} - \frac{p_0}{2\alpha_r} \tag{11}$$

The corresponding optimal employment level is given by:

$$p_r^{\bullet} = p_0 + \alpha_r t_r^{\bullet} = \frac{(p_0 + \alpha_r)}{2} \tag{12}$$

These two expressions resemble the expressions (6) and (7) derived for the central training and placement policies. There is, however, one fundamental difference: Following the argumentation above, we can expect that

$$a_r > a_f \tag{13}$$

Consequently:

$$t_r^{\bullet} > t_f^{\bullet} \tag{14}$$

$$p_r^{\bullet} > p_f^{\bullet} \tag{15}$$

$$Y_r^{\bullet} > Y_f^{\bullet} \tag{16}$$

In other words, the fact that the productivity of training and placement activities is higher leads to more resources being spent in this field. Therefore, the net income per person employed is lower. The resulting losses in income are, however, overcompensated by the fact that the employment level that can be reached is higher. This means that the higher productivity caused by decentral control can reduce unemployment considerably and despite the higher tax rate yield a higher net income for the members of society.

This can be shown by differentiating the formula for net income (8) with respect to α. The resulting derivative is positive for all situations in which $\alpha^2 > (p_0)^2$. If this does not apply, the optimal tax rate is 0 and thus training and placement activities are inefficient regardless of the institutional arrangement under which they are pursued.

Up to now, we have concentrated on decentralized training and placement and the efficiency gains due to decentralization. So far, the results suggest that these activities should be decentralized.

3 Unemployment Insurance and Spillovers

3.1 INTRODUCING THE INSTRUMENTS

Apart from training and placement activities, most countries have installed a scheme of unemployment benefits.[1] Their purpose is to cushion the loss of income the individual faces when it loses its job. Basically, those inhabitants who are currently employed pay taxes which are then used to cover the benefits for the unemployed. In order to grant unemployment benefits, an insurance premium must be collected from the employed. Let b denote the insurance premium the employed have to pay (expressed in percent of their income). λ denotes the so-called replacement rate. It states the percentage of unit wage a person receives when he is unemployed. Due to the budget restriction, the following relationship between λ and b must hold:

$$p \cdot b = (1 - p) \, \lambda \tag{17}$$

where: $\lambda << (1\text{-}t\text{-}b)$.

Thus it always pays to be employed. In this case, p is independent of b and □. In other words, unemployment insurance and taxation do not set negative incentives to work. On the other hand, the net income is not affected by the unemployment insurance scheme.

Now, how does the unemployment insurance influence the government's decision concerning training and placement and thus the tax rate t? We start out by discussing its impact on the federal level.

3.2 FEDERAL TRAINING AND PLACEMENT

In order to answer the question above, we have to look at the equation of the federal income:

$$Y^{net} = p \, (1 - t) \tag{18}$$

Without unemployment insurance, this is all the income which is available for consumption. Adding the unemployment benefits for the unemployed and subtracting the insurance premium payments of the employed yields the following expression:

---

[1] The basic construction of the model of unemployment insurance derived below is based on Büttner (1999), Kurz (2000) and Neugart (2005).

$$Y^{net} = p\,(1 - t) + (1 - p)\,\lambda - p\cdot b \tag{19}$$

Since all the funds the employed have to pay are transferred to the unemployed within the federation, the net income is not changed by the introduction of the unemployment insurance. Consequently, the optimal tax rate for the central level remains unchanged. It is still given by expression (5).

$$t^* = \frac{1}{2} - \frac{p_0}{2\alpha} \tag{20}$$

Employment level and net income also remain unchanged.

3.3 Decentralization and Spillovers of Training and Placement

The next step is to analyze how the unemployment insurance affects the optimal tax rate on the regional level. For this purpose assume two identical regions 1 and 2. They are identical with regard to all the parameters set constant in the model and to population size. Decentralization as discussed above means that each region can autonomously set the tax rate t_1 and t_2 respectively. Consequently, the regional employment rates p_1 and p_2 can differ:

$$p_i = p_0 + \alpha_r\cdot t_i \quad i = 1,\,2 \tag{21}$$

The full net income that is available for consumption in region r is now given by the following expression:

$$Y_i^{net} = p_i\,(1 - t_i) + (1 - p_i)\,\lambda - b \cdot p_i \quad i = 1,\,2 \tag{22}$$

The net income consists of three terms. The first term represents the total net income of region 1 in the case when there is no unemployment insurance. This is the net income that we used to derive t_r^* in section 2.3. The second term denotes the net influx in income from the unemployment benefits and the third term represents the outflux of income due to the insurance premium payments of the employed population within region 1. The budget restriction for the unemployment insurance is defined for both regions and not for each region separately. Consequently, the influx of unemployment benefits does not necessarily equal the outflux of premium payments. In other words, it is possible that:

$$(1 - p_1)\, \lambda \neq b \cdot p_1 \tag{23}$$

In the theory of fiscal federalism, these flows of income are called spillovers. Generally speaking, spillovers are economic consequences in one region of economic activities of another (Oates (1972), p. 46). We can differentiate between horizontal and vertical spillovers. Horizontal spillovers affect an entity on the same level of government. In our case, the activities of region 1 affect the activities of region 2. In the case of vertical spillovers, the economic activities of a region affect the federal level or vice versa. In addition, we can differentiate between negative and positive spillovers. In the case of positive spillovers, the region benefits from the activities of another. In the case of negative spillovers, it is harmed (e.g. Keen (1998)).

In the equation below, we can see that the fiscal interrelations between the two regions and the federal unemployment insurance comprise different types of spillovers. In term 2, we have a positive vertical spillover. The higher the federal level sets the replacement rate λ, the more resources flow into region 1 for a given unemployment rate. Second, we can see negative vertical spillovers in term 3. The lower the unemployment rate within region 1, the more resources it must transfer to the unemployment insurance on the federal level. Finally, the third term also comprises positive horizontal spillovers from region 2 into region 1. The more resources region 2 spends on the training and placement of its unemployed, the lower the total unemployment rate and thus the lower the sum of payments that the employed in region 1 have to transfer to the federal unemployment insurance.

Spillovers mean that the passive entity has costs or benefits which it cannot influence directly while the spillover-producing entity produces costs or benefits which do not affect its own residents. If we assume that each regional government is merely concerned with the costs and benefits that occur within its own borders, it will not take these spillovers into account. This will lead to inefficiencies in the allocation of resources. In our case, it will have a negative impact on the incentives of regional governments to provide training and placement.

The effects can be shown mathematically if we write equation (9) in terms of the regional tax rate t_1.

$$Y_1^{net} = \left(p_0 + \alpha_r\, t_1\right)\left(1 - t_1\right) \;+\; \left(1 - p_0 - \alpha_r t_1\right)\lambda \;-\; \left(p_0 + \alpha_r\, t_1\right) \cdot \frac{\left(1 - p_0 - \dfrac{\alpha_r}{2}\left(t_1 + t_2\right)\right)}{\left(p_0 + \dfrac{\alpha_r}{2}\left(t_1 + t_2\right)\right)} \cdot \lambda$$

We reach this equation by substituting expression (12), which expresses the regional employment rate p_1 in terms of the regional tax rate t_1, into the equation for the net income.

Just like above, we have to differentiate (9) with respect t+o the tax rate, in our case t_1. Under the assumption that the replacement rate is exogenous and constant ($\lambda = \overline{\lambda}$), this yields the following expression

$$\frac{\delta Y_1^{net}}{\delta t_1} = \alpha_r - p_0 - 2\alpha_r t_1 \quad - \alpha_r \overline{\lambda} \quad - \left(\frac{\alpha_r \left(1 - p_0 - \frac{\alpha_r}{2}(t_1 + t_2)\right)}{\left(p_0 + \frac{\alpha_r}{2}(t_1 + t_2)\right)} + \frac{\frac{\alpha_r}{2}(p_0 + \alpha_r t_1)}{\left(p_0 + \frac{\alpha_r}{2}(t_1 + t_2)\right)^2} \right) \cdot \overline{\lambda}$$

This expression can be used to point at two facts:

First, the relationship between this derivative and the ones used above is of interest. Abolishing the unemployment insurance by setting λ and b as zero reduces the expression to the first term of the derivative. This is identical to expression (10).

The spillovers caused by the unemployment insurance are captured in the second and third term of the derivative. Both are functions of the training and placement activities carried out by the regions and thus depend on t_1.

To show how these spillovers affect the regional tax rate, let us concentrate on the second term. This term shows the impact that an increase in the regional tax rate t_1 has on the influx of unemployment benefits. We see that the relationship is negative. This is intuitively plausible: The more training and placement activities a region provides, the lower its unemployment rate and the lower consequently the unemployment benefits for its residents. When we take this effect into account, we get the following optimal tax rate:

$$t_1' = \frac{(\alpha_r - p_0 - \lambda)}{(2\alpha_r)} = \frac{t_r^* - \lambda}{(2\alpha_r)} \tag{25}$$

We can see that this tax rate is lower than the one that would exist without the unemployment insurance. The regional tax rate will be lower the higher the unemployment benefits and the replacement rate λ are.

The third term of the derivative captures the positive spillovers which result from the unemployment insurance. The more region 1 reduces its unemployment rate, the lower the insurance premium b its citizens have to pay for the unemployment insurance.

However, this spillover is not large enough to overcompensate the negative spillovers resulting from the unemployment benefits. Consequently, region 1 has an incentive to underinvest in training and placement activities.

This leads us to the following question: What tax rate and thus what level of employment and net income will region 1 set if it takes the spillovers into account?

The answer depends on the expectations concerning the behavior of region 2. The higher t_2, the lower the insurance premium b and the more it pays for region 1 to set a low tax rate. In other words, region 1 can chose to become a free rider with respect to the training and placement activities of region 2. However, region 2 will try to do exactly the same with respect to the training and placement activities of region 1. Here, game theory comes into play if we want to predict the expected level of t_1 and t_2. Assuming two identical regions, the reaction functions of both regions can be sketched in a (t_1, t_2)-graph (see Figure III - 1).

Figure III - 1: Nash-equilibrium of regional tax rates

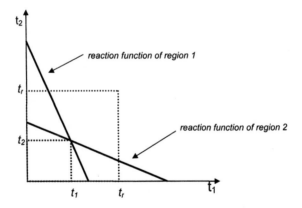

The Nash-equilibrium is given by the point where the reaction functions of region 1 and 2 intersect. If the difference between α_r and α_f is moderate, the Nash-equilibrium yields lower tax rates, employment probabilities and a lower net income:

$$t_r^* > t_f^* > t_1''$$
$$p_r^* > p_f^* > p_1''$$
$$Y_r^* > Y_f^* > Y_1''$$

In order to achieve substantial gains in productivity (i.e. α_r), it is necessary to create more than 2 regions. However, the more regions are built, the more important the spillovers become. In a federation of 16 regions, like the German Länder or Polish voivodships, $t_i'' = 0$ even if $\alpha_r = 2\,\alpha_f$. Thus, decentralization leads to a dilemma: By trying to exploit gains in efficiency from decentralization, we destroy the incentives to engage in active labor market policy.

Even though the analysis above is restricted to a very specific set of policies, the basic argument holds for different types of policies which reduce unemployment. One very important type of policy concerns the sector of public education in schools and universities. Here, we have the same dilemma as described above. It is to be expected that schools and universities are more efficient in educating our children and youth if the sector is decentralized and if there is competition between these institutions. At the same time, there are massive spillovers of good education, because not all students educated in one region start working within that region after graduation. Even if they stay, the benefits, e.g. in terms of income tax payments etc., spill over to other regions. We therefore have imperfect incentives for local and regional governments to invest in education.

3.4 Possible Solutions

Given this dilemma of decentralization, the question of institutional design is the following: Is there an institutional design which combines the best of both worlds in such a way that we can exploit the higher productivity of decentralization and, at the same time, prevent the spillovers from destroying the incentives to fight unemployment on the regional level? Below, two benchmark solutions are presented.

Decentralizing the Unemployment Insurance

By decentralizing the unemployment insurance, it is possible to avoid all spillovers. Therefore, the regions can be expected to set the efficient tax rate. At the same time, training and placement activities will be conducted efficiently.

However, this solution is problematic for two reasons. First, insurances become cheaper the larger the insured population is. This phenomenon can be explained with the law of large numbers. If the unemployment insurance is decentralized, these economies of scale cannot be used. As a consequence, the unemployment premium will be higher than it would be on the central level. Second, the unemployment insurance is an instrument of interregional distribution. It transfers resources from the rich to the poor regions. Under a decentralized unemployment insurance, this form of regional redistribution is no longer feasible. The regional differences in income and employment are likely to increase. Furthermore, the poor regions will have to set higher unemployment premiums and higher tax rates than the rich regions. This will destroy their chances to catch up (cp. Kurz (2002), Koller/Stichter-Werner (2003), and Reissert (2003)). In addition, this option will lead to migration and brain drain (Brown/Oates (1987), Cremer et al. (1996)). Especially for countries which start off with large interregional differences in income, industry structure and infrastructure, this solution is not advisable.

Regional Autonomy and Vertical Grants

The second, more feasible solution leaves the unemployment insurance on the central level. However, in order to increase productivity in the public sector, regions are granted far-reaching autonomy with respect to their training and placement activities. They can decide autonomously which training schemes to invest in and how to organize the placement of the unemployed. To cover the costs, each region is granted a vertical transfer from the federal government which must be spent on training and placement activities only. In addition, regions are also granted disposable transfers. These transfers are larger the more successful a region is in reducing its unemployment. The free transfers internalize the regional spillovers from the unemployment insurance and reward successful policy (e.g. Breton (1965), Dahlby (1996)).

4   Labor Market Policy in Germany – A Critical Overview

4.1   A BASIC CLASSIFICATION OF LABOR MARKET POLICY INSTRUMENTS AND THE ASSIGNMENT OF RESPONSIBILITIES TO THE FEDERAL LEVELS IN GERMANY

In the past 20 years, and increasingly since the reunification, unemployment has become the most virulent economic problem in Germany. Next to public investments to improve public infrastructure, the government applies labor market policy to address the problem. Under the chancellorship of Gerhard Schröder, Germany witnessed a far-reaching reform in the way that labor market policy was conducted. The reform affected the mix of instruments in both the active and the passive labor market policy. In addition, the government reformed the assignment of tasks and responsibilities within the federation.

Generally, since 2005 the assignment of tasks in the field of labor market policy reflects the basic distinction between short-term and long-term unemployment. The responsibility for the short-term unemployed who receive unemployment insurance benefits, is clearly assigned to the federal level. In Germany, it is a central authority, namely the Federal Employment Service Agency ("Bundesagentur für Arbeit", herafter BA), that is in charge of the administration and management of the unemployment insurance as well as of implementing the active labor market policy that goes along with the former.

Next to the BA, regional and local authorities pursue active and passive labor market policies. Their part in passive labor market policy has been reduced by the Hartz-reforms. The counties are now – together with the federal level – in charge of supporting individuals who have been unemployed for more than twelve months or who are not entitled to unemployment insurance benefits and, additionally, are not available for the job market (e.g. Lohse (2004)).

The following passages sketch the post-reform situation of the German labour market policy. Section 4.2 describes the Federal Employment Service Agency. Section 4.3 briefly discusses the role of the regional and local government. A critical assessment of the current division of tasks and responsibilities is conducted in section 4.4.

4.2 CENTRAL LABOR MARKET POLICY – THE BUNDESAGENTUR FÜR ARBEIT[2]

4.2.1 Organisational Structure

The "Bundesagentur für Arbeit" (BA) is one of the largest institutions under public law in Germany, and it carries out the largest part of labor market policy in Germany. Basically, its tasks are twofold. First, it administers the German unemployment insurance, i.e. by collecting the contributions and paying unemployment benefits. Second, it is in charge of active labor market policy, which aims at helping currently unemployed clients to find a new job. For this purpose, the BA can offer a set of active labor market policy measures that will be described in detail below. While its discretionary freedom with respect to the first task is limited, the BA has considerable freedom when it comes to the allocation of means for active labor market policy.

The federal secretary of labor-related affairs has the formal supervision of the BA. Despite recent efforts to delegate decisions to subordinate units, the BA is a highly centralized institution (e.g. Mosley/Schütz/Schmid (2003)). All strategic decisions, including the regional distribution of funds, are decided upon on the central level, i.e. in the BA's headquarters in Nuremberg. The BA is managed by an executive board,

---

[2] Until 2004, the "Bundesagentur für Arbeit" was called "Bundesanstalt für Arbeit".

whose management practice is in turn monitored by a supervisory committee. A characteristic feature of its inner structure is the so-called "third-parity", the term designating a system in which government, employers and employees participate in the administration of the unemployment insurance on an equal basis. It is according to this "third-parity" rule that the members of the decisive supervisory committee are appointed. The government delegates are appointed by the federal government. The board members representing employees and employers respectively are in most cases direct delegates of the federal labor unions and employers' associations respectively. As this committee appoints the executive board and controls its policies, the federal government, labor unions and employers' associations exert a strong influence on labor market policies in Germany.

The BA subdivides into 10 regional offices and 178 local employment service offices. In general, the geographical delimitation of those regional offices follows the division into 16 states ("Laender").[3] At the same time, the regional distribution of the funds reserved for active labor market policy and, thus, the decision of *where* exactly those funds are spent, lies largely in the hands of the executive board on the central level who in turn have to follow fundamental regulations made by the supervisory committee. State governments have no formal way to influence how much money the BA spends in their region. At the same time, the funds coming from the BA have a noticeable influence on the regional purchasing power and on the regional labor market. Thus, the regional distribution of funds controlled by the BA is an important factor in regional labor market policy.[4]

4.2.2 Instruments and Budget

The BA was initially founded to administer the funds of the German unemployment insurance. This is still its primary task. Membership in the German unemployment insurance is mandatory for all employees (except for civil servants ("Beamte") and people employed in certain small-scale work contracts). The unemployment insurance pays unemployment benefits for a maximum time period of twelve months.[5] Its aim is to

---

[3]   Some small states do not have a regional office but share one with a neighboring state.

[4]   The BA has published an official statement on how the regional distribution is determined. Though this statement is detailed with respect to the relevant indicators, it does not specify the weight these different indicators have in determining the regional distribution of funds. This crucial issue is a "political question" and thus left to the BA's executive board (e.g., Blien 1998 and Blien 2002).

[5]   Under certain conditions, the maximum period can exceed twelve months.

protect individuals against a major decline of their personal living standard. The individual amount an unemployed individual receives therefore depends proportionally on his previous wage. Only individuals who have paid their unemployment insurance premium for a certain time period are eligible for unemployment insurance benefits. It is by paying these contributions that one becomes entitled to unemployment insurance benefits in case one loses one's job. Because unemployment insurance benefits are not an "act of grace" but a matter of legal claims, short-term unemployed people entitled to unemployment benefits do not have to prove that they are in fact needy.

There are five fundamental ways to achieve that:[6] First, public placement activities render the matching of the unemployed and vacant positions more probable and less costly for both the unemployed and the potential employers. In Germany, the BA runs a nationwide information system that gathers firms' job offers and applications of the unemployed. At the respective local BA agency, a jobless person can feed an individual application into the system and request suitable job offers. The local agency's service is not only limited to providing job offers that stem from the BA's own database; rather, it also comprises advice and counselling that includes searching non-BA-sources like the appointments section in local newspapers or online "jobletters". Second, publicly funded training schemes serve to adjust the unemployed person's qualifications to the necessities of today's labor market. The BA offers a wide variety of courses in fields like IT, foreign languages and soft skills to improve the skills of unemployed clients. Furthermore, for people with very low qualification, the BA offers the opportunity to get a basic school degree and serve an apprenticeship. Third, public authorities can pay wage subsidies to employers who hire unemployed applicants with low qualifications. Currently, there is an intensive political debate about the need for wage subsidies in Germany. Some wage subsidy programs have been tested in recent years, and a nationwide scheme is expected to be introduced within the next one or two years. Fourth, job creation schemes are implemented in order to preserve human capital and in order to give jobless people the opportunity to prove their employability and employment willingness to potential employers. The term "job creation measure" stands for publicly funded jobs – usually in the social and/or environmental sector – that are supposed to be "additional". That means politicians who opt for such measures try to avoid the crowding out of private enterprise jobs by publicly funded ones. During the 90s, job creation measures have been used extensively in Eastern Germany. Because they continue to face heavy criticism, the number of such programs has, on the one hand, been cut down significantly. On the other hand, they seem to experience

---

[6]   For a slightly different classification of active labor market policy tools cp. OECD (1993), p. 71f.

a revival in the form of the "one euro jobs" described below. Fifth, special active labor market policy measures can be implemented in order to turn jobless people into entrepreneurs. Currently, there is an intensive political and scientific debate in Germany about a program called "Ich AG" (translated literally: "I Inc.") which was introduced during the most recent labour market reforms (2003-2005). Table III -2 provides an overview of the number of people who took part in the BA's respective programs in 2005.

Table III - 2: Participants in the BA's active labor market policy programs (annual average)

	2005	2004
Placement	116,554	105,083
Training	629,074	755,982
Wage subsidies	93,005	160,273
Job creation	287,097	131,624
Entrepreneurship programs	322,474	234,299

Source: Bundesagentur für Arbeit (2006)

The active as well as the passive labor market policy measures of the unemployment insurance scheme are primarily financed through contributions paid by the employed and their employers. If, however, the contributions do not provide sufficient cover for the cost of active and passive labor market policies – for example at the peak of a recession – , the unemployment insurance's budget is balanced by a tax- (or debt-) financed transfer from the federal government. Table III - 3 displays the main components of the BA's budget in 2004 and 2005.

Table III - 3: Composition of the BA's budget in 2004 and 2005 (billions of Euro)

	2005	2004
Active labour market policy	13.6	18.7
Passive labour market policy	29.7	30.5
Total	43.3	49.2

Source: Bundesagentur für Arbeit (2006)

4.2.3 The Efficiency and Effectiveness of Active Labor Market Policy Measures Carried Out by the BA

Numerous papers evaluate active labor market policies in general (e.g. Martin/Grubb (2001) and Hujer et al. (2002)) as well as with special regard to Germany (e.g. Jacob/Kluve (2006)). Authors who merely analyze the success of a given ALMP measure (whatever the definition of "success" may be) focus on the effectiveness of ALMP. Other authors include the costs of ALMP in their considerations (whatever the definition of "costs" may be) and carry out a cost-benefit-analysis. They focus on the efficiency of ALMP.

It is evident from this basic distinction that the result of each study depends to a high extent on the respective definition of the success and – in the case of efficiency evaluations – on the definition of the costs of ALMP. Definitions vary considerably in the literature on this subject. For example, success can simply mean that a participant of an ALMP measure gets a new job. A more sophisticated approach compares the job market performance of the participants of a certain ALMP program to that of a control group of jobless individuals not taking part in any ALMP measure. In addition, one would need to assess the quality of the job obtained by the ALMP participant – e.g. with respect to the qualification requirements, the wage level and etc. When making a cost-benefit-analysis (and thus evaluating the efficiency of ALMP programs), the benefits of a scheme have to be compared with its costs. As the definition and measurement of the variables under consideration is difficult, every statement on the efficiency or effectiveness of ALMP measures crucially depends on the underlying assumptions and definitions (e.g. Calmfors (1994)). Consequently, different studies evaluating the same type of ALMP measures can produce contradictory results. Nevertheless, we will at least try to give an insight into the central results of recent studies which evaluate the effectiveness of training schemes, wage subsidies, job creation measures and entrepreneurship programs.

As regards training schemes, the effectiveness depends on the duration of the respective program (Fitzenberger/Speckesser (2005)). Programs that do not exceed six months are conducive to enhancing the participants' employment probability. In contrast, programs that last longer than twelve months significantly reduce the participants' employment probability. Obviously, employers expect jobless people who have taken part in training schemes for more than twelve months to be not productive. This phenomenon is called "lock-in-effect" (e.g. Lechner (2005)).

Wage subsidies tend to raise the employment probability of the respective individual significantly. By subsidizing the wages of disadvantaged jobless people (long-term unemployed, disabled people, unemployed without any formal qualification, unemployed with very low qualifications etc.), they enable employers to hire people with low or at least uncertain qualifications. Those hired have the chance to prove their skills in a "real life"-environment. This is why their employment probability rises significantly.

In contrast to wage subsidies, job creation measures face heavy criticism among ALMP experts. According to them, the measures are supposed to stigmatize the participants. Employers perceive such participants as unproductive, because they have spent too much time in an artificial "laboratory environment" called public work program. In addition, job creation programs are expected to crowd-out private activity. This is why the respective empirical literature comes to a general negative assessment of such programs (e.g. Caliendo/Hujer/Thomsen (2005)).

While wage subsidies find general approval and job creation schemes are generally rejected, the assessment of entrepreneurship programs is not as clear-cut. On the one hand, there are studies that show them to be highly effective. On the other hand, it remains to be seen whether or not the newly established enterprises will survive in the long-run.

4.2.4 The Political Economy of the BA

In many cases, essential decisions concerning passive labor market policy are made by the federal government and the "Bundesrat" (Federal Council). When it comes to active labor market policy, the major decisions are made by and negotiated within the BA. Three groups of agents (i.e. labor unions, employers' associations, federal government) may influence the regional distribution via the BA's supervisory committee. Employers' associations and especially labor unions benefit from high expenditures for training schemes because they run large agencies which offer them. At the same time, they can be expected to disagree when it comes to expenditures on other instruments. With respect to the regional distribution of funds, partisan motives can be expected to play a dominant role. In other words, the three groups of agents may try to support high expenditures on active labor market policy in a region whose government they consider worth supporting. Labor unions can be expected to favor left-wing governments while employers' associations may prefer conservative governments.

On the part of the federal government, it is obvious to assume that it will try to support the administration of those states which are governed by its own party or an identical party coalition respectively. By supporting "friendly regional governments", the federal government can improve the chance that its own political convictions become effective. If high expenditures for regional labor market policy help the regional government to be re-elected, the federal government can – through its influence on the regional distribution of these funds – also influence the composition of the "Bundesrat". This second parliamentary chamber consists of delegates from the regional governments and decides on a number of important issues in federal politics. The higher the number of "friendly regional governments" in the "Bundesrat", the more likely it is for the federal government to put through its own convictions. Thus, the federal government faces incentives to use its position within the BA to redirect funds to regions which are governed by "friendly regional governments".

Finally, the BA may be regarded as a large bureaucratic institution whose employees try to pursue their own interests. Following the seminal work of Niskanen (1971), each regional office within the BA can be expected to try to maximize its regional budget. Given the substantial asymmetry in information between regional offices and the headquarter, regional offices will find it easy to back their demand for additional funds with at least questionable arguments which however appear plausible to the executive board in Nuremberg. Since total funds are limited, the regional distribution of funds is a zero-sum-game with respect to the regions at large. In this game, regions which are governed by "friendly governments" – from the point of view of the federal government – can expect a favorable treatment. Depending on the relative power of labor unions and employers' associations within the executive board, regions with a left-wing government may have an advantage or disadvantage. Regardless of these partisan factors, one might expect to find a stickiness in funds. This means that changes in the regional distribution of funds from t to t+1 occur at a slower pace than justified on normative grounds. In particular, the funds are not redistributed from regions with a declining unemployment rate to regions which witness an increase in unemployment.

4.3 Labor Market Policy on the Regional and Local Level

As pointed out above, the local level (i.e. the counties) is – at least theoretically – responsible for supporting the long-term unemployed by paying welfare payments and by providing active labor market policy measures. Yet the 2005 reform of labor market policy in Germany is a compromise. It is the result of a political bargaining process between counties, *Laender* and the federal government. Consequently, the current assignment of responsibilities to the levels of government in Germany reflects the specific characteristics of German federalism: It is very complicated, and it is constantly a matter of debate. This holds true especially for labor market policy measures geared towards the long-term unemployed. This task is assigned to both the counties and the federal government who are obliged by law to cooperate closely in order to administer welfare payments to the recipients and, ideally, reduce long-term unemployment. In each county, the BA's respective local branch and the county's welfare administration department have established a joint venture that is in charge of administering welfare payments and running active labor market policies which aim at reducing long-term unemployment.

What are the basic features of active and passive labor market policy measures carried out jointly by the federal and the local level? The fundamental distinction between an unemployment insurance scheme and a public welfare system causes a significant difference between unemployment insurance benefits and welfare payments. As explained above, welfare payments do not result from a legal claim. Instead, they reflect the public opinion that each member of society should be able to live in dignity. Welfare payments are therefore not designed to enable the individual to sustain its living standard, but enable the needy to live a humane life. Consequently, welfare payments are lump-sum transfers the level of which equals the subsistence level. The current level is 345 Euro. In addition, the recipient's accommodation cost is paid for by public welfare authorities.

In contrast to unemployment insurance benefits which are paid to unemployed people who have acquired legal claims by paying unemployment insurance contributions, the critical prerequisite for receiving welfare assistance payments is neediness. This has two consequences: First, the jobless and other members of their household are not allowed to earn additional income that exceeds a certain maximum level. Second, they and other members of their household are not allowed to possess assets, like for example real estate or saving accounts, that exceed a certain maximum level.

Since 2005, welfare assistance payments for the long-term unemployed are funded jointly by the respective local authority in charge and by the federal government. More specifically, the federal budget contributes funds for the "Arbeitslosengeld II" and the active labor market policy measures, while the local level pays for the accommodation cost. Table III – 4 provides a comparison between the federal and the local level's expenses for active and passive labor market policy measures (for long-term unemployed people) in 2005. Because assisting the needy is a public task, welfare payments and the respective active labor market policy measures (see below) are not financed by unemployment insurance contributions. Instead, the funds for this kind of ALMP stem from the general public budgets.

As far as active labor market policy measures are concerned, there are no fundamental differences between fighting short-term and long-term unemployment respectively. Generally, public authorities offer short-term unemployed the same ALMP measures that are provided to long-term unemployed. Yet the long-term unemployed suffer to a disproportionally high extent from specific problems – e.g. drug addiction, very low qualification, mental disabilities etc. – which worsen their chance to get a new job. At the same time, even long-term unemployed people without these specific individual challenges face the risk that the longer they are unemployed, the less valuable their qualification becomes. Therefore, employers often assume that long-term unemployed are unproductive and they tend not to hire them. All this makes for a vicious circle. Against this background, German law offers some specific tools that are tailored to the specific needs of the long-term unemployed. These tools are applied in order to preserve an unemployed person's employability and in order to signal his willingness to be employed to potential employers. The most prominent of these tools is called "one euro jobs". Jobless individuals who have a "one euro job" take part in public work programs – for example social or environmental activities. In return, they receive 1 to 2 Euros an hour in addition to the usual welfare assistance payment.

Table III - 4: Federal and municipal expenses for labor market policies directed at supporting long-term unemployed people (2005, billion Euros)

Counties		Federal Government	
Cost Category	**Expenses**	**Cost Category**	**Expenses**
Accommodation	8.6	Welfare Payments (*Arbeitslosengeld II*)	25.6
Administration	0.5	Active labor market policy measures	3.6
Other expenses	0.4	Federal share in accommodation cost	3.5
		Administration	3.1
		Other expenses	0.1
Total	**9.5**	**Total**	**35.9**

Source: Deutscher Landkreistag

4.4   A Critical Assessment of the Assignment of Tasks and Competences

How can the distribution of responsibilities be assessed against this background? From a welfare economics perspective it makes sense to assign the responsibility for the UI scheme to the federal level. Because of significant economies of scale, only one single scheme on the national level can be expected to work efficiently. In addition, a national UI scheme automatically transfers funds from prospering to poorer parts of the federation. Thus, it prevents the latter from getting on the slippery slope of low employment and high UI contribution rates, which in turn raise labor costs and lower the poorer regions' competitiveness even further.

The same applies to the responsibility for supporting the long-term unemployed by active as well as passive labor market policy measures. If each region had to fund the welfare payment for "its" long-term unemployed on its own, poorer regions would not be able to bear this massive burden without imposing excessive taxes on their citizens and enterprises – which would inevitably lead to further deterioration of the region's economy. At the same time, this responsibility should not be assigned exclusively to the national level, because there are – as derived above – good reasons for decentralizing this task at least partly: Small, decentral entities do not only have better access to the necessary information about the situation of the local job market and the specific problems of the jobless; moreover, the competition between the decentral entities can be expected to generate better solutions. Thus, at first glance, the current assignment of responsibilities in the field of active labor market policy seems like a suitable compromise, too. However, two central points of criticism cast serious doubt on this conclusion:

First, the participation of counties is restricted to the handling of the long-term unemployed, while the efforts to bring the short-term unemployed back to work are still largely concentrated in the hands of the BA. However, the short-term unemployed will regularly require more than just transfer payments and information about vacant positions. In the current situation, the BA and their regional offices are in charge of assisting them in their search for a new job. Hence, the advantages of a decentralized assistance are not utilized.

The second point regards the way in which the BA and the counties cooperate when jointly supporting the long-term unemployed. This cooperation is not only completely inefficient, but also quite ineffective, because the respective delegates of the BA's local office and the municipal department of social affairs are forced to use a significant part of their resources to coordinate the cooperation. Fortunately, the BA's local office and the respective county officials are not forced to work together in all counties. Instead, 69 counties have opted for running the active and passive labor market policies for the long-term jobless completely on their own – with financial support from the federal budget. While the latter guarantees that each of the 69 so called "option counties" is able to bear the burden of supporting the long-term unemployed, the county officials can act much more freely than the "Arbeitsgemeinschaften" in the other counties. The way labor market policy is organized in these 69 counties could prove a model for a future reform of the assignment of responsibilities for active and passive labor market policy in Germany.

Solving the two problems would require further steps along the road of decentralization. Next to the arguments already put forth above, these steps could help to reduce the concentration of power in the hands of the BA. The strong position of a central, quasi-monopolistic institution could thereby be restricted to those fields of labor market policy where the negative aspects of this concentration are outweighed by the benefits of such a centralist solution. Beyond these fields, however, the BA would lose its strong position. This is likely to break up the sometimes overly bureaucratic procedures within the BA and increase the speed at which the set of instruments used in active labor market policy is adjusted in response to empirical studies which assess their effectiveness and efficiency. In addition, the groups controlling the BA would no longer be able to control the flow of funds and direct parts of them to programs which serve their own interests rather than that of the unemployed.

5   Conclusion

This paper deals with the allocation of tasks and responsibilities of active labor market policy in a federal state. The analysis has shown that while the decentralization of training and placement activities will increase the productivity of these policies, the federal unemployment insurance caused spillovers that reduce the incentives for regions to spend resources on training and placement. The emerging dilemma can, however, be overcome by intelligent institutional design. In particular, decentralization, when combined with an adequate set of incentives, can substantially increase the efficiency in the public sector.

In recent years, Germany has undergone substantial reforms with respect to the assignment of tasks and responsibilities for labor market policies. While some reforms point in the right direction, the overall degree of centralization is still much too high. Regional and local agencies are not given sufficient autonomy and incentives to exploit the efficiency gains from decentralization and the quasi-monopolistic structure of the BA is not revised. The lessons learned from the Public Choice theory discussed in section 4.4 suggest that keeping up this structure gives away potential gains in efficiency.

6 References

Bailey, S. (1999): Local Government Economics : Principles and Practice, London 1999

Boadway, R./Cuff, K. (1999): Monitoring Job Search as an Instrument for Targeting Transfers, in: International Tax and Public Finance, Vol. 6, S. 317-337

Boadway, R./Cuff, K./Marceau, N. (2003): Redistribution and Employment Policies with Endogenous Unemployment, in: Journal of Public Economics, Vol. 87, S. 2407-2430

Breton, A. (1965): A Theory of Government Grants, in: The Canadian Journal of Economics and Political Science, Vol. 31, S. 175-187

Brinkmann, C. (1998): Regionalisierung der Arbeitsmarktpolitik, in: Informationen für die Beratungs- und Vermittlungsdienste der Bundesanstalt für Arbeit, Heft 17/1998, S. 1763-1771

Brown, C./Oates, W. (1987): Assistance to the Poor in a Federal System, in: Journal of Public Economics, Vol. 32, S. 307-330

Bundesagentur für Arbeit (2006): Amtliche Nachrichten der Bundesagentur für Arbeit, Vol. 54, Sondernummer „Arbeitsmarkt 2005" (24.8.2006), Nürnberg 2006

Büttner, T. (1999): Regional Stabilization by Fiscal Equalization? Theoretical Considerations and Empirical Evidence from Germany, ZEW Discussion Paper, Mannheim 1999

Büttner, Th./Prey, H. (1998): Does Active Labor-Market Policy Affect Structural Unemployment?, in: Zeitschrift für Wirtschafts- und Sozialwissenschaften, Vol. 118, S. 389-413

Caliendo, M./Hujer, R./Thomsen, S. (2005): The Employment Effects of Job Creation Schemes in Germany – A Microeconometric Evaluation, IZA Discussion Paper, Vol. 13/2005

Calmfors, L. (1994): Active Labour Market Policy and Unemployment – A Framework for the Analysis of Crucial Design Features, in: OECD Economic Studies, Vol. 22, S. 7- 47

Cremer, H. et al. (1996) : Mobility and Redistribution – a Survey, in : Public Finance, Vol. 51, S. 325-352

Dahlby, B. (1996): Fiscal Externalities and the Design of Intergovernmental Grants, in: International Tax and Public Finance, Vol. 3, S. 397-411

Downs, A. (1957): An Economic Theory of Democracy, New York 1957

Eichenberger, R. (1994): The Benefits of Federalism and the Risk of Overcentralization, in: Kyklos, Vol. 47, S. 403-420

Fitzenberger, B./Speckesser, S. (2005): Employment Effects of the Provision of Specific Professional Skills and Techniques in Germany, IAB Discussion Paper, Vol. 21/2005

Hagedorn, M./Kaul, A. (2002): Langzeitarbeitslosigkeit in Deutschland – Fakten, Ursachen und Bekämpfung, Discussion Paper Nr. 680, Forschungsinstitut zur Zukunft der Arbeit (IZA), Bonn 2002

Hirschman, A. (1970): Exit, Voice, and Loyalty, Cambridge 1970

Hujer, R. et al. (2002): Macroeconomic Evaluation of Active Labour Market Policies in Germany – A Dynamic Panel Approach Using Regional Data, Discussion Paper Nr. 616, Forschungsinstitut zur Zukunft der Arbeit, Bonn 2002

Inman, R./Rubinfeld, D. (1996): Designing Tax Policy in Federalist Economies: An Overview, in: Journal of Public Economics, Vol. 60, S. 307-334

Jacob, L./Kluve, J. (2006): Before and after the "Hartz Reforms": The Performance of Active Labour Market Policy in Germany, IZA Discussion Paper, Vol. 2100/2006

Keen, M. (1998): Vertical Tax Externalities in the Theory of Fiscal Federalism, in: Int. Monetary Fund Staff Papers, Vol. 45, S. 454-484

Koller, M./Stichter-Werner, A. (2003): Modellrechnungen zum „verdeckten" Finanzausgleich in Deutschland, Beiträge zur Arbeitsmarkt- und Berufsforschung, Nr. 276, Nürnberg 2003

Kraft, K. (1998): An Evaluation of Active and Passive Labour Market Policy, in: Applied Economics, Vol. 30, p. 783-793

Kurz, C. (2000): Regional Risk Sharing and Redistribution by the Unemployment Insurance System: The Case of Germany, Paper Presented at the 15th Annual Congress of the European Economic Association from August 30 to September 2 2000

Kurz, C. (2002): Regionale Arbeitslosigkeit, Risikoausgleich und staatliche Transfersysteme: Theoretische Überlegungen und empirische Evidenz, Aachen 2002

Lechner, M. et al. (2005): Long-Run Effects of Public Sector Sponsored Training in West Germany, IAB-Discussion Paper 3/2005, Institut für Arbeitsmarkt- und Berufsforschung, Nürnberg 2005

Lohse, T. (2004): Die aktuellen Reformen der Sozialleistungen, in: Wirtschaftdienst, vol. 9/2004, S. 576-581

Martin, J./Grubb, D. (2001): What Works and for Whom: A Review of OECD Countries' Experiences with Active Labour Market Policies, in: Swedish Economic Policy Review, Vol. 8, S. 9-56

Mosley, H./Schütz, H./Schmid, G. (2003): Effizienz der Arbeitsämter – Leistungsvergleich und Reformpraxis, Berlin 2003

Neugart, M. (2005): Unemployment Insurance: The Role of Electoral Systems and Regional Labour Markets, in: European Journal of Political Economy, Vol. 21, S. 815-829

Niskanen, W. (1971): Bureaucracy and representative government, Chicago/New York 1971

Oates, W. (1972): Fiscal Federalism, New York 1972

Oates, W. (1996): Taxation in a federal system: The tax-assignment problem, in: Public Economics Review, Vol. 1, S. 35-60

Oates, W. (1998): On the Welfare Gains from Fiscal Decentralization, Working Paper 98-05, University of Maryland, Department of Economics, Baltimore 1998

Oates, W. (1999): An Essay on Fiscal Federalism, in: Journal of Economic Literature, Vol. 37, S. 1120-1149

OECD (1990): Labour Market Policies for the 1990s, Paris 1990

OECD (1993): Employment Outlook, Paris 1993

OECD (1998): Decentralising Employment Policies – New Trends and Challenges, Paris 1998

Penz, R. (2002): Institutioneller Wandel in der Arbeitsmarktpolitik – Das Beispiel der Reform von Arbeitslosenhilfe und Sozialhilfe, in: Priddat, B./Hegmann, H. (Ed.): Finanzpolitik in der Informationsgesellschaft, Marburg 2002, p. 185-204

Petrongolo, B./Pissarides, C. (2001): Looking into the Black Box: A Survey of the Matching Function, in: Journal of Economic Literature, Vol. 39, S. 390-431

Reissert, B. (2003): Zentrale oder dezentrale Finanzierung eines Nachfolgesystems für Arbeitslosenhilfe und Sozialhilfe? Eine Untersuchung zu den regionalen Stabilisierungseffekten der Arbeitslosenunterstützung, Schriftenreihe der Senatsverwaltung für Wirtschaft, Arbeit und Frauen, Vol. 62, Berlin 2003

Salmon, P. (1987): Decentralization as an incentive scheme, in: Oxford Review of Economic Policy, Vol. 3, S. 24-43

Sen, A. (1995): The Political Economy of Targeting, in: van de Walle, D./Nead, K. (Hrsg.): Public Spending and the Poor – Theory and Evidence, Baltimore 1995, S. 11-24

Sinn, S. (1992): Taming the Leviathan: Competition among Governments, in: Constitutional Political Economy, Vol. 3, S. 177-196

Stigler, G. (1962): Information in the Labor Market, in: Journal of Political Economy, Vol. 70, S. 94-104

Taheri, J. (2000): On the Alternative Explanations of Persistence of Unemployment in the OECD Countries, in: Applied Economics, Vol. 32, S. 1051-1057

Thomsen, S. (2006): Evaluating the Employment Effects of Job Creation Schemes in Germany, Heidelberg 2006

Voigt, S. (1997): Positive Constitutional Economics – A Survey, in: Public Choice, Vol. 90, S. 11-53

IV. REFORM PROPOSALS FOR THE POLISH FISCAL SYSTEM

REFORM PROPOSALS FOR THE POLISH FISCAL EQUALIZATION SYSTEM DERIVED FROM THE THEORY OF FISCAL FEDERALISM

LARS PONTERLITSCHEK

1 Introduction

The reform proposals presented here are based on the analysis of the Polish fiscal equalization system and derived from the theory of fiscal federalism. Starting point is the analysis and evaluation of the expenditure assignment in Poland. After that, the social security system and the current tax assignment will be criticized. Finally, the problems of the existing transfer system are analyzed and reform proposals are presented in order to tackle the analyzed weaknesses.

The proposed reforms within the expenditure assignment scheme will bring about the need to finance additional activities for the subnational governments, particularly for the voivodships. Additional (tax) revenues need to be generated at all subnational levels of government. The local governments typically are not allowed to collect enough tax revenues to fully cover their expenditures. On the other side, the central government usually will have more tax capacities than it needs to fulfil its duties, it will give vertical transfers to the local governments.

2 Reform Proposals for the Expenditure Assignment

2.1 PROBLEMS OF THE CURRENT SYSTEM

In most instances, the expenditure assignment in Poland is in line with the theory of fiscal federalism. The decentralization process in Poland has resulted in a system where tasks which entail economies of scale and produce spillovers are mainly

291

assigned to the central government and in certain cases also to the voivodship governments. Typical 'local tasks' with limited spillovers and economies of scale are performed by gminas, cities with poviat rights, and poviats, following the principle of subsidiarity.

However, even after 17 years of reforms and decentralization efforts, the public finances in Poland remain rather centralized. The central government still has a dominating role. It executed 67 % of all budgetary public expenditures in 2005 in comparison with e.g. Germany, where the central level executed 42 %. The local governments' expenditures are mainly made by the communes and cities with poviat status (79 % of local and 26 % of all budgetary expenditures in 2005). Poviats and voivodships have very small budgets and low expenditure competencies. This situation leads to the question which level of government should be responsible for tasks with regional spillovers like agricultural policy, regional labor market policy, environmental policy, or higher education. In a federal country, the intermediate level (US States, Länder, Kantone) usually plays an important role in the execution of such tasks. In Poland, contrary to the principle of subsidiarity, these tasks are under control of the central government. This may explain why many voivodships are confronted with low development of the regions, poor infrastructure (especially roads and environmental infrastructure), and inefficient agriculture.

One problem which could be observed during the decentralization process in Poland are the so-called 'unfunded mandates'. When tasks are decentralized, the central government must make sure that the local governments receive sufficient revenues for the execution of these tasks (see article 167 of the Polish constitution). At present, this 'principle of connectivity' is not always followed in Poland. For example, local expenditures for education are higher than the educational part of the general subsidies that the local governments receive. Even if parts of the appropriated allocations are given to finance educational duties, there is still a considerable gap to be financed from the communes' own revenues. The connection between received grants and actual expenditure needs from obligatory and delegated tasks is not appropriate, not only for educational tasks.

Moreover, the observed domination of obligatory and delegated tasks means that large parts of the TSGs' budgets are absorbed by duties they cannot freely decide on. As a result they do not have enough capacities for their own tasks and thus not enough real decision-making autonomy.

Another problem is the sharing of responsibilities for several tasks and the fact that the actual assignment is often different from what it appears to be. For example, in the field of education, even though local governments execute more than 90% of the expenditures for primary and secondary education, most of the key decisions in education policies are made at the central level. The Ministry of Education and Science remains responsible for curriculum design and teacher training. Thus local autonomy is limited. Issues similar to those in the education sector arise in other fields such as health and social welfare. However, the sharing of responsibilities, which is quite common in fields like education or health care, does not necessarily lead to inefficiencies, as long as the central government confines itself to setting standards or defining aims for particular public services and does not prevent local competition by providing detailed rules for every task.

Concerning the structure of expenditures, Poland spent only 2.0 % of GDP on knowledge in 1999, which was one of the lowest values of all OECD countries. Expenditure per student for tertiary education in Poland was the lowest of all OECD members in 2001. For primary, secondary, and post-secondary education, only the Slovak Republic spent less per student than Poland in 2001. On the other hand, Poland has higher social expenditures in relation to GDP than the average of all OECD countries. Especially the pension system is relatively expensive in Poland, compared with other OECD countries.[1]

2.2 REFORM PROPOSALS

First proposal

As mentioned above, many voivodships are confronted with low development of the regions and poor infrastructure. Thus the regions need to be strengthened by granting them more decision-making autonomy for all tasks which entail regional, but not national, externalities and which are carried out by the central government today. A first step for higher independence from the central government should be to reduce the central government's influence at the regional level. The Voivod should no longer be assigned by the Prime Minister, but elected by the voivodship council. The voivodships are already responsible for tasks like structural policy, regional development, et al. which entail large benefit spillovers and/or economies of scale as recommended by economic theory. But at the same time, voivodships have rather small budgets and low expenditures compared to other territorial self-government (TSG) units. They only had 7.3 % of all local self-government expenditures and merely 2.4 % of all public expenditures in Poland in 2005. Compared to other countries, the low expenditures at the regional level signal that voivodships do not have sufficient autonomy and

---

[1]   CF. World Bank (2003), pp. 39-44.

independent decision-making power to execute necessary regional development and structural policies. Additionally, following the subsidiarity principle, voivodships could take over (more) responsibilities from the central level in fields like higher education, extracurricular vocational education, health care, agricultural policy, housing/dwelling economy, regional labor market policy, and environmental policy.

Second proposal

Subnational governments at all levels should be given enough financial means for the execution of obligatory and delegated tasks so that they enjoy some scope for the execution of their own tasks. Concerning the tasks they already execute, subnational governments should have wider scope, i.e. further deregulation is necessary.

Third proposal

Having compared the public expenditures for several tasks in Poland with other OECD members, it seems recommendable to increase public expenditures on knowledge, primary, secondary, and tertiary education in Poland, even though it is not possible to define one universally valid optimal level of spending for education.

Fourth proposal

Expenditures on social security and particularly pensions seem too high in Poland and should therefore be reduced.

Fifth proposal

Finally, the consolidation of extrabudgetary special funds and entities into the state budget or local governments' budgets would be desirable. A reduction of the vast number of extrabudgetary funds at the local level, but also the abolishment of the large funds associated to the central level, by bringing them into the appropriate budgets would subject their programs to the same degree of parliamentary and ministerial oversight as other government activities[2]. Abolishing these funds and integrating their activities into the budgets could also help reduce administrative costs.

---

[2] In Poland, Regional Accounting Offices (RIO) are responsible for supervision and control of local government finances.

3 Reform Proposals for the Social Security System

3.1 PROBLEMS OF THE CURRENT SYSTEM

Concerning the social security system there are some features that should be discussed and eventually reformed:

- As already mentioned above, Poland has a rather expensive social security system in comparison to other EU members;

- Poland has rather liberal disability criteria that were not tackled during the 1999 reform of the social security system;

- Different retirement ages cause gender inequalities within the old-age pension system;

- Poland is the only transition country with a separate system of social insurance for farmers (KRUS). Benefits paid out by KRUS are to the largest extent not financed from contributions, but from state budget subsidies;

- The existence of separate sickness and health insurance systems is a problem that has not been addressed in the 1999 reforms.

3.2 REFORM PROPOSALS

The first problem mentioned above has twofold implications. First, employees liable to contributions have to transfer large shares of their incomes to the social security system. Second, the central government has to pay large transfers from the state budget to the social security system. Thus cuts of the social security system's expenditures seem necessary. There are several possibilities for expenditure reductions in the current system. For example, disability pension benefits should be made less generous by tightening eligibility criteria. Spending on sickness leave could also be reduced as there is scope for abuse in the currently generous system. Moreover, the replacement rates for short-term sickness could be reduced (e.g. from 80 to 70 % of salary).

An overall reduction in ZUS contribution rates payable by employees would clearly boost job creation. Expenditure reductions would also disburden the state budget.

Further reform options aimed at resolving structural and organizational shortcomings of the current system include equalizing the pension age for both sexes to 65 years and reforming the social insurance for farmers by including large farmers into the ZUS system. Small (part-time) farmers should stay with the KRUS system.

4   Reform Proposals for the Tax Assignment

4.1   PROBLEMS OF THE CURRENT ASSIGNMENT

The nominal tax assignment in Poland corresponds to the theoretical literature. Taxes with redistributive effects, like income taxes, are levied by the central government. The revenues of indirect taxes, including VAT also go to the central government. This is reasonable in a unitary state considering the administrative problems connected with VAT taxation on the local level. Local governments on the communal level impose taxes on immobile tax bases by making use of property taxation.

Currently, the central government's revenues mainly consist of tax revenues from indirect taxes, i.e. VAT and excise taxes (64.0 % of total revenues), the personal income tax (13.6 %), and the corporate income tax (8.8 %), as shown in table IV - 1:

Table IV - 1: State budget revenue 2005 (in m PLN)

TOTAL	**179,772**	**100.0%**
Tax revenue	**155,860**	**86.6%**
Indirect taxes	115,672	64.3%
VAT	75,401	41.4%
Excise tax	39,479	22.0%
Income taxes	40,185	22.4%
CIT	15,762	8.8%
PIT	24,423	13.6%
Non-tax revenue	**21,060**	**11.7%**
Receipts from customs duties	1,271	0.7%
Payments from the profit of NBP	4,168	2.3%
Revenue of the budgetary entities	10,844	6.0%
Foreign revenue	**405**	**0.2%**
Transfers from the EU	**2,447**	**1.4%**

Source: GUS (2006), p. 422.

As table IV - 2 shows, only gminas and cities with poviat rights have sources of own tax income. The situation of poviats and voivodships is less satisfactory. They have to rely heavily on grants and do not have any important revenues from own taxes for which they can set the base and/or rate. Moreover, they receive shares in PIT and CIT, but do not have any influence on these shares, nor on the tax rates or bases of these taxes. The revenues from tax sharing are somewhat misleadingly classified as 'own revenues' in the budgets, probably because the revenues can theoretically be spent according to the voivodships' and poviats' preferences.

Table IV - 2: Territorial self-governments' revenues (in m PLN) in 2005

Type of revenue	Gminas	Cities with poviat status	Poviats	Voivodships
Own revenues	20,558	23,379	3,379	4,417
Share in income from CIT	443	1,155	91	3,338
Share in income from PIT	6,270	9,089	1,805	599
Agricultural tax	950	17		
Tax on real estate	6,995	4,674		
Forest tax	136	1		
Tax on means of transport	385	277		
Tax paid by small firms in the form of tax card	58	62		
Tax on inheritances and gifts	81	145		
Tax on civil law transactions	438	756		
Stamp duty	294	225		
Exploitation fee	185	20		
Market place fee	151	93		
Revenue from property	1,622	2,438	210	64
Appropriated allocations	7,433	3,961	3,046	1,128
General subsidies from the state budget	16,080	8,325	6,699	1,351
Revenue from non-budgetary sources	1,742	605	280	170
Total	45,813	36,270	13,763	7,066

Source: Ministry of Finance (2007), GUS (2006), pp. 429-430.

With respect to their own taxes, gminas and cities with poviat status cannot decide independently on the tax rates and bases. The central government defines the tax bases and sets maximum tax rates. The local governments are allowed to set rates below these maximum rates. These ceilings restrain the revenue autonomy of the local entities. Moreover, there seem to be very low incentives for local tax effort in the current system. For example, many gminas reduce tax rates to 0 % for the real estate tax today. Finally, the fact that the agricultural sector has reduced VAT rates and is exempt from the PIT has negative effects on the revenue system.

4.2   REFORM PROPOSALS

Increased autonomy should be given to all entities of the territorial self-government in taxation decisions. Every subnational level of government should have at least one truly own source of tax revenue on which it can decide (tax base and/or rate), so that local governments are able to build their own tax base over time. Above mentioned exemptions for the agricultural sector should be abolished so as to broaden the tax base. Moreover, the centrally defined maximum tax rates for local taxes should be abolished. However, tax coordination/harmonization may be reasonable to avoid ruinous tax competition.

The gminas' share of revenues from "truly own" revenues, i.e. without revenues from shared taxes, in total revenues amounted to a little more than 30 % in the year 2005. For cities with poviat status, the share of truly own revenues is 36.0 %. This means that revenues from local taxes and charges for communes are not sufficient to fulfill their obligatory and delegated tasks. In order to be able to fulfil their tasks, it is therefore necessary to assign communes other sources of revenues such as shares in the central taxes or intergovernmental grants, i.e. not truly own revenues. Nevertheless, on the communal level the problem today is not the structure, but the overall size of the revenues in relation to their tasks/expenditures. Thus local authorities should either be allowed to make more use of own taxes (e.g. local governments could make even more use of property taxation), which would also enhance their independence from the central government, or they need to receive higher shares in PIT/CIT, or they need larger transfers from the central government.

One possibility for improving the local governments' revenue situation often mentioned in the literature is to eliminate tax sharing for PIT and CIT. Therefore, the central tax rates on these taxes should be reduced and the local governments should be allowed to impose flat supplementary tax rates on the central government tax base for PIT and CIT.[3]

5   Reform Proposals for the Transfer System

As the subnational governments are not typically allowed to collect enough tax revenues to fully cover their expenditures, and usually the central government will have more tax capacities than it needs to fulfil its duties, it will give vertical transfers to the local governments. In Poland, both unconditional grants (called 'general subsidies' in official statistics) and conditional grants (called 'appropriated allocations') are widely used. The theory of fiscal federalism suggests using unconditional grants for closing vertical fiscal gaps and for equalizing horizontal disparities across local governments.

---

[3]   CF. World Bank (2003), p. 33.

Conditional matching grants should be used to internalize benefit spillovers by inducing the receiving local governments to spend the correct amounts on certain tasks.

5.1 PROBLEMS OF THE CURRENT SYSTEM

5.1.1 Conditional Grants

The following table illustrates the importance of both types of grants for the financial situation of the Polish local governments:

In table IV - 3 we can see that conditional grants (appropriated allocations) have different weights for the local governments. In gminas and voivodships, they account for 16.0 % of total revenue. In cities with poviat status, their share is only 11.0 %, while for poviats conditional grants are the second most important source of revenue with a share of 22.0 %.

Conditional grants are transferred to a large extent for the execution of local governments' own tasks, as table 28 shows. Compared to 1999, however, the share of allocations granted for the execution of own tasks has declined from 38.0 % to 27.7 %. It stands out negatively that the share of investment grants has declined from 15.8 % in 1999 to only 9.0 % of all conditional grants in 2005:

Table IV - 3: Territorial self-governments' revenues (in m PLN) in 2005

	Gminas	Cities with poviat status	Poviats	Voivod-ships
Total revenues (m PLN)	**45,813**	**36,270**	**13,763**	**7,066**
of which:				
Own revenues	30.2%	36.2%	13.4%	6.8%
Shared taxes	14.7%	28.2%	13.8%	55.7%
Share in the corporate income tax	1.0%	3.2%	0.7%	47.2%
Share in the personal income tax	13.7%	25.1%	13.1%	8.5%
Appropriated allocations	16.2%	10.9%	22.1%	16.0%
General subsidies from the state budget	35.1%	23.0%	48.7%	19.1%

Source: GUS (2006), pp. 429-430.

Table IV - 4 does, however, not include information whether the different levels of local governments receive different shares of appropriated allocations for investment tasks.

The share of conditional grants given to gminas, cities with poviat status, and poviats for investment tasks was rather low in 2005 with values of 3.8 %, 7.4 %, and 10.5 % of all allocations respectively. Only in voivodships, where investment transfers accounted for a share of 52.0 %, the fostering of investment projects through conditional grants was performed substantially.

Table IV - 4: Breakdown of appropriated allocations from the state budget to all local governments (in m PLN)

	1999	%	2001	2003	2005	%
Total	**13,726.40**	**100.0**	**16,588.00**	**11,985.40**	**13,921.30**	**100.0**
On tasks delegated by law	7,814.10	56.9	10,872.60	6,509.80	9,837.50	70.7
Current tasks	7,765.30	56.6	10,599.50	6,098.70	9,590.30	68.9
Investment tasks	48.9	0.4	273.1	411.2	247.2	1.8
On tasks delegated by contracts	700.5	5.1	184.5	133.9	229.7	1.6
Current tasks	303.3	2.2	117.4	118.3	152.5	1.1
Investment tasks	397.2	2.9	67.1	15.5	77.2	0.6
On own tasks	5,211.80	38.0	5,530.90	5,341.70	3,854.10	27.7
Current tasks	3,500.90	25.5	3,728.50	3,959.10	2,931.00	21.1
Investment tasks	1,710.90	12.5	1,802.40	1,382.60	923.1	6.6

Source: MINISTRY OF FINANCE (2007).

5.1.2 Unconditional Grants

Furthermore, large unconditional grants are given for the financing of gminas and poviats, where they contribute to 35.1 % and 48.7 % of all revenues respectively. The amounts given to cities with poviat status and voivodships, where unconditional grants only contribute to 23.0 % and 19.1 % of their total revenues, are considerably smaller.

Unconditional grants are divided into different parts that, with the exception of the equalizing part, try to take into account the financial needs of the local governments. Table IV - 5 gives an overview of the composition of the unconditional grants given to the different local government units. Clearly the educational part is the most important one, accounting for 80.4 % of all unconditional grants. Also the equalizing part plays some role with a share of 14.6 %. The other elements do not have much influence on the revenues of the local governments.

Table IV - 5: Breakdown of the general subsidies

GENERAL SUBSIDIES	2005 (in m PLN)	%
Total	32,455.7	100.0%
Educational part	26,097.4	80.4%
for gminas (excl. cities with poviat status)	12,139.5	
for cities with poviat status	7,851.2	
for poviats	5,542.2	
for voivodships	564.5	
Compensatory part (discontinued)	11.8	0.0%
for gminas (excl. cities with poviat status)	7.3	
for cities with poviat status	4.5	
Equalizing part	4,731.5	14.6%
for gminas (excl. cities with poviat status)	3,609.8	
for cities with poviat status	45.5	
for poviats	637.2	
for voivodships	439.0	
Balancing part	909.7	2.8%
for gminas (excl. cities with poviat status)	304.1	
for cities with poviat status	210.8	
for poviats	394.8	
Regional part for voivodships	314.5	1.0%
Supplement to general subsidies	390.9	1.2%
for gminas (excl. cities with poviat status)	19.6	
for cities with poviat status	213.5	
for poviats	125.3	
for voivodships	32.5	

Source: Ministry of Finance (2007).

The calculation of the educational part of the unconditional grant is very complex in Poland. There are various factors which determine the amount of the educational part given to the local governments. The most important factors are the number of pupils, the formal qualification of teachers employed by the government entity, and the share of pupils located in rural areas in the total number of pupils in the self-government entity. Thus there are rather complex but improper measures of need in the calculation of the educational part of unconditional grants. Moreover, it is doubtful whether the valorization of pupils in rural communes can be justified by the actual costs they generate compared to urban pupils. Other measures should be found to support small rural gminas.

The second part of the general subsidies that is worth analyzing more thoroughly is the equalizing part. The equalizing part follows theoretical considerations which suggest using unconditional grants for filling fiscal gaps and for equalization purposes. It is given to gminas that have less than 92 % of the average fiscal capacity from own revenues of all gminas and to poviats and voivodships which have per capita tax revenues below average.

This part of the general subsidies clearly – as the name suggests – has a strong equalizing effect. For the poorest gminas which have tax revenues below 40 % of the average gmina before equalization, the fiscal gap is filled until they have between 76.9 % and 80.8 % of the average income. Gminas which initially have tax revenues between 40 % and 75 % of the average, receive the equalizing part so that the gap is filled until they have revenues between 81 % and 87.8 % of the average gmina. Finally, gminas which have tax revenues between 75 % and 92 % of the average, receive the equalizing part so that the gap is filled until they have at least 88 % of the income of the average gmina. Gminas with 92 % or more of the fiscal capacity of the average gmina do not receive this part of the general subsidies.

The allocation of the equalizing part is less complex for poviats and voivodships as only one formula is used, irrespective of their financial situation. After receiving the equalizing part, each poviat has at least 88 % of the average income of all poviats. Voivodships which receive the equalizing part will have at least 70 % of the average fiscal capacity of all voivodships.

The balancing part is granted to gminas and poviats that have specific expenditure needs. This part is financed by contributions of wealthy gminas and poviats to the state budget and thus has some equalizing impact. The regional part of the general subsidies is given to voivodships with specific expenditure needs. The total distributable amount of this part consists of contributions of wealthy voivodships to the state budget and therefore has an equalizing effect on the voivodships' total revenues. Due to the way the balancing and regional parts are financed, they are a form of *horizontal* equalization via the state budget. The overall effect of these parts is rather small, however, according to the size of these transfers.

To sum up, Poland uses unconditional grants that try to take into account the expenditure needs of subnational governments. But the chosen indicators for local need seem inappropriate. Only local expenditures for education are considered, although these only account for approx. one third of the local governments' total expenditures. Expenditure needs for social welfare, transport and communications, etc. are either not considered at all or in an intransparent manner within the balancing / regional part. At any rate, they are under-represented in the design of the general subsidies.

Poland does already use a formula-based transfer system. In this respect, it is better developed than most of the East European transition countries, where in some cases the intergovernmental grant system is negotiated year by year between the central and local governments. The equalizing part of the grants is designed effectively – it considerably diminishes disparities across local governments. Particularly in poviats and voivodships, fiscal capacities are nearly completely equalized. This seems to be justified because at these levels, differences in revenues do not result from different tax efforts, but from the distribution of the local shares in PIT and CIT.

The changes in the financing of the Polish territorial self-governments introduced in 2004 brought about positive and negative effects. On the one hand, they point into the right direction because of the increase of local governments' 'own' revenues by granting them higher shares in the PIT and CIT. This was a positive change in the structure of revenues, but still subnational governments have insufficient financial means for the fulfillment of their tasks. On the other hand, the reforms led to an increase in disparities across local governments, especially in cities with poviat status and voivodships. Particularly in voivodships the increased disparities are problematic as they do not result from different tax efforts, but from unequal distribution of revenues from PIT and CIT, which are not entirely equalized by the transfer system.

Altogether, Poland uses unconditional grants in line with theoretical considerations. They are used for filling vertical fiscal gaps, particularly by transferring the educational part of the general subsidies to all levels of local governments. Here, further reforms of the transfer system seem necessary, particularly concerning the measurement of fiscal need and fiscal capacity of the local governments. Unconditional grants are also used for equalization purposes via the equalizing part of the general subsidies. Conditional non-matching grants are used for fostering defined tasks of the local governments, while theory prefers applying matching elements.

5.2 REFORM PROPOSALS

5.2.1 Conditional Grants

Conditional grants (appropriated allocations) should not be transferred to finance local governments' own and delegated tasks in the form of non-matching grants. In such a case, the transfer-receiving community will spend the full grant on the respective task, but it might also reduce its own expenditures for this task, which is not the desired reaction. Therefore, it is recommended to design conditional grants in such a way that the recipient local governments have to match the transferred amount with own sources. Moreover, conditional grants should be used more than they currently are for fostering capital and infrastructure spending. The share of investment-related conditional grants in Poland should be higher for all local levels except for the voivodship level.

5.2.2 Unconditional Grants

As far as the equalizing part of the subsidies is concerned, the design of this part seems to be effective. One could ask whether the competition between gminas could be encouraged by reducing the 'redistributivity' of the equalizing part for this government level. The existence of the balancing and regional parts could be reconsidered as the amounts transferred within these parts are rather small (together only 3.8 % of all unconditional grants) and the equalizing effect could also be achieved by integrating the contributions of the local governments with above-average revenues into the amount of the equalizing part to be distributed. This could reduce the administrative expenses of the system.

The biggest issue in the transfer system is the way that fiscal needs and capacities are measured within the educational part of the general subsidies. Poland needs to find feasible measures of fiscal capacity and better/more comprehensive measures of fiscal need in order to design a transfer system which guarantees subnational governments the necessary funds to perform their tasks. Theory calls for giving unconditional grants subject to the fiscal capacity and fiscal need of the receiving jurisdiction, with "fiscal strength" being the difference or ratio between the two. However, the largest part of the general subsidy, namely the educational part, is given to all local governments without taking their fiscal capacities into account. Thus this part of the general subsidies should be reformed and be given inversely to the jurisdiction's fiscal strength. Unconditional grants should be increased if local expenditure needs rise, and they should be cut if the potential local fiscal capacities rise. Presently, however, voivodships and poviats do not really have any fiscal capacity, if we define this as the ability of a government to raise revenues from its own sources and if we do not count shared taxes as own sources.

In the case of the regions, fiscal capacity could be proxied by per capita income. On the municipal level, the task is more difficult as fewer data are available. Measuring fiscal need is much more complicated. A comparison of actual to average expenditures on education, social welfare, health, sewage, and roads could be a starting point.

High dependence of gminas on grants (general subsidies and appropriated funds) may entail low incentives for their efforts to collect own taxes. Thus unconditional grants must be designed in a way that they do not discourage local governments' efforts to collect 'own' taxes and user charges.

In the following subsections, possible arrangements for vertical (equalization) transfers will be discussed in more detail. Therefore, in a first step, a few considerations about the different possible types of grant formulas will be presented. In a second step, some possibilities for measuring fiscal need and fiscal capacity at the local level are proposed. In the final step, the impact of a formula-based approach of a fiscal equalization scheme on local tax effort will be shortly assessed.

5.2.2.1 Types of Transfer Formulas

In practice, there are four different types of formulas for vertical equalizing transfers[4]:

Formulas which consider not only the equalization of fiscal capacities, but also take into account the expenditure needs of different subnational governments (SNG) are typically as follows:

$$TR_i = N_i - C_i - OTR_i$$

where TR_i is the vertical equalization transfer from the central, N_i is the fiscal need of the ith SNG, and C_i is the fiscal capacity of the ith SNG. $N_i - C_i$ measures the gap between fiscal need and capacity (i.e. own sources of revenue). OTR_i represents other transfers, e.g. specific grants, which the ith SNG receives from the center. This formula, however, is rather demanding in terms of data requirement, especially with regard to those on expenditure needs. The advantage of this formula is that the central government will fill the gap between each SNG's fiscal need and capacity to ensure that the SNGs are able to provide a reasonable level of public services.

The second formula only considers the equalization of fiscal capacities. This type of formula has relatively weak requirements for data and can be implemented easily. But it ignores the potentially large differences in special expenditure needs across SNGs:

$$TR_i = P_i (B/P - B_i/P_i) t$$

Pi is the population, Bi is the tax base of the ith SNG. P is the total population, B is the total tax base of the country, and t is the country's average effective tax rate on the tax base. $B/P - B_i/P_i$ measures the gap between the national average per capita tax base and the ith SNG's per capita tax base. This formula implies that the central government will bring the fiscal capacity of below-average SNGs up to the national average. Above-average SNGs can be forced to contribute to the pool for transfers of the central government. The intensity of the equalization effort can vary between full equalization and a certain percentage of the national average.

---

[4]   The subsequent illustrations summarize a World Bank paper by Jun Ma.

This approach is basically applied in Poland for the equalizing part of the general subsidies.

The third approach distributes equalization transfers based on certain needs indicators. Here, fiscal capacity is not taken into account, often because such data are very difficult to obtain. There are various indicators that can be used to reflect the fiscal needs of SNGs, and the choices are dependent on the political objectives of the central government. Typical indicators used to identify SNGs' fiscal needs include:

- area,
- poverty incidence,
- unemployment rate,
- population density
- per capita income level

- infant mortality,
- life expectancy,
- school enrolment rate,
- infrastructure (e.g. length of roads or railways),
- other indicators of development level (e.g. electricity consumption or number of telephone lines)

Which indicators should be chosen to measure fiscal need and how much weight each indicator should be given are very sensitive questions and need to be answered with simulations and in cooperation with the receiving SNGs.

This type of formula is used in Poland for the educational part of the unconditional grants, but only for one type of expenditure needs, namely education. Although this is the most important type of expenditure for Polish local governments, a broader approach like that discussed in section 5.2.2.2 for measuring local needs should be applied.

The last possibility is to distribute transfers on an equal per capita basis. Compared to the first three types of transfers, this type is least demanding for data, but it has relatively weak equalization effects:

$$TR_i = P_i \, (TT/P)$$

Where TT is the total pool for transfers and P is the total population eligible for the transfer program. Equal per capita transfers cannot fully equalize but can mitigate disparities in fiscal capacity among SNGs.

Altogether, the first type of formula provides the potential for full equalization. It is the most complex and most accurate one in measuring horizontal fiscal gaps, but it is very demanding in terms of data requirement. Types 2 and 3 each ignore one important aspect, i.e. need or capacity, of the horizontal equalization, and thus are less effective in addressing disparity issues among SNGs.

5.2.2.2   Measuring Fiscal Need and Capacity

The above subsection mentioned the terms fiscal need (N_i) and fiscal capacity (C_i) of a SNG several times. This subsection will present some ideas how to estimate these variables.

Measuring Fiscal Need

Determining fiscal needs of subnational governments is a difficult task which requires many information and data. Subsequently, an approach, which divides the expenditures of a subnational government into different categories and for each category estimates the need of this government, is presented. The total fiscal need of a subnational government is the sum of the estimated needs for all these categories. This approach involves the following steps:

Step 1: Divide the SNG's expenditures into several categories. The most commonly used categories include:

- education,
- Health,
- transportation,
- police and fire,

- telecommunications,
- social welfare,
- environmental protection,
- other services,

Of course, depending on the country's existing budgeting rules and data availability, the division of expenditure categories can have many variations. One can combine transportation with telecommunications, separate police from fire, divide social welfare further into many smaller items, divide education into primary, secondary, and post-secondary educations, etc.

Most countries' equalization transfer formulas take into account the needs for current expenditures (including maintenance of capital projects) but exclude those for new capital projects. Their expenditure needs may vary significantly from year to year; and it is difficult to find appropriate indicators that reflect the needs for new capital projects.

Step 2: Calculate the expenditure need for each category and then sum up these needs to get the SNG's aggregate fiscal need. An illustrative example is discussed below.

The general formula for calculating expenditure need in category i can be written as:

N_i = Measurement Unit * Average Per Unit Cost * Adjustment Index

where i stands for the ith expenditure category, such as education, health, transportation, etc. Measurement unit refers to the number of units that receive services from the respective subnational government. Average per unit cost is defined as total local expenditure on category i divided by the measurement unit (e.g. the average per unit cost of primary and secondary education is the ratio of the total expenditure on primary and secondary education to the total number of students in the country). Adjustment index is a combination of factors that differentiate the per unit cost of the service in the SNG from the national average.

Below, two examples for the application of such an approach are given:

(a) Primary and Secondary Education

Measurement unit = population of school ages (e.g. age 7-18).

Average per unit cost = the country's per capita public expenditure on primary and secondary education.

Adjustment index = $a_1WI + a_2RCI + a_3SDI + a_4PFI$

where WI (wage index) = the ratio of teachers' wage level in this SNG to the national average;
RCI (rental cost index) = the ratio of per square rental cost in this SNG to the national average;
SDI (student disability index) = the ratio of the percentage of students with physical disabilities in this SNG to the national average;
PFI (poor family index) = the ratio of the percentage of students from low-income families in this SNG to the national average.

The weights attached to the four factors should add up to one, i.e. $a_1 + a_2 + a_3 + a_4 = 1$. These weights can be derived from an econometric estimation using cross-region or panel data (cross-section and time series) from the past years. Many countries try arbitrary values of weights based on the designers' intuition about the importance of different factors in affecting the costs of services. Assigning these weights can also be a method for the designers to emphasize certain factors in grant distribution.

(b) Health Care

Measurement unit = total population in this SNG

Average per unit cost = the country's per capita public expenditure on health care

Adjustment index = $a_1HPI + a_2IMI + a_3ILEI + a_4IPDI$

where HPI (health price index) = the ratio of health care cost in this SNG to the national average;

IMI (infant mortality index) = the ratio of infant mortality rate in this SNG to the national average;

ILEI (inverse life expectancy index) = the ratio of national average life expectancy to life expectancy in this SNG;

IPDI (inverse population density index) = the ratio of national average population density to that in this SNG;

$a_1 + a_2 + a_3 + a_4 = 1$.

The above method to calculate regions' fiscal needs requires substantial information on a large number of factors that affect the costs of providing public services. Much of this information may not be available in some countries. This being the case, a feasible solution is to use fewer variables to directly estimate a region's aggregate fiscal need.

Measuring Fiscal Capacity

Fiscal capacity is defined as the ability of a government to raise revenues from its own sources. There are several ways to measure the fiscal capacity of a subnational government. In many developed countries, fiscal capacity is measured by using figures of major tax bases and standard (average) tax rates. The following method measures the fiscal capacity of a SNG by revenue that could be raised in that SNG if the subnational government taxes all the standard tax bases with the standard tax effort. The formula is as follows:

$$C_i = \Sigma_j B_{ij} {}^* t_j \qquad (*)$$

where C_i is the ith SNG's tax capacity, B_{ij} is the ith SNG's jth tax base, and t_j is the standard (e.g. national average effective) tax rate on the jth tax base. It is important to apply the standard tax rate to the SNG's tax base rather than the SNG's own effective tax rate, in order to ensure that the SNGs with high tax efforts are not penalized and those with low tax efforts are not encouraged. In other words, if the SNG's effective tax rates are higher than the national averages, the transfer it receives does not decrease as a result; if the SNG's effective tax rates are lower than the national averages, the transfer it receives does not increase as a result.

It is important not to use the SNGs' actual revenue figures to measure their fiscal capacities. If the actual figures are used, the transfer a SNG receives from the center becomes largely a variable controlled by its own tax effort. The SNGs would thus have the incentive to under-collect their own revenues in order to attract more transfers from the center. The reason is straightforward: the more a SNG collects from its own sources, the higher the measured fiscal capacity, and the less transfer it will receive.

Such an approach would currently only be applied to determine the fiscal capacities of Polish gminas, as poviats and voivodships do not have any truly own tax sources.

5.2.2.3   Influence of Equalization Transfers on Local Tax Effort

A frequently heard criticism of equalization transfer schemes is that equalization may adversely affect localities' effort to collect revenue. The rationale is that because an equalization scheme redistributes revenue from revenue rich regions to revenue poor regions, the former may purposely reduce their tax effort in order not to be penalized by the transfer scheme. This reasoning is, in most cases, a false impression of fiscal equalization.

Consider the formula described by equation (*). In this formula, local fiscal capacity is calculated using the previous year's tax bases and standard tax rates set by the central government. Therefore, fiscal capacities are independent from tax effort (the actual tax rates). If a locality increases its tax effort by raising its tax rates above the standard rates, the transfer that it will receive does not decrease. If the locality reduces its tax rates to levels below standards, it will not receive more transfer as a result. In other words, such a formula does not encourage low tax effort, and does not discourage high tax effort. The additional revenue collected due to a locality's higher effort will be kept by itself. In this sense, this formula encourages local tax effort.

Of course, if a locality's tax base increases, its transfer will decrease. However, it is important to note that, if the formula is appropriately designed, the magnitude of the decline in transfer can be rather small relative to the benefits a locality can gain from the increase in tax base. As a result, localities do not have the incentive to reduce tax bases simply for the purpose of attracting more transfers.

6   Bibliography

GUS (2006): "Concise Statistical Yearbook of Poland", GUS,
    http://www.stat.gov.pl/english/ opracowania_zbiorcze/maly_rocznik_ stat/2006
    /10 _ chapters.pdf, found 31/07/2006.

Ministry of Finance (2007): "SPRAWOZDANIA BUDŻETOWE", http://www.mf.gov.pl /
    index.php?wysw=4&sgl=2&dzial=229, found 15/01/2007.

World Bank (2003): "Poland - Toward a Fiscal Framework for Growth", in: World Bank
    Report No. 25033-POL. Washington, D.C.

PROPOSALS FOR THE IMPROVEMENT OF THE POLISH LOCAL FINANCE SYSTEM

TOMASZ URYSZEK

RADOSŁAW WITCZAK

We have to point out that, compared to poviats and voivodships, communes and cities with poviat rights have more own sources of revenues. Poviats and voivodships are almost entirely under the control of the central government. So the system of revenues of subnational governments in Poland only relies to some degree on their own revenues. In fact poviats and voivodships do not have fiscal autonomy in Poland. That is why many changes ought to be implemented into the present system. The suggested changes consider both the local authorities' own revenues and grants.

The future system of local revenues should be based more on the local authorities' own taxes and user charges. There are some possibilities to give more financial autonomy to the local authorities: reform of real estate tax, imposing of surcharges on some taxes, assigning of some of the central taxes to local authorities, transferring more power in the assigning of local taxes.

The reform of real estate tax is one of the ways to increase the financial autonomy of local authorities. The market value of real estate should become the tax base. It could increase the revenues of local authorities. Implementing the market value of real estate as tax base would facilitate a change of the system of local revenues. Such local taxes could be assigned not only to the communes but also to other subnationals.

Imposing surcharges on some taxes can increase the autonomy of local governments as well. In Poland there are no surcharges imposed on any taxes. It is advisable to levy them on personal income tax. Subnational governments could levy surcharges on the income of individuals living in their jurisdiction but in such a case the problem to solve is the administration of that tax. We would recommend the central tax administration to collect it. We have to remember that the high contributions of social insurance can be an obstacle to the implementing of surcharges. Imposing surcharges on corporate income tax and VAT should also be considered.

Due to fact that poviats and voivodships do not have any taxes of their own, we think that it is necessary to assign some taxes to them. One solution would be to assign the lump sum income tax on business activity to poviats and voivodships. It should still be collected by the central tax administration. Tax-sharing arrangements between poviats and voivodships could be implemented.

Local authorities should receive more power with regard to the assigning of local taxes. They ought to set the tax base and tax rate, especially in the case of property taxes like the inheritance and donations tax. They should have the power to impose their own property taxes and user charges.

As for unconditional grants, we can say that a relatively significant number of the particular parts of the grants given to the different levels of the local and regional governments, the frequent changes in the legal acts and very complicated ways of calculating these parts make the system of intergovernmental grants in Poland non-transparent. It is necessary to introduce the transparent system of grants. Besides, the system of calculating the particular parts of the grants should be simplified.

A very high share of the conditional and unconditional grants in the structure of the local and regional revenues points to the very strong dependence of local governments on the central level. This should be changed. The decrease of the share of conditional grants in the structure of the revenues of local and regional governments is particularly necessary to make these governments more independent. The decrease of both conditional and unconditional grants and the increase of the authorities' own revenues would be the best solution for the structure of financing local and regional governments in the long run.

Despite the high share of intergovernmental grants in the revenues of local governments the value of those grants is not enough to cover necessary expenditures. The transfer of tasks from the central to the local level is not followed by the transfer of the relevant financial means. That is why we can say that the transfer of tasks follows the theory of fiscal federalism but the transfer of financial sources does not. Besides, it is hard to show clearly that the local and regional governments receive "too small" sums of financial sources. To improve this, the social needs should be calculated. The integral system of calculation of social needs should be introduced.

However, the analyses of revenues of the selected local and regional governments indicate that the changes that took place after 2003 head for the increase of independence of local governments. We can observe that (at least in the field of intergovernmental grants) these changes are favorable for the raise of the level of self-reliance of these governments.

SELF-GOVERNMENT FINANCE
RECOMMENDATIONS FOR POLAND

WOJCIECH MISIĄG,
MARCIN TOMALAK

1   Introduction

The aim of the recommendations proposed below is to strengthen the position of the self-government in the Polish political and financial system and to guarantee the maximum level of financial and organizational independence. When formulating the recommendations, we must take into account that the Constitution and the European Charter of Local Self-Government[1] should be treated as the legal basis for the recommendations[2]. It means, in particular, that:

- the scope of the public tasks performed by the self-government units should – in general – be determined by the statutes,

- new taxes can only be established by the parliamentary act,

- self-governments from the lower level cannot be subordinated to the higher ones.

We must underline that the necessary reforms of the organization and financial system of the self-government should be treated as part of a larger program of the general government sector in Poland. We must also state that the current state of public finance, and namely:

- the amount of the Polish public debt (ca 50% of GDP),

---

[1]   The European Charter of Local Self-Government was ratified by Poland and – in consequence – must be treated as part of Polish law.

[2]   In particular, we must remember that, according to the Constitution of the Republic of Poland of the 2nd of April 1997: the principle of subsidiarity in the strengthening of the powers of citizens and their communities is declared in the Constitution as one of the basic principles determining the organization of state, Poland is an unitary state (Art. 3 of the Constitution), the territorial system of the Republic of Poland should ensure the decentralization of public power (Art. 15 paragraph 1 of the Constitution), gmina is the basic unit of local government.

- the large state budget deficit (more than 4% of GDP) should be taken into account when formulating the recommendations.

2   Recommendations

The competencies and financial resources of the self-government units are not sufficient to correctly fulfill the public tasks assigned to the self-government. In addition, the financial system of the self-government does not fully comply with the provisions of the Polish Constitution and of the European Charter of Self-Government – the new tasks are transferred to the self-government units without the adequate financial resources, the financial independence of self-government is strongly limited. These problems can be treated as strictly legal, but – in fact – they influence the effectiveness of the use of public resources and the quality of public services provided by the self-government. That is why the reform of local finance should be treated as an integral part of the large program of the public sector reform.

The reform of the local finance should include:

- changes in the catalogue of the self-government units' revenue, increasing the level of their financial independence,
- abolition of excessive regulations, in order to enable the self-government units to manage their financial resources more freely.

Our recommendations concerning the necessary changes in the political and financial systems of self-government can be divided into three sections: (1) general rules of fiscal and regional policies, (2) organization of the self-government, (3) local finance.

In the field of the general rules of fiscal and regional policies, concerning the self-government units, our recommendations are as follows.

1. The tax system and social insurance system for the agriculture should be improved.
2. The role of self-government units in the system of programming and managing the use of EU funds should be increased.

In the field of the organization of the self-government we recommend:

3. The role of the *voivods* should be reconsidered and the scope of the *voivods'* tasks should be limited to the functions of the government representative and the supervising authority for the self-government units.
4. Self-government on the voivodship level should be organized as the union of the gminas and not as the community of citizens.
5. The existence of the poviats should be reconsidered.

6. The tasks delegated to the self-government units by the statutes (acts) should be converted into the obligatory own tasks of appropriate self-government units.

In the field of the financial system of the self-government we recommend:

7. Two separate systems of the own revenue and financial equalization should be applied to rural communities and to towns.

8. The following revenue of the central government should be transferred, together with the public tasks, to the appropriate self-government units as their own revenue:

    • contributions to the Labor Fund, the State Fund for the Rehabilitation of Disabled Persons, and to the National Health Fund,

    • income of the State Agricultural Property Agency.

9. The algorithm for calculating the total amount of the general subsidies should be introduced, and the algorithms used to calculate the general subsidies should be simplified significantly.

10. The total revenue from the CIT should be the own revenue of the voivodships, or – at least – the share of voivodships in the CIT income should be significantly increased.

11. Financing of the self-government units' own tasks by conditional grants should be prohibited.

12. The voivodships should have the right to establish their own systems of financial equalizations (transfers between the voivodship budget and the gminas).

13. The self-government appropriate funds should be incorporated into the budgets of the self-government units.

14. The share of the self-government units in the distribution of the Environment Protection Funds' revenue should be significantly increased.

3 General Rules of the Fiscal and Regional Policies

3.1 TAXES AND SOCIAL INSURANCE IN AGRICULTURE

The system of taxes and social insurance contributions paid by the Polish farmers can be characterized by two facts:

- the contributions paid by the farmers to the KRUS (state social insurance agency for farmers) cover 5% of the social benefits for farmers,
- the revenue of gminas from the agriculture tax (simplified form of taxation, replacing PIT from the farmers) is less than the contributions paid to the farmers from the state budget and the budget of the EU.

This system is the main factor determining the financial situation of the rural gminas. In order to improve the tax system and to increase the financial capacity of the rural gminas, the following measures should be taken:

- the personal income from agricultural activity should be included in the PIT system,
- at least part of the farmers (owners of greater farms generating significant income) should be obliged to pay the social insurance contribution according to the rules which are in force in other branches.

3.2 USE OF THE EU FUNDS

The self-governments of the voivodship level should play an important role in the process of programming and managing the use of the funds from the EU budget during the new financial perspective 2007 – 2013.

The boards of voivodships will be the managing institutions for 16 regional programs financed from the European Fund of Regional Development. It is also important that the voivodship self-governments will participate in the programming and managing of the use of the resources coming from other European structural funds, like the European Social Fund and the European Agriculture Fund for Rural Development[3]. In our opinion, an active participation of regional and local self-governments is one of basic conditions of the successful use of European funds in Poland.

---

[3] The programs using the resources of these funds will be formally managed by the Minister of Regional Development and the Minister of Agriculture.

4 Organization of the Self-Government

4.1 ROLE OF THE VOIVODS

The role of the *voivods* should be limited to the functions of government's representatives, as it was proposed in the early version of the administration reforms, finally introduced in 1999. Such a change will strengthen the voivodship-level of the self-government and will allow avoiding the problems which have arisen from the existence of two parallel administrations (voivod and self-government) in the voivodships.

As a consequence of a new role of the voivod, the subordination of the voivodship controlling agencies should be reconsidered.

4.2 ORGANIZATION OF THE VOIVODSHIPS

All kinds of entities have the same structure in the Polish model of self-government. The self-government entity is the community (created by law) of citizens residing in a defined territory. Although this definition describes the character of a gmina very well, it is not adequate to describe a poviat or especially a voivodship.

Regional development programming and coordination of self-government interlocal projects are fundamental tasks of a voivodship. The regional self-government is not the public authority which would have any superior powers in gminas and poviats. This rule is one of the bases of the current Polish model of self-government. Moreover, a voivodship does not have enough financial capacity to be a partner for much stronger gminas, especially big cities. Paradoxically, the authority of the self-government voivodship has to carry out tasks which are important for the whole region (from 2007 onwards, the significant part of the European Union funds will be granted to and governed by voivodships), although it has very limited influence over gminas and poviats.

In our opinion this problem can be solved by the change of the voivodship's self-government formula. We propose that the voivodship's self-government should adopt the form of the gminas' union, rather than the community of inhabitants. The range of voivodship tasks should be reconsidered. New principles of decision made by voivodship bodies should be introduced to avoid domination of the biggest gminas and facilitate coordination of the region's interest as a whole, including the interests of individual gminas.

The changes in the organization of the voivodship's self-government should be introduced simultaneously with the changes recommended in paragraphs 4.1 and 4.3.

4.3 EXISTENCE OF POVIATS

Since their establishment in 1999, poviats have been the weakest element of the self-government system – both in the sense of activity range and financial capacity. After the 2003 act on self-government revenue came into force, poviats have only been one category of self-government whose own revenue is lower than 50% of the total revenue.

According to initial assumptions of the self-government reform, the poviats' main activity had to be concentrated on health care and educational tasks. Finally, another organizational model of health care was decided and from that moment on, the establishing of poviats became very controversial. Moreover, one should remember that the first conception of the reform assumed that 120 – 150 poviats would be created. Meanwhile, their actual number is much higher, which means that a significant part of poviat capitals have been located in small towns which do not even have the necessary infrastructure to play the role of local centers for neighboring gminas.

Figure IV - 1: Share of the own revenue in the revenue of the self-government units in the years 1991–2005

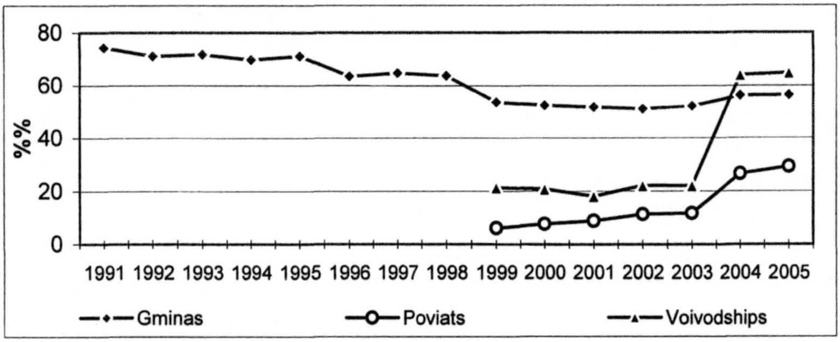

Source: authors' own calculations based on Ministry of Finance data

In conclusion, we recommend reconsidering the usefulness of the existence of poviats as a separate level of self-government and of the public administration. In our opinion the bigger part of the poviats' tasks (including education, culture and social service) could be taken over by gminas (mainly cities), and the other tasks (e.g. state administration tasks that are delegated by law or by contract) could be transferred to the administrations of the self-government voivodship. According to the principle of subsidiarity, voivodships should have the right to delegate their tasks to gminas by contract agreements. After applying the recommendation, self-government authorities will be able to set down a more flexible and independent policy with regard to the tasks' execution. This change in self-government organization will strengthen both gminas and voivodships, as well as result in cost savings on administration.

In our opinion such a change in the organization of the self-government will, at the same time, cause a strengthening of the self-government on gmina and voivodship level. In addition, the abolition of poviats should reduce the administrative costs of self-governments.

4.4 DELEGATED TASKS

We recommend a conversion of all state administration and other tasks which are delegated to the self-government by law into the self-government entities' own compulsory tasks. In our opinion, there is actually no argument for such delegated tasks at present.

Self-government entities are a part of the pubic administration system in Poland. Besides, the public administration system consists of the state bodies (e.g. the president, Sejm, Senat and public institutions subordinated to them), and the state administration. All the public tasks which are attributed to the self-government by law are in some sense state tasks (or more precisely public tasks) entrusted to the self-government. The self-government entities should bear responsibility for the execution of all tasks within the limits of standards which have been set by the state.

When delegated tasks for gminas were created at the beginning of transition, the introduction of transitory forms between the state administration's tasks and the self-government's own tasks was justified both by administrative principles of the state and relationships between the state administration and the self-government in the early 1990s. The reasons for an introduction of delegated tasks were no longer valid in the late 1990s. At that time the new constitution of Poland was approved and the administrative procedures concerning citizens' appeals regarding decisions made by the local authority were changed. Nowadays, there is no reason to treat delegated tasks as a category which is different from the obligatory own tasks of self-government. The abolition of delegated tasks would not change the actual range of self-government tasks. It will make this range more transparent according to the principle of responsibility for the execution of public tasks.

The abolition of delegated tasks would facilitate changes in financing rules for these tasks. It must be added that transforming delegated tasks into own tasks does not mean that the state authority has no possibility to control the execution of these tasks or intervene when the law is broken. Since 1997 state intervention has been limited to cases where self-government breaks the law, both for own and delegated tasks.

5 Local Finance

5.1 OWN REVENUE AND EQUALIZATION SYSTEM

The differences in the level and structure of revenue and expenditure in municipal and rural gminas are the main obstacle to increasing the share of the own revenue in the total sum of the self-government units' revenue.

The main source of the big gap between the rural and urban gminas is the Polish taxation system, and more precisely, the system of taxes paid by the farmers. As we stated earlier, the farmers do not pay PIT, and the rates of agriculture tax are much lower than the rates of PIT and real estate tax. Another reason for the bad financial situation of Polish rural gminas is the lack of a well-developed sector of services for agriculture.

The financial data also show the important differences in the level of expenditure (per 1 inhabitant) in the rural and urban gminas, caused mainly by such factors as:

- higher costs (per pupil) of running the rural schools, caused by a smaller number of pupils in one class and by the costs of driving (busing),
- higher costs of municipal tasks in the cities,
- costs of local transport in the cities,
- higher costs of running cultural institutions in the cities,
- higher density of roads in the cities.

For these reasons we propose to radically change the system of the self-governments' revenue and to replace one uniform system of gminas' revenue by two (or three) different systems for – at least – rural gminas, taking into account:

- the different revenue capacities of rural and urban gminas,
- differences in the "standard" level of expenditure.

The existence of some parallel financial systems for gminas will allow the significant increase of the share of their own revenue in the structure of total self-government revenue – in such a system cities can obtain higher shares in PIT and CIT, and – at the same time – the general subsidies to the cities can be reduced.

The systems should be diversified by:

- the sets of the own revenue,
- the algorithms employed to calculate the amount of general subsidies (it should be "more equalizing" then now, especially for cities),
- the shares of income taxes and – alternatively – VAT).

5.2 NEW SOURCES OF REVENUE

The catalogue of the self-governments' own revenue should be enlarged. First of all, the public revenue collected today by the state administration and transferred to the self-government units, as for example:

- contributions to the Labor Fund,
- contributions to the State Fund for the Rehabilitation of Disabled Persons,
- fees and fines collected by the National Fund for the Environmental Protection and Water Management,
- should become the own revenue of the self-government units.

The self-governments should also have the right to retain all the revenues from delegated tasks.

5.3 ALGORITHMS FOR THE CALCULATION OF GENERAL SUBSIDIES

Two important changes should be introduced to the system of the general subsidies.

First, the rule establishing the calculation of the total sum of the general subsidies should be defined.

At the same time, the system of calculating the amount of the general subsidies due to separate self-government units should be simplified considerably. In particular, we recommend:

- to reduce the number of parts of the general subsidies (a liquidation of the educational part is most important),
- to reduce the number of parameters used to calculate the general subsidies for the separate self-government units,

- to liquidate the contributions paid by the "richest" self-government units to the state budget.

5.4 SHARES IN CIT

Shares of self-government units in the revenue from the personal income tax should be increased. In particular, we recommend increasing the shares assigned to the voivodships.

5.5 FINANCING OWN TASKS

Appropriated allocations have a decreasing share in self-government revenue. In 1999 the share of these allocations equaled 21.2% and in 2005 it decreased to 13.5% of the total revenue. Even in poviats, which were always the most financially dependent entities in self-government sector, the share of appropriated allocations was limited to 18%. In gminas and voivodships the share is smaller than 13% of the total revenue.

Appropriated allocations on gmina tasks mainly concern: family payments (66.5% of allocations), social benefits (10.5%), social aid centers (5.1%) and benefits for pupils (3.6%). Most of the allocations are transferred to gminas for social service activities. Poviats are mainly given appropriated allocations for (i) social service tasks like community homes (33.3% of allocations), social payments (10.6%) or common hospitals (3.1%) and (ii) for some public services like fire brigades (34.7%) and (iii) public roads (3.0%). More diversified financing by appropriated allocations occurs in voivodships. The allocations for voivodships mainly finance drainage works (15.9% of allocations), medical internships (14.0%) surcharges to railway tickets (11.4%), common hospitals (10.8%), investment needs after natural disasters (8.3%), benefits for pupils (6.5%), public roads (5.1%).

Self-government entities are fully responsible for the execution of foregoing tasks, even of those delegated by the state administration. As we recommend transforming all delegated tasks into the self-governments' own tasks, there is still the problem of financing them. According to the charter *grants to local authorities shall, as far as possible, not be earmarked for the financing of specific projects*. The decreasing share of appropriated allocations in TSG total revenue, transferring poviat tasks to gminas and voivodships and creating a new system of gminas revenue equalization are the arguments for the abolition of conditional grants. The tasks which are now financed by the appropriated allocations have to be executed by force so that there is no need to relate expenditure on it to specific public funds.

5.6 INTERNAL VOIVODSHIPS' EQUALIZATION ALGORITHMS

The voivodships (in their new form, described in paragraph 4.2) should have the right to establish their own equalization systems. In order to establish the source of financing such transfers from the voivodship level to the gminas, the equalizing part of the general subsidies should be divided into two parts:

- the part transferred directly from the state budget to the gminas,
- the part transferred to the voivodships, but designed to finance the transfers to the gminas.

5.7 SELF-GOVERNMENT APPROPRIATE FUNDS

There are four self-government appropriated funds: the Social Fund of Countryside (FSW) in gminas, the Agricultural Land Protection Fund (FOGR) in voivodships, the Environmental Protection and Water Management Fund (FOŚ) and the Geodesic and Cartographic Resources Management Fund (FGZGiK) – both in gminas, poviats and voivodships. Only the voivodship FOŚ has legal character and its own governing body, the other funds are dependent on self-government executive bodies. The appropriated funds have their own revenue sources which can only be used to finance the specified tasks. *FOŚ* resources are only used to finance environment protection projects, *FGZGiK* recourses are used to update and conduct public geodesic and cartographic resources, and *FOGR* resources are used to protect and improve the quality of agricultural land. Sources collected by *FSW* are too small to finance any bigger task.

In 2005, revenues of appropriated funds in gminas equaled 0.7% of the gminas' total revenue. In poviats it equaled 1.8% of the poviats' total revenue and in voivodships it was 14.3% of the total revenue. Relation of the funds' revenues to self-governments' revenues in gminas and poviats are so small that there is no danger to protected activities. A bigger problem could develop at voivodship level, where significant parts of public sources are governed by FOŚ. However, if the law regulates self-government duties related to countryside development, environment protection or the updating and conducting of public geodesic and cartographic resources, the self-governments will have to execute these tasks regardless of the appropriated funds' existence. Moreover, self-government will get an opportunity to adjust expenditure to needs according to community preferences.

All local self-government appropriate funds should be liquidated and their revenues should be included directly into the local budgets. At the same time, the tasks financed today from these funds should become the self-government units' own tasks.

We also recommend reconsidering the distribution of shares of today's revenues of the Environmental Protection and Water Management Funds between the self-government units and the state administration in order to increase the local share of these revenues.

5.8 THE STATE FUND FOR REHABILITATION OF DISABLED PERSONS

The State Fund for Rehabilitation of Disabled Persons (*PFRON*) is a state legal person. Obligatory contributions from enterprises and other legal persons are the main revenue of the fund. *PFRON* is made up of the central administration and 16 voivodship branches which coordinate different social programs for disabled persons.

In 2004 *PFRON* expenditure was 2.7 billion PLN, 2.2 billion PLN of which were divided among branches. Voivodships were given 90 million PLN and poviats 659 million PLN for their statutory tasks. Besides that, self-government units like job centers obtained some funds from *PFRON* on programs coordinated by the central administration and the branches.

We recommend transferring the responsibilities and funds from *PFRON* branches to voivodships. The implementation of this idea will strengthen the position of the voivodship as a coordinator of the social development policy in the region. At present, a strong center for the social policy development in regions does not exist, as responsibilities and sources are divided among different institutions. The position of voivodships in the Polish political system predestines these entities to be such a center. Transferring the *PFRON* branch tasks and funds to voivodships will be an important step on the road to a strong regional self-government. *PFRON* would still exist as the central administration which will coordinate programs for disabled people on a national level.

List of the authors (in alphabetical order)

Dr. Ivo Bischoff

Professur für Volkswirtschaftslehre II
und Öffentliche Finanzen
Justus-Liebig-Universität Gießen

Prof. Dr. Armin Bohnet

Zentrum für internationale Entwick-
lungs- und Umweltforschung (ZEU)
Justus-Liebig-Universität Gießen

Piotr Bury

Institute of Economics
Świętokrzyska Academy, Poland

Magdalena Godek

Institute of Finance, Banking and
Insurance
University of Lódz, Poland

Kai Hofmann

Referat Grundsatzfragen der
Finanzpolitik, Finanzplanung,
Subvention
Hessisches Ministerium der Finanzen,
Wiesbaden

Marta Mackiewicz

Gdańsk Institute for Market Economics
Warsaw, Poland

Elżbieta Malinowska-Misiąg

Gdańsk Institute for Market Economics
Warsaw, Poland

Dr. Wojciech Misiąg

Gdańsk Institute for Market Economics
Warsaw, Poland

Andreas Kienemund

Kommission von Bundestag und
Bundesrat zur Modernisierung der
bundesstaatlichen Ordnung
Bundesministerium der Finanzen,
Berlin

Lars Ponterlitschek

Zentrum für Internationale Entwick-
lungs- und Umweltforschung (ZEU)
Justus-Liebig-Universität Gießen

Prof. Dr. Wolfgang Scherf

Professur für Volkswirtschaftslehre II
und Öffentliche Finanzen
Justus-Liebig-Universität Gießen

Marcin Tomalak

Gdańsk Institute for Market Economics
Warsaw, Poland

Tomasz Uryszek

Faculty of Economics and Sociology
University of Lódz, Poland

Radosław Witczak

Institute of Finance, Banking and
Insurance
University of Lódz, Poland

Schriften zur Internationalen Entwicklungs- und Umweltforschung

Herausgegeben vom

Zentrum für internationale
Entwicklungs- und
Umweltforschung
der Justus-Liebig-Universität Gießen

Band 1 Hans-Rimbert Hemmer / Rainer Wilhelm: Fighting Poverty in Developing Countries. Principles for Economic Policy. 2000.

Band 2 Lorenz King / Martin Metzler / Tong Jiang (eds.): Flood Risks and Land Use Conflicts in the Yangtze Catchment, China and at the Rhine River, Germany. 2001.

Band 3 Ingrid-Ute Leonhäuser (ed.): Women in the Context of International Development and Cooperation. Review and Perspectives. Selected Papers and Abstracts presented at the Justus-Liebig-University Gießen 26.–28. October 2000. 2002

Band 4 Margit Schratzenstaller: Internationale Mobilität von und internationaler fiskalischer Wettbewerb um Direktinvestitionen. 2002.

Band 5 Armin Bohnet u.a.: Theoretische Grundlagen und praktische Gestaltungsmöglichkeiten eines Finanzausgleichssystems für die VR China. Unter Mitwirkung von Chen Biyan, Chen Shixin, Ge Licheng, Ge Naixu, Ge Zhuying, Ma Shuanyou, Markus Peplau, Yang Zhigang, Zhu Qiuxia. 2003.

Band 6 Armin Bohnet / Matthias Höher (eds.): The Role of Minorities in the Development Process. 2004.

Band 7 Thi Phuong Hoa Nguyen: Foreign Direct Investment and its Contributions to Economic Growth and Poverty Reduction in Vietnam (1986–2001). 2004.

Band 8 Andreas Böcker / Roland Herrmann / Michael Gast / Jana Seidemann: Qualität von Nahrungsmitteln. Grundkonzepte, Kriterien, Handlungsmöglichkeiten. 2004.

Band 9 Christina Mönnich: Tariff Rate Quotas and Their Administration. Theory, Practice and an Econometric Model for the EU. 2004.

Band 10 Reimund Seidelmann / Ernst Giese (eds.): Cooperation and Conflict Management in Central Asia. 2004.

Band 11 Claudia Ohly: Das Steuersystem im ungarischen Transformationsprozess. Ein Beitrag zur Transformationstheorie. 2004.

Band 12 Nicole Mau: Umweltzertifikate. Der Einsatz von Umweltzertifikaten in der Landwirtschaft am Beispiel klimarelevanter Gase. 2005.

Band 13 P. Michael Schmitz (Hrsg.): Water and Sustainable Development. 2005.

Band 14 Ira Pawlowski: Die Wettbewerbsfähigkeit der ukrainischen Milchwirtschaft. Messung von Marktverzerrung und Politikeinfluß im Transformationsprozeß. 2005.

Band 15 Kirsten Westphal (ed.): A Focus on EU-Russian Relations. Towards a close partnership on defined road maps? 2005.

Band 16 Andreas Langenohl / Kirsten Westphal (eds.): Conflicts in a Transnational World. Lessons from Nations and States in Transformation. 2006.

Band 17 Rosemarie von Schweitzer: Home Economics Science and Arts. Managing Sustainable Everyday Life. 2006.

Band 18 Dörthe List: Regionale Kooperation in Zentralasien. Hindernisse und Möglichkeiten. 2006.

Band 19 Michael Gast: Determinanten ausländischer Direktinvestitionen. OECD-Länder als Investoren und besonderer Aspekte der Ernährungswissenschaft. 2007.

Band 20 Kim Schmitz: Die Bewertung von Multifunktionalität der Landschaft mit diskreten Choice Experimenten. 2008.

Band 21 Kerstin Kötschau / Thilo Marauhn (eds.): Good Governance and Developing Countries. Interdisciplinary Perspectives. 2008.

Band 22 Armin Bohnet (ed.): Poland on its Way to a Federal State? 2008.

Band 23 Johannes Harsche: Regionale Inzidenz und ökonomische Bestimmungsgrößen der Gemeinsamen Europäischen Agrarpolitik. 2008.

www.peterlang.de

Gerhard Robbers (ed.)

Reforming Federalism – Foreign Experiences for a Reform in Germany

Reports of a Symposium held in Trier on December 2nd to 4th, 2004 hosted by the Institute for Legal Policy at the University of Trier in Cooperation with the German Bundesrat

Frankfurt am Main, Berlin, Bern, Bruxelles, New York, Oxford, Wien, 2005.
148 pp., num. fig. and tab.
Legal Policy Symposium.
Edited by Bernd von Hofmmann and Gerhard Robbers. Vol. 3
ISBN 978-3-631-54621-5 · pb. € 36.20*

Germany's federal order is, according to all political parties and social groups, under pressure of reform. An inter-parliamentary commission has been surveying all areas of federalism and was to propose models of reform late in 2004. The symposium's aim was to analyse other federal systems, which are currently undergoing or have already undergone reforms in their federal orders. The Institute for Legal Policy therefore invited experts from various countries to discuss their experiences with problems and reforms of federalism. The results thereof are explored for the German perspective.

Contents: Horst Risse: The Bundesrat in the Federal Legislative Process · Bicameralism in Germany · *Andre Alen and Koen Muylle:* The Belgian Senate in a Federal State – Origins, Practice and Reforms · *Beniamino Caravita di Toritto:* Bicameralism in Italy: Its Past, Present and Future Outlook · *Hans W. Kopp:* Fiscal Federalism: Switzerland · *Peter Bußjäger:* Reforms on Fiscal Federalism in Austria · *Arthur Gunlicks:* State and Local Government Finance in the United States · *Jean Leclair:* Reforming the Division of Powers in Canada: An (Un)Achievable Endeavour? · *Eliseo Aja:* The Debate about Competencies in Spain

Frankfurt am Main · Berlin · Bern · Bruxelles · New York · Oxford · Wien
Distribution: Verlag Peter Lang AG
Moosstr. 1, CH-2542 Pieterlen
Telefax 00 41 (0) 32 / 376 17 27

*The €-price includes German tax rate
Prices are subject to change without notice
Homepage http://www.peterlang.de